CW01433524

De la Pole, Father and Son

De la Pole, Father and Son

The Duke, the Earl and the Struggle for Power

MICHÈLE SCHINDLER

AMBERLEY

For Elena

First published 2022

Amberley Publishing
The Hill, Stroud
Gloucestershire, GL5 4EP

www.amberley-books.com

British Library Cataloguing in Publication Data.
A catalogue record for this book is available from the British Library.

ISBN 978 1 3981 0618 5 (hardback)
ISBN 978 1 3981 0619 2 (ebook)

1 2 3 4 5 6 7 8 9 10

Typeset in 10.5pt on 12.5pt Sabon.
Typesetting by SJmagic DESIGN SERVICES, India.
Printed in the UK.

Contents

Family Trees

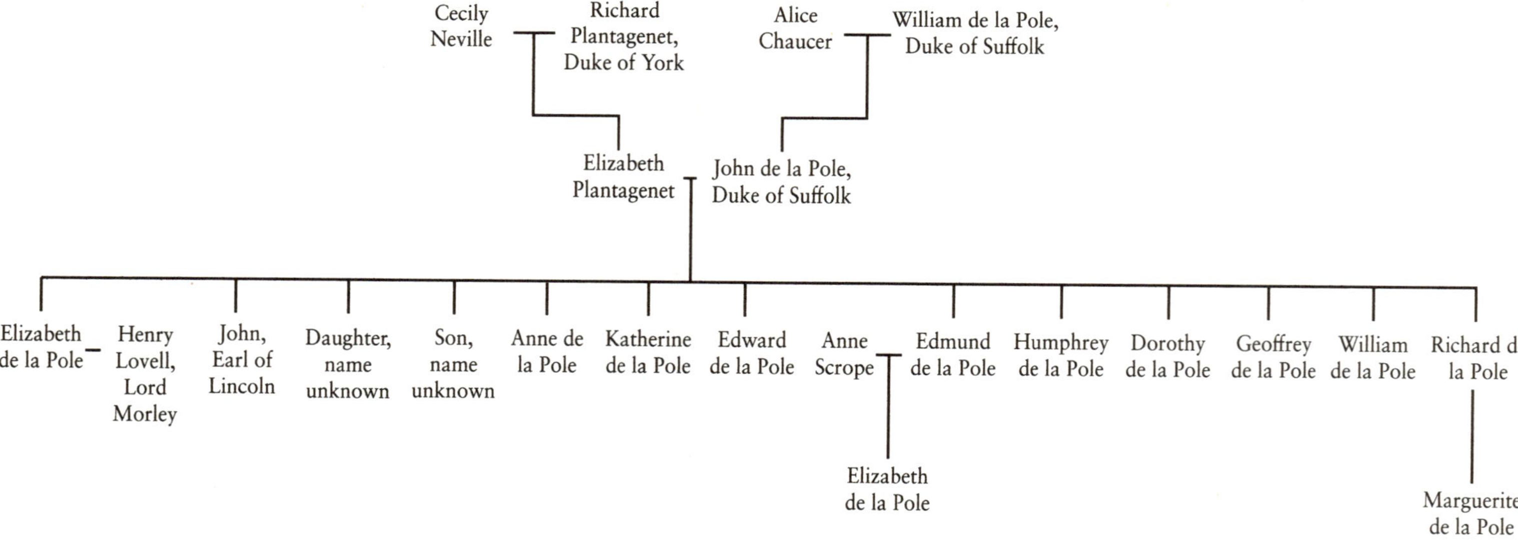

Family Trees

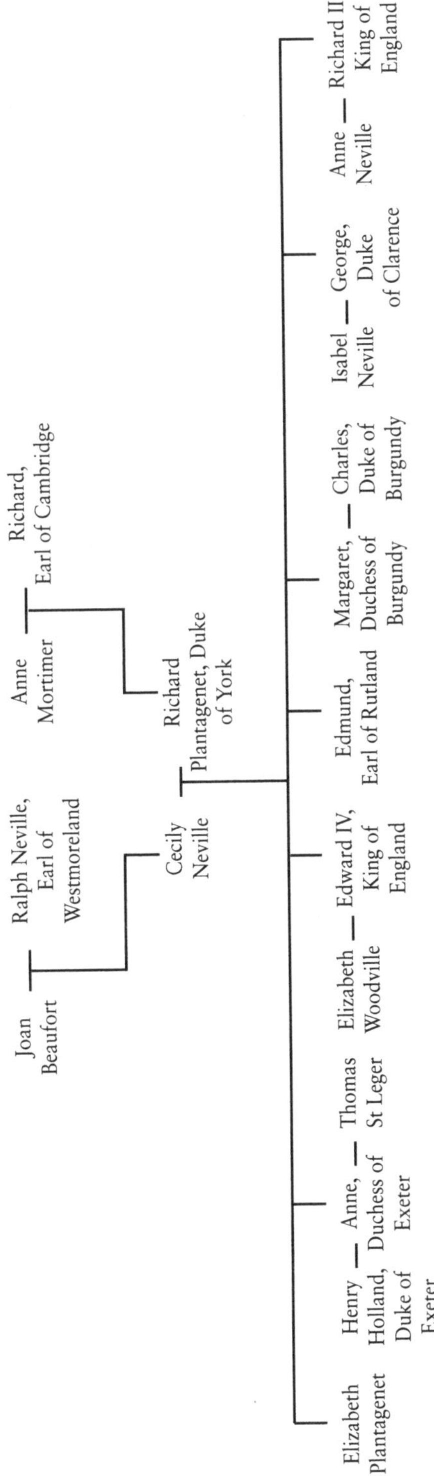

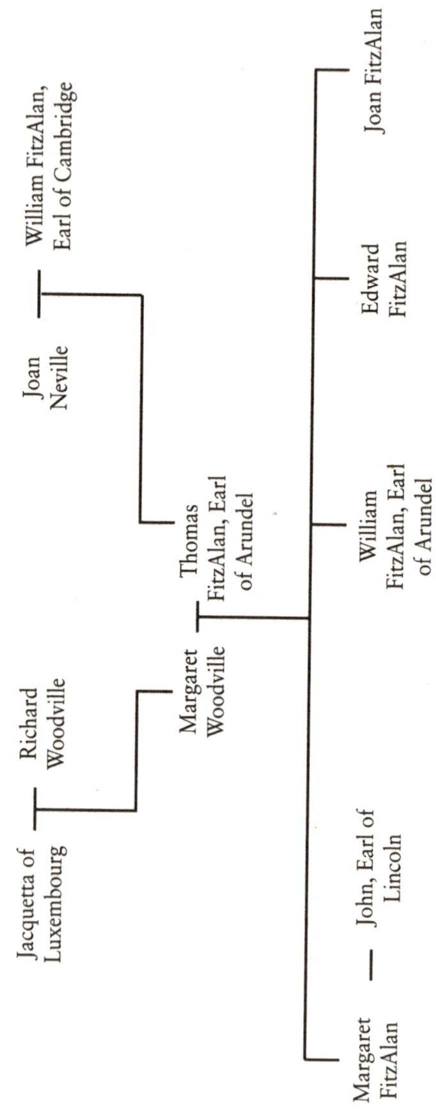

Jacquetta of Luxembourg
Richard Woodville
Joan Neville
William FitzAlan, Earl of Cambridge
Margaret Woodville
Thomas FitzAlan, Earl of Arundel
Margaret FitzAlan
John, Earl of Lincoln
William FitzAlan, Earl of Arundel
Edward FitzAlan
Joan FitzAlan

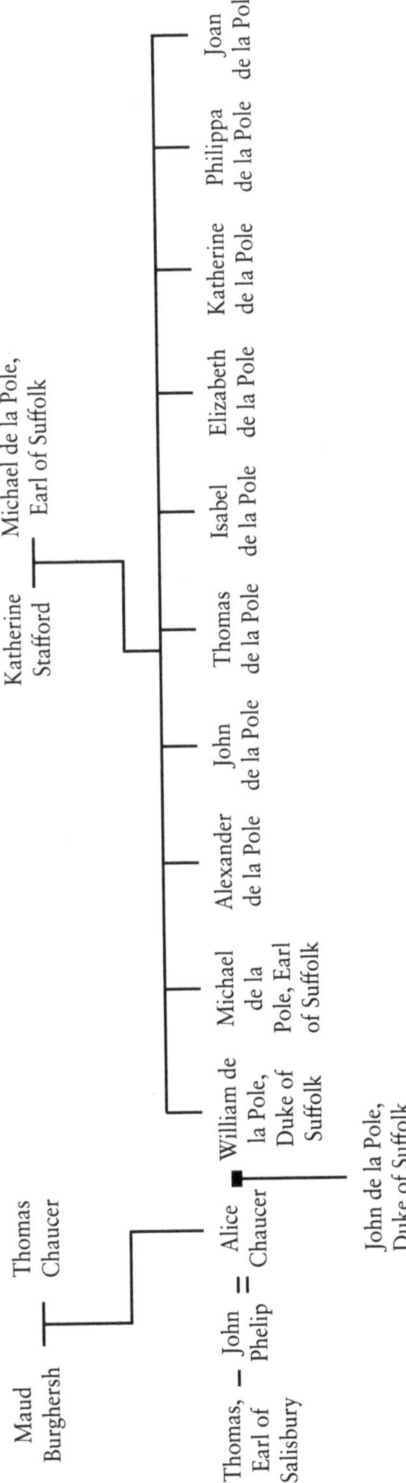
Maud Burghersh
Thomas Chaucer
Katherine Stafford
Michael de la Pole, Earl of Suffolk
Thomas, Earl of Salisbury
John Phelip
Alice Chaucer
William de la Pole, Duke of Suffolk
Michael de la Pole, Earl of Suffolk
Alexander de la Pole
John de la Pole
Thomas de la Pole
Isabel de la Pole
Elizabeth de la Pole
Katherine de la Pole
Philippa de la Pole
Joan de la Pole
John de la Pole, Duke of Suffolk

Introduction

John was their miracle baby.

Born to a thirty-eight-year-old mother and a forty-six-year-old father, their first child after twelve years of marriage, his birth must have seemed like the answer to all their prayers.

Delivered into this world on 27 September 1442 as the son of William de la Pole, Earl of Suffolk, and his wife Alice Chaucer, a lot of hopes and expectations would have rested on little John de la Pole. His parents would have known that it was probable he would remain an only child, and they would have focused all their love and care on him. Whatever they envisioned for his future, however, they would not have been able to foresee that John would grow up to be brother-in-law to two kings, husband to a princess and even, for a while, father of the heir to the English throne. However, though a rise to such heights would have seemed all but impossible when little John was born, his family history was marked by upward mobility. Both his parents had risen from comparatively humble beginnings to their present, important, position.

William de la Pole's Early Life

Though both the de la Poles and the Chaucers were well-known, well-respected and important families in the late fourteenth and early fifteenth centuries, neither William de la Pole nor Alice Chaucer could boast unusually noble ancestry, and their importance was the result of the connections they made throughout their lives, not mere birthright.

The de la Poles were what we would call a self-made family. William's namesake great-grandfather had been an untitled if wealthy merchant, a man who knew how to use his wealth to become powerful and important.[1] Said to have been 'second to no other merchant in England',[2] he gave loans to Edward III and thereby came into close contact with not only the king himself but also important nobles. Though he died without title, his son used his father's fame to gain himself an earldom.[3]

However, the family's position was always precarious. William's great-grandfather knew the value of the king's favour but his son died in disgrace, stripped of his title, only narrowly escaping execution for treason.[4] William's father, Michael, tried everything to get his father's earldom back, showing his loyalty to king and country, but he was insecure of himself and his position. With the family's wealth largely drained in his father's downfall, he might have hoped that supporting the king in a difficult situation would help him regain his father's old position. Such ambition very nearly destroyed him too.

This crisis was off in the future when William was born on 16 October 1396 in the town of Cotton in Suffolk[5] as the second son of Michael de la Pole and his wife Katherine. He had one older brother, named Michael after their father, who was some two years older than him, and probably several older sisters. Over the next few years, he would be joined in the nursery by three more brothers and several sisters.

William was baptised on the day he was born, and many details of the event survive.[6] His godfathers were William Wynkefeld and William Burgate, and it is possible he was named after one of them, though it is equally possible he received his name in honour of his great-grandfather. Though William was only a second son, his baptism was a great occasion. According to an eyewitness, 'many men and women' of Cotton attended the ceremony and were 'infected by the great joy' of it, despite the fact that this day witnessed 'such a great and strong wind that men and women of the aforesaid town feared that the building of their homes was too weak'.[7]

William's godfathers gave him generous gifts for his baptism. Wynkefeld presented him with a silver bell and gave his wet nurse six shillings and eight pennies to 'nourish' him, while Burgate gave him 'a cup with a gilded coverlet' and twenty shillings for his wet nurse.[8] This generosity, allied with the great fanfare that accompanied his baptism in the town, suggests that William was expected to become a great man.

He certainly would have been raised with this sense of destiny, though his early childhood is poorly documented. All that can be said for a fact is that he and Michael were soon joined by three more brothers – Alexander, John and Thomas – and several more sisters, though the exact ages of neither the brothers nor the sisters are recorded.

As was normal for children of nobles, William and his siblings would not have been cared for by their parents but by servants tasked with raising them and seeing to their well-being. Naturally, this would have been supervised by their parents, but the children might not have seen them very often, as their day-to-day care would have been provided by others.[9]

Apart from this obvious difference, William's routine as a toddler might not have been too different from that experienced by his modern-day counterparts as he learnt skills such as walking and talking. Despite his nobility, at this age he would not have been expected to understand his father's role, nor the state of the kingdom at large. It was no doubt a cause for great happiness among the family when Michael finally got back his father's earldom in 1398,[10] but William would have been too young to understand.

Michael's happiness was not to last. In 1399, the sitting king Richard II was deposed by his cousin, Henry of Bolingbroke, who assumed the throne as Henry IV.[11] William would still have been too young to realise what this meant, for the kingdom and for his family, but he might have sensed the tension and sadness of those around him when Henry IV quickly reversed all of Richard II's recent rulings.[12] The decision to return to Michael his father's earldom was among those overturned.[13]

Perhaps it was simply this disadvantage to him and his family that made Michael decide to oppose Henry IV, or maybe he really felt loyalty to the deposed king. Whichever it was, he was involved in several plots against Henry IV,[14] something that William would not have realised at the time but surely understood and learned from as he grew older. The failure of these rebellions and the fact that his father eventually found prosperity in serving the new king[15] no doubt taught him the value of loyalty to the reigning monarch.

It was not until 1405 that Michael finally found his place under Henry IV. The king, seeking to make peace with a largely dissatisfied nobility, began making amends. Among his decisions at this time was the return of Michael's earldom once more.[16] This was to prove a wise decision, for Michael was a loyal subject from then on and raised his sons to follow his example. Aged nine when his father received the earldom again, William would have at the very least understood the basics of what was happening, and perhaps, seeing his father rejoice at the largesse of the king, would have felt warmly towards his ruler. Certainly, William's own loyalty towards the king and his progeny never wavered.

In some history books Michael has received criticism for his behaviour,[17] apparently motivated too much by personal gain, but it is clear that by choosing to be pragmatic rather than idealistic he saved himself and secured his family's future. With his sizeable brood Michael could not afford to chase after shadows; better to show the king his worth as an ally.

He was not mistaken about the value of his support. Though his struggle to regain the earldom of Suffolk had taken up most of his time since his father's death, he still had important connections that could be useful to the king. Henry finally recognised this, and allowed Michael to become an influential man in his reign.[18] As a result, William enjoyed life as part of a wealthy and important family from his ninth year onwards. However, if he was under the illusion that unswerving loyalty to the king brought only advantages, he was to be disabused of this notion in a brutal fashion.

Despite the upheaval in the country and despite his father's troubles, William's early years were most likely uneventful for the most part. He would have been brought up together with his siblings in one of the family's manors in Suffolk. As he grew up, he would have been instructed more and more by his father. Some of this education would have been conventional, his father simply choosing tutors to school him in martial arts and other subjects essential to a noble boy of the time. A marriage was arranged for Michael Jnr,[19] William's older brother, and Michael would certainly have considered a match for William too, though these designs came to naught for now.

In other ways, Michael might have been less conventional, choosing to allow his son to accompany him to court occasionally, observing the workings of the government up close. Even if he did so, however, there is no evidence of William being connected to king or court in any way until 1411, when he was fifteen. That year he was clearly considered old enough to be of a certain importance because he was knighted by the king himself.[20] It is another occasion that might have filled William with gratitude and loyalty towards the king. From now on, William was a young man to be reckoned with. Any doubts about this would be dissolved two years later, when Henry IV died and his son took over the throne as Henry V.[21]

Henry IV's attempts to win popularity and distract from his lack of a claim to the throne had forced him to focus on internal politics. Battling against domestic intrigue, he had little time for crises outside the borders of England and was unable to unite his restive subjects against a common enemy abroad.[22] However, Henry V soon did just that. He was to perfect this policy by focusing on England's claim on several French lands, which had been handed down for over two hundred years and over which the two countries had been at war for several generations. This was the perfect distraction, and Henry V duly succeeded in using patriotic fervour to distract from internal problems.[23]

It would be unfair to Henry IV to say he simply failed to do what his son now did to such great effect. Henry IV was a usurper. Though he had eventually been accepted, if somewhat grudgingly, by most, it was always a fact that hung over his head. Henry V, however, had inherited the throne. Though the way his family had come to rule was far from forgotten,[24] and would come back to haunt his own son in turn, Henry V nonetheless had more legitimacy than his father had ever had, and this put him in a better position to rally his subjects.

Naturally, French kings did not take kindly to the English claiming what were in practice (though not entirely legally) their lands, and there were often retaliatory attacks on lands held by the English in what is today French territory.[25] Soon after taking the throne, Henry V made it his policy to stop these attacks and claim all of France as English territory, launching a military campaign to topple the French monarchy completely and to unite the French and English crowns in his own person.[26]

The conflict between France and England had already been rumbling on for nearly sixty years when Henry V took the throne.[27] Now known as the Hundred Years War, it had been started by the English king Edward III, who claimed the French throne through his mother Isabella of France.[28] His successors, all descended from him, maintained the claim.

Soon after taking the throne, in autumn 1414,[29] Henry V made it his policy to do what the three successive kings before him had not been able to do and claim the French throne as well as all French lands as English territory. To achieve this, soon after ascending the throne, he launched campaigns to defeat the French monarchy and its military forces.[30] It was during these campaigns that William first emerged from a sheltered if possibly troubled childhood and adolescence to fight in France for his king. His experiences there would shape him. When he first crossed the Channel, William was likely in complete agreement with Henry V and his policies, truly believing that the English kings had a divine right to the French crown. He was only eighteen. Like many young men before and since, he was probably fired up to fight for something he considered glorious, only to find out a shameful and terrible truth on a muddy French battlefield.

William's father, Michael, agreed to raise 160 lances for the king in early 1415. He gave the command of twenty to each of his two oldest sons.[31] This would have given them command of over a hundred men each. Surely this must have been exciting for both of them, but any exhilaration they felt was not to last. While everything was ready for the campaign, with all the men William, his father and brother had gathered waiting together with other nobles and their troops for the passage to France, news broke that a plot against Henry V had been uncovered. Fingers were pointed at some of the most powerful men in the country, such as the Duke of York's brother Richard of Conisburgh.[32]

Perhaps this, in itself, put a bit of a dampener on the mood of the men, showing as it did that Henry V, who had presented himself as the avenger of English honour, was not seen as such by everyone, and that even some with a lot of power and very noble blood disagreed. Conversely, it might have whipped these battle-ready forces into an even greater frenzy. The traitors were executed after a short trial.[33] This decisive action was not surprising, but Henry V would have been disappointed: on the eve of his bloody quest to conquer France, here was a sign that his was not a united country.

It seems, however, that the treason against him only made Henry V more eager to show his mettle in battle, and with the executions over and done with he and his men boarded ship for France.[34] It was probably the first time William had left England. If he still expected to find glory on the battlefield, he was soon to learn better. Henry V's French campaigns were brutal, violent, gory and without the slightest bit of honour; they were anything but glorious. But it was not Henry V's ruthless and brutal nature, which was extreme even for the time, that would show William the cost of war so soon after arriving in France. It was a much more personal blow.

Henry V had decided that the best course of action would be to first attack and destroy the French town of Harfleur, to deal a massive blow to French trade along the River Seine,[35] and so it was there that his men marched once they landed in France. The townspeople saw them coming; those who could flee did so. The others closed up the city and prepared for a siege for which the English seemed almost too well prepared – something that nearly spelled their downfall.

Henry V's army was massive, too big for a siege of a town as small as Harfleur. Too many men, well over ten thousand, had to camp together on muddy ground as they besieged the city. This made the camp the breeding ground for disease;[36] those not hurt by any of the French defences found themselves at risk of contracting 'the bloody flux' – dysentery – or other diseases associated with such camps. Even while his men were battling sickness, Henry V insisted the bombardment of the city go on day and night.[37]

William was in the heat of the action, and it was there that he, only weeks after arriving in France, was injured.[38] The nature of his injury is not known, but it must have been serious. He was removed from the immediate camping ground of the besieging army to be nursed by the physicians the English army had brought along.[39] Quite possibly this saved his life, as it meant he was somewhat removed from the campground teeming with disease, which eventually did for William's father. Michael died of dysentery while his second son was still recuperating from his injury, two days before the siege was finally successful.[40]

Michael de la Pole, 2nd Earl of Suffolk, did not see the English victory, which had come at a price of nearly two thousand English lives and countless French ones. Of the English, most had died of dysentery, like Michael. It had not been the glorious death William might have envisaged for him or any of his relatives during the campaign. It was a painful, undignified end, and if William had still been under any illusions about the nature of war and battle after his own injury, without a doubt his father's death would have taken them from him.

William was still too weak to fight, so after the city of Harfleur had been taken by the English he was among the men sent home to England to recuperate.[41] He travelled back to his newly widowed mother in England with his father's body.[42] Without a doubt, his father's death would have saddened him, and maybe it also began seeding his first doubts about the necessity of the English campaigns in France; such misgivings would eventually grow into a conviction that it was useless, something that should be ended. If so, it was still a long time before he started showing signs of this belief.

Apart from such personal worries, little would have changed for William himself. His older brother, who had survived the siege of Harfleur unscathed and was still with the English army in France, had become the third Earl of Suffolk with their father's death, and it was his life that would have been expected to change drastically once the English army had crushed the French.

It was never to come to that. Michael would never get to enjoy his earldom in any peace. He marched on with the English army to meet the French forces gathered against the invaders. The size of the English army, such an inconvenience to them during the siege of Harfleur, seemed much less impressive in the face of the massive French force mustered to meet them.[43] Eventually, the two armies met near a small town called Azincourt, often Anglicised to 'Agincourt' in English history books, and engaged in battle. This battle has since gone down in history, famously being celebrated as a roaring success by William Shakespeare in his play *Henry V*, and has served as a rallying point for English and even British war efforts over the centuries.[44]

Naturally, the truth was less glamorous.[45] While it was a startling and unexpected victory for the English forces, it was much uglier in real life than in Shakespeare's famous play. While some of what is presented by the play is correct, such as the fact that the English archers won the day, and that the French forces, much like the English at Harfleur, were too numerous and bogged down in the mud, this version leaves out a lot. For one, it all but glosses over the massive loss of French life. This might be said to be expected for a battle, but a lot of those lives were not lost in combat. Henry V was anything but a graceful winner, and even at the time attracted a lot of criticism for his cruel decision not to ransom Frenchmen taken prisoner by the English forces, instead giving orders to kill all but the most noble of them.[46] It has often been explained, even excused, by there being too many prisoners for the English to hold. Even so, it was extremely uncommon to kill prisoners, and at the time it was practically unheard of to do as Henry did and order the deaths of the foot soldiers, who were only drafted to follow orders.[47] Of course, such actions were not discussed in England at the time, where the win at Agincourt was seen as miraculous, and the men who had fought there were celebrated as heroes.[48] Since few English fighters died in this battle, the overwhelming feeling would have been one of triumph, but it was unlikely that William de la Pole shared the enthusiasm. His brother Michael was one of the few English casualties of the battle.[49]

Michael left a wife and three young daughters,[50] the oldest of whom was four. Whether because of her youth or her sex, or both, her father's earldom did not fall to her upon Michael's death but instead to her uncle William. Just a day shy of his nineteenth birthday, William de la Pole became Earl of Suffolk when his older brother died on a muddy, bloody battlefield in France.[51]

Earl of Suffolk, 1415–1430

William's life would remain turbulent. Naturally, his earldom meant new responsibilities he would never have expected to bear. He had been unencumbered before his brother's death, his future uncertain. Now he was an earl, a man of vast possessions, head of the family. He does not seem to have been prepared for this role, nor does it seem he particularly cared about it.[52] In any case, he did what was expected of him, entering his lands when he attained his majority in 1417,[53] and for the next few years the centre of his life was in France, in the service of the king. These were no easy years, and sadly for him and for so many others, the Battle of Agincourt did not mean the end of the fighting. Henry V, knowing that his actions at that battle had left the French crown drastically weakened, pursued his plans to take all of France.[54]

In 1417, in a campaign that William may or may not have joined, Henry V led his men to take most of Normandy, including the important town of Caen.[55] If William was not there, perhaps due to obligations in England after attaining his majority,[56] he was definitely present as the campaign progressed and the English army took the town of Rouen in early 1419.[57] By that time, he had been earl for nearly four years; he had spent most of this time in Henry V's army, and would have had a thoroughly realistic view of warfare and his king's nature. Indeed, Henry's cruelty did not only show itself at the Battle of Agincourt; he showed a lack of regard for civilian life that was shocking even in his own time.[58] William's thoughts about this are not recorded, but it is not far-fetched to assume that even if he was completely convinced of the righteousness of the English cause he would have welcomed the chance of peace when it presented itself in late 1419, when the Duke of Burgundy took advantage of the French king's preoccupation with the English threat and took Paris.[59] Henry V allied himself with the duke,[60] leaving the French king, Charles VI, with little choice but to pursue peace.

Henry V and Charles VI met in 1420 at Troyes to discuss the conditions of a possible peace treaty.[61] Naturally, this was mostly ceremonial; Henry V was in a position to dictate terms, and he did. The agreed solution was that Henry would marry Charles's daughter, Katherine.[62] This was not a new idea; such a match had been considered by Henry IV, who had died before anything could come of it. However, the conditions attached to the marriage were now much more favourable to the English than anything Henry IV would have proposed. It was agreed upon that the firstborn son of Henry and Katherine would be made heir to the throne of both France and England. Katherine's brother, who had been the Dauphin of France, crown prince of the country, was declared illegitimate.[63]

If William, like many others, hoped this would mean the end of the Franco-English wars, he was to be disappointed. Perhaps unsurprisingly, the treaty was a recipe for disaster. Though the marriage between Henry V and Katherine went ahead on 2 June 1420, it did not at all mean peace between the two countries. The disinherited dauphin was not content to accept the change in his fortunes. He had many supporters who agreed with him, and so he led the fight against the English interloper.[64]

The dauphin, who would in due time become Charles VII of France, was a formidable enemy, and the war he waged would cost the English crown dear, as it had already cost the French. Even as a married man, Henry V's focus lay more on conquest and war than on ruling his own country, seeing to domestic issues or showing any interest in his wife. William must by then have been a seasoned fighter, and whatever his personal feelings were, he was a loyal man who stayed in France to fight with the king's army even on the rare occasions when Henry himself left the army to go to England.[65]

This was what happened during March 1421, and it would end in disaster. Having left his brother Thomas, Duke of Clarence in charge, Henry had gone to spend time with his queen and attend to English internal affairs. Against the advice of his men, Thomas, perhaps eager to show his mettle, charged into battle against a battalion that was 5,000 strong.[66] He was killed in the battle, in which William also took part, on 21 March 1421.[67] His body was recovered by the Earl of Salisbury,[68] which at least spared the English the humiliation of seeing the body displayed, but it must have been a shock to the troops. At the same time, it was surely a boost for French morale – the English were not invincible.

Henry V returned to France upon hearing of the death of his brother.[69] He was never to return to England again, though perhaps news a few months later that his queen was pregnant shored up the flagging English morale. William may have been among the first to hear the news, as he seems to have been close to Henry V for the rest of his time in France.[70] He joined Henry when he visited Paris, Chartres and Gatinais, and was part of the army when the king decided to attack the town of Meaux,[71] which was loyal to the dauphin. The town proved difficult to take. The campaign started in October 1421 and lasted until May of the following year,[72] exhibiting many of the same problems experienced at the siege of Harfleur some six years before. Too many men were crammed into too little space, besieging a town that proved more resistant than expected. Without a doubt, it would have brought up painful memories for William, but they must have remained private.

There is no indication that William allowed himself to question Henry V's plans. We cannot say whether this was because of his early lessons about loyalty or a more straightforward faith in his king's policies. In any case, presumably it was happy news for him and the other men of the army, and naturally Henry V himself, to hear in December 1421 that the queen had given birth to a son, the promised child whose right to hold both the English and the French crown was the purpose of their fighting.[73] Perhaps this son, a tangible reason to fight, provided much-needed inspiration. Though men were once more dying of dysentery in their thousands, the siege was continued until Meaux surrendered in May 1422.[74]

Henry was not to enjoy his victory for long, though he did not know it. He sent for his wife, who joined him with her father Charles and his court as he retired to Senlis.[75] This was obviously a show of unity between the two monarchs, but it was to absolutely no avail. Henry, with William and others, soon set off from Senlis to attack another town, but they never made it. The king became sick. William must have been among the first to realise what was happening and what it meant. Henry V had contracted dysentery, like so many of his men during his campaigns to conquer France, and like so many of them, including William's own father, he died of it in August 1422.[76]

This would have been a shock to the English fighters and a boon to the dauphin. Though Henry V had left his brother John, Duke of Bedford in charge of his French campaigns on his deathbed,[77] it was clear that English morale would all but collapse after the loss of the warlike king; worse still, his successor was not yet a year old.

If William had such thoughts he kept them inside, staying in France to help any battle efforts. He was almost twenty-six years old when Henry V died, had been Earl of Suffolk for seven years, and had spent most of this time as a soldier in France. Quite possibly, he had become used to this life and found it hard to imagine something else. Certainly, he was starting to make connections in France, making a name for himself as a good fighter,[78] and centred his life around his service in France.

It was not all doom and gloom for him, and this very fact points towards him starting to become closer to the French population than was perhaps thought fitting by Henry V. Around 1422, he started an affair with a French woman[79] who is often claimed to have been a nun. This may very well have been true, but for William she was clearly not a quick distraction from army life. Whoever she was, they must have had a relationship. She gave him a daughter called Jane, and William would take good care of her until his death.[80]

Despite this, William apparently did not show any interest in getting married and producing an heir for his earldom. There is no telling why he neglected to do so. It cannot have been that he considered it unimportant due to there being plenty of alternative heirs; his youngest brother, Thomas, was a clergyman, and while the middle brothers John and Alexander could marry, neither of them had yet done so; moreover, both of them had joined the king's army in France and so were at risk of death.[81]

William seems to have had a rather unconventional approach to marriages, as he would also demonstrate in later life.[82] However, he would have attended several weddings as he started making connections with his fellow soldiers and may, for instance, have been present when Thomas Montacute, Earl of Salisbury, who had fought alongside him for almost all of the seven years and seems to have become close to him, married his second wife Alice, daughter of Thomas Chaucer and granddaughter of the poet Geoffrey.[83] Perhaps this wedding was the first time William met Alice, but he would certainly see her more often over the following years, as she often accompanied her new husband to France.[84]

Thomas Montacute probably hoped that he would get to stay in England more often with his new wife, and William quite possibly hoped to be able to go home more often too, but it was not to be. Despite Henry V's death, and that of Charles VI soon afterwards, the battles in France went on. William was present at the Battle of Verneuil,[85] during which the English once more thoroughly defeated the French. It seems there was some hope that this would be the last of the dauphin's efforts, but the French regrouped and there soon emerged a figure, a young commoner woman, who would deal a deadly blow to English ambitions and go down in legend: Joan of Arc.[86]

Much has been written about Joan elsewhere, but it cannot be denied that she inspired French fighters and made them believe God was on their side.[87] The dauphin, by then calling himself Charles VII of France, may have himself believed it, or maybe he just thought she was useful. Joan was definitely a talented soldier and leader. The victory that was to propel her to her legendary status happened in Orleans, in the winter of 1428/9.[88] William and his brothers John and Alexander were present when the English laid siege to the town of Orleans,[89] and all of them were present at Orleans when the leader of the English forces, William's friend Thomas Monatcute, Earl of Salisbury, died after having been hit by a cannon ball.

William and his brothers were lucky to avoid any injuries, as well as the diseases rampant in the English camp, but none of them were prepared for the arrival of the peasant woman who took over the defence of Orleans and repelled the English. As the English retreated, harassed by French forces, Alexander was killed in the fighting.[90] William and John escaped with their lives and fled to Jargeau, where they were taken prisoner after a battle that took place there soon after.[91] John died in that fight, but William lived. According to legend, he surrendered to Joan herself, saying that she was the most remarkable woman God had ever created and that he would surrender to no one else, but there is no corroborating evidence. In the face of cold, hard facts, it seems unlikely he had any choice to whom he surrendered.

Having been captured, William was imprisoned, albeit honourably, in the Bastard of Orleans's castle.[92] He was thirty-two. He had been Earl of Suffolk for thirteen of those years but had never shown any interest in the earldom, or even in producing an heir for it. It was only during his imprisonment in 1429, after the death of his friend Salisbury, that William started thinking about marriage. His chosen bride was Salisbury's widow, Alice Chaucer.

Alice Chaucer's Life until 1430

Alice Chaucer was born to Thomas Chaucer and Maud Burghersh in the year 1404, though the month and date of her birth are lost to history. Like William's family, Alice's was not of particularly noble lineage, but hers was famous even then: Alice's paternal grandfather was the poet Geoffrey Chaucer, still well known today for his ground-breaking work *The Canterbury Tales*.[93] Geoffrey Chaucer had several children by his higher-born wife Philippa Roet, but Alice is his best-known grandchild. Her father, though not of the nobility, was a politically active man, being a Speaker of the House of Commons and having a lot of trading interests in France.[94] His wife, Maud, was landed gentry.[95]

Alice was born to the couple after several years of marriage, and seems to have remained an only child. If she had siblings who died in infancy or childhood, we no longer know about them. Certainly by 1415 she was their only child, for when a marriage was arranged for her she was stated to be her parents' sole heiress.[96] Though Alice's pedigree was far from flawless and she did not have a lot of noble blood, she was still a good marriage prospect. The family money and their connections to some of the highest and mightiest in the realm were sufficient to get her a great match with the thirty-year-old John Phelip,[97] younger brother of William, Lord Bardolf, as his third wife. Naturally, as Alice was still a child of only eleven years when the marriage was made, this was to be in name only until she was old enough to live with John. Such an arrangement was not uncommon at the time, and there would have been no reason to doubt that despite the age gap theirs would be a perfectly functional marriage once Alice reached her majority.

Sadly, this was never to happen. Only one year after their wedding, John died at the siege of Harfleur, like Michael de la Pole a victim of the dysentery rampant in the English camp.[98] Despite the fact that they had only been married for a year, and in name only, John had not failed to make arrangements for his wife in the event of his death. He was very generous in those arrangements, leaving her several of his possessions to hold for the rest of her life, such as the priory of Grovebury.[99] At just eleven years old, Alice was already a rich widow.

It seems unlikely that John Phelip and Alice saw much of each other. On the few times they met they would hardly have found common ground, but Alice seems to have remembered him fondly and, in the years to come, would grow close to his brother William; they would remain friends until William's death nearly thirty years later.[100] Though her marriage to John never really had a chance to take root, Alice was to profit from the wealth and connections it brought for the rest of her life.[101]

Alice must have been aware of this, and probably started using both the wealth and the connections for her own good as she grew up, but she did not hurry to remarry, nor did her parents make her do so. For the next seven years, she remained living in her parents' household until, at the age of eighteen, she found a second husband.

Alice's first marriage had been a good, suitable match for her; her second marriage, to Sir Thomas Montacute, Earl of Salisbury, was splendid.[102] Though Alice was rich, well connected through her father and not low-born, marriage to an earl was a steep rise for her. Like Sir John Phelip had been when Alice married him, the earl was a widower, some sixteen years her senior. He had one daughter, also called Alice, who was only three years younger than his new wife.

This time, Alice was old enough to become the earl's wife in all ways immediately after their wedding, and as soon as they were married they set up their household together.[103] Without a doubt, Salisbury hoped his new young wife would give him a son and heir, but it was not to be. Though there is evidence Alice gave him a child, it was a daughter born after Thomas's death. There was no child born to them in the six years of their marriage, and is no way of saying if this was due to fertility issues or if she had miscarriages, but in any case it seems Salisbury did not hold their childlessness against Alice, and the marriage appears to have been successful otherwise.[104] Alice often accompanied her husband to France when he went there, perhaps already knowing the country from her own father's visits.

Alice soon made a name for herself in France, becoming known as a very beautiful and very temperamental woman. One story that encapsules her spirit occurred in Paris in 1424, after the English took Verneuil. The Duke of Burgundy, Philip the Good, had arrived to celebrate the English victory with the English commanders at a wedding of two of his nobles. Alice's husband Thomas was one of them, and she attended the festivities with him. William de la Pole, Duke of Suffolk, was also there.[105]

It was a great celebration, but for Alice it soon turned sour. Philip appeared captivated with her, and 'made a pass' at her. Alice rejected him, but Philip was used to being successful with women. He persisted, trying to flirt. As he would not take no for an answer, Alice openly made a scene, rejecting him loudly and clearly. This was recorded in several sources,[106] which suggests it actually happened rather than being salacious court gossip. Tellingly, everyone agreed that Alice had been justified in making a scene.[107]

Perhaps because of this incident, the relationship between Alice's husband Thomas and Duke Philip cooled remarkably. Soon afterwards, Thomas and his friend William de la Pole chose to go against Duke Philip's interests by joining the force that was to besiege Orleans.[108] This decision was to prove fatal for Thomas, and disastrous in other ways for William.

We cannot know if William sided with Thomas's decision because of conviction, friendship or simple pragmatism. Perhaps he too was insulted by the way the Duke of Burgundy had treated his friend's wife. He and Thomas were good friends then, often together, and since Alice often accompanied her husband, she and William must have known each other well. We do not know how they felt about one another, but Alice probably liked William. He, however, may have felt more for her than simple affection, though presumably he would have assumed that any feelings of love or lust he had towards her were to remain his secret, never acted upon. Certainly, he never acted in any way untoward to her, and he and Thomas remained good friends.

When Thomas and William committed to the siege of Orleans, neither of them would have known it was to be their last venture together. William, as we have mentioned, was captured and imprisoned. Thomas, however, was killed, leaving Alice a widow for the second time. She was just twenty-four or twenty-five.

Like Sir John Phelip, Sir Thomas Montacute, Earl of Salisbury had been very generous to his wife. Though naturally his title fell to his daughter, Alice was treated equally to her in all other possessions. Thomas left her half his net worth in his will, as well as 1,000 marks in gold, 3,000 marks in jewellery and plate, and lordship over his Norman lands.[109]

It was upon this wealthy widow that William de la Pole, Earl of Suffolk, set his sights when in prison, his thoughts turning towards love and marriage. He made contact with her, at first presumably only to express his sympathy for her loss, and later to woo her. He wrote her love poems from captivity and had them sent to her.[110]

It is often claimed that these poems show William was romantically and sexually interested in Alice,[111] and not simply motivated by the prospect of a good marriage. This is certainly possible, but it does not have to be the case. Alice was a good catch. As mentioned above, she was extremely wealthy. In addition to that, she had connections which would be useful to any man whom she chose to marry. Through her stepdaughter, Alice Montacute, she was closely related to the powerful Neville family; through her first marriage, she was on good terms with the Phelip and Beaumont families; and through her father she had connections with many merchants.[112] All of this would have sufficed to make William interested in her by itself, and though she had, in six years of marriage, not given Salisbury a child, William would have heard by early 1429 that she had given birth to his posthumous daughter, which would have dispelled any doubts on her ability to bear children. It is perfectly feasible that William simply considered the advantages marriage to Alice would bring, just as it is possible that he might have developed romantic feelings for her and, since she was of good standing and a reasonable match for him, decided to pursue a marriage with her. It is feasible that for William this was outweighed by the advantages marriage to Alice would bring, just as it is possible that he might have developed romantic feelings for her and, since she was of good standing and a reasonable match for him, decided to pursue a marriage with her. His poems to Alice might have been a genuine expression of feelings, a conventional way of wooing a prospective bride from a distance, or even a calculated way to convince Alice to marry him.

Alice had less to gain from the marriage than William did. Already a dowager countess, her status would not increase by marriage to him. Nor had she any need for financial security, and William would not have been able to offer this anyway. The birth of her daughter in 1429 meant that the pull of motherhood is unlikely to have convinced her to marry William. If William wanted Alice to marry him, he would have needed to convince her she would be happier as his wife than she would be as a widow.

However he did it, he accomplished his goal. Alice agreed to marry him. But she was not a lovestruck girl. Whether love and affection were involved in her decision, or whether she simply did not like the thought of remaining alone from her mid-twenties onwards and considered William's offer the best she was going to get, she did not go into the marriage unprepared. Her father had seen to it that she was secure and received all the possible perks from her first two marriages,[113] and Alice seems to have inherited his sense for good business and ensured a similar arrangement when she married William. She would not lose any privileges while married to William. She would retain complete control of her money and assets, while William would need her assent to spend any of her money. Despite this, he would be wealthier than before the marriage.[114] William agreed to her terms, and arrangements for the marriage were made.

William would have been in need of wealthy relatives, and was presumably happy to have a rich fiancée, for it was clear that securing his freedom would require a hefty ransom to be paid to the Bastard of Orleans. A sum of £20,000 was agreed on,[115] representing well over £10 million in modern times.[116]The Bastard of Orleans must have known there was no way William would be able to obtain such a sum in captivity; to raise it he would need to sell lands, and to do that he would need to be out of prison. The Bastard of Orleans therefore agreed to give him conditional freedom. William was not the first such case, and the normal arrangements for such circumstances were made. A prisoner exchange was agreed on, and William's youngest brother, Thomas, a priest, eventually arrived at the Duke of Orleans's castle in late 1430 and agreed to take William's place in prison while he raised the money to buy his freedom and married his intended.[117]

Perhaps William thought that raising the money would be easier once he was married to Alice and thus connected to many wealthy and noble families, or perhaps the couple were simply eager to be united. As soon as William was free and had arrived in England, the two applied to the king to secure a marriage licence for themselves. It was issued in November 1430,[118] from which point William and Alice might have married at any time. Given the gargantuan nature of William's mission to raise his ransom money, it is likely neither he nor Alice wanted to wait until that was done, knowing it could quite possibly take up to a year, if not more.

Early Years of Marriage, 1430–1442

William and Alice's honeymoon phase was a short one. Within months of their wedding, they must have begun to fear that theirs was to be a tragically short-lived union, for in April 1431 William took sick. He was 'seized with the plague',[119] and for a time was thought likely to die. In the end, it did not come to that. William was lucky; despite being so seriously ill, he survived without any adverse effects, and before the month was out he was considered completely recovered.

Once he had recuperated, in the summer of 1431, he returned to France with his new wife.[120] Their actions there are not recorded. William might have gone to see his brother Thomas and his captor, the Bastard of Orleans, and informed them how far he had progressed raising the money. If they arrived in France as early as May, it is likely they went to see the burning of the nineteen-year-old Joan of Arc, against whose forces William had lost the siege three years earlier. Despite what is often assumed, Joan was not executed for witchcraft but heresy.

Their presence at Joan's execution is often assumed but not confirmed, and with William seriously sick only in April, not to mention his efforts to raise the money to free his brother, it is quite possible they arrived in France only in the weeks after this most famous of executions. If so, this would have been rather symptomatic, for in the following years William, and Alice with him, began spending more and more time in England and less and less in France, involved in the war.

It seems that William, once he was married, became more focused on establishing his place as an earl in England. He may well have reasoned that his fifteen years of military service in France had amply demonstrated his support for the military concerns of the English crown.[121] It is possible he originally thought to join the army again once he had raised all the money he needed to free Thomas, but when Thomas died in prison in 1432[122] William seems to have considered his concerns in France as mostly over; he also grew more interested in peace. Possibly this was in part due to the Bastard of Orleans's courteous behaviour in agreeing not to take another prisoner and abstain from claiming more money. Perhaps it was the mere fact of his brother's death in itself; Thomas was William's fourth brother to die in France, and he might have now decided the price for war was too high to pay. Equally, it could have been that his marriage changed his focus, and he wished to stay with his wife rather than be involved in military campaigns, and also to finally concentrate on his position in England, which had gone neglected for so long while he had been fighting in France.

Whether this was his motive for losing interest in military actions in France or not, it was certainly what occupied him in the years to come. He became part of the royal court, being made a royal councillor,[123] though his steep rise in the king's favour would come only later. In the 1430s, especially during the early part of the decade, William's main interests seem to have been attending to his marriage and building up his own connections through his wife.

William and Alice appear to have had a good relationship. William became close to her parents, especially her father, and it seems that in the first four years of their marriage the couple often stayed with them, until Thomas Chaucer's death in 1434[124] and his wife's death shortly afterwards. Thomas left his daughter, granddaughter and son-in-law his ancestral manor in Ewelme, where in the following years the couple would stay most often, and where sadly his Montacute granddaughter died in the mid-1430s.

William and Alice had the manor renovated, practically turning it into a palace. They also had a very famous almshouse built there, for which royal licence was granted in 1437.[125] It was at that time that William began finding his place in the court of the young king Henry VI. He soon became a favourite, and at first this was not considered a problem. A war veteran, William was in a good position to advise Henry, and though his influence would come to cause more and more resentment as the years passed, there was none of that in the 1430s.

In the first decade of their marriage there were few clouds in the sky for William and Alice. It was perhaps the most peaceful period of their married lives. Tales survive to suggest theirs was a carefree life then, even joyful. There is an account of Alice causing some outrage in the 1430s by dressing up as a merchant's wife and 'desport[ing]' herself with two of her servants.[126] No further details are offered, but the suggestion is clearly that there was a lot of free time for Alice and her husband to enjoy themselves in those years.

And of course the couple tried to have children. Before his marriage to Alice, William had had two illegitimate children. It seems he took care of them; quite possibly, they lived in his and Alice's household. One of them, Jane, married Thomas Stonor, an Oxfordshire neighbour of the Earl and Countess of Suffolk in Ewelme, which suggests at least a close association of father and daughter.[127] What happened to her sister, William's other illegitimate daughter, is not known. It seems certain, though, that William was a good father to them. Such fond feelings aside, it is virtually certain that William would have wanted and tried to have children with Alice, to have an heir to his earldom if nothing else.

In 1438, they had a font built in the church belonging to their Ewelme palace[128] and in 1440 they acquired a papal licence to use it to baptised any children they might have,[129] suggesting they had concrete hopes of having a child soon. Sadly, they were mistaken. Either their hopes came to naught or Alice suffered miscarriages. Whichever it was, it must have caused them pain, and as Alice became older they must have feared their hope of having children would never be fulfilled. This does not seem to have affected their marriage, however. They still seemed to be a close couple at the end of the 1430s and the beginning of the 1440s, seeking each other's company and taking joy in their shared projects.

William began to spend more and more time at court, and often Alice accompanied him. Christmas 1441, however, they spent at Ewelme, observing the Christmas festivities there and remaining at the manor until late February 1442.[130] It must have been during this time that Alice conceived their only – or perhaps only surviving – child.

Going by her son's birthdate, it seems likely Alice first became aware of her pregnancy in February, and maybe this is why she did not accompany her husband when he went to court again on 22 February 1442, because like many women she felt unwell in the first stages of her pregnancy.[131] Another possibility is that she was wary of travelling for fear that if she overexerted herself she might lose this longed-for pregnancy.

Alice turned thirty-eight at some point during 1442. She was old for a pregnancy, and all precautions will have been taken to provide security for her and her unborn baby. From Christmas 1441 until the birth of her baby, Alice travelled much less than usual.[132] William, for his part, spent less time at court than in previous years, and a lot of time at Ewelme with her.[133]. It is easy to imagine them being torn between joy as the pregnancy progressed, apparently without any problems, and fears of a late miscarriage, complications during the birth, or the deaths of mother and baby.

In August 1442, following the custom of the time, Alice would have gone into confinement to prepare for the birth. Perhaps, as she would arrange for her daughter-in-law over twenty years later, she brought books to entertain herself.[134] Evidence suggests that she had her chambers decorated with tapestries showing biblical scenes, among them one of Saint Anne, mother of the Virgin Mary.[135] Perhaps Alice took special comfort from this saint, who in the Bible is said to have been married three times and to have given birth late in life,[136] echoing Alice's own experience.

However she might have comforted herself and passed the time, Alice's pregnancy had a happy outcome. She carried her baby to term, and on 27 September 1442 she gave birth to a healthy boy. She and William decided to name him John, after William's late brother. Baby John was baptised in the font they had built at their church in Ewelme.[137]

1
Early Life

Son of an Earl

We no longer know the identity of John's godparents. It was custom at the time for a boy to have two godfathers and one godmother, and for girls to have two godmothers and one godfather.[138] While it was a rule that the godparents were not meant to be related by blood or marriage to the child, it was a rule more honoured in breach than observance for children of John's noble birth.[139] Partly, this was simply out of necessity, as most nobles were related in some degree and therefore it would have been extremely difficult to find a suitable godparent, let alone three. Equally, it was also due to the fact that relatives of such a child were often of extremely high standing, best positioned to give them all they could need in their life, and as such considered good godparents.

In John's case, at least, it seems likely that his godparents were not close relatives. His mother had been an only child, so no maternal aunts or uncles existed to stand as godparents for him, and his father's brothers had all died long before his birth. William did, however, have several living sisters when his son was born. Quite possibly one of them was his godmother, but naturally this is sheerest guesswork. All we can say with certainty is that that the men and the woman chosen to be godparents would have been of high standing.

There are many noble men and women closely connected with William and Alice who could have feasibly been asked to fulfil this task for little John. Perhaps even King Henry VI himself stood godfather to the small boy. Even if he did not, he showed happiness at his birth, sending congratulations to the new mother and father and probably a christening present. His most valuable present came later, though, when John was two, granting Alice joint guardianship of her son with William, which meant that in the event of something happening to William the boy would remain in his mother's care, to be raised in her household, his wardship not granted to another.[140]

Little John doubtlessly grew up sheltered. His parents would have known that, given his mother's age at his birth, he would almost certainly remain an only child. All their hopes would have centred on him, and amid all their joy at his birth and his eventual growth into a healthy toddler, they also would have feared for this precious life. Child mortality was high; for both personal and dynastic reasons, they must have been afraid of losing their only child, and surely protected him as best they could. It seems as if little John was not allowed to travel for the first seven years of his life, for fear of something happening to him. Though we have no details of his first years, it is almost certain they extended the same care to all other aspects of his early existence. All the servants employed to take care of him would have been carefully watched for signs of illness.

Speaking of servants, there would have been many; even a noble infant needed a lot of attention. Nicholas Orme in his book *Medieval Children* details the sort of household a boy like little John would have had.[141] If Alice chose not to flout conventions and breastfeed her son herself, which is possible but unlikely, little John would have had a wet nurse to feed him. He would have had his own nursery, supervised by a nurse and staffed with at least one rocker who changed and dressed him and did other menial tasks. Without a doubt, William and Alice would have been very careful in choosing these servants, seeing to it they were healthy, strong and trustworthy. John's wet nurse would have been given the same good food as his parents to ensure the quality of her milk.[142]

These precautions worked; John prospered. It seems that he was a strong child. During his first years, his upbringing would not have been too different from that of modern toddlers. He would have learnt how to walk and talk, examining and discovering the world around him, always under a close eye. Only after he had mastered such basic skills would his education have begun, his routine now diverging from those of modern toddlers and his commoner contemporaries. Around the age of three or four he may well have been considered old enough to start preparing for his future work as an earl.[143]

It seems as if Alice made most of the decisions about little John's education, William giving her free rein. In fact, it seems that he was not very involved in the decision-making process. It was not unusual for mothers to have the power to decide over their small child's upbringing and education until a certain age, and to have a say even later, but few men gave their wives such complete control as William gave Alice.[144] Indeed, William seemed very little involved himself in his son's upbringing. This might have been due to him not considering his toddler son to be very interesting, but more likely it was because his responsibilities at Henry VI's court were growing as time passed.[145]

Little John presumably did not see his father often in his first years of life, though Alice often chose to stay close to the boy at Ewelme. Though she did occasionally accompany her husband to court in the first years of John's life, she did so less often than in the years before his birth. This might have been out of sentimentality, a desire to be close to her child, but in the context of the times in which they lived it seems unlikely. She might have been motivated out of fear for her only surviving child, preferring to keep a watchful eye on all that was happening around him and guarding against problems. The household ordinances for the future Edward V, made in 1473, give a hint as to what such problems could have been in the raising of a noble child.[146] Like Edward, he might have been kept away from 'people who swore, were sick or could be a bad influence'.[147]

It is notable that from 1444 Alice accompanied William to court more frequently, leaving little John in the care of his nurses and caretakers, so it may very well be that, having assured herself as to his safety and well-being, and having seen him grow up healthy and strong in the first one and a half years of his life, Alice considered it safe to leave him be.

While William, like many parents of the time, was a rather distant father by necessity, it is possible his lack of interest was not emotional detachment from his son but rather enforced through his work at court. Alice appears to have chosen to be unusually close to her son, staying with him more often than was usual for parents at the time, but even she saw no cause for constantly staying with him.

Due to this, little John saw little of his parents that year. At the age of two, he could not yet have had any formal education, as can be seen by the arrangements for various Princes of Wales; even heirs to the throne of England did not start having lessons before the age of three.[148] Alice was a woman who valued education, but there is no reason to assume she wanted to give her son a schooling that went above and beyond that received by heirs to the throne.

John's days would have followed the simple routine he had followed ever since he could walk and talk. He would have been encouraged to learn the simple skills even a toddler could learn and would not have known, or been able to understand had someone told him at that age, that his father was involved in trying to arrange and king's marriage and this was why he and his mother barely at home. Presumably, it would not have mattered to him either, as he did not know anything else. It was very common for medieval nobles to rarely see their children, so even as he grew old enough to understand the absence of his father and, less frequently, his mother, he is unlikely to have seen anything wrong with it. However, his father's actions in the years to follow were to have profound repercussions on John's life in the not too far off future.[149]

It was his undertaking to arrange the king's marriage that would make William the unpopular man he became. Unlike many others, William was eager to bring England's long war with France to a close, and therefore he supported a marriage which would bring this about. Naturally, the idea did not originate with him. Knowing that Henry VI favoured peace, and that it would be the best for the English, whose military heyday in France was over, Charles VII of France suggested a peace treaty, which would include a marriage for Henry.[150] On the face of it, this was the best for both sides. It would allow the English to stop their incessant warring in France without losing face, and it would stop the expensive and brutal attacks on French lands which had cost so many lives. It would also remove a rival claimant to Charles VII's throne. From a modern point of view, the issue seems black and white; peace is always being the preferable choice. But in the context of the times, both sides had a point.

Charles VII was entirely right in pointing out, and William in agreeing, that there was no longer any realistic chance of the English seizing the French throne by military victory. Thirty years after the Battle of Agincourt, England had lost all its advantages. Though Henry VI had been crowned King of France in Paris in 1429[151], this was only nominal by 1444.[152] Charles VII had long since been crowned himself and had assumed his powers as king. It has sometimes been postulated that if Henry had been a stronger king, more like his warlike father, he could have made such a joint monarchy work, but most likely it would have just meant more battles fought and more lives lost. Others have speculated that Henry VI´s famous mental illness was worsened, if not caused entirely, by the stress of having this nearly impossible task hanging over him since earliest childhood. In any case, Henry was not the man for this task. In the long years of his minority, France had regained a lot of the lands won by the English, and as the monkish, gentle Henry came of age his weakness and unsuitability as a ruler was exploited to encourage the French fighters.

William, an experienced warrior, most likely saw the writing on the wall. He also knew the terrible human cost of war first hand, having lost all his four brothers and his father during the conflict in France in some way. It is very understandable that he wanted the war to stop, and from a modern perspective he was completely in the right. However, the peace came at a price, and many feared that it would too steep for England to pay. William nonetheless appears to have considered it worth paying when weighed against the humiliation of an inevitably military loss. Doubtlessly, some of the opposition to William's hopes and plans was also rooted in xenophobia and hatred of the French, but it is possible to overstate this and ignore the validity of the arguments against the match suggested for Henry. His mother Katherine of Valois had been accepted as Henry V's wife despite her French nationality, so perhaps this kind of prejudice only reared its head when the English were to be disadvantaged. Whichever it was that motivated most of those arguing against the match, however, those arguing for it were to have their way.

In March 1444, William, accompanied by Alice as well as others of Henry's court like Keeper of the Privy Seal Adam Moleyns, secretary Richard Andrewe and John Wenlock, a nobleman who would earn infamy in later years, travelled to France to meet the fourteen-year-old girl suggested by Charles VII to become Henry VI's wife and queen – Charles's niece Margaret, daughter of René, Duke of Anjou.[153]

While his parents travelled abroad, the not-quite-two-year-old John stayed at Ewelme, with his own staff. He would still have been too young to even understand what was happening, and would definitely have been seen as too young to make such a journey to France when there was no pressing need for it. Arrangements would have been made for his care in the absence of his parents, but while this would not have differed much, if at all, from the preparations usually made for him when neither of his parents were in residence, there would have also been other measures taken in case something happened to his parents. This was a real danger, as ships sometimes sank, and it is probable that both William and his wife wrote wills before setting off on the journey.

Any fears they might have had thankfully came to naught. The royal entourage travelled to Tours, where on 4 May they met the young Margaret.[154] The meeting was a success, and it was agreed that the marriage would go ahead soon.

The men Henry VI had sent to France had been given instructions in the event that they considered Margaret a suitable wife for Henry and wished to secure a quick alliance. This was an outcome that had been expected to occur before they had ever left England, and William had been given the perhaps most important task of all: he was to be the bridegroom in a proxy wedding.[155] Margaret of Anjou was to wed Henry not in a ceremony with the king himself but with William, who was instructed to stand in his place. This was not an unusual practice, especially for royal weddings, and was often used so the bride could start the journey to her new country as a married woman, removing the threat that she could be kidnapped and forcibly married to someone else to thwart the alliance.

Henry, too, could not come to France to marry. There were concerns about him leaving a power vacuum in his absence, allowing his enemies to seize power, or establishing a regency council that was bound to displease one important faction or another. It was also feared that Henry's life might be in danger should he go to France. The only sensible decision, therefore, was a proxy wedding.

It went ahead on 24 May 1444, Margaret making her vows to William in lieu of Henry.[156] Naturally, the marriage was not yet completely binding. Once in each other's presence, Henry and Margaret would have to make their vows to one another and then consummate the marriage, but it was still a binding promise. Four days after the proxy marriage, a truce was signed between France and England, again with William acting in Henry's stead again.[157] He had Henry's permission to negotiate the terms of this truce,[158] but it was not to be a very favourable one. Either William didn't dare to negotiate more firmly with Charles VII or was unsuccessful when he did; either way, William's truce neither fulfilled Henry's hopes or served England well. Unlike what Henry had hoped, it was not a perpetual peace agreement but one lasting for just twenty-three months, albeit with the possibility of being extended.[159] The matter of who was rightful King of France had not been touched upon but postponed, and, perhaps most shockingly for the English, William had not objected to a stalwart English ally, the Duke of Brittany, being named a French vassal.[160]

Henry VI seemed happy with William when he returned home, buoyed by the news that he was now a married man. Perhaps the king, much like William, did not care how unfavourable the terms were as long as they meant peace, or maybe he thought it was the best William could do under the circumstances. Whatever he thought, he was certainly pleased with William, and rewarded him.

One reward given to William would concern little John. Almost exactly one year before William signed the truce with France, on 31 May 1443, a baby girl called Margaret had been born to John Beaufort, Duke of Somerset and Earl of Kendall, one of the wealthiest and, together with William himself, most powerful men in the country.[161] Almost exactly a year after the birth of his small daughter, however, on 27 May 1443, a day before the Franco-English truce was signed, John Beaufort died under somewhat mysterious circumstances.[162] As had happened when William's brother Michael had died, Somerset's titles did not fall to his young daughter. The dukedom of Somerset fell to John's brother Henry, while the earldom of Kendall passed out of the family. It was given to Jean de Foix as a reward for his staunch support.[163] Since Foix was the husband of William's niece, it seems probable William was involved in this decision. He, and especially little John, were to profit in other ways from John Beaufort's death.

Beaufort's daughter, though she remained untitled in her own right, inherited all his lands and money, becoming a very rich heiress though she wasn't yet one year old. As was usual in such cases, her wardship fell to the king, who had the choice to either keep it and all the revenues it brought until she came of age or married a man of his choosing, or else to give these privileges to someone he wished to reward. Though when little Margaret was born the king had originally agreed to allow her mother to keep her wardship in the event of her father's death,[164] the duke's subsequent failures in France had lost him favour with the king, and Henry VI thus chose to pass little Margaret's wardship to one of his greatest and most beloved advisors, William de la Pole.

The full text of the grant show just how much he and Alice profited from this, and how high William stood in the king's favour by then:

> And forasmuch as our cousin the Duke of Somerset is now late passed to God's mercy, the which hath a daughter and heir to

> succeed him, of full tender age called Margaret. We considering the notable services that our cousin the earl of Suffolk hath done unto us, and tendering him therefore the more specially as reason will, have of our grace and especial proper motion and mere deliberation granted unto him to have the ward and marriage of the said Margaret, without anything.[165]

It has sometimes been assumed that this was more than a simple reward for William. Due to her parentage, Margaret had royal blood, albeit diluted, and as such was considered to be a possible focal point for rebels who might try and use her parentage to unseat the king.[166] By handing her wardship to William, whose own son was roughly her age, Henry VI might have hoped to stop any such plans before they could even take off; if William married little John to Margaret, she was safely allied to a family loyal to king and crown, while her wealth ensured the future of his closest advisor's progeny.

Over sixty years later, Margaret's confessor John Fisher would claim that her money and royal blood meant that William 'most diligently worked to procure her for his son and heir',[167] but this statement was probably heavily tinged with hindsight. Not only is there no evidence of William being very eager for such a marriage between the two children, he also showed remarkably little interest in Margaret's wardship otherwise.

It was quite common for those who had the wardship of a child to also have custody of the child, though William and Alice decided against that. In this case, the Suffolks chose to let baby Margaret stay in her own household with her mother. Given that their only child was a boy, perhaps they felt Margaret's mother would be better equipped than them to bring up a little girl. Perhaps, they thought it was the best option for all involved, as it would allow little Margaret to grow up under the supervision of her mother and they would not have to pay for the upkeep of a duke's daughter while still profiting from the income of her lands. Conversely, perhaps Margaret's mother paid the Suffolks for the privilege of having her daughter remain in her household, or William remembered Henry VI's broken promise and allowed her to keep her daughter. Whichever it was, little John and little Margaret would not have much to do with one another in these early stages of their lives.

There is one contemporary source which states that William and Alice chose to marry Margaret and John as soon as they received her wardship, in order to create an alliance between the families.[168] However, this does not seem all too likely. For one, all surviving documentation regarding this marriage, such as the papal dispensation, indicates that it was only made in early 1450. Moreover, in early 1444 John was a toddler of twenty months while Margaret was a baby of one year. It is unlikely either of them were old enough to talk well enough to give the right responses during a wedding service. It was not at all unusual for very young children to be married in the fifteenth century, but at such a tender age they could not have performed even the simplest duties of bride and groom during a wedding ceremony. They would have had to be married by proxy, and while such proxy marriages sometimes happened, they had to be affirmed by bride and groom themselves soon after to validate the marriage. John and Margaret would not have been able to do this for some time yet in 1444, undermining the purpose of any ceremony to secure their alliance.

It is possible that they intended to hold a marriage ceremony as soon as the children were old enough, perhaps four or five, and considered them engaged, but other plans eventually intervened, and it has to be pointed out that William never seemed all too eager to marry the two children. Since William also never showed a lot of interest in his son's education, leaving all details of his care and upbringing to Alice, it might very well be he considered his duties to king and country more important, or else he trusted in Henry enough that he felt no need to rush.

Certainly, it must have seemed to William that his position at Henry VI's court was secure. The valuable wardship of Margaret Beaufort was not the only reward the king gave his chief advisor, after all. While it is certainly interesting that little John's future was considered a very important reward for his parents, Henry had also a more immediate reward for William, elevated him from earl to marquis,[169] which meant he was above all other earls in the country, among the most noble men of the realm. Little John thus became the heir of one of the highest-ranked men in the country. Whether or not this changed his upbringing we cannot know, but even at only two years of age he would have known he was set to become an important man.

Son of a Marquis

William's elevation to marquis came at the price of little John rarely seeing his parents during his early years. Though the marriage of Henry VI and Margaret of Anjou had been formalised in Tours, the preparations for her coming to England and becoming queen consort had only just begun. Henry VI began having palaces restored so they would meet the standards expected by a queen,[170] as well as planning a suitable entourage to meet her when she finally made her way to England. William was deeply involved in these preparations, and given the important part she would play in the coming ceremonies it stands to reason that Alice was too.[171] This, of course, meant they had little time for their small son; he would almost certainly have spent his second birthday without his family.

To modern ears, all this sounds rather sad. At the time it would have seemed quite ordinary, and John himself would have been too young to even question the circumstances of his life. Between the ages of one and three, he would have almost never seen his parents. However, their continuing rise in royal favour affected him as well, and clearly the king was aware of his importance to his parents. On 4 November 1444, Henry VI made an important grant to John which his parents must have hoped would never become relevant:

> Grant to William de la Pole, marquis and earl of Suffolk, and Alice his wife, in consideration of his long stay in the parts of France at his great costs for the treaty of peace between the king and his uncle of France and his realms, lordships and subjects, and for the king's marriage, that, if he died, his heir being within age, Alice and his executors shall have the keeping of the heir with his marriage and so from heir to heir etc.[172]

This grant is illuminating in several ways. For one, it was clearly stated to be a reward for William's work in bringing about the marriage between Henry and Margaret of Anjou. It is very interesting that the well-being of William's wife and son after his death was seen by Henry as the best reward for him, rather than something more concrete he could use during his own lifetime. Even though his parenting looks rather distant through modern eyes, the nature of this gift suggests William must have cared deeply for his son as well as his wife.

It is, however, also interesting that Henry VI made such a grant to William less than a year after he had broken a similar promise to John Beaufort. Possibly, it helped William to know that in the event of his death, his wife and son had not only a promise but an actual grant to affirm their right to stay together. In any case, the grant obviously shows that little John's well-being and education was so important to his parents that retaining control of it was considered a great reward. The boy himself would have been too young to understand such precautions and too young even to be told, and he would have had little with which to console himself as they remained largely absent through 1444.

Despite this, William and Alice obviously worried about their son and made arrangements for his comfort. In 1444, they gave orders for their living quarters to be renovated to conform to their wishes. Little John was the one who got the benefit of this most of all, for in early 1445 his parents had to leave the country again, while John remained in his nursery in Ewelme.

After her proxy wedding to Henry, Margaret of Anjou had spent most of the year with her family in Lorraine preparing for her new life in England. It was not until March 1445 that she finally left.[173] On the first leg of the journey, from Lorraine to St Denis, her brother Jean accompanied her. At St Denis he left, and the Duke of Orleans took over as head of her entourage. He stayed with her until they arrived in Pontoise, where she was received by the English entourage Henry VI had organised.[174] Henry VI had not stinted on his new wife's reception. The group tasked with honourably accompanying her to England was 300 men strong and cost 5,000 pounds.[175] Many noblemen were in this entourage, such as the king's cousin Richard, Duke of York, and his wife, but it was headed by William and Alice. Quite possibly, Margaret was glad about this. Though she naturally did not know them well, they were at least familiar faces from the proxy wedding, and it was perhaps at this time that their famous closeness began to take root.

Margaret travelled to Rouen with her new entourage, but she was not well. In fact, by the time they arrived in Rouen, she was so poorly that she could not take part in the festivities that had been staged for her arrival.[176] If little John, back in England, was told of the festivities in Rouen it must have sounded like a fairy tale to him, with his parents as the lead characters; due to Margaret's illness, a substitute had been chosen to play the part of the queen for her, travelling into the city of Rouen in a chariot covered by cloth of gold. The replacement for the queen was Alice.[177]

Apparently, Alice played her part well. The reception came off without a hitch, and on 3 April the new queen and her entourage left for England. The sea crossing did not help Margaret's recovery, and legend has it that she was so weak when her ship landed in England that she could not walk, and William gallantly carried her ashore.[178]

Henry VI was happy with William's service and would once again reward him well. He was definitely the king's favourite by now, and he would become one of the queen's favourites as well, as would his wife. They were present on 24 April 1445 when Margaret and Henry married in person,[179] and appear to have stayed at court for most of the rest of the year, becoming more closely acquainted with the queen and strengthening their bond with the king.

It has sometimes been suggested that Margaret, who was only fifteen in 1445, saw Alice and William as substitute parents in the strange land that was to be her new home, and that they in turn treated her as a daughter in many ways.[180] In fact, this seems fairly likely and makes sense of all their behaviour. Margaret had been born in the year of William and Alice's wedding; they were certainly old enough to be her parents. Certainly they helped Margaret figure out her new position, and it may very well be that in the first year of her queenship they saw more of her than of their actual child. They were so often at court in 1445, though, that it is quite possible they even brought little John with them on at least one occasion. Either way, John was not the main focus of attention in those years.

Despite this, William's work at court was also to have a positive effect on John in the long run. Already, he had become heir to a marquis and his parents had been given a wardship that could have, should they choose to exploit it, financially secured his future before he was old enough to count. However, William obviously had other plans for his son's future. He must have considered the possibility, but for whatever reason, he and Alice decided not to marry little John to their ward. In 1446, another wealthy little girl's wardship fell to the king: that of Anne Beauchamp, the two-year-old Duchess of Warwick.[181] Like Margaret Beaufort, she was one of the richest heiresses in the realm, and like Margaret she would have been considered a very good marriage prospect.

William and Alice were aware of this, and clearly considered little Anne to be a better match for their son. In the summer of 1446, William bought the wardship of the little girl from the king. In the Calendar of Patent Rolls it is stated on 16 September 1446 that 'William, marquis and earl of Suffolk, bought of late the keeping of Anne, daughter and heir of the said duke [Henry Beauchamp, Duke of Warwick]'.[182] It is not known what William paid to the king for the wardship, but given Anne's wealth it must have been a hefty sum.

William might not have bought the wardship solely with little John's future in mind. Anne was only two years old; whoever held her wardship would profit from the revenue of all lands she possessed for well over a decade, until she was either married to a man of his choosing or came of age unmarried at fourteen. It would be naive to assume that William did not think of this, even if perhaps his son's future was foremost in his mind when he made the purchase.

Holding Anne's wardship did not nullify their possession of Margaret Beaufort's wardship. In autumn 1446, William and Alice could choose between two very good marriage prospects for their son. William was later to claim that his intention had always been to marry John to Anne, rather than to Margaret. Though his circumstances when he made this statement suggest that he might have been lying to save himself,[183] as anything else could have been taken as an admission of guilt in various matters, circumstantial evidence indicates he was telling the truth. Even if one assumes that William did not purchase Anne's wardship explicitly to marry her to his son, he and Alice showed rather more interest in her than they had in Margaret Beaufort from the first.

They took custody of the toddler girl and had her brought up at Ewelme together with John.[184] Only one and a half years apart in age, the two children would have got to know each other well. Perhaps it was a relief for John to finally have a playmate of his own standing, somebody who was not alienated by his significance. It seems that Alice, still responsible for John's upbringing, arranged for Anne to receive a similarly good education.

William and Alice never arranged an actual wedding between their son and little Anne. However, the children were both still very young in 1446, and perhaps John's parents were simply waiting until both were old enough to fully understand what was happening before they arranged such a ceremony. Anne was definitely treated with honour and given as much care as little John, and the circumstances very much suggest the two toddlers were being raised to become husband and wife one day. For Margaret Beaufort, there are no such indications.

First Signs of Trouble

Once Anne Beauchamp had settled in her new life, and John had become used to having her around, the children would have continued their calm existence at Ewelme while life for William and Alice grew increasingly turbulent.

Now the king's closest and most beloved advisor, as well as a favourite of the queen, who was rapidly becoming unpopular,[185] William was widely thought to run the government after his own gusto for the weak-minded Henry.[186] He became more and more powerful, but also gained a lot of enemies, especially when one particular aspect of the marriage contract between Henry VI and Margaret of Anjou was discovered. The marriage treaty had included a secret clause that England would give their occupied lands of Anjou and Maine back to France.[187] This didn't just mean that the French would regain something most Englishmen considered rightfully theirs, but also that all English settlers in those lands would have to leave. This naturally caused a lot of resentment, not only in those directly affected but also across England as a whole. William, seen as the architect of the treaty, bore the brunt of the criticism.[188]

This is somewhat simplistic. While William technically was the one who agreed to the contract, even as Henry VI's closest advisor he never had anywhere near the power to agree on something like this without explicit instructions from the king to do so. He can be fairly maligned for his support for the policy, but the notion that he was its author is patently false.

Such details are usually lost on any angry mob, and so they were in this instance. Since it was extremely common for the perceived failures of a king to be blamed on his advisors, William would have always been a convenient scapegoat for anyone wishing to criticise the king's policies without directly insulting the monarch. In the case of Henry VI, who was thought – with some justification – to be little suited to the position of king, and malleable as well,[189] it was even easier for William's enemies to blame him for all the government's failures.

Though William's association with Margaret of Anjou and his role in the marriage negotiations has since dominated all discussions about his rise to power and his downfall, that was not the whole cause of his unpopularity. Henry VI's government was notoriously indebted;[190] his advisors, William among them, had to make do with what little money there was to try and help Henry run the government. However, this deficit was also blamed on William with the logic that the crown was only in debt because William used its funds for his own gain. This is easily disproved by historians,[191] but in the 1440s, with few having any access to any detailed information about the treasury and William's exact government work, such a rumour would have had far more sticking power.

As he grew up, John might have slowly come to realise that while his father was noble and favoured by the king, not everyone liked him. This truth would have been kept from him for the most part, but if he was an inquisitive child, he would have heard some of it. And he certainly would have caught wind of the scandal of early 1447 when the king's uncle Humphrey, Duke of Gloucester was arrested for suspected treason and died in custody.

Duke Humphrey had been an influential politician in the early years of his nephew's reign, though even at the time he was far from uncontroversial, arguing with his own brother and developing a reputation as a violent man in a quarrel. He had lost his political influence some time before when his second wife, Eleanor Cobham, was accused and convicted of witchcraft and trying to kill the king in 1441.[192] Perhaps recognising that the tide was turning against him, Humphrey had then retired from politics, though he remained a popular man among the English commoners.[193] When he was suddenly accused of treason on 20 February 1447 and arrested, many at the time imagined William's hand, suspecting him of wishing to remove a man who might threaten his influence.[194] That Duke Humphrey died only three days after his arrest gave rise to new rumours that he had been poisoned before he could be brought to trial,[195] his enemies fearing that such a trial might turn in his favour and backfire against those who had framed him. Once more the finger was pointed at William, though there is no evidence Duke Humphrey was poisoned at all.[196]

Perhaps, if he heard of it, John was scared and puzzled, but most likely he would still have been too young to truly grasp it, though at four and a half years old, he would have been old enough to understand that his father was in trouble and that many people did not like him. It was, in fact, a dangerous situation for William, especially after Duke Humphrey's death, but it seems that he was either not fully aware of the dangers or, perhaps more likely, ignored or underestimated them. This may have been easy, cosseted as he was in a court that favoured him while his enemies lost power.

In 1448, Henry VI, typically inept at reading the mood of the population, unwittingly gave his enemies more ammunition by rewarding his most favoured advisor in an extravagant fashion: he chose to make him a duke.[197] This was the highest title he could have given his favourite, and it was usually reserved for members of the royal family. For a man as comparatively lowborn as William, it was a dazzling, almost unbelievable honour.

Son of a Duke

Little John, not quite six years old, was heir to a dukedom from then on, and perhaps just old enough to appreciate this. If so, he would have felt very important, and so might have little Anne Beauchamp. Though her father's dukedom had been in the male entail and she was only a countess, it is quite possible that, had she lived, this could have been set aside and she and her husband might have become duke and duchess twice over at some point in the future.

It seems, however, that William became aware of the dangers and the ill-will towards him shortly before his elevation, which happened in June that year. Or possibly he simply wanted to make sure he had his affairs in order. At fifty-two, he was no longer a young man. Many of his contemporaries had died at a younger age of natural causes. With this in mind, William might have wanted to make sure that when he died, whenever and however that happened, his family would be taken care of. Whatever he was thinking, in 1448, he decided to write his will. It was not the first time he did so. We know he had already written one in 1446 (it is referenced in the 1448 version), perhaps when he received Anne Beauchamp's wardship, and he might made others before then as well. Possibly, in one of those wills, little John was mentioned prominently. In the will he wrote after his elevation to a dukedom, it seems William thought more of Alice than John:

> In the name of the Father, Son, and Holy Ghost, one God in three Persons, Be it known to all Christian men, that these presents shall hereafter have, or see, that I, William de la Pole, Dile, Marquis and Earl of Suffolk, in good health of body, and in my good mind, the seventeenth day of January, the twenty-seventh year of King Henry the Sixth, and of our Lord 1448, make my testament in the wise that followeth.
>
> First, I bequeath my soul to the highness and mercy of Him that made it, and that so marvellously bought it with His precious blood; and my wretched body to be buried in my Charter-house at Hull, where I will my image, and stone be made, and the image of my best-beloved wife by me, she to be there with me if she lust; my said sepulture to be made by her discretion in the said Charter-house, where she shall think best, in case be that in my days it not be made, nor begun, desiring, if it may, to lie so, as the masses that I have perpetually founded there for my said best-beloved wife and me, may be daily sung over me.
>
> And also the day of my funeral, and the day of my burying, that the charge thereof be byset upon poor creatures to pray for me, and in no pomps, nor pride of the world.
>
> Also I will, that my lands and goods be disposed after that that I have disposed them in my last will of the date of these presents. And only ordain my best-beloved wife my sole executrix, beseeching her, at the reverence of God, to take the charge upon her for the weal of

> my soul, for above all the earth my singular trust is most in her; and I will for her ease if she will, and else not, that she may take unto her such one person as she lust to name to help her in the execution thereof, for her ease, to labour under her, as she would command him.
>
> And last of all, with the blessing of God, and of me as heartily as I can give it, to my dear and true son, I bequeath between him and his mother, love and all good accord, and give him her wholly. And for remembrance, my great balays [ruby] to my said son.[198]

This will suggests, as do the arrangements for John's care, that while William loved his son, he was not very interested in the details of his upbringing, and his focus lay much more on his wife. Interestingly, his bequest to John of his valuable ruby ring echoes the bequest his own father, Michael, had made to him and each of his younger brothers. Since William had not been his father's heir, he had received only his father's blessing and a ring.[199] John, naturally, would eventually have inherited much more than his father had ever expected to inherit, but it is interesting to note that despite this, the only bequest to John spelled out in his will was almost identical to what his own father had left him.

Of course, John would have known nothing of the contents of his father's will at the time he made it, and possibly he never read it at all. Perhaps he did when he was older, after his father's death, and felt rather left out and unappreciated. Whichever it was, at the time that it was made, neither William, nor his family, and nor the king and queen would have made concrete plans for William's death, hoping he would live for many years yet. But from 1448 on, more and more rumours about William started circulating, rumours that were at best unflattering and usually outright hostile. With his elevation to a dukedom, the resentment against him, already massive after Duke Humphrey's death, reached a new pitch, and for the first time people openly wished for his death.[200]

For many, his elevation to a dukedom must have seemed like a reward for working against what were popularly thought to be England's best interests. Despite this, it seems that neither he nor the king and queen, who continued favouring him, grasped the depth of popular hatred against William. But by 1449, less than a year after William's elevation, his star truly began to fail.[201] It has been suggested that Alice could not deal with the hostility of the public, and that this was why she chose to spend more and more time away from court and William, instead staying with her son and his intended bride at Ewelme.[202] This is certainly possible, but in the light of how she would later act when under pressure and faced with hostility,[203] it is not the most likely explanation. More probable is that she was afraid the wrath expressed by large parts of the population towards her husband, and already extending to her by association, would also be directed at her son.

The Catastrophic Years: 1449–1450

At almost seven years of age, John was old enough to know something bad was happening, affecting his parents, though probably not old enough to understand the details. Probably, his mother and tutors would have tried to shield him from the extent of the trouble, but 1449 was to prove a dramatic year for the little boy, who found himself drawn more and more into the turmoil around his father's person. He must have sensed the danger around him, but it may well have felt distant. Soon, however, the family was struck by a tragedy that was to affect him personally.

In June 1449, little Anne Beauchamp, his intended bride and his playmate of the last three years, died at the tender age of five.[204] The cause of her death is not known, but sadly, child mortality at the time was very high and it was not uncommon for children to die suddenly and unexpectedly. It may have been John's first experience of the death of someone close to him, and no doubt it was a shock and a personal blow. It was also a blow to his parents' plans for his future, and it came at a most inconvenient time for them.

Plans were now openly made for William's downfall, with other powerful nobles voicing their support.[205] William and Alice were no longer in a position to cheerfully make plans for the future in the secure knowledge they would go as they intended, as had been the case in 1446. Their every move was watched for missteps, for a reason to accuse William of various crimes.

Most likely because of this, in the first months after little Anne's death, they made no other arrangements for John's future marriage, perhaps hoping that the frenzy and hatred would die down over time. Perhaps they were also afraid of drawing any attention to themselves and especially their young son by making fresh arrangements. It was a tense time for John, grieving for his little playmate and frightened by the violent hatred against his parents, which affected plans for his own future.

The opprobrium levelled at William did not die down as he might have hoped and as his caretakers might have told John it would; on the contrary, the situation worsened. Men were beginning to disobey William; tenants in his lands began acting lawlessly, which was blamed on him, multiplying the problems. Popular resentment against William was now felt by all associated with him. In November 1449, as Henry VI's parliament opened, William's treasurer was forced to resign under immense pressure.[206]

William seems to have realised that he could only make the situation worse, and that inactivity was therefore the best cause of action. When parliament was adjourned over Christmas, he removed himself from court and did not spend Christmas 1449 with the king and queen, instead staying with his wife and son at Ewelme. Though they would have celebrated Christmas, it must have been a very tense time. William and Alice probably feared that they had little time left to spend together or to secure their son's future.

It was probably because of this anxiety that they made arrangements for John to marry Margaret Beaufort, whose wardship they still held, and who was by then six years old. William had apparently been hesitant to connect John with the girl's family, but by the end of 1449 it was the only sensible option left for his son, promising the boy a degree of security even should something happen to his father. Margaret was very rich in her own right, and her family's connections to William's enemies would have most likely been seen as a way to make sure John could eventually find a place at the king's court even if William's fortunes turned against him, his possessions confiscated and his name besmirched.

In January 1450, a hasty wedding was planned for the two children.[207] It was not before time; William's treasurer was murdered by an outraged mob on 9 January,[208] and perhaps William realised that he too would have to face the music soon. Due to the children's close degree of consanguinity, it was necessary to apply for a papal dispensation allowing them to marry. This was sent for in early January,[209] suggesting the marriage was a sudden decision, made only when William and Alice realised there were no other options left to give their son the wealth and standing they wanted for him.

There was no time to wait for the dispensation to come from Rome; the marriage would have to be validated later. Everyone involved knew the ceremony would have to go ahead without it, and it did. Sometime between 9 January and 28 January 1450,[210] John and Margaret were wed. They were by then old enough to understand their parts in the ceremony and what it would mean for their futures. They were not the youngest children to ever marry; marriages between four-year-olds are recorded. Their age nonetheless did damage the validity of the match, however. When the dispensation came, it described them as having 'formally contracted marriage *per verba legitime de presenti*'[211] –'at the moment legitimised by words'.

This meant the marriage would need to be affirmed again when they were older, then confirmed by consummation. Theirs was considered as more than an engagement but less than a marriage, then. Nevertheless, John's future was as secure as his parents could make it under the circumstances.

Nothing would change in day-to-day life for the newlyweds. Margaret stayed in her mother's household and John stayed with his parents.[212]

Perhaps, had the circumstances been different, Margaret would have joined John in his parents' household, but her mother, though keen on the alliance that would one day make her daughter a duchess, may not have wished to have her daughter physically close to the disgraced Suffolks.

By the time the marriage went ahead, it must have been clear to everyone but the children that the situation was rapidly coming to a head. The wedding ceremony might have been the last time John saw his father. With his son taken care of, William chose to face his enemies head-on. He was isolated by now; all his erstwhile supporters had abandoned him.[213] He would have to fight alone.

On 22 January,[214] openly accused of treason not only by his political enemies but by many commoners, William made a speech to Henry VI, essentially throwing himself on his mercy. He stressed his and his family's losses in Henry V's service and firmly asserted his loyalty to the king. The entire speech is recorded in the Parliament Rolls.[215] It was a brave and impassioned speech, but it was of no avail. On 28 January 1450, William was impeached by Parliament. Shortly afterwards, he was arrested and imprisoned in the Tower of London.[216]

A duke's heir just days ago, John was now a traitor's son.

William remained imprisoned for a while. He was not in a dungeon; the outer circumstances of his imprisonment likely resembled those he had endured in France two decades before. But back then he had few attachments to worry about; now he had a wife and a son. His illegitimate daughters were married, so he at least would not have needed to worry about them. John and Alice, however, were endangered by his situation. His imprisonment satisfied neither his political enemies nor the angry mob.

On 13 March, William had to appear before the king to answer charges of having 'falsely and traitorously plotted, contrived, proposed, envisaged, performed and committed various high, great, heinous and horrible treasons'.[217] The court of public opinion had already declared him guilty. John must have been aware of this; there was no way of sheltering a seven-year-old boy from the reality of his father being accused of treason, nor the fact that, if he was found guilty, he would be executed, his possessions and title forfeit to the crown. He and his mother would have been virtual prisoners at Ewelme if this happened, and if they ever ventured outside they would have been met with hostility. Sheer association with William was enough to imperil them, as the fate of William's treasurer had proved.

Given this backdrop, it is unlikely that Alice travelled to watch her husband's meeting with the king. She and John likely learnt through messengers, at a later date, of the exact accusations against William. Perhaps most shocking for them would have been the charge that William had intended to make John king after Henry VI's death, disinheriting any child of Henry's queen, Margaret. John may not have fully understood the repercussions of this, though it must have baffled and quite possibly frightened him to be mentioned in such accusations. For Alice, however, it would have been terrifying; with her son drawn into the proceedings like this, John came into focus for the angry mob. While most would not have held anything against a small boy of his tender years, the danger was always there that some would consider harming him a suitable revenge against William. It stands to reason that Alice and the household nurses would have tried to keep such fears from John, and perhaps they also tried to conceal other details that could only upset and frighten him.

Despite the terror and stress, it is even possible that William's wife and son were proud of his composure when they heard of his reaction to the accusations, which is recorded in the Parliament Rolls. Notably, while he said that all the charges were 'false and untrue',[218] he specifically addressed the charge concerning the marriage between John and Margaret: 'It is contrary to law and reason to consider the said Margaret so close to the crown; and for his acquittal, he had told to a large number of the lords that if the duke of Warwick's daughter had lived he had intended to marry his son to her and not to the said Margaret.'[219]

William made his case well. It is interesting to note that the only charge involving his son that he formally addressed pertained to the boy's marriage to Margaret. He did not explicitly answer to the charge of wanting to make John king, perhaps because he considered it best not to draw too much attention to his son in the process, or possibly because he considered those charges to be obviously absurd whereas the others needed clearer and more concrete proof against them.

Though William did his all to provide proof of his innocence, it was to no avail. Henry VI believed him; he loved his best advisor and did not want him to die. But the cries for William's blood were too loud, too widespread. Henry VI's love and trust could not save William completely. While the king declared William innocent of high treason and safe from execution, telling him that 'regarding the great and dreadful charges contained in the said first bill, the king holds you neither declared nor charged',[220] he was not completely off the hook. Henry's declaration went on:

> And as regards the second bill submitted against you touching misprisions which are not criminal, the king, by force of your submission, by his own advice and not resorting to the advice of his lords, nor by way of judgment for he is not in place of judgment, puts you to his rule and governance: that is to say, that you, before 1 May next comming shall absent yourself from his realm of England; and also from the said 1 May until the end of the next following and fully complete five years you shall refrain from living in his realm of France or in any other lordships or places which are under his [col. b] obedience, wheresoever they be. And that you shall not show nor

> impute, nor no man for you as far as you may prevent it, any malice, evil will, harm nor damage to any person of whatever degree he is, or to any of the commons of this parliament, in any manner at all, for anything done to you in this said parliament, or elsewhere.[221]

Though it was better than death by beheading, this verdict and the punishment must still have come as a blow to William, as well as to his wife and son when they heard of it. At best, they would not see their husband and father for five long years, languishing in England deprived of whatever protection he could offer. Even then, while John might have initially believed that his father would return after an admittedly sad absence, William and Alice would have been all too aware that the danger had not yet passed.

William seemed to believe he would die before he saw exile, or at least considered this a very likely possibility. The king's decision was not a popular one, and there was violence against William's servants when the news spread. An angry mob assembled in front of the Tower of London to await William's emergence.[222] Had he fallen into their hands, he would have been killed. To avoid such a fate, in April he left the Tower under the cover of night, riding for Dover.[223] He had a safe conduct with him,[224] but nobody would have believed this protected him from the mob, least of all William himself. He had to be careful, and before he arrived in Dover he spent a week laying low in his ancestral home of Wingfield. While there, he wrote a letter to John:

> My dear and only well-beloved son, I beseech our Lord in Heaven, the Maker of all the World, to bless you, and to send you ever grace to love him, and to dread him, to the which, as far as a father may charge his child, I both charge you, and pray you to set all your spirits and wits to do, and to know his holy laws and commandments, by the which you shall, with his great mercy, pass all the great tempests and troubles of this wretched world.
>
> And that also, knowingly, you do nothing for love nor dread of any earthly creature that should displease him. And there as any frailty maketh you to fall, beseech his mercy soon to call you to him again with repentance, satisfaction, and contrition of your heart, never more in will to offend him.
>
> Secondly, next him above all earthly things, to be true liegeman in heart, in will, in thought, in deed, unto the king our aldermost high and dread sovereign lord, to whom both you and I be so much bound to; charging you as father can and may, rather to die than to be the contrary, or to know anything that were against the welfare or prosperity of his most royal person, but that as far as your body and life may stretch you live and die to defend it, and to let his highness have knowledge thereof in all the haste you can.

Thirdly, in the same way, I charge you, my dear son, always as you be bounden by the commandment of God to do, to love, to worship, your lady and mother; and also that you obey always her commandments, and to believe her counsels and advices in all your works, the which dread not but shall be best and truest to you. And if any other body would steer you to the contrary, to flee the counsel in any wise, for you shall find it naught and evil.

Furthermore, as far as father may and can, I charge you in any wise to flee the company and counsel of proud men, of covetous men, and of flattering men, the more especially and mightily to withstand them, and not to draw nor to meddle with them, with all your might and power; and to draw to you and to your company good and virtuous men, and such as be of good conversation, and of truth, and by them shall you never be deceived nor repent you of.

Moreover, never follow your own wit in nowise, but in all your works, of such folks as I write of above, ask your advice and counsel, and doing thus, with the mercy of God, you shall do right well, and live in right much worship, and great heart's rest and ease.

And I will be to you as good lord and father as my heart can think.

And last of all, as heartily and as lovingly as ever father blessed his child in earth, I give you the blessing of Our Lord and of me, which of his infinite mercy increase you in all virtue and good living; and that your blood may by his grace from kindred to kindred multiply in this earth to his service, in such wise as after the departing from this wretched world here, you and they may glorify him eternally amongst his angels in heaven.

Written of mine hand,
The day of my departing from this land.
Your true and loving father[225]

Despite the promise that he would be as good a father to John as he could, the letter strongly suggests William did not expect to see his son again. Putting aside the threat of murder at the hands of the mob, at almost fifty-four years of age William might have simply feared a death by natural causes before his five years were up.

Reading this letter, it is clear that William loved his son. However, the letter was not just intended as some parting fatherly advice; it was something rather more selfish as well. William had the letter sent to John, but he also had copies made to be circulated in England.[226] This loving, touching letter to John was also an attempt to polish his own image in the eyes of the hostile population, a kind of PR stunt. It is unlikely that it was successful if so, as several of the charges levelled against William concerned the notion that he wanted to put his son on the throne.

Reminding the public of his fondness for his son was therefore not the best way to rehabilitate his image.

On the contrary, given that being linked to William could get a person murdered, his decision to circulate the letter was reckless. If indeed he made it to exile, out of reach of the mob, his son might have been the next best target, and William had just drawn attention to him. Though it may have been intended as a harmless gesture, by choosing to publicise the letter William effectively painted a target on his son's head.

John presumably did not understand this; it is likely he was happy to receive his father's letter. Alice might not have been so happy. Whatever she thought of her husband's decision, she saw to it that her son was as safe as he could be under the circumstances. When William left the Tower of London, she and John left Ewelme to stay in one of her other manors, not associated with William, though we do not know which. There they would have awaited news of William's safe arrival in France.

Such news was never to come. William had been seen off by an angry crowd when he boarded a ship at Dover, but his journey was to be a short one. They had barely set out when his ship was cut off by one from the royal fleet, the *St Nicholas of the Tower*. William was made to leave disembark and board the *St Nicholas*, where he was reportedly greeted with the words, 'Welcome, traitor.'

William must have known then that he would die. He had his safe conduct from the king with him, but it was taken from him and ripped apart. He was then given a mock trial, with the predictable outcome: he was found guilty of treason and sentenced to death.[227]

It was 1 May 1450. William was given a day of respite before the death sentence pronounced by the mock court would be carried out. He was not given any material to write to his wife or his son, and it is not known if a priest was present to take his confession. As the new day dawned, he was ordered off the ship and on to a small boat. There he knelt before one of the crew of the *St Nicholas* who was acting as headsman. With five strokes of a rusty sword, William de la Pole, Duke of Suffolk, was beheaded.[228]

William's body was dumped ashore at Dover, his head supposedly set on a pole beside it. His body had been stripped of all valuables.[229] It was a brutal and undignified end. Who was responsible is still a topic of debate, though the very fact that his executioners had commanded a ship of the royal fleet suggests that his death had not been mob 'justice' but the work of one of his powerful political enemies, perhaps Henry Beaufort, Duke of Somerset or Richard Plantagenet, Duke of York.[230] We may never know.

2

A Father Murdered

In His Mother's Wardship

William's body was soon found, and the king and queen were notified.[231] Henry gave orders to remove his body with honour.[232] Soon afterwards, Alice and John were informed of what had happened too. It must have been a massive blow for both of them, not only sad but also scary, and almost incomprehensible to a small boy. Alice would have understood it better, but that would only have made it more frightening. She would have known that whatever powerful man she thought or suspected of having given the orders to kill her husband would be unlikely to wish harm on her or John, but that did not mean they were safe. The real danger to them came from the common people, who blamed William for the loss of the war in France and whose hankering for revenge was not stilled by William's death.

There were attempts to despoil William's body.[233] Alice soon made arrangements for an honourable burial; she had to have it moved at night for fear of attack, but this passed without incident. Following William's wishes as stated in his will, Alice had him buried at Hull. It has since been claimed that she had him buried at Wingfield,[234] either because it was easier under the circumstances or because she did not care about his wishes, but this is not true. She and John left their stay in one of her manors. Alice was to travel to Hull for William's funeral, but it is not certain that John accompanied her there. Circumstantial evidence suggests that Alice had him brought to the one person he was safe with: to the king at the royal court.

It is hard to imagine the effect this must have had on John. He was only seven years old; in the last year, he had lost his intended bride and playmate, seen hostile crowds turn against his parents, been a virtual prisoner in one of his parents' manors for his safety, been married to a small girl he did not know, had his father accused of treason and finally had to come to terms with the fact that his father had been murdered. It would have been traumatising for an adult; for a child it must have been all but unbearable.

The nightmarish situation still wasn't over. When John and his mother travelled, either to court or to his father's funeral, they were not able to move about openly during daytime, in luxury, as had been their habit; instead they had to travel under cover of darkness to protect against an attack from the mob. Given all that had happened and the imminent danger, Alice would not have been able to keep the truth from her son as to why they had to do this; he must have been scared and bewildered. Accustomed to the life of a duke's cosseted and adored only son, he had become a half-orphan whose future was uncertain and whose very parentage put him in harm's way.

There can be no question that John's experiences in those days affected him for the rest of his life. In fact, it is often postulated that he stayed out of national politics for most of his life because he wanted to avoid the same fate that had befallen his father.[235] Though his later actions do not indicate any fear of authority, it is possible that his disdain for national politics stemmed from his experiences as a scared and hunted little boy.

As if the grief and the danger was not enough, John also had to contend with the fact that, at the tender age of seven, he was now a duke. Henry VI did what he could for John, though in the immediate aftermath of William's death he confiscated most of his belongings.[236] This may have been a kindness; if he did not do so, the prospect of a child with such vast wealth could only whip up a frenzy of hatred against William and his family even more. Even so, the very fact that John got to keep the dukedom caused a lot of anger.

Mostly, however, the wrath was still directed at William; his death had not been able to calm it. Though John's inheritance of his father's titles and goods caused some outrage, he himself was not openly spoken about in hostile tones, presumably because of his youth. Instead, his mother Alice bore the brunt of hostility in the wake of her husband's death.[237] As an adult she could more easily be accused of various crimes, but she was also known to be close to the unpopular queen and to have supported her husband. Perhaps most importantly for the outraged mob, Alice had made it clear that she had affection for her husband until his death. William's funeral might have been a peaceful affair, but for Alice the troubles had only just begun.

Only a few weeks after William's death, there was a rebellion by dissatisfied commoners. This has sometimes been said to have been the real start of the conflicts now known as the Wars of the Roses,[238] and certainly this revolt, known as Jack Cade's Rebellion, was very sympathetic to the men who would later become Yorkists. Its leader, Jack Cade, in fact claimed to be called Edmund Mortimer and to therefore be closely related to Richard, Duke of York.[239]

The latter disavowed all knowledge of the rebels' plans, openly condemned them and even claimed to have lost jewels and other valuables when the rebels raided one of his manors.[240] This might have been true, but it could also have been an event staged to provide plausible deniability if the rebellion failed. We do not know the truth, but it is not inconceivable that Richard, Duke of York, perhaps justifiably feeling side-lined,[241] instigated or supported the rebellion to test the waters. Either way, the rebellion caused a lot of trouble in the summer of 1450.

The rebels had a long list of complaints. As was standard at the time, their grievances were not levelled directly at the king but at those close to him, with the implication that these advisers were an evil influence. In this case, it may have been more true than usual. Henry VI was a notoriously weak king, easily influenced.[242] Given that many historians have called William the 'effective governor' of England between 1446 and 1450,[243] it would make sense if people at the time felt that William's fall had so undermined Henry's government that he could be driven in another direction by rebellion. Unsurprisingly, Alice was one of the prime 'councillors' the rebels wanted to see punished for treason.[244]

Had she actually been found guilty of treason, Alice still would not have had to fear being executed as she was a woman. Nonetheless, it would have meant possible imprisonment for her, and certainly it would have meant she would be stripped off all her belongings. For a powerful woman, who had been actively involved in politics and given prominent roles including the constableship of castles,[245] such a fall would have been painful.

Even more alarmingly, however, such a development would have left little John without an inheritance, at the mercy of whatever guardian the king chose for him, and, as the child of two hated and supposedly treasonous parents, in danger of being attacked and 'punished' for his parents' supposed infractions. Though John may not have understood the whole scope of the situation, he would have understood he and his mother were in danger. It must have been jarring to go from a luxurious and sheltered childhood to a summer in hiding. Alice did not officially turn up at court that summer, though it is possible she brought John there for the funeral; the rebels declared her a traitor and attainted her in her absence. Had the rebellion succeeded, it would have had dire consequences for her and John.

However, luckily for them, the rebellion was beaten down soon afterwards. Henry VI never followed any of the rebels' demands and Alice was out of danger of being declared a traitor by autumn, though resentment against her was still so bad that the House of Commons named her first in a list of people they wanted banned from court and Henry's presence.[246] The charge used in this petition was that 'the persons named hereafter in this bill have been behaving improperly around your royal person and in other places, by whose improper ways your possessions have been greatly diminished, your laws not executed, and the peace of this your realm not observed nor kept, to your great harm and the distress of the liege people of this your realm and the likely subversion of the same without your good and gracious attention to this matter in all appropriate haste',[247] and the suggested actions against them was 'that neither they nor any of them may approach your said presence by the distance of twelve miles, upon pain of forfeiture to you of their goods and lands that they have or any person has for their use, or for the use of any of them in fee-simple held directly of you. And also to forfeit all the lands and tenements that they or any of them, or any other person has for the use of any of them in fee-simple held directly of other persons, to the persons that the said lands or tenements have thus been held from; saving to every one of your lieges and their heirs, other than the said persons thus named as behaving improperly, their right, title and interest that they have in the said lands and tenements.'[248]

The petition failed. Henry VI had his chancellor make an announcement:

> his highness is not sufficiently appraised of any reason why they should be removed from the presence of his highness; nevertheless, his highness has agreed by his own volition and by no other authority that save for the person of any lord named in the said petition, and also save for certain persons, who are few in number, who have been accustomed to wait continually upon his person, and who know how and in what way they may best serve him to his pleasure, his highness has agreed that the rest shall remove themselves from his high presence and from his court for the period of a whole year; within which time any man who can and will make any objection against any of them by which it might be considered reasonable that he should be removed from his high presence and service and from his court, he who so objects will be patiently heard and listened to, saving always that if it happens the king takes to the field against his enemies or rebels, that than it shall be lawful for him to use the service of any of his liege people, this notwithstanding.[249]

Though this may have been seen as a partial victory by the House of Commons, it did not affect Alice. She was among those who were exempted for being 'a lord', or rather, in her case, technically a lady. With the rebuttal of her banishment from court, Henry VI had made his position clear. That, in addition to the failure of the rebellion, made it unlikely that anyone would dare act against her, and the hope would have been that anger against William would fade, and be directed against other nobles.

First Years as Duke: 1450–1453

That autumn, John turned eight years old. A lot had changed for him since his seventh birthday, and he was almost certainly traumatised by what had happened. No one had ever threatened him openly, but he would have experienced fear such as is hardly imaginable today. At only eight years of age, John had experienced all the dangers of being prominently involved in politics as a highborn.

It is certainly possible, as is often assumed, that this sparked his desire to have a fairly calm life, setting his own concerns and that of his family over those of affairs of state. It seems a reasonable deduction, though of course we cannot really know. Perhaps it was simply in his character to be more interested in his own immediate concerns than in those of the state and other people. In modern histories he is often mocked for it, even labelled as 'feeble' or 'cowardly',[250] but it was to prove a good course of action for him and his family, so it could be argued that he learnt the right lessons from his father's fate.

Apart from his father's death and the fact he was now duke, once the dust had settled in the autumn of 1450, John's life probably went on much as before. His marriage would not have changed anything – his bride did not live with him and never would. John probably hardly knew her, having met her only the one time at their wedding.

Despite this, both Alice and Margaret's mother were eager to keep up the marriage arrangement for the children's future benefit, and in August 1450 a dispensation came from the Vatican in answer to a petition supposedly written by the children themselves in which it was said that they 'formerly contracted marriage *per verba legitime de presenti*'[251] in ignorance of their relation 'in the fourth and fourth degrees of kindred', and that if this was to be cause for a divorce 'grave dissensions and scandals would probably be stirred up between their parents and friends'.[252] The petition achieved its aim. John's and Margaret's marriage was declared valid by the pope, who stated that they were allowed to 'remain in the said marriage, notwithstanding the said impediment. The Pope hereby decrees their offspring, if any, and that to be born legitimate.'[253]

This decision probably would not have mattered much to John. Perhaps he and Margaret were encouraged to write each other polite letters, as sometimes happened in such cases, but if so they have not survived to this day.

In the meantime, John would have taken up his formal education again, which by necessity would have been neglected during the summer of 1450, with him and his mother in hiding. What we know suggests that it centred less on martial arts and more on what we today would call the humanities. He learnt French, Latin, English, writing, maths and music. In the mid-1450s, Alice had Vincent of Beauvais's *De morali principis institutione* copied by a clergyman at Oxford named John Courteys.[254] The subject of the text – moral instructions for a prince – suggests that it was copied for the use of her son, which gives us a good insight into what sort of education Alice gave him. In addition to Beauvais's text, John would have been made familiar with the work of his great-grandfather Geoffrey Chaucer alongside other important works of literature, and we know from his library as an adult that he could at least read French and Latin in addition to English.[255]

It can also be assumed, albeit without evidence, that John would have learnt how to use weapons and lead men among other military skills. Perhaps influenced by his mother's decisions early in his life or else by the knowledge of what had happened to his warrior father, he was never to be a very enthusiastic fighter, his focus more on humanities. Even in quarrels, violence seemed to be his last resort and he preferred outsmarting his opponents. Though it was not his main area of knowledge, however, he nonetheless knew how to fight.

Usually this sort of education was considered a matter for men, and it is possible that William had intended to arrange something for his son before he died. Indeed, with John turning seven in September 1449, the age at which children were usually considered old enough to leave the nursery, it is possible William had already made arrangements before his downfall. As it stood after his death, Alice was left to either make or confirm the decisions. There is no suggestion he lacked a proper education, so Alice probably knew what she was doing; John would grow into a very educated man, well-read and interested in scholarship. It seems that while she kept close to the king and queen, Alice's main interest in the months and years after her husband's death was her son and his education. They would stay very close for the rest of Alice's life, and it seems very likely the closeness was forged in his childhood, after the loss of their husband and father.

It is clear that, after the traumatic year of his father's death, John experienced a calm upbringing. Meanwhile, in the kingdom, the situation worsened. Richard, Duke of York first aired his grievances with the government and the king in 1452,[257] when John was nine years old. It did not end well for York, whose enemies took power and forced him to apologise. Henry Beaufort, Duke of Somerset, uncle of John's bride Margaret, took over the reins at court. In some ways, Somerset was viewed as stepping into the void left by William, especially as the king's favourite.

Annulment

Somerset's rise to power was to affect John directly. At the beginning of 1453, he convinced Henry VI to annul his niece's marriage to John.[258] Little Margaret's wardship, which Alice had still held until that point, was instead given to the king's half-brothers Edmund Tudor, Earl of Pembroke, and Jasper Tudor, the former marrying her in 1455 when she was twelve years old.

A later legend, first related by Margaret's confessor John Fisher at her funeral in 1509, said that Margaret, when 'not fully nine years old', which would mean in early 1452, was asked to choose between staying married to John or having the marriage annulled and eventually marrying Pembroke. After she had prayed for guidance, St Nicholas was said to have 'appeared unto her arrayed like a bishop, and naming unto her Edmund [Pembroke] had take him unto her husband'.[259]

Though the story came from Margaret's confessor and therefore seems more trustworthy than many such legends, it is unlikely to be true. Apart from the obvious inaccuracy regarding the year in which this happened, it would have been all but unheard of to let a child decide for themselves which marriage they wanted. If anything, Henry Beaufort influenced his niece and tried to sweeten the sudden change in her future by telling her about Pembroke's supposed advantages as a prospective husband and John's supposed disadvantages. Moreover, as this story was first told at Margaret's funeral, in front of her grandson Henry VIII, it may not have been a story Margaret had misremembered and told her confessor but instead a fabrication for political ends, suggesting the beginning of the Tudor dynasty was blessed and intended by God and his saints.

Even if Margaret actually got to choose, she would not have made such a decision based on any personal feelings for either John or Pembroke. She had never met Pembroke that we know of, and would have been unlikely to be interested in a man nearly twice her age. As for John, he and Margaret had probably met only once, at their wedding three years before the decision was made. It would have been a rational decision, one almost certainly made between Henry VI and the Duke of Somerset. Henry VI's brothers were on the up, while John was only a disgraced duke's son.

Irrespective of the children's feelings, Margaret's marriage to John was annulled. For Margaret, her future was changed but must have seemed fairly clear. She would make a good marriage to one of Henry's half-brothers and endow him with her lands. For John, the future was suddenly uncertain once again, his marital and financial future different to what he would have grown to expect in the previous three years. Aged ten, he would have been old enough to understand this, though not yet old enough to make any plans to improve his situation, even had he been in the position to do so.

Alice would have considered new marriages and potential brides for her son, but, perhaps seeing the writing on the wall, did not seem to immediately want to tie their twin futures to one of the warring factions. Conversely, perhaps she tried but failed to secure an alliance in those years. It is possible that despite his dukedom John did not seem like much of a good marriage prospect thanks to his father's disgrace and the fact that he was not particularly wealthy.

Whichever it was, John was to remain unmarried for five years after his first marriage to Margaret was annulled. In fact, neither John nor Margaret seemed to consider themselves to have been truly married to each other. In her will, made in the 1470s, Margaret was to describe Pembroke as her 'first husband'.[260] John, meanwhile, seemed to regard his next wife as his one and only.

A lot was happening in England in 1453 that might have hampered any marriage arrangement Alice was hoping to make for John. Henry VI suddenly lost his mind in the early part of the year, becoming catatonic.[261] Naturally, a power struggle immediately broke out. Queen Margaret, finally pregnant after eight years of marriage, favoured the Duke of Somerset and those supporting him, while the other most important nobleman at court, the king's cousin Richard, Duke of York, made his own bid for power.[262]

Eventually, despite his recent disgrace, it was York who won. Somerset was imprisoned. Fortunately, with her son's connection to Somerset's family recently annulled, Alice was no longer considered to be on the side of the thwarted duke, though she was still close to the queen. This appears to have caused some trouble, and at some point during the year a man closely connected with the Duke of York, Sir John Howard, and his nephew the Duke of Mowbray, broke into one of her manors, ransacked it and even beat some servants. Though this would have been frightening for her, or at least for John, it does not seem to have been a particularly significant event; it was just one of many minor outrages committed as England slid towards civil war.

Most people did not see Alice's support for the queen during her pregnancy as any kind of political act; after all, Alice had not been at court much at all since her husband's death. She was present when the queen gave birth to a baby boy in October 1453, helping her during her labour.[263] This was perfectly normal for noble ladies, and Alice was far from the only one. As she had acted *in loco parentis* for Margaret on many occasions during her first years of queenship, it is hardly surprising that the queen wanted her to be there for the birth of her first – and, as history was to show, only – child.

Predictably, it seems that John, then eleven, did not join his mother at court. In fact, Alice appears to have made an effort to keep him well away from king, queen and court. Possibly she did this to stop him from building connections that would see him emulate his father's involvement in politics once he was old enough, or else it was to stop him from being associated with one of the sides warring at court. Another possibility is that Alice did not wish people to see her son as William's boy, with all the baggage that came with that, preferring to give him the chance to establish himself as his own man by being a blank slate for the court until he was old enough to make his own decisions and be considered a force in his own right.

The Wars of the Roses Begin

Whatever Alice's reasons for keeping her son away from court, it was to turn out a wise choice as it kept him out of the conflicts at court that would grow into the Wars of the Roses.

We actually know very little about John's life in the early and mid-1450s, though he was by then old enough to follow what was happening in the centre of power, perhaps even to contemplate where he would fit in once he was old enough to play a part. Despite his lack of personal involvement he may well have followed the news from court with interest, and might have had his own opinion when he learnt that on Christmas 1454 Henry VI had recovered suddenly and unexpectedly from his catatonia, released Somerset from the Tower and dismissed York from his post as Lord Protector.[264]

Though York cannot have expected to keep the post once Henry recovered, he did not take kindly to being removed from all other positions as well, and over the next few months he and Somerset faction became embroiled in a vicious power struggle. It first escalated in May 1455 when a battle was fought in the town of St Albans, widely considered the first of the Wars of the Roses. York's forces were victorious on this occasion, giving him the upper hand once more.

Alice kept well away from all the political upheaval, and by 1455 was no longer seen as the queen's woman. In fact, she was not seen as particularly important at all then, meaning that there was also no particular interest in winning her adolescent son over to one party or the other. His loyalties were uncertain at this stage. Still, as he grew up, he was expected to carve out his place in society. Shortly before he turned fifteen, in 1457, he was first expected to involve himself in the concerns and working of the kingdom. It was then that he first received an order to be on a commission of peace for Oxfordshire[265] led by John, Baron Lovell, an Oxfordshire neighbour some nine years his senior. However, it seems that this appointment was nominal for John, as fourteen was still unusually young to have been active in such a commission and there is no evidence he was involved. All the appointment meant was that he was slowly coming into his own, recognised as someone who would eventually hold a lot of power and who was expected to make his mark as an adult.

Elizabeth of York

Meanwhile, as the conflicts in the country intensified, John's mother made a decision that would affect the course of his entire life. In late 1457 or early 1458, Alice decided that it would be best for her and her son to have a foot in both camps, using her former closeness to the queen as an 'in' with the Lancastrian side while leveraging her son's availability to gain favour with the Yorkists. It must have already been in late 1457 that Alice indicated a willingness to arrange a marriage between her son and a daughter of Richard, Duke of York. Understandably eager to win allies, the duke was equally willing, and so the two agreed that their children would marry. York's oldest daughter, Anne, was already married to the Duke of Exeter, but Elizabeth and Margaret, two and three years younger than John respectively, were as yet unmarried.

As neither was promised to anyone, and it was common for older sisters to married before their younger siblings, Elizabeth was chosen to be John's bride. She was almost exactly two years younger than John, having been born on 21 or 22 September 1444.[266] Thirteen years old in late 1457, it seems that, unlike John, Elizabeth had not been promised to anybody else beforehand. All we know for sure is that, by the end of 1457, she was free to marry. Alice and the Duke of York arranged the details of the marriage. Elizabeth's dowry was to be £1,533 13*s* 4*d* and was to be paid to Alice in instalments over the next four years. A number of Richard, Duke of York's men entered bonds to secure these payments, with the condition that if Elizabeth was to die childless before these payments were made the bonds would be void.[267]

These bonds were recorded on 1 and 2 February 1458. Once they were done, the wedding followed immediately. We do not know the exact date, but in early 1458 John and Elizabeth were married. A papal dispensation, which was needed for their match because of their relation through the Beaufort family, must have already been procured by that time, though it no longer exists. Once the bonds were entered in and recorded, there was no impediment to the match. Unlike the first time John went through a marriage ceremony, there was no rush; if anything had still impeded the marriage, the wedding could have waited until it was resolved.

John and Elizabeth were now husband and wife. This affected both their lives right away, as Elizabeth promptly moved into Alice and John's household.[268] The newly married couple did not get their own place yet, but they were clearly meant to get to know each other and she to learn about her new life as a wife in her husband's household, while he was to learn about his new life as a husband in his wife's presence.

It is possible that the marriage was consummated immediately following the wedding, but it does not seem too likely. Though famously the age of consent at the time was twelve for girls and fourteen for boys,[269] and the new bride and groom therefore qualified, most people considered this far too young. While cohabitation at their age was normal, consummation was usually delayed until both parties had turned sixteen.[270] The birthdates of John and Elizabeth's children suggest they chose to wait.

The young couple would have been in the privileged position of getting to know each other before having to run a household on their own or have sex with one another. They were lucky, too, that they were of a similar age and might therefore have had similar interests. Of course, we cannot know their thoughts about each other and their relationship at first, but theirs would be a close and successful marriage. Perhaps, given their young age, they would still have had tutors. Alice was a very educated woman, and Elizabeth as well,[271] so it is perfectly possible they even had lessons together. Fifteen and a half at the time of his marriage, John would also have been considered old enough to begin visiting his properties and establishing himself as a regional power. His presence on the commission of the peace in Oxford, if only nominally, supports this assumption.

Elizabeth was to hold quite some sway as she grew up,[272] so it is quite likely she would have accompanied her youthful husband on such trips quite regularly, the two of them establishing themselves as lord and lady to all their tenants. This may have been done in the face of adversity, for it seems that due to John marrying Elizabeth there was a motion to strip him of his ducal title for his apparent closeness to the rebel Yorkists. John Benet's Chronicle stated that it had actually been taken from him,[273] but other sources do not support this. In the Calendar of Patent Rolls, an order for him to be on commissions of the peace for the counties of Suffolk and Norfolk in 1460 described him as 'Duke of Suffolk'[274], and contemporaries also called him that during those years.

John might have been aware of the risks his new marriage would bring. Some modern authors have lambasted John as stupid for marrying Elizabeth and 'risking' the king's fury,[275] but even putting aside the fact that he did not get to choose his wife, no one is recorded as having expressed such an opinion at the time. Even John Benet's Chronicle took the match as a deliberate decision by his mother, not his own folly. In 1458, it is likely he would have fostered resentment in one faction or other regardless of his chosen wife. If John heard of such grumbling, he did not openly react.

Shortly after John's marriage to Elizabeth, the so-called Love Day took place in London. Arranged by Henry VI and the Archbishop of Canterbury to engender peace between the warring factions,[276] it was put on in large part for John's father-in-law, as well as for Elizabeth's brother-in-law the Duke of Exeter, but there is no evidence John and Elizabeth were present. However, despite his absence John was slowly starting to make his mark.

As would be the case for most of his adult life, his focus was largely on regional politics. He made his acquaintance with neighbours and tenants, and from fairly early on seems to have followed a rather belligerent fashion to claim those lands and manors he considered his property. This seems to have been designed in large part by Alice.[277] John seems to have been motivated more by principle than money in this respect.[278] In fact, despite his efforts he and Elizabeth often had money troubles.

Predictably, he crossed a few people in his pursuit of his perceived entitlements. Though he established a good, functional relationship with his half-sister's husband Thomas Stonor and her entire family,[279] he and the famous Paston family were to become staunch enemies. This has oftentimes been claimed to be wholly John's fault,[280] but this is not entirely fair. While John's actions could be unpleasant, so could those of the Pastons, whose word is usually believed over John's by historians for no reason. Though John had more power because of his status, the Pastons gave as good as they got, and the enmity seems to have been mutual. Moreover, the quarrel was not started by John but inherited. Even before his birth, his father and especially his mother had unfriendly dealings with the Pastons, which their famous letters demonstrate.[281]

In fact, John often appears to have followed his mother's lead, and later, when he was old enough to make his own decisions, he decided to act in the same way as her, prompting Margaret Paston to write, in 1462, of the still-young John and Alice that 'the young duke and his mother are not popular'.[282] This has often been taken at face value but cannot be proven one way or another. While those affiliated with the Pastons or in possession of belongings claimed by John obviously had reason to dislike him, there is no evidence of a widespread dislike outside of the Paston quarrels.

Interestingly, John's wife Elizabeth was not mentioned by Margaret, though she seems to have supported her husband enthusiastically. The couple seem to have established a pattern between them whereby she was the peacemaker while he was the more belligerent one in pursuing their interests. Evidence from later years also suggests that she was the only one able to make him change his mind once he had come to a decision, and that he trusted her to make decisions in both their interests, even if those decisions went against his own ideas.[283]

It is quite possible that for most of 1458 and 1459, during which years we have little evidence about John and Elizabeth, they established themselves as duke and duchess in their territories and worked out the dynamics of their marriage between themselves. As they did so, the fighting across the country worsened. Though John may not have been overly interested, his wife would have been due to her close familial connection to the Yorkist side. Through her, John would have become more closely involved than he was before the marriage, if only emotionally.

In 1459, after a failed attempt to overthrow the king's chief adviser, John's father-in-law had to leave for exile with his son Edmund, Elizabeth's brother,[284] while her oldest brother Edward left for Calais together with his cousin Richard Neville, Earl of Warwick. She would presumably have had an opinion on that, and perhaps she was influencing her husband to support her father. Alice's preferences may have lain elsewhere; certainly this was speculated in a letter written to the Paston family in 1460.

Two letters from October 1460 show the uncertainty about Alice's preferences. The first of those, written by one Friar Brackley to John Paston, appears to have been penned just after several Yorkist victories in the summer of that year had made it possible for Richard, Duke of York to return from exile in Ireland. In it, the friar stated that 'the Lady of Suffolk hath sent up hyr sone and hise wyf to my Lord of York to aske grace for a schireve the next yer'.[285] This at the very least suggests that Alice was aware of the importance of being on good terms with her son's father-in-law and was eager to secure advantages for herself and her family through the connection, if only in the relatively modest form of being allowed to instate a sheriff in this case.

However, the letter writer very obviously did not consider this to be proof she leaned to his side in the civil war. On the contrary, in another letter written that month the friar stated that Alice, with 'other aforementioned persons', was the 'leader of those most inclined towards [Queen Margaret] with all their strength',[286] which Brackley found to be lamentable.

Whether this was true or simply based on Alice's former closeness with the queen we do not know. Though she did not do anything to get involved, it is perfectly possible she was also trying to influence her son to support the king and queen. Equally, it is possible, judging by her sending John and Elizabeth to plead with Elizabeth's father for boons, that she wished him to support his father-in-law while she kept up her good relationship with king and queen so that, whoever won, they would have a good and favourable relationship with the winner.

If Alice influenced her son to side with king and queen, it is perfectly possible he was being influenced in two different directions by the two women closest to him, as Elizabeth would have doubtlessly sided with her father. Possibly, under these circumstances, John did not know what to do, and this is why he waited so long to get involved in the conflicts. Equally possible is that John wished to support his wife's family but, keeping in mind his father's last letter to him, found the decision to actually go against Henry VI rather difficult. This will only have been harder when, after returning from exile in late 1460, Richard, Duke of York claimed the throne for himself. On the other hand, perhaps John simply had no interest in who was king.

Most likely perhaps is that Alice, having married her son to the Duke of York's daughter, supported the Yorkists more than the Lancastrians, or considered them more likely to emerge victorious, but did not wish to be seen to be involved in case the fortunes of war turned against York. Since John was always close to his mother, he would have probably sought her advice on how to deal with the whole situation, but at eighteen years of age he was old enough that her word alone would not have made a decision for him. He would also have discussed it with his wife, and possibly others close to him as well.

3

Adulthood

By autumn 1460, John was clearly seen as an adult. In October that year, Friar Brackley wrote about John and the fact that he had not yet committed himself to one side in the conflict, which he considered overdue, though he did not make any outright criticism: 'Item, it would be good if the young Duke of Suffolk, with his soldiers and squires, would be spurred and used and now tried in war to whom he would be faithful, either meat or fish.'[287] It is an interesting letter, making it clear that John had now established himself as a force to be reckoned with should he choose to become involved, despite the fact he and his wife were apparently still living in Alice's household. Those firmly committed to a side in the conflict – Friar Brackley was an ardent Yorkist – obviously wished for his support.

However, if John heard such demands he did not immediately yield to them. Perhaps he still wasn't interested, or maybe personal reasons kept him from the conflict. Perhaps he was too concerned with the more immediate changes for him and his wife that autumn. That September, Elizabeth turned sixteen, which was usually considered the suitable age to consummate a marriage. This would also have meant they would be expected to have their own household. In fact, couples often had their own household at a younger age. John and Elizabeth do not seem to have begun establishing their own immediately after her sixteenth birthday and his eighteenth, as they were still in Alice's in October 1460, but it seems highly likely they had already started arrangements by then. It may well be that John, who was never to show much of an interest in national politics, considered this immediate change to his and his wife's family to be of more importance than making a choice and becoming involved in a civil war.

There are, however, other possible explanations as well, suggested by instances when he actually did become involved. In the winter of 1460/1, the short-lived calm after the resounding Yorkist victory of the summer had already been broken. A truce had been negotiated over Christmas, but it was broken on 30 December 1460 when the Battle of Wakefield took place.[288] It was a catastrophe for the Yorkist side. John's father-in-law Richard, Duke of York was killed in battle, while one of his strongest supporters, Richard Neville, Earl of Salisbury – incidentally the husband of Alice's stepdaughter from her second marriage – was captured and executed.

Most horrifying of all, York's seventeen-year-old second son, Edmund, Earl of Rutland, was captured after the battle and killed. Though victors often captured their enemies after battle, and in some cases executed them afterwards, downright killing a captive on the spot was unusual. This fact, coupled with Edmund's youth and the fact that his death did not promise any end to the conflict, caused a lot of outrage.[289]

Combat

It might well be that this deed was what eventually caused John to commit himself to the Yorkist side, either out of anger at what had been done to Edmund or out of family feeling for his wife's older brother, whose death presumably would have affected her deeply. However, there is another possible reason why it was only after the Battle of Wakefield that John finally chose a side: fear for the entire York family. After the deaths of York and his son, there seems to have been concern about further punishment. Certainly, York's widow Cecily had such fears, and she did not take any chances. She sent her two youngest sons, eleven-year-old George of York and eight-year-old Richard of York, away from England to Burgundy, where they would be safe from Lancastrian machinations.

Perhaps John thought a policy of zero tolerance against even innocent members of the York family would be dangerous for any sons he and Elizabeth might have in the future, and therefore chose to become involved to protect these as-yet unborn children. However, there another possibility: that John believed, as so many others had, that Richard, Duke of York had been responsible for ordering his father's murder, and while convinced of York's superior claim to the throne and therefore unwilling to fight for the Lancastrian side he did not want to fight for someone he considered his father's killer. With York's death, this problem of conscience was solved. In any case, in early 1461, John finally made his decision.

He did not choose in a hurry. After the battle at Wakefield, the next clash between the warring Lancastrian and Yorkist factions, the so-called Battle of Mortimer's Cross, took place on 2 February, over a month after the deaths of Richard, Duke of York and Edmund of Rutland, but John does not appear to have participated. The battle is not particularly well recorded, so it is possible that he was actually there, but if so it seems highly likely that those contemporary sources that do exist would have mentioned his presence. Furthermore, circumstantial evidence suggests that he was with his wife at that time rather than fighting for her brother.

It was in February 1461 that John finally became involved in the civil war. Though he probably missed the Battle of Mortimer's Cross, he was present at the Second Battle of St Albans, which took place only two weeks later on 17 February. The *English Chronicle* includes him in the list of fighters.[290] This was an inauspicious blooding for John. Unlike Mortimer's Cross, the Second Battle of St Albans ended in a loss for the Yorkists. What John did during the fighting is not recorded; it seems he comported himself well enough as he was neither injured nor captured, although he did not merit mention for bravery.

John continued his involvement in the Yorkist campaign after 17 February, his forces probably meeting and joining together with those of his brother-in-law Edward, Duke of York at some point. Upon his father's death Edward, formerly Earl of March, had assumed his father's dukedom and his claim to the throne. Though the late Richard's claim to the throne in autumn 1460 had not been a particularly popular move,[291] events since then had made it clear that there was no turning back. Edward fought to become king, and John supported him in the battles that were to follow, specifically at Ferrybridge and, a day later, at Towton.

Since called the bloodiest battle ever fought on English soil, the Battle of Towton, which took place on 29 March 1461, was a brutal melee fought for hours during a snowstorm. When it finally ended, anywhere between 20,000 and 50,000 men lay dead. A firm victory was won by the Yorkists,[292] all but winning the throne for Edward, Duke of York (though he dated his reign from 5 March, the day of his triumphant entry into the City of London).[293]

We know that John was involved in the Battle of Towton because, once more, the *English Chronicle* records his presence.[294] However, his performance does not seem to have been remarkable. Once on the battlefield, he seems to have done what was expected from him – nothing more and nothing less.

Building Relationships

Edward taking the throne meant that John's wife Elizabeth had become a true-born princess. John's own children, as soon as he had them, would therefore be in line to the throne. However, it does not seem that John was particularly interested in this; none of his actions after Edward's coronation suggest a man taking pride in his close connection to royalty.

While Edward took up the reins of government, John returned home to his wife Elizabeth. It was perhaps his first time in their own household. It is reasonable to assume that Elizabeth was happy about her brother becoming king, though she would never show any signs of closeness to him. Even so, her mother and sisters were now of much higher status than they had been before, and her two younger brothers could return from Burgundy as Prince George and Prince Richard to become important magnates in the years to come. Perhaps Elizabeth also hoped to see royal favours heaped upon her husband. All we can say for sure is that she and John were not overly concerned with her brother and his new government.

Even at this early stage, their primary interest was their own duchy, and the privileges and duties that came with it. One of those duties was, of course, producing an heir. By the time her brother became king, Elizabeth was sixteen while John was eighteen. Both were, by the standards of the day, old enough to have children, and in fact it seems that Elizabeth was already newly pregnant when her brother became king, probably having conceived just before her husband left to fight.

By late spring 1461, John must have known he was to become a father for the first time. By the time of Edward's coronation as Edward IV in Westminster Abbey on 28 June 1461, Elizabeth might have already shown. John was prominently involved in the coronation, though his actual place in it is only referenced in one contemporary source, the *Brief Notes of Occurrences Under Henry VI and Edward IV*, which states that 'in the year of our Lord 1461, the 27 [*sic*] of June … the coronation of King Edward IV, Earl of March, son of Richard Duke of York, at Westminster by two archbishops with great solemnity. For there were more bishops, the duke of Norfolk, Marshall of England, the Duke of Suffolk the Steward of England, Lord George the king's brother, Duke of Clarence, Lord Richard his brother, etc.'[295]

John did not seem to hold the position of Steward of England for long after the coronation, suggesting it was a kindness provided to reflect his great standing during the ceremony. Sadly, there is no description of the actual coronation ceremony. However, the grant of the stewardship of England for his coronation seems to have been the only honour bestowed upon John by the new king.

Two days before his coronation, Edward had knighted both his younger brothers and had made Prince George – his heir presumptive until he had legitimate children – Duke of Clarence,[296] but there were few other honours or gifts of any kind for any other member of Edward's family. The king had to strike a balance between rewarding his family and friends and winning over nobles from the Lancastrian fold. Despite the lack of new titles, Edward did grant John and Elizabeth the constableship of Wallingford Castle,[297] which John's father had held from 1434 until his death, and the stewardship of the castle as well as St Waldric and Chiltern.[298] This honour came with £40 for them annually, and £40 for whoever they chose as their lieutenant.[299] This was a fairly generous grant, probably encouraging them to expect further advancements as time went on.

In November 1461 Edward also granted a dukedom to his youngest brother, Prince Richard, who was then just a month past his ninth birthday.[300] As with his grant to John and Elizabeth, this suggests that he was not ignoring all his relatives save for his heir presumptive but simply trying to avoid the appearance of a new king playing favourites.

4

Starting a Family

By the time her youngest brother Richard was told he would receive a dukedom, Elizabeth was heavily pregnant. In late October 1461 she travelled to London without John, perhaps intending to go on to Westminster for Richard's elevation, when it seems she was surprised by the onset of labour. Perhaps Elizabeth had miscalculated, or perhaps this was a premature birth. Elizabeth was the capital, going into labour, with no lodgings prepared. She wrote a rather panicky letter to John Paston:

> On to Jon Paston, in haste.
> Master Paston, I pray you that it may please you to leave your lodging for three or four days til I may be purveyed of another. For God's sake, say me not nay, and I shall do as much for your pleasure; and I pray you recommend me to my lord chamberlain.
> Your friend, Elizabeth[301]

The letter is not dated but mostly likely came from a time before the relationship between her husband and John Paston had soured, so it cannot have been penned much later than 1463. The year 1461 is also suggested by Elizabeth asking Paston to intercede on her behalf with Lord Chamberlain William, Baron Hastings, as Hastings was closely connected to the Suffolk family by 1643, at which point Elizabeth could have written to him directly.

Paston seems to have granted Elizabeth's request. Apart from its unexpected onset, the birth seems to have gone well, and Elizabeth was delivered of a daughter, named Elizabeth after her mother. Though John would not have been present at the birth, it stands to reason that he would have ridden to London as soon as he heard the news, and though he might not have arrived in time for the baptism, he and Elizabeth would presumably have already discussed naming the child.

John, Future Earl of Lincoln

Little Elizabeth Jnr was presumably baptised in London, perhaps in a private chapel of the manor where her mother had given birth. As was the norm at the time, the baptism would have happened in the days immediately following her birth, perhaps even on the day of the birth itself if she was small, sickly or – as seems to have been the case – premature.

No details survive of Elizabeth Jnr's baptism, neither the date nor the chosen godparents. It would have been expected for her uncle, King Edward, to be one of her and perhaps this was one convention John and Elizabeth chose to follow. However, this cannot be said with any certainty. If Edward was godfather, he might have travelled from Westminster to London to attend the baptism, though there is no record of him leaving Westminster at that time. He might also have chosen to be godfather in absentia, unwilling to interrupt his work at court to meet his niece. At least one of the godparents is likely to have been present, though we don't know who they were. It was quite common for noble babies to be godchildren to their relatives, and unlike her father, Elizabeth Jnr had many close male relatives who could have taken the job.

Though nothing explicitly survives about Elizabeth Jnr's baptism, descriptions of his siblings' baptisms can be used to make some inferences. If hers was anything like theirs, Elizabeth Jnr was carried to the font on a 'long cushion of red cloth of gold of damask',[302] doubtlessly in an expensive christening gown, perhaps made from 'blue cloth of gold velvet ... furred with ermine and powered'.[303] As she was not her father's heir it is natural to assume that the ceremony for her baptism was somewhat less grand, but the preparations made for one of her younger siblings at the end of 1466 suggest the opposite – that John and Elizabeth celebrated each new arrival with a lot of pomp. It is therefore likely Elizabeth was greeted with as much happiness and celebration as her brother had been, though perhaps there was less outside interest in her birth.

It is also virtually certain, however, that Elizabeth Jnr's parents were delighted, personally and because it made their position as duke and duchess more secure. Possibly, John carried his daughter to show him off to neighbours and curious bystanders after her baptism, something we know was often a custom even for landed gentry. Even as an infant, her clothing and her surroundings would have reflected his standing. If Elizabeth was given the same finery as her sibling born at the end of 1466 or the beginning of 1467, her nursery would have included 'a pane [cloth covering] and headsheet for the cradle of scarlet, furred with miniver'[304] and a 'tapestry of red warste'.[305] Other finery included 'swathing sheets of Rennes'.[306] Though such items had probably been purchased in expectation of Elizabeth Jnr's birth, some might not have been readily available during her first few months in London, before he was old enough to be moved to a nursery in Wingfield Castle.

Like any father, John must have been proud of his daughter. The birth of an heiress might have given him the chance to be taken a bit more seriously as a duke and magnate. At only nineteen, he was not even in possession of his own lands as he had yet to reach his majority. For that reason, he also had not been summoned to Edward's Parliament, which opened on 4 November 1461,[307] probably only a few days after Elizabeth Jnr's birth. However, John was much luckier than many in a situation similar to his own. While others saw their lands exploited for profit by rapacious guardians, his lands were held by his mother.

Family Life

This seems to have been a happy time for John and Elizabeth. In fact, the new parents seem to have been eager to grow their family, and soon after Elizabeth Jnr's birth Elizabeth was pregnant again. Though we do not know exactly when she gave birth to her second child, we can narrow it down using what knowledge we have of John's and especially Elizabeth's movements. For noble women, it was usual to go into confinement around six weeks before the expected birth date[308] – unless, of course, they had miscalculated or the baby came earlier than expected, as with Elizabeth Jnr. Confinement then lasted until forty days after the birth of the baby, when the mother went through the cleansing ritual of 'churching' and could once more take part in normal life. This means that Elizabeth would not have been able to travel until six weeks after her second baby's birth. It seems that most of the time, however, women who had given birth waited a bit longer than these six weeks before doing something as physically exhausting as travelling, and Elizabeth would likely have followed this convention as well.

Since we do know that she and John were travelling by December 1462,[309] the birth of her second child must have taken place in mid October 1462 at the very latest, more likely somewhat before that, perhaps in August or September. If so, it means that their second child was probably conceived while Elizabeth was still in confinement after Elizabeth Jnr's birth, or, at the latest, immediately after she came out of confinement. Technically, it was forbidden by the Church for a couple to have sex while a woman was still in confinement. In fact, a man was not allowed to be in his wife's presence at all while she was in confinement. While this appears to have been a rule more honoured in breach than observance,[310] babies were seldom conceived during this time, suggesting that John and Elizabeth found themselves to be very sexually compatible and enjoyed the physical side of their union. As a result, Elizabeth may have been pregnant again when she and John returned from London to Wingfield with their baby daughter and established their small family in Suffolk.

John appears to have spent most of his time in 1462 feuding with the Pastons over several possessions; this quarrel would go on over nearly twenty years.[311] Interestingly, though this dispute is nearly always assumed to have been started by John, there is some circumstantial evidence against that. As early as 10 May 1461, John Paston the elder received a letter in which he was advised to seek the support of Richard Neville, Earl of Warwick, or another noble lord, against the sale of the lands which had belonged to the deceased Sir John Falstof to 'the Lord of Suffolk or another great lord',[312] suggesting that whoever purchased these lands would have earned the ire of the Pastons. John's actions in 1462 were not at all violent, though he was regarded with distrust by the Paston family. He simply showed himself as the lord of the manors of Hellesdon and Drayton, which he had purchased in 1461.

Little Elizabeth Jnr would naturally not have been in any way affected by the quarrel. Though even infants were sometimes nominally chosen to be arbiters in disputes – or conversely, possessors of manors – that did not happen in this case. Elizabeth Jnr was taken care of in her nursery, with no responsibilities attached to her name, and while Elizabeth appears to have joined her husband on several of his visits to his manors and lands during the first part of the year, in the second part of 1462 her pregnancy would have made it much more difficult for her to leave Wingfield Castle very often. Perhaps she chose to stay put to avoid a repeat of her first childbirth.

While at Wingfield Castle, Elizabeth would have been able to supervise her daughter's care. It is interesting to note that while Elizabeth and John made decisions about Elizabeth Jnr's upbringing and education together, apparently with some input by Alice, they did not feel the need to keep as close an eye on things as Alice had in John's childhood. In fact, while it seems that the education of John Jnr and his siblings closely resembled that experienced by their father,[313] their wider lifestyle was much more closely modelled on what Elizabeth had known during her childhood.

They had presumably always planned to have several children, and though it does not seem that they intended to conceive again so quickly there is no reason why they should not have looked forward to having a second baby. Elizabeth Jnr was still too young to realise what was going to happen, and perhaps John was happy that his daughter would never be able to remember a time when she was alone in the nursery without a playmate, as had been the reality for him during large parts of his childhood. Instead, Elizabeth Jnr would grow up as her mother Elizabeth had, surrounded by siblings. John appears to have been present at Wingfield when Elizabeth gave birth to their second child. It was a little son, named after his father. Their choice indicates their priorities; it would have been no surprise had they named the baby Edward after the new king, but instead their focus was very clearly on their duchy, not on the kingdom as a whole.

Like his older sister, he would have been baptised immediately after birth or soon afterwards. It is almost certain that this infant, the new heir to the duchy of Suffolk, would have been shown off after his baptism. The more high-born a child, the grander the ceremony to celebrate their birth and baptism. Royal births were often greeted with bonfires. Naturally, the celebrations for John Jnr's birth would not have been nearly as lavish, but even so they would have been grand. John Jnr was not only a duke's heir; he had royal blood as the son of a princess, and he was the new king's first nephew. It is reasonable to assume that his birth would have aroused some interest in the kingdom at large, though no mention of it survives in contemporary sources.

At just twenty years old, John was a father of two. He was still not of age, but he already had a lot of responsibilities, among them the constableship of Wallingford Castle and the upkeep and defence of his newly purchased manors of Hellesdon and Drayton. And though he was still too young to become involved in the workings of the government, he was certainly considered an important man by the powers that be. King Edward had started taking more notice of him. In late December 1462,[314] John accompanied Edward while travelling north to meet some Lancastrian rebels and marauding Scots. His presence was noted; Elizabeth's was not, although she may have travelled with him. Certainly she joined him at Norwich in January 1463, during the election of the knights of the shire.[315]

Though there is no contemporary information about this occasion, it is known that Edward asked Sir Robert Conyers 'that he should await upon his well-beloved brother the Duke of Suffolk at Norwich on Monday next coming, for to be at the elections of the knights of the shire', and that not only Conyers but 'every gentleman in Norfolk and Suffolk that be of any reputation has writing from the king in like wise'.[316] It is interesting to note Edward's obvious care to make this a special occasion for his brother-in-law, and it can be assumed he was treated with all respect due to him. Probably, many of those attending thought that John, who was by then approaching his twenty-first birthday, would only continue rising in the king's favour and the ranks of his advisors.

Such assumptions would only have gained traction at another grand, if infinitely sadder, event that took place less than a month after John's election to the Order of the Garter, and was attended by most of

England's nobility: the funeral of Richard Neville, Earl of Salisbury, his wife Alice Montacute and their son Thomas.

Salisbury, Elizabeth's uncle, and his son Thomas, her cousin, had been killed on the same day as her father and her brother Edmund,[317] so this occasion might have been rather emotional for her. However, not only she was closely related to the deceased; Alice Montacute and her husband had been John's stepsister and stepbrother-in-law through his mother's second marriage, though we do not know how well, if at all, they knew each other.

The funeral of the Salisburys was a large one. A primary sources states that their 'son and heir, the Earl of Warwick' led the procession, followed by his brother 'the Lord Mountague, on foot, upon the right hand':

> and the Lord Latymer's son on the left; with divers other Knights to the number of sixteen; His banner and standard borne next the chair. A mile without the town there met the corpse two Kings of Arms, and two Heralds, going at each corner of the chair until they came to the place of burial, where met them the Bishop of Exeter, Chancellor of England; the Bishops of Salisbury and Saint Asaph, and two Abbots mitred, with solemn procession, accompanied with the Lord Hastings, Chamberlain to the King; the Lord Fitzhugh, and divers other Knights and Esquires, conveying the son before the father into the quire, and so laid within the hearse, which was there prepared for them, in most solemn wise as appertain. And above that, nearer to the high altar, was one other hearse, wherein was the Lady Countess, his wife, who was brought thither not half an hour before, the pall and perelose of her hearse covered with white, where within sat the Ladies which followed it, viz; the Duchess of Suffolk, the Lady Fitzhugh, the Lady Hastings, the Lady Stanley, the Lady Margaret of Salisbury, and the Lady Montague, with many and divers other Ladies and Gentlewomen about the hearse.[318]

Of all these attending nobles, John seems to have been considered a particularly important one, for he was stated to have followed the coffins in a carriage, in which 'sat the Dukes of Clarence and Suffolk, the Earls of Warwick and Worcester, and the Lords Montague, Hastings, and Fitzhugh, with divers other Knights and Esquires about it'.[319]

The next day, when the ceremony itself took place, 'the Duke of Suffolk, and his wife together' were noted to have offered 'a groat', while John alone offered three 'cloth of gold and baudekyn unto the corpse then present'. Interestingly, the source also states that John paid for two of the five cloths of gold offered by his teenage brother-in-law, the Duke of Clarence.[320] There is no hint of particular interest in either of them in the above-quoted source, which suggests they simply did as expected without drawing any attention to themselves, but it still contains some interesting titbits about them. For one, it is the only contemporary source that records John and his young brother-in-law George, Duke of Clarence working together. Though this would have been co-ordinated in advance, at the very least it shows the two were on good terms then. Perhaps more notable, however, is that John is the only man, noble or otherwise, recorded to have given his offering to the deceased together with his wife. None of the other men present at the ceremony did so, not even the sons of the deceased, nor any of the other dukes. It was clearly not strange enough to cause a shock, but for someone assessing John's character it is nonetheless notable, suggesting that from early in the marriage he considered his wife his equal – a rather unusual stance for the time, but one he would show again in the years to come.

Though the source shows no particular interest in the person of John, it can be assumed that his fellow nobles were more intrigued by this young duke, if only because he would soon attain his majority and was expected to become a major player in national politics soon after. John himself never seems to have had any ambitions to become anything but a regional magnate, but he no doubt eagerly anticipated the rights that would come with his full adulthood. In fact, he explicitly worked for them. Exactly six months before his twenty-first birthday it was recorded 'at the request of John, Duke of Suffolk' that on '7 May, 28 Henry VI [1450]' a writ of *diem clausit extremum* had been issued 'on the death of William, Duke of Suffolk', and that 'on 12 October, 29 Henry VI [1450]' an inquisition 'that the said duke held in his demesne as of a fee a messuage in Deptford, county Kent … worth 6 shillings 8 pennies, yearly' and that William and 'Alice his wife, who survives him, held in their demesne as of fee in her right the manor of Westgrenewich, county Kent, held of the king of his castle of Dover by the service of rendering 5 shilling yearly at the same castle at Michaelmas, and worth 20 pound yearly'. This statement also mentioned that the inquisition in October 1450 had found that William 'died on 2 May and John, now duke, is his son and heir and was of the age of 8 years on 27 September last'.[321]

It seems that Edward gave John permission to enter his lands at this time, freeing him of the necessity to prove his age. By doing so, he gave his brother-in-law control over his possessions some months earlier than would otherwise have been the case. Interestingly, this grant was not recorded either in the Calendar of Patent Rolls nor anywhere else; we know of it only because John took possession of his lands in early 1463 in his own right. It seems that Edward gave him permission informally, though why he chose to do so can only be guessed at. Perhaps it was a genuine gesture of good will; such a theory is supported somewhat by the record mentioned above, which affirmed John's rights at his own request.

Whatever Edward's motivation, we can rule out financial gain. John did not pay for the privilege; even had he wanted to, his finances were always rather paltry. It must have been Edward's decision. He also reaffirmed John's dukedom,[322] securing it in law in Parliament a year later.

Since he was consistently called 'Duke of Suffolk' in all but one primary source from 1458 onwards, this was not a special grant by Edward returning something lost through marriage to Elizabeth, though some modern commentators have suggested this. Instead, it appears to have been an attempt to counteract rumours that he had lost his dukedom, establishing his stature so that he was in a confident position to make deals and manage his lands in his own name.

Until that time, John's relationship with the king appears to have been conventional. Edward had not favoured him and Elizabeth in any notable way, but he had given them some signs of his goodwill, and John appears to have been close enough to him to make requests and complaints with the expectation of being heard. However, it seems that their relationship soured after 1463, and Edward was not to make any other selfless grants to John again until 1478, when it seems their relationship recovered somewhat. The permission for John to enter his lands before his twenty-first birthday without having to prove his age, then, was the last sign of goodwill John received from his brother-in-law for well over a decade. Cynically, it could be pointed out that it had been an easy and meaningless gesture for Edward; it did not take anything away from him and did not require him to do anything but give the necessary instructions. Nonetheless, for John it was significant. For the first time in his life he had control over both his lands and his destiny.

Despite this pleasant surprise, John soon found himself in a situation that would prove familiar. He was too poor to truly maintain his status as duke, and so was perpetually in debt. Edward did nothing to change this; he did not grant John any of the lands and privileges taken away from his father after his murder. This probably wasn't malicious; in all likelihood he simply did not think to improve John and Elizabeth's situation.

It seems that John spent most of 1463 establishing himself in his Suffolk territories. Perhaps this was the year in which his rather vicious quarrel with the Paston family truly began, but nothing survives to confirm this. On the whole, it seems likely that John did not have strife on his mind in 1463 but instead simply wished to gain recognition as a local power. In this, he was no different than any other lord in the fifteenth century, and 1463 seems to have been a peaceful year for him and his family. Their main manor at the time was Wingfield Castle, and John may well have enjoyed seeing his baby son and toddler daughter whenever he wished, close enough to watch them grow even as he was establishing his own position in his native Suffolk.

The married couple had clearly decided on more than two children, as indeed most at the time did. By mid-1463, Elizabeth was pregnant again, expecting her third baby. The exact birth month is not known, though it seems to have been before April 1464.[323] Perhaps most likely is that this baby was born around a year after John Jnr's birth. Obviously, John and Elizabeth were very fertile, and it was very common for many couples at the time to have one child every year. In fact, Elizabeth's mother had done so several times. If Elizabeth had her third child a year after she gave birth to John Jnr, she would have conceived shortly after she was churched. By the time she prepared to give birth again she must have had a certain routine, and perhaps John, too, was less nervous.

Whatever they were feeling, at some point during autumn or winter 1463, John and Elizabeth welcomed another daughter. Her name is sadly lost to history. Though we have records of four of their daughters – Elizabeth Jnr, Katherine, Anne and Dorothy – none of what we know about their lives fits with a birth this early. It seems most likely that the little girl born in late 1463 or early 1464 did not survive childhood and was therefore not mentioned by name in any source that has survived to this day. Of course, when Elizabeth gave birth to her all this was still in the future, and both she and her new baby survived the birth without any problems. Like her siblings, John's second daughter would have been baptised shortly after her birth, and was perhaps named after her grandmother Alice, who, despite her recorded closeness to her son and daughter-in-law, is not known to have had a granddaughter named after her.

The little girl thrived in the beginning. She and her older siblings were apparently raised in the same nursery. John Jnr would by now have started walking and talking, and since all evidence suggests he and his father were close, John probably took a special interest in his son's development and was proud of his achievements. However, soon after their third child was born, the Suffolks' peaceful, family-oriented equilibrium was upset.

Battle and Illness

By early 1464, Edward IV had been on the throne for three years but still not everyone accepted him. Though recent years had seen nothing more than skirmishes disputing his rule, by 1463 a more dangerous situation arose[324] at court. Edward was keen to make peace with former Lancastrians, and in pursuit of this policy he had pardoned Henry Beaufort, Duke of Somerset. The two appeared to become close, spending a lot of time in each other's presence. It does not seem that Edward trusted him completely, however; he was careful not to give him much power.[325] Through his physical closeness to Edward at court alone, though, he would have been privy to a lot of information. It seems that this was what Henry was after, for in early 1464 he once more joined the Lancastrian side.

In late April 1464, Lancastrian rebels led by Henry Beaufort assembled an army,[326] hoping to unseat Edward IV and return the still fugitive Henry VI to the throne. Edward reacted as soon as the news reached him, seeing to it that men were raised in his name to fight against the Lancastrians. This force of men was led by John Neville, Earl of Northumberland,[327] cousin of Edward and brother of the famous Earl of Warwick. John, Duke of Suffolk, was among the men gathered to fight for Edward,[328] which stands in stark contrast to the common notion that he avoided conflict, preferring to wait things out and then support the winning side.

It seems there was never any doubt about him becoming involved in this particular battle, and he rode with the Yorkist forces to meet the Lancastrian makeshift army. On 28 April, a group of Yorkist fighters, led by Northumberland, met a group of Lancastrian fighters and defeated them,[329] but this did not spell the end of the hostilities. Beaufort was not involved in the skirmish in April, and he gathered his men and met the Yorkist forces near Hexham, where on 15 May they engaged in battle. It was a vicious fight, but eventually the Yorkists emerged victorious.[330]

Henry Beaufort was captured and summarily executed on the orders of John Neville,[331] who had been given authority to issue such orders by Edward IV before the engagement. Most importantly for the Yorkist future was another outcome of the battle, however. Many Lancastrian fighters who had still been at large, like John de Vere, Earl of Oxford, were taken prisoner.[332] With their capture, the danger of another Lancastrian attack in the near future was diminished significantly.

Once more, what part John, Duke of Suffolk played in the battle itself was not recorded by any source, suggesting he comported himself well without drawing any attention to himself, either by outstanding bravery or any cowardice. It seems, then, that he acted the same as he did in the other battles he had been involved in in his life. However, the Battle of Hexham was to have lasting consequences for him. In a letter dated 8 June 1464, some three weeks after the battle, Margaret Paston wrote to her husband about the conflict. She reported the actions of John Howard, Lord Howard, and John Woodville, Lord Scales, both of whom were clearly still busy with the consequences of the battle: 'And Sir John Howard is come home, and it is said that the Lord Scales and he have a commission to enquire why they of this county that were sent for came not hastily upon after they were sent for.'[333] In the same paragraph of the letter she stated that 'it is told that the Duke of Suffolk is come home, and either he is dead or else right sick and not like to escape'.[334]

No further details are offered, and we know that John was neither dead nor dying in June 1464, which suggests it was either an exaggeration or even a baseless rumour. The latter, however, seems somewhat unlikely, as Margaret was right about everything else she reported in her letter, including the enquiry by Howard and Scales. Because of this, there may well be some truth to the notion that he was very sick when he returned home after fighting at Hexham.

Despite the context in which Margaret couched this information in her letter, it could of course be that John's sickness was unrelated to the battle, that it was similar to his father's reported serious illness in 1431. If so, it is unlikely it was an illness typical of life on campaign, such as dysentery, for there is no report of anyone else, noble or commoner, being stricken with such ailments. There is one fact that is rather telling, however: John never fought again. He would not be present at any of the battles still to come in his lifetime.

Though on the face of it this might have been his own decision, one notable fact argues against it: John was never in his lifetime accused of cowardice, or of deliberately sitting on the fence. Though this accusation has often been levelled at him in histories written in the centuries after his death, with his supposed nickname of 'the trimming Duke'[335] being used as evidence, there is no such accusation found in any contemporary source. The unflattering nickname itself is a later invention, not one used in his lifetime. After 1464, it seems that no one ever expected of John to do anything more than gather men in his name and send them off to fight when war reared its head. While the notoriously indecisive Thomas Stanley was heavily criticised at the time, no such opprobrium was directed at John after 1464, very much pointing towards him being physically unable to fight.

Of course, it is always possible that his inability to fight after 1464 had nothing to do with his illness following the Battle of Hexham; perhaps it was instead caused by an unconnected accident, such as a bad fall off a horse at any time between 1464 and 1469. But perhaps this would be too great a coincidence. The most likely theory is that John was critically injured during Hexham, in such a way that he retained some sort of disability after recovering, such as a slight limp, which rendered him unable to fight but otherwise able to continue his life as usual. For instance, he could have suffered an open break, which could very easily have made him so sick that he was thought likely to die but would not, once it had healed, have left much more than a slight limp or a weak arm. We can only guess at the precise nature of such an injury, but evidence of him using crossbows in 1466 might suggest an injury to his legs rather than his arms.

In any case, it must have been a tense time for his entire family. For a while after John returned it must have seemed possible, even likely, that he would die and John Jnr, only one and a half years old, would become Duke of Suffolk. Such a prospect must have been scary for a little boy, but the situation would have been even worse for his mother. If he died, she could not be sure that her brother would allow her to keep custody of her small son as Henry VI had allowed Alice to keep custody of John.

It seems that Elizabeth travelled from Wingfield Castle to Ewelme to be with her husband,[336] though her children, John Jnr included, would have been left behind in the care of their nurses and caretakers. The children would have been considered too young to travel if there was no necessity, and, more importantly, Elizabeth might have feared that they might catch something from their father, as contagion was poorly understood at the time. When John recovered after several weeks it must have been a massive relief for everyone, and any small disabilities he retained must have seemed a very small price to pay for his survival.

How quickly John recovered is unknown, but it seems he was able to take up the running of his estates again by summer 1464, though he might still have avoided travelling. Given that he was so sick he was considered likely to die, it can be assumed his recovery lasted well into the summer. He was nominated to a commission of the peace for Suffolk in August 1464, and though this nomination may very well have been nominal, it seems obvious that by this time he was considered likely to survive, and perhaps able to work again.

Interestingly, John being unable to take care of his affairs for at least three months before and after the battle presumably means that Elizabeth took on these tasks for him. It would have been her first chance to show her mettle. As she was not yet twenty years of age and had spent most of the last three years pregnant, and so was not in her husband's presence while he saw tenants and managed his lands, it would have been impossible for outsiders to tell how she would take to the responsibility.

Even though it is reasonable to assume Alice helped Elizabeth to run the estates, the final decisions would have been Elizabeth's. Similar to how it would not have been obvious to any outsiders which of John's decisions were influenced by his wife, it would not have been obvious to anyone but those very close to them which of Elizabeth's decisions during this time were her own and which influenced by her mother-in-law. Perhaps, when John finally recovered, Elizabeth decided she had enjoyed being more involved in the running of his estates and wished to take her place at his side more often in the coming years. If so, perhaps they made a conscious decision not to try for another baby for a little while.

Whether due to this or for some other reason, Elizabeth did not immediately conceive again. It could even have been due to John's illness. This possibility seems rather unlikely, though, for he seemed perfectly recovered and able to take up his normal life by autumn 1464, and whatever injury he might have sustained during the Battle of Hexham, it obviously did not cause him any trouble in that regard in later years. Elizabeth, too, seemed to be in good health, having survived her three pregnancies with no ill effects that we know of, so the most likely explanation is not that they stopped having sex but simply that she did not conceive as readily as she had with her previous three children. If she and John hoped to have another child soon, it was not for lack of opportunity to try that it did not happen, as they appeared to spend the rest of the year together.

Political Intrigues, Part 1

Whatever their decisions regarding their sex life, or possible concerns about her not conceiving as quickly as she had before, such personal matters would have been dwarfed by the news that broke in September 1464. At a meeting in Northampton, Edward IV announced that in May 1464[337] he had married a widow, an Englishwoman, without telling anyone. John and Elizabeth were present when this announcement was made, and presumably they were as shocked as everyone else. The marriage was a breach of all custom, not simply because it had been made in secret but also because it had been kept that way for several months. Moreover, during the time Edward had been married, his closest advisor, his cousin Richard Neville, Earl of Warwick, had been in France negotiating a marriage between Edward and the French king's sister-in-law, Bona of Savoy.[338] Naturally, Warwick was enraged at having been made to look like a fool, negotiating a marriage for someone who was already married.

Warwick's wounded pride was not the biggest issue with the marriage, however. There were legitimate concerns about the reaction of the French at a time when a fragile peace was forming; predictably, they did not take kindly to Lady Bona being treated with such callous disregard.[339] Even the Spanish monarchs were to later say that they had been insulted by Edward negotiating for a marriage with them only to then prefer an Englishwoman of no pedigree.[340] Edward's marriage had all the makings of a disaster for both domestic and foreign politics.

Moreover, not only the circumstances, but also the person of Edward's bride was contentious. Elizabeth, Lady Grey, a daughter of the Woodville family, was the widow of a Lancastrian fighter who had died at the Second Battle of St Albans. She was some five years older than Edward and had two sons by her first husband, plus a very large family of five sisters and six brothers.[341] Her mother, Jacquetta, was a high-born woman of foreign nobility who had been sister-in-law to Henry V through her first marriage, but her father, Richard, was only a member of the gentry.[342] Elizabeth brought no dowry or useful connections to her marriage with Edward, and the most common assumption, then as now, is that Edward only agreed to marry her because she would not otherwise yield to his seduction.

None of this, of course, was the new queen's fault, but she would soon prove an unpopular queen in other ways that had more to do with her actions.[343] This was still in the future in autumn 1464, however, and what John and Elizabeth thought about that marriage is absolutely unknowable. Unlike many of the nobility, they did not express any surprise or shock, nor did they become enemies of the Woodvilles in the coming years. However, they didn't make friends either. They were some of the very few nobles who did not seem to mind the Woodvilles one way or another, possibly because they generally preferred not to involve themselves in national politics, and therefore rarely crossed paths with the Woodville clan. On the rare occasions that they did, John and Elizabeth were successful in keeping up friendly relations without ever becoming close or, in reality or the public mind, associated.

Despite this and despite the fact that the marriage did not have an obvious fallout on them as it did on others, the Suffolks were to suffer under Edward's marriage. This was not directly the fault of the Woodville family or even Elizabeth Woodville herself, and most likely it would have happened even had Edward married a foreign princess as had been expected of him. Knowing he had to furnish his wife with lands, Edward chose to confiscate some of John's lands to give to her, in addition to some other lands he himself had held previously.[344] There is no saying why Edward chose to do this, and it seems extremely cruel. His brother-in-law and sister were already too poor for their status, in fact even too poor to properly maintain an earldom, so they would have keenly felt the loss of any lands. It may be that Edward considered them the least likely of any nobles to act against him in response, but if so it reflects very badly on him. Only months after John had apparently been critically injured while fighting for him, Edward visited this poor treatment upon him in return.

It might be that the king realised this, because shortly afterwards he granted John and Elizabeth £100 yearly.[345] He might also have been motivated by the fury of his mother, who wouldn't wish to see her daughter impoverished on top of the humiliation of her son's clandestine union. On the face of it, £100 was a generous amount, but it barely covered the value of the lands taken from them. Moreover, the grant was given on the condition it only continued until Elizabeth's death. It is obvious that for some reason, by 1464, Edward had come to deeply dislike John, so much so that in the event of his sister's death he would prefer to have his own nieces and nephews grow up with too little money to cover their expenses rather than give John anything, even in compensation for what he had taken from him. As far as we can tell, John had not done anything that would warrant such strong feelings against him; indeed, it was not even a year since John had nearly lost his life to keep Edward on the throne. John, never given to public displays of feeling, showed no indication he disliked Edward while the latter was alive. Perhaps he knew some forgotten reason for Edward's antipathy, or maybe he simply accepted it as something he could not change.

Edward's terrible behaviour towards his brother-in-law has rarely if ever been discussed, either in his lifetime or in the centuries after his death, and modern historians have nearly all squarely blamed John for Edward's mistreatment of him. John has been described as 'a feeble character'[346] or even 'an ineffectual non-entity'[347] to explain away Edward's actions and frame him as reasonable for doing what he did. In actuality, however, Edward's behaviour was shameful and John's acceptance of his mistreatment shows a rare inclination to keep peace that few of his contemporaries would have shared. John might have thought he could only lose if he fought back. He chose to keep away from court as much as he could, and it is not surprising to find that the Suffolks did not spend Christmas 1464 there. They had returned to Ewelme by autumn of 1464, although in November John travelled to Westminster again to be present as Parliament was opened; it was his first session. There is no indication he got involved in any way, though he did his duty and was present.

It is easy to imagine John was glad when Parliament was adjourned for Christmas, at which time he travelled to Ewelme to spend Christmas with his wife and mother. In January, Elizabeth travelled to Wingfield to be with her children,[348] whom she had probably not seen since she had travelled to be with John while he was sick at the end of May or early June. John did not accompany her; we do not know why, though we do know it was not because of any disagreement with his wife, as they were on very good terms then. A letter from 17 January 1465 suggests that John's motivation was not that he wanted to be away from his wife or had no interest in seeing his children again, but simply that he hoped to avoid going to court again soon. The letter is a response by one of John's servants, a man called Wadehill, to a letter written by John's brother-in-law Thomas Stonor. Though Thomas's letter no longer survives, its contents can be gauged from the answer:

> Worshipful and my right good master, I recommend me to your good mastership, and like you to know that my lord, and my lady his mother also, have commanded me to write unto you that they both heartily desire and pray you, if you may in any wise on your going to London, you will take the labour as to come hither to speak with my said lord and lady for diverse great matters and causes that they would speak unto you of. And if you may not come hither, than that you will find the mean to my lord chancellor as to excuse my lord of his coming not to London at this time, like as my said lord was written unto by a privy seal which was delivered to him on Monday last passed at six of the clock within night at Ewelme, which as your mastership knows well was right short warning, remembering that the more part of my lord's servants were sent into Suffolk to the household there against Christmas, and the remnant of his servants, that were here awaiting, your mastership knows well been forth with my lady, my lord's wife, into Suffolk to bring her thither, for God knows she thought fill long from the young lord and the young ladies her children, that been there. And so my lord might not come at London himself at this time to his worship, and his servants from him: for I dare say he has here at this day awaiting upon his lordship not a dozen persons.
>
> Nevertheless with God's grace my said lord puproses and will be and attend at Parliament as other lords shall, for by that time his said servants that be now absent will be with my said lord again here.
>
> Written in haste this Thursday, 17th day of January.
>
> Your servant Wadehill.
>
> To my right worshipful master,
> Thomas Stonor.[349]

Obviously, John had no intention to come to court in January 1465, not even when formally asked to do so by the king. Though he was right in stating that it would not be appropriate for a duke, especially one married to the king's sister, to be seen with such a small retinue and the 'not a dozen' servants would not have been able to keep up a household such as would be expected for a duke attending court, it is hard not to see this as a planned and construed excuse.

Both John and Elizabeth would have known such an invitation was likely to come before Parliament resumed in late January or early February. When Elizabeth left John in early January to go 'into Suffolk', both would have known that taking the majority of their servants meant John would not be able to attend court while making sure he could attend Parliament as would be expected of him. The conclusion that this was John's intention cannot really be avoided. It might be that this was the reason why Elizabeth went to see 'the young lords and the young ladies' on her own.

It is, of course, equally possible he did not really feel a need to see them. John made it clear he loved them, but at the time this would not have meant he was expected to see them very often. However, both John and Elizabeth usually made a point of seeing their children whenever they could, so it seems very out of character for him to simply have no interest in accompanying his wife. Going by the evidence available, it seems that when Elizabeth decided to go see her children John decided not to come along so that they could arrange it between themselves in such a way that he would have an excuse to avoid court without it being considered an affront to the king. Had he accompanied his wife, he would have had enough servants around him in Suffolk to create a suitable retinue and hence would have had to go to London with them or else appear openly disobedient. Had he gone with Elizabeth, he would also have barely had the chance to see his children before having to leave again, largely rendering his journey pointless.

The letter, which comes off as somewhat tetchy, is interesting in that it marks the first appearance in the surviving historical record of a trait John would show more often from now on: polite disobedience. This sort of completely truthful yet irreverent answer to someone in power asking him to do something, refusing to do it on grounds which were obviously avoidable, was to become something of a trademark and it stands in stark contrast to the reputation John has among most modern-day historians as a spineless yes-man. Rather than somebody who did whatever he was told by his superiors, it seems rather the opposite was true about him. He tended to do only what he wanted to do, but he was polite and deferential in his refusal to do something he had no wish to do. It generally worked in his favour, and this case was no exception. Edward did not insist on him coming to court, and there were no consequences for him.

It has often been claimed that this letter was written in 1471, as it is only dated to Thursday 17 January with no year given, and 1465 and 1471 are the only years between 1463 and 1475 in which the 17 January fell on a Thursday.[350] 1471 is usually assumed because it was the year of the Lancastrian readeption – Henry VI's return to the throne – and John wishing to avoid court in such an uncertain time would fit his modern reputation as a turncoat trying to stay on the fence. It being written in

1471 would also explain why Elizabeth had left London, not wanting to be present for the parliament of a government that had replaced her brother's.

The details speaking against such a dating are often brushed aside. In the Stonor letter volumes annotated by Charles Lethbridge Kingsford it is offered that if it was written in 1471 this would 'involve[s] a reference to an otherwise unknown meeting of the Parliament of the Lancastrian Restoration', and therefore dating it to that year is 'difficult'. Nevertheless, it concludes that John, 'who was married to a sister of Edward IV, would naturally desire to keep away from Court in 1471' and therefore the letter was written then.[351]

However, other details from the letter make it perfectly clear it cannot have been from 1471. For one, it states very clearly that John and Elizabeth's children are 'the young lord and the young ladies' at that point – John Jnr, Elizabeth Jnr and their little sister, whose name has sadly been lost to history. By 1471, John and Elizabeth had more children. While their birth order has never been properly established, we know for a fact that their son Edward de la Pole was born by January 1471, meaning that their children would have been described as 'the young lords and the young ladies'. If only three of their children had been in Suffolk in January 1471, and the others staying with their father in Ewelme, there would have been more than barely twelve servants in John's household when he received the letter, and their inability to form a retinue for Parliament would have been explained by them needing to care for his children. Moreover, it seems that by 1471 the children's main nursery was in Ewelme,[352] so Elizabeth would not have needed to travel to Suffolk to see her children. The presence of at least two daughters mentioned in the letter makes it clear that their residence in Suffolk was not used as a separate household for their oldest son and heir but was simply the location of their children's nursery.

Another detail that speaks against the letter being from 1471, though one not as indicative as the details mentioned above, is that John Jnr held a title in his own right by that time.[353] Despite this, his father's servant would not necessarily have used that title in such a letter. Even when he was an earl, in the context of the letter 'young lord' would still have been a perfectly acceptable way to refer to him.

In the face of all this evidence, it is clear that the letter was written in 1465. It is therefore an important piece of evidence even about John and Elizabeth's children, since it is the only contemporary source we have for them having two daughters but only one son in January 1465, when traditionally it has been claimed that they had only two boys by that time. For most of John's children who survived childhood we have approximate dates of birth and death, but for his second little girl we do not even have a name. All we know is that, given her mother's movements, she must have been born in late 1463 or very early 1464, and that she was still alive in January 1465 and was raised with her older brother and sister.

Despite sharing his nursery with them, John Jnr would have been raised knowing of his special position as their father's heir. When their mother visited in early 1465, he was two years old. He had passed his second birthday in autumn without his parents, much as Elizabeth Jnr had spent her third, but it is doubtful the children expected anything else. At two years of age, John Jnr was still in the nursery, in the care of women, but it is likely that plans were made that once he had reached his third birthday he would have first started receiving lessons. Elizabeth's brothers had done in their childhood, and presumably so did she, though we know less about her upbringing than that of her brothers. John, as discussed above, probably received lessons at a very young age as well, and though we sadly know less about John Jnr's early childhood than his father's, it seems likely he would have followed his parents' example.

Though still a very small boy, John Jnr's education would have already been planned by January 1465, and possibly, those of his older sister would have already begun. This would obviously have been with easy lessons that could be followed by a toddler. John and Elizabeth were an intelligent and extremely educated couple, and presumably they would have wanted their children to receive an equally good education.[354] What concrete form this took for John Jnr and his siblings at that young an age can of course no longer be said, but some clues can be found in the education of his cousin, who would in due course, albeit briefly, become King Edward V. Though obviously little Edward would have been prepared for an entirely different life than his older cousin, it has been suggested that Edward's upbringing and education was modelled closely after that given to his father and uncles by his grandparents.[355] Since Elizabeth, like her brother, appears to have chosen to model her offspring's childhood after her own, the two cousins presumably had a very similar experience of education in their first years of life. John Jnr would have been read to and, even as a toddler, been instructed how to read and write.

There is no indication how the boy took to this. Though several of his brothers and at least one of his sisters were to turn out very scholarly – Edward de la Pole, who was born some nine years after John Jnr, was said to have a particular aptitude for learning[356] –there is no saying if that was also true for John Jnr. He grew up to be an intelligent man, but there is no indication he was particularly scholarly or had an interest in learning. In fact, what is known of him suggests a very practical man, which perhaps suggests his unusually thorough education was more of an annoyance than a pleasure for him.

In 1465, of course, any such contemplations still lay in the future. John Jnr was still only a toddler, and his behaviour and understanding of the world would have been similar to that exhibited by toddlers today. When his mother arrived to see him and his sisters in January of that year, he might have barely understood who she was, not having seen her for so long.

5

1465–1470

Landholdings and Resulting Difficulties

It seems unlikely John came to see his wife and children after Parliament was over. If he did not, Elizabeth cannot have stayed with her children in Suffolk for more than three months before going back to her husband in Ewelme, for at some point in the spring of that year she became pregnant again. She must have already been with child by May 1465, when her sister-in-law, her brother Edward's wife, was crowned as Queen Elizabeth on 26 May 1465, though she might not yet have been certain of it. Whether she knew it or not, it did not seem to affect her adversely. She was reportedly in good health when the coronation took place, her new pregnancy not hindering her.

Though Elizabeth had not played a significant part in her brother's coronation, she was more involved in that of her sister-in-law. A contemporary source states that her aunt 'the Duches of Buk[ingham] thelder [the elder] bare up the Quenys trayne' and that directly behind her 'followed nexte the Queene of ladys the Duches of Suff[olk] & my lady M[ar]grete her sister and the Duches of Bedford'. This is confirmed by another source. During the coronation ceremony, Elizabeth is noted to have 'attend[ed] the crown reverently' and 'at certain times of response held the crown on her [the queen's] head' together with the Duchess of Bedford, the queen's mother.[357] Elizabeth's position, though of high honour, was not a special favour from the king but in fact a role that was her due as his sister and the new queen's sister-in-law. That she, rather than Margaret, was given the task of holding the crown over the new queen's head was most likely simply due to her higher standing as duchess, and not due to any preference by Edward or the new queen herself.

John's part in the coronation was somewhat less spectacular than his wife's, though not insultingly unimportant. Instead, it simply reflected his standing well, without giving him any special honour such as he had received at Edward's coronation: '[T]he duq of Suff[olk] beyng on hir [the queen's] right hand bering in his hand the septor of Seint Edward.'[358] It is possible that John had hoped for a more prominent part in the ceremony, but there is no indication of him ever saying so or even being speculated to have had such thoughts. Except for the mentions in the sources attesting to their presence and activity during the coronation, there is no indication of them doing anything, or even being expected or rumoured to do something during them that aroused any interest, and perhaps both of them preferred it that way.

If John and his wife were, in fact, wary of such big celebrations and preferred a quiet life in Wingfield Castle, they must have been glad to get away from court again and return to rural Suffolk. However, their summer there was to prove rather turbulent, for it was then that John's quarrel with the Pastons, which had been smouldering over recent years, first escalated. In fact, that trouble was coming was already clear in early 1465. On 8 April that year, Margaret wrote a letter to her husband stating that one of her men 'had told Dorlet [another servant] that he had suche a deed as he supposed that would done ease in purveying of the title that the Duke of Suffolk claims in Drayton, for the same deed that he sent me the seale of armys is like onto the copy that I send you, and nothing like to the Duke of Suffolk's ancestors'.[359] We do not know if this coat of arms actually proved the Pastons' claim to the manor of Drayton as Margaret seemed to think it would, but apparently, in that month, she seemed positive about her family's chance of claiming the disputed manors. In the same letter, she also stated she had been sent word that 'Barker and Herry Porter told him in council that the Duke of Suffolk has bought on Brytyeff right, the which makes a claim onto Heylysdon, and the said Duke is purposed to enter within short time after Easter; for in so much the said Russe felt by the said Barker and Porter that all the feoffees woill make a release onto the Duke and help him that they can into their power, for to have his good lordship'.[360]

It is interesting that Margaret's early letters do not point towards any misbehaviour by John. On the contrary, the letter suggests that while there was a quarrel about the ownership of the manor of Drayton, it was one that she expected to solve with proof that possession had always been in her family whereas he felt he had purchased the rights to the manor of Hellesdon. That she reported hearing that the feoffees would help him 'to have his good lordship'[361] without any mention of dissent suggests that there was nothing actually wrong with John's behaviour, though obviously Margaret considered it to be threatening her family's interests. The letter also makes it obvious that John had established himself as local power in such a way that he was considered a valuable ally – and a formidable enemy.

Though we do not know of any actions taken by either John de la Pole or John Paston in April or May to secure their possession of these manors, it seems that something happened, for on 3 May Margaret Paston wrote another letter to her husband, including some warning words:

> Sundry folks have said to me that they think verily but if ye have my Lord of Suffolk's good lordship while the werd is as it is, ye can never live in peace without ye have his good lordship; therefore I pray you with all mine heart that ye will do your part to have his good lordship and his love in ease of all those matters that ye have to do, and in easing of mine heart also, for by my truth I am afraid else, both of these matters the which ye have in hand now, and of other that not be done to yet, but if he will do for you and be your good lord.[362]

Though this letter suggests that Margaret was very much afraid of the repercussions of being in opposition to John, again there is no indication of wrongdoing on his part. If anything it suggests that John Paston had done something, or was rumoured to intend doing something, that would turn John against him.

Interestingly, these two letters rather contradict the modern take on John's quarrel with the Pastons, for they make it clear that despite his mother's quarrels with the Paston family he was not opposed to them from the first, nor was his dislike of the Paston family, as is so often claimed, random and unprovoked.[363] In fact, the letter of 3 May suggests the opposite: that John Paston had been acting in a way his friends advised him against for fear of offending John, rather than simply reacting to his actions. This therefore put John, rather than his opponents, in the position of reacting to offence.

It was not to remain that way. Those advising Margaret Paston were right about one thing: John did not take kindly to others laying claim to what he considered rightfully his. Even as John was making his way, together with his wife, to Westminster to be present at the new queen's coronation, on 10 May 1465, Margaret was reporting her plans to put off a possible attack by John's men once he returned from the festivities, as well as rumours of what John intended to do. None of this can have been very reassuring for John Paston. She stated that 'on Wendnesday last passed Dabeney, Naunton, Wykys, and John Love were at Drayton for to speak with your tenants there, to put them in confort and for to ask money of them also',[364] without detailing why the tenants needed comforting, though her implication is that it was because they feared an attack by John, possibly because, as she had already reported a month earlier, 'it is told me that the Duke of Suffolk has bought, or shall be in haste, the right that on Brighttylhed has in Hellesdon etc'.[365]

Again, this letter, though obviously fearful of John and his reaction to the Pastons' claims and actions, does not actually report any misbehaviour by John, nor even rumours of such, rather the future prospect of it.

However, in the same letter, Margaret reported misbehaviour by their own men: 'And Piers Warren, otherwise called Piers at Sloth, which is a flickering fellow […] he had a plow going in your land at Drayton, and there your said servants at that time took his plougher […] and brought them to Hellesdon, and there they be yet'. She then reports that as revenge, one Master Phillip, allied with Piers, had 'come to Hellesdon with a great number of people, that is to say eight men and more in harness, and there too from the person's plow two horses, price four mark, and two horses of Thomas Stermyn's plow, price 15 shilling, saying to them that there was taken a plant against them in the hundred by the said Piers for taking of the foresaid plougher at Drayton'. She reports that the said Master Phillip was questioned by her husband's men as to whether he had taken horses from workers in Hellesdon, which he answered in the affirmative, stating that he would only bring them back if 'they would bring back home their detresse that was taken of Piers Warren'. She also stated that Master Phillip had gone on to state that 'if you [John Paston] or any of your servants took any distress in Drayton, that were but the value of a hen, they would come to Hellesdon and take there the value of an ox therefore, and if they cannot take the value thereof there, that then they would do break your tennants houses in Hellesdon and take as much as they would find therein'.[366]

This prelude to the big escalation of the quarrel between John and the Paston family provably happened before John got involved, before he gave any orders to in any way threaten, frighten or blackmail anyone into affirming his right to either of these manors and their corresponding lands. Margaret Paston herself admits that the quarrel she reports on 10 May started with misbehaviour by her husband's own servants, though she then records that she considers it most likely that John would support the enemies of their family. She therefore once more cautioned her husband that 'he saide that if you tale upon you to let them so for to do, that they would go into any livelihood that you had in Norfolk or Suffolk and take a distress in likewise as they would do at Hellesdon'.[367] Perhaps as a consolation, or a warning, she also added that it 'shall never lie in your power to [allow them to steal from John's servants], for the Duke of Suffolk is able to keep daily in his house more men than Dabney had hairs in his head if him lust [if he wants]'.[368]

On the whole, Margaret's letter does not sound very positive for her family's cause, though naturally she is very biased in its favour. Interestingly, at the end of the letter, she also reported that 'it is told me that Thomas Elys of Norwich, which now is chosen major, said at Drayton that if my lord of Suffolk need a hundred men, he would purvey him thereof, and if any men of the town would go to Paston he would lay him fast in prison'.[369] From this, it can be concluded that John had made arrangements, seeing to it he had important support in case his quarrel with the Paston family escalated, but it is equally possible that

Thomas Elys had made the decision to support him by himself, without any bribery beforehand, in the hope of preferment by John. In fact, this is the more likely version; Elys was newly elected, and while it is possible that John saw to it any possible candidate was well-disposed to him, he did not usually have the ready money to offer bribes. Since he had, until that time, done nothing illegal whereas the servants of the Paston family had done, he may not have considered it necessary.

However, only two weeks after Margaret reported this statement, she had better news for her husband:

> Your tenants at Drayton, as I can understand by them, they be right good, and true-hearted to you to their powers, and full fain would, that ye had it again in peace: for they had as lief almost be tenants to the Devil as to the Duke, except Will Herne, Piers at Sloth [Piers Warren] and one Knott of the same town, for they be not good. All your tenants at Hellesdon and Drayton, except these three, be right glad that we are there amongst them, and so be many others of our old neighbours and friends.[370]

Later events would show that Margaret had been somewhat too positive about the tenants' feelings towards her family and against John. However, she probably recorded what she perceived to be the truth at that moment, and it may very well be that John, hearing of public opinion turning against him and in the knowledge of the pledge of support by the mayor of Norwich, decided to act in a rather warlike manner once he returned from the coronation festivities. He probably acted almost immediately after returning to Suffolk, for by 11 June 1465, Margaret Paston was writing another letter to her husband reporting the newest developments in this situation. Sadly, we do not have all their correspondence in this matter, for Margaret references a letter her husband wrote her in the meantime, referring to her husband telling her he had heard from a messenger that she had let him know 'that the Duke's men were not so busy as they had been before, no more they were not at the time', but then she added that 'since then they have been busier'.[371] She went on to state that 'what comfort that they have I cannot have no knowledge as yet, but I suppose, and all your fellowship were good, they should not have so great comfort as they have, or else they would not be so busy as they have been'.[372]

This is the first reference to any wrongdoing by John in this conflict, and it is only speculation by Margaret Paston. In fact, it seems that even by mid-June 1465, with some Paston servants having attacked his own, and his men having mounted a retaliatory attack, John was not inclined to escalate the matter – something that, curiously, Margaret Paston sounds rather disapproving about: 'Great boast they [John's men] make that the Duke should have Drayton in peace, and after this Hellesdon, and that within a short time.'[373] Margaret's letter suggests she did not take this boast very seriously, instead speculating that 'they are much the bolder, I suppose, because that you are where as you are', and hoping that her husband 'if [he] may by any worshipful or reasonable mean, come over there as soon as you may, and come among your friends and tennants', as she thought it would 'be to them greatest comfort that they may have him' there. She also considers her husband's presence would be 'the contrary [of comfort] to your enemies'.

Having made this plea, she then goes on to report that 'it is said here that the Duke of Suffolk shall come to Coshay in haste and lodge there for a season',[374] something she considered obviously threatening in some way. However, once more she did not state that this would be in any way dangerous to anyone, instead apparently fearing that it would allow John to achieve his goal of taking the manors peaceably. To counteract this, Margaret repeated her plea to her husband to beat John at his own game: 'I feel well by your tenants that if you were peaceably possessed and your court holden in peaceable wise, and that they might be in peace against the other many, than they would take actions against them for such wrongs as have been done to them.'[375] This sentence is perhaps the most interesting one of the whole letter, for in all the correspondence between Margaret and her husband from early April to 11 June, it is the only non-speculative reference to John's men doing something wrong and harming Paston's tenants in some way. However, Margaret does not elaborate on these wrongs, instead going on to state that if her husband did not show up 'they say that they dare not take it upon them, for they dwell so near to the other many that they know well they should never be in ease if they did so while that they dwell among them'.[376]

Obviously, the conflict was escalating in earnest by then, with both parties thinking that if they approached it peacefully they would stand apart from the enemy faction. Probably because of this, and in spite of the servants of both clearly being more violently disposed than either patriarch at that point, the two were apparently still intending to take the quarrel to court. Margaret writes of one of her servants that 'he is so called upon by Wayte and others of the Duke of Suffolk's council that he know not where to hold him [John], and he is put in so great comfort, as I am informed, to receive money for the land, and that tempted him right sour'.[377]

This, once more, seems to suggest that John was trying to solve the problem as he had in previous years by ensuring that his purchases secured his rights. In the light of his always straitened circumstances, this suggests that the manors in question were important to him, although we don't know why he was so steadfast in refusing a compromise with the Paston family. It is possible that he did not trust them, but it is also possible – in fact, given what we know of his character it is rather likely – that it was sheerest stubbornness that made him dig in his heels on this issue.

Immediately following Margaret's statement that John wished to purchase some lands to shore up his possessions in Drayton, she then stated, rather intriguingly, that the man she had spoken to 'told John Strange that ... you have up an inquest to disprove their witness, and therewith he is sore moved'.[378] The next bit of the letter is sadly missing, so we cannot know why this man was 'sore moved', though given his explicitly mentioned money trouble the suggestion is that he was motivated to help John Paston in exchange for money. That would doubtlessly put John Paston in the wrong, but since it cannot be confirmed it would be unfair to lambast him for this. However, it is obvious that by this time the two Johns were growing somewhat desperate to prove their rights and take certain possession of the manors.

By 27 June, John had apparently lost his patience, for in yet another letter John Paston reported to his wife:

> Word [is] that Master Phillip has entered in Drayton in my lord of Suffolk's name, and had other purpose to enter in Hellesdon, and he asked my advice, which is that you comfort my tennants and help them til I come home, and let them know that I shall not lease it; and that the Duke of Suffolk that last did would have both it of Falstof, and for he might not have it, so he claimed the manor, saying it was on Polis, and for his name was Poole [*sic*] he claimed to be his. He was answered that he come nothing of that stick, and how someone were kin to the Polis that owns it, it hurt not for it was lawfully bought and sold, and he never claimed it after.[379]

This part of the letter is particularly illuminating, not only showing that the quarrel was in fact inherited from John's father but also the weakness of his claim.

Despite John's men having taken possession of the manors, John Paston did not seem very worried, apparently considering his own claim unshakeable and certain to win eventually. He stated that he was:

> ... in purpose to take assistance against them at this time, and else I would have sent the others straight a letter of attorney to enter in my name. Nevertheless you are a gentlewoman, and it is worship for you to comfort your tenants, wherefore I would you might ride to Hellesdon and Drayton and Sparha [...] and tarry at Drayton [...] and speak with them, and bid them hold with their old master til I come, and that you have sent me word but late, wherefore you may have no answer yet. And inform them as I have written to you [...] within and say openly it is a shame that any man should set any lord on so [...] a matter, and special [...] and let them know as soon as I am come home I shall see them.[380]

This letter definitely suggests that John Paston had not only expected John to act as he did but had also made arrangements for it. It is interesting, given that modern history books often criticise John for entering the manors, that John Paston did not consider it in any way unusual or as anything more than an annoyance, and that he himself expressed a wish to do so.

However, perhaps thinking it was best to outwit John rather than use violence, or perhaps thinking of the support pledged to John and his servant's assertion of how many men he could have, Paston went on:

> or distress for rent or farm, though the Duke has title, as he has not, he may not ask til the next rent day after his entry, that is Michaelmas. And say that you will be paid your pain, and ask them it, and make much of men of Cossey because they were our well-willers when we were neightbours there, and them them know that the beginnings of such metters had never worship nor profit of me, nor shall, and desire god will or your neighbours, etc, and find […] all other men that you can to please the people. And let your tenants know that the Duke may never by law compel them to be torn from me, and do all so well as you can. And if any entry be made in Hellesdon […] shove him out and set some man to keep the place […] if need be, notwithstanding […] it longes not to the manor.[381]

Though John Paston sounds very secure in the legality of his claim, it is interesting to note that he doesn't seem at all confident that everyone would agree with him. He clearly considered it necessary to instruct his wife as to what she should tell people to win them to his side.

In fact, though he appears rather concerned for his tenants initially, it has to be noted that he does not state any sort of concrete fear of danger to them from John's men taking possession of the manor. If anything, given that he considered it possible and saw no difficulty in 'shove[ing] out' John's men should they attempt to take Hellesdon, he clearly did not think them too much of a danger. This was to prove a misconception, but the impression of him feigning concern for his tenants to win them over to his side is strengthened by the ending of the letter, in which he first stated that he would 'fain have some man to be bailey of Hellesdon and Drayton etc., that might go among the tenants and else I will than Richard Charrlis to go among them til I come home, and also Richard Call when he may … he sent me word that the tenants of Drayton will not come to the Duke's court, and if they will be so stead[…]fast to me, and keep them strong and forward from the Duke's council, all this matter shall turn to a jape and not hurt them nor, and if they … be wavering … it shall hurt them.'[382]

It could, of course, be argued that by this rather ominous warning John Paston referred to any likely misdeeds he expected from John. However, given that there is no reference made to John wanting to force anyone to come to his court, and John Paston explicitly refers to them 'wavering', suggesting their own free will, it sounds rather like a threat from him, showing he was not averse to threatening violence against those not working to further his aims.

The conflict was coming to a head by then. On 8 July, Margaret reported back to her still absent husband what had happened since he had last sent her instructions to act against John. She had not been at all successful in making his men leave the manor of Drayton, but apparently her efforts had had an effect, for John personally became involved. John Paston's wife reports that she was 'informed for certain the Duke of Suffolk raises great people both in Norfolk and Suffolk to come down with him to put us to a rebuke and he may, wherefore I would in any wise that ... make you as strong as he can within the ... place, for I and others much suppose that if they find you not here they were seek you here by arms'. She went on that she would like it if her son 'John Paston the younger, should ride against to my lady of Norfolk and be with her still til we have other tidings, and he may do some good, after that he hears tidings, in going forth to his father or in some other place where we may have remedy'.[383]

Though Margaret had been very optimistic in previous letters, she was clearly worried now. It would turn out that she had good reason. She was also correct in her warning of March 1465 that there would be no peace for the Paston family unless they were on good terms with John. Though he had been patient for some time, John was becoming a bad man to have as enemy. Margaret reported that 'it is ... told me that there are come to Cossey onward more than two hundred and there is coming as it is said, more than a thousand'.[384] This sounded ominous, but if John had hoped to impress the Pastons by sheer numbers he was to fail. Margaret, though obviously worried, set about planning a resistance, pleading with her husband to send their son so she might 'send him about on my errants', as well as asking him to 'send me word how that you do by some of the tennants that are not known'.[385]

By this time the Pastons were ready to do all they could to keep the manors from John's hands, even apparently threatening tenants who were not known to be wholly committed to them. Though this sounds quite shocking given modern history books portray the Pastons as helpless victims in the quarrel, their fears were well grounded. Within a day of this letter, John's men arrived in Drayton. The occasion was recounted in a letter by Richard Calle, one of John Paston's agents, to Paston himself. At first there was nothing very notable about the force's arrival, which reads a lot like any other attempt by a nobleman to seize some manors which he saw as his by right:

> The bailiff of Cossey, with others of my Lord of Suffolk's men, on Monday last past at afternoon were at Hellesdon, with the number

> of three hundred men, for to have entered, notwithstanding they said they came not for to enter; but without doubt, and had they been strong enough for us, they would have entered.[386]

This has often been taken as fact, but there is no evidence to show that Calle was correct in his assumption. It is possible that John's first intention was not to have his men enter by force but instead to simply make a show of force, and Calle even admits that his assumption is coloured by what came later. He reports that John and Margaret Paston were within the manor of Hellesdon, together with sixty armed men, so they were not attacked by John's men.

In fact, it seems that John's men were fairly peaceful at first, waiting while the mayor of Norwich, who was well disposed towards John, 'sent thither Master John Salett and Master John Bulleman for to treat, and so they did; and the Duke's men said they had a warrant for to attach John Daubeney, Wykes, Calle, Hunworth and Blickling, and other, which they would have; and my master, Sir John [Paston] answered them, and said, that they were not within, and though we had been, they should not have had them. And so they desired one of our men, and so Naunton stood by my mistress, and asked whom they would have, and said, if they would have him, he would go with them, and so he did. And on the next day they carried him forth to my Lord of Suffolk to Claxton, through Norwich: and there we had found a remedy for him for to have let him, and he would not, but needs go forth with them, but like a gentleman he was entreated amongst them.'[387]

Though this event naturally upset the writer, who was one of those John had asked for, it is notable that the men acted like gentlemen in this case, explicitly treating their hostage well, taking John Paston at his words as to the whereabouts of the men they had been sent to arrest and generally acting with as little violence as possible, an impression that is reinforced as in the next part of the letter. Calle goes on to report that 'Harleston desired at Hellesdon to speak with my Master, Sir John; and so he did, and said to him, it were right well done that he rode to my Lord of Suffolk, and desired him in any wise that he should do so, and said, that it was his duty so for to do, inasmuch as my Lord was come to country, and that he would ride with him, and bring him to my Lord. And he answered, and said to him, when that he understood that my Lord were his father's good Lord, and his, that then he would see his Lordship, and else he had none errand to him; and so they departed. And then appointment was taken that they should send home their men, and we should send home ours.'[388]

This peaceful state of affairs was not to last. For all their gentlemanly behaviour, John's men did not keep their word, for Calle goes on to say that 'now my Lord of Suffolk's men come from Claxton to Norwich, and face us, and fray upon us, this daily. There fell upon me before Swaine's door twelve of his men, eight of them in harness, and there they would have mischieved me, and the Sheriff letted them and other, and they make their avaunt, were that I may be gotten, I should die, and so they lie in await for to mischief me, Daiibeney, and Wykes. And so I dare not ride out alone without a man with me.'[389]

As if this was not bad enough, Calle reports, 'I understand there is coming an Oyer Determiner to inquire of all riots, and my Lord of Suffolk and Yelverton be commissioners, and so they say as many of us as can be taken shall be indicted, and hanged forthwith.' He does state though that 'the people here are dismayed with their rule, wherefore that it like you to send word how my Mistress shall do at Hellesdon, and we in all other matters: and whether ye will that we fetch again the flock of Hellesdon, for they are now driven to Causton, and there go they on the heath, and my Lord of Suffolk will be at Drayton on Lammas-day, and keep the court there, wherefore ye must seek a remedy for it, or else it will not do well'.[390]

There are two points of note in this particular letter. Most obvious is the escalating violence, which was even turned against the tenants of Hellesdon to the outrage of the people, especially since it appears to have been very petty, hurting men and stealing from them in a way that could hardly have been considered a sensible reaction to whatever Paston's men had done to John or his men. Secondly, however, the note is interesting because, for all his antipathy to John, the put-upon Richard Calle apparently considered appealing to him a solution and did not seem to regard the threats as having been ordered by John himself. A letter from Margaret Paston, written some two days later, seems to support this. It reaffirms Calle's letters in almost all details:

> Right worshipful husband, I recommend me to you, praying you heartily that ye will seek a mean that your servants may be in peace, for they be daily in fear of their lives. The Duke of Suffolk's men threaten daily Daubeney, Wykes, and Richard Calle, that wheresoever they may get them they shall die; and affrays have been made on Richard Calle this week, so that he was in great jeopardy at Norwich among them, and great affrays have been made upon me, and my fellowship, here on Monday last past, of which Richard Calle tells me, that he hath sent you word of in ' writing, more plainly than I may do at this time, but I shall inform you more plainly hereafter. I suppose there shall be great labour against you and your servants at the assizes and sessions here, wherefore me seems, saving your better advice, it were well done that you should speak with the Justices, before they come here. And if you will that I complain to them, or to any other, if good fortune me life and health, I will do as ye advise me to do, for in good faith I have been simply entreated among them, and, what with sickness, and trouble

> that I have had, I am brought right low, and weak, but to my power I will do as I can or may in your matters.
>
> The Duke of Suffolk and both the Duchesses shall come to Claxton this day, as I am informed, and this next week he shall be at Cossey; whether he will come further hitherward, or not, I know not yet. It is said that he should come hither, and yet his men said here on Monday, that he claimed no title to this place. They said, their coming was but to take out such riotous people as were here within this place, and such as were the King's felons, and indicted, and outlawed men, nevertheless they would show no warrants whereby to take none such, though there had been such here. I suppose, if they might have come in peaceably, they would have made another cause of their coming.
>
> When all was done, and they should depart, Harleston and other desired me that I should come and see mine old Lady [Alice] and sue to my Lord, and if any thing were amiss, it should be amended. I said, if I should sue for any remedy, that I should sue further, and let the King and all the Lords of this land to have knowledge, what has been done to us, if so were that the Duke would maintain that has been done to us by his servants, if you would give me leave.
>
> I pray you send, me word, if ye will that I make any complaint to the Duke, or the Duchess, for as it is told me, they know not the plainness that hath been done in such things as hath been done in their names.[391]

It is more than interesting that Margaret admits, even in the face of an outrage done by John's men, that neither John nor his wife had wished to do this, as well as that the claim by his men that traitors to the king had hidden in Drayton was correct.

However, understandably, it was not that with which John Paston was concerned in his answer to his wife's letter, on 13 July 1465, but first and foremost that 'you avowed that you kept possession at Drayton'. Clearly not considering the danger past yet, he asked her to 'make your word good if you may, and at the least let my adversary not have it in peace if you may'.[392] Quite obviously, he was just as prepared, if not more so, than John to use violence. In fact, while the terrible behaviour of John's men is clearly recorded and mentioned above, this was explicitly stated to not have been John's intention. John Paston can hardly be blamed to have decided to react with violence should they try and take a manor he considered his, but it is once more notable that he did so, when there is no explicit order for it known from John.

In fact, despite what had happened, John Paston was very certain of his success in claiming the manor as his own, going on to state that 'I shall have the manor securely to me and mine than the duke shall have Cossey, doubt you not.'[393]

Perhaps to explain this certainty, he then said that 'as for that it is desired that I should show my title and [?] to the duke, my thi[...]ks that he had [...] council to enter in upon me trusting [...] I should show him [...]'. Them, apparently thinking that it could not hurt to try and convince those who had sided with John to side with him instead, he told his wife that 'you seem it may do you good or ease, let my lord of Norwich know that the manor of Drayton was a merchant of London's, called John Hellesdon, long before any of the Poles that the said duke comes of were born to any land in Norfolk of Suffolk', adding, perhaps for Margaret's benefit, or as a pointer what she should say to the major, 'if they were at that time born to no land, how may the said duke claim Drayton by that pedigree?' Giving his wife all the information he either had or wished her to make the major believe, he goes on '[A]s for the said John Hellesdon, he was a poor man born, and from him the said manor descended to Alice his daughter, his estate I have, and I suppose the said duke comes not of them.'[394]

In order to stave off any questions, or perhaps simply to explain to Margaret his claim and his rival's supposed lack thereof, he then went off on a rather long tangent as to the 'pedigree of the said duke', elaborating that 'he is son to William Pole, Duke of Suffolk, son to Michael Pole, Earl of Suffolk, son to Michael Pole, the first Earl of Suffolk of the Poles, made by King Richard since my father was born. And the said first Michael was son to William Pole of Hull, which was a worshipful man grown to fortune of the world, and he was first a merchant and after a knight, and after he was made bannaret.'[395] This explanation is entirely correct, suggesting that John Paston had taken pains to make exact enquires, which made him rather secure in his own right, for he then stated that 'if any of these had the manor of Drayton, I will lose 100 pounds, so that any person for the duke will be bond in as much to prove the contrary'.[396]

Despite what had happened, this letter sounds almost triumphant. Certainly it doesn't suggest anxiety, nor does it sound as if John Paston really blamed John; on the contrary, he seems to have held what had happened to be Alice's fault: 'And I know well the said duke's council will not claim to the said manor by the title of the father of the said William Pole. And what that father of the said William was, as by the pedigree made in the said last duke's father's days, I know right well; wherefore I informed Harry Boteler to tell my old lady of Suffolk, because he is of her council, and more will I not tell in this matter but if I am desired or compelled.'[397] He does not explicitly state why he wants Alice, rather than John himself, informed of this, but the impression given is that he thinks she counselled her son to send men, possibly because she had previously had quarrels with them about lands, going back to before John's birth.

Curiously, while John Paston does not once mention the violence of John's men, his letter suggests he was very eager to win over the support of the mayor of Norwich, taking up the subject again towards the end of the letter, asking his wife to 'let my lord of Norwich know that it is not profitabl … nor becoming well of gentlemen that any gentleman should be completted by an entry of a lord to show his evidence or title to his land, nor I will not begin that example of [?] of gentleman nor of other'. Though this announcement stands in stark contrast to him claiming he had enough evidence for his claim to the manor and was ready to show it, he apparently considered his statement that 'it is good a lord take sad council, or he begin any such matter' to be sufficient explanation for why he would not.[398] Paston finishes the letter by stating that 'as for the Poles that own Drayton, if there were a hundred of them living, as there is none, yet have they no title to the said manor' – a rather curious statement, which he does not at all explain.

Though he does not once actually refer to the theft by John's men, it seems that Margaret did indeed bring the matter before the king, who heard it. Apparently, Edward IV was at first inclined to agree with the Pastons in this matter as a draft for a message from him to one of John's men, William Yelverton, exists, detailing the 'instructions for the messenger' to William:[399]

> That you greet wll Sir William Yelverton, letting him know in our behalf that we are informed that certain persons in the name of the right worshipful our cousin the Duke of Suffolk, have entered in the manor of Drayton that was Falstof's, and have driven from the said manor and other[s] 13 sheep and other beasts pastured upon the said manor, notwithstanding we marvel greatly that the said Sir William, his sons and servants, as it is said, assist and comfort the said persons so entering and withdrawing the said cattle, saying that he is named both feoffee and executor; and well be it so that there is variance between him and our well-beloved John Paston in our court, concerning as well the said manors as other goods that Sir John Falstof, whom God assoil, yet it may not accord with worship and conscience for the said Sir William to assist the destruction of the said manors and goods in the meantime. Wherefore we desire him that he will do his devour effectively to help save the said manors from all such pretence or title, and to cause the said cattles to be restored to the manor's aforesaid and not to be withdrawn and destroyed as they are, and that he do his faithful part in this behalf according to the trust he was put in, as we may do for him in time to come.[400]

This was a fairly calm response by the king, favouring neither side. Recognising that the theft was wrong, he obviously wished this to be redressed, but there was otherwise no punishment for Sir William, and he did not otherwise show any willingness to get involved. In fact, it seems he never did, leaving John and John Paston to work out their differences between them, violence notwithstanding.

The king's message apparently did not do much to solve the quarrel between John and John Paston. Sadly, however, regarding the first part of the quarrel we have only the Pastons' descriptions of happened, and any picture gleaned from them is by necessity biased. However, even so, facts can be discerned, and it is from their letters that we know that even after the escalation of July 1465 neither John nor John Paston were ready to give up their claim or even compromise. On 7 August 1465, Margaret Paston wrote to her husband that she 'sent on Lammase Day to Drayton Thomas Bonde and Sir James Gloys to hold the court in your name and to claim your title, for I could get no other body to keep the court nor that would go there but the said Thomas Bonde, because I suppose they were afeared of the people that should be there of the Duke of Suffolk's part'.[401]

Such fear was not unfounded, for Margaret went on to state that 'the said Thomas and James, as the Duke of Suffolk's men, that is to say Harlesdon, the parson of Salle, Master Phillip, and William Yelverton, the which was steward, with 50 persons or more by estimation, and the tenants of the same town, some of them having rusty poleaxes and [?], come in to the manor to keep the court, meet with them and told them that they were come to keep court in your name and to claim your title. Wherefore the said Harlesdon, without any more words or occasion given of your men, committed the said Thomas Bonde to the keeping of the new bailiff of Draxton, William Dokket, saying that he should go to my lord amd do his herals himself notwithstanding that Sir James gave the errandes to them and had the words, wherefore they took the said Thomas without occasion.'[402]

Curiously, Margaret sounds more outraged about this rudeness than she had sounded about anything that John's men had done in July, even though it was hardly unusual or unexpected behaviour. It is interesting to note that despite Margaret's claims from three months earlier that the tenants of Drayton were on her husband's side, and Calle's claims that he and his wife had won a lot of favour during the attack of John's men for their bravery, the tenants had apparently not only accepted John taking the manor but actively supported him.

John appears to have decided that once the situation had already escalated there was no saving it, and instructed his men to be rough, if not unusually so. Margaret reports the consequences of this, stating that John's men 'would have made the said Thomas to have the words, and the said James told them that he ... had them because he was the more possible man, whom afterwards they bodies avoid, and since then led forth Thomas Bonde to Cossey, and bound his arms behind him with whip-cord like a thief'. She claims that these men 'should have led him forth to the Duke of Suffolk, had it not been that I had spoken with the judges in the morning ... and informed them of such riots and assaults as they had made upon me and my men, the bailiff of Cossey and all the

Duke of Suffolk's council being there present and all the learnt men of Norfolk and William Jeney and much ... people of the county, the judge calling the bailiff of Cossey before them all and gave him a great rebuke, commanding the sheriff to see what people they had gathered at Drayton, which came after to Hellesdon to see the people there, with which ... he held him well content. And from thence he rode to Drayton to see there people which were avoided before he came, and there he desired to have delivered the said Thomas Bonde to him.'[403]

However, it seems either that John expected Margaret to take the matter to court and gave orders to counteract her efforts, or that his men simply anticipated his wishes and reacted accordingly. Margaret's statement that 'they excused them and said they had sent him to the Duke of Suffolk, notwithstanding afterwards they sent them to Norwich with them, desiring him that he should deliver him not without he made a fine because he troubled the king's people' rather suggests the latter, as it does not seem a very organised defence. Margaret managed to convince the judges of her standpoint without any trouble: '[A]fter that I understood it I sent Daniel of Marshland and Thomas Bonde to inform the judges how the said Thomas was treated amongst them, and so he did, and the judges were greatly ... with the duke's men and forthwith commanded the sheriff to deliver the said Bonde without any fine made ... saying that he ought none to make. And in good faith I found the judges right gentle, and favourable to me in my matters, notwithstanding the duke's council had made their complaint to them or ... that I come in the wort wise, no saying us of great gathering of people and many riots things done by me and your men.'[404]

Again, this is a confession by Margaret that often goes overlooked by those analysing the feud, who typically blame John for all that occurred.[405] It is notable, though, that with what had happened in July it seems most of those holding any power in Suffolk were inclined to side with the Pastons rather than with John, as Margaret's letter suggests: '[A]fter I informed the judges of their untruth and of their [?] and of our [?] in like wise, and after the judges understood the truth he gave the bailiff of Cossey before me and many others a passing great rebuke, saying without he amended his condition and governance they would ... inform the King and help that he should be punished.'[406]

This would be punishment by proxy for John, which was not uncommon. However, it seems that despite all that had happened, Margaret seemed mostly to blame the men and not John himself. Curiously, despite her fairly triumphant letter, it does not seem she achieved everything her husband had asked her to achieve: 'And whereas you advices me ... a fellowship to keep the court at Draton with easy cost, it was thought by your council it were ... better otherwise and not to gather no people, for it was told me that the duke's men had the number of 500 men, and your council advised me to a get a fellowship to keep my place at Hellesdon, for it was told me that they should come and pull me out of the place, which caused me to keep the place the strong at the time.'[407]

This fear was, it seems, unfounded. It may even be that it was a rumour sowed to keep Margaret from keeping a court in her husband's name at Drayton. If not, it was certainly the effect of these rumours, and Margaret was realistic about it: '[A]s for keeping of any court for you at Drayton, I cannot know how it could be brought about without help of other, but if there should grow great inconvenience of it.'[408]

Curiously, for all her success convincing the local judges of the righteousness of the Pastons' cause and the failure of John's men to do the same for him, she does not consider it very likely that courts outside of Suffolk would agree with them, and in fact feared punishment for the Pastons' men if the case was heard anywhere else: 'And at the assizes ... made great labour to indight your men, notwithstanding it was let.'[409] However, her and her husband's men were trying to convince the judges of the righteousness of their cause, and were apparently succeeding: 'And as for the writs of replain they were delivered openly before the judges to the sheriff and also other writs which James Gresham brought, and after that Richard Calle spoke with the high sheriff for the serving of them, and so promised to serve it and to send men of his own to serve it. And so he sent two of his men with Richard Lynsted and with two of your ... shepherds to Cossey for the sheep, and there they were answered ... that Elverton claimed the property, and so were they answered in all other places where as any cattle was, and so they departed and came to the sheriff and informed him, and I understand the sheriff take it for an answer.'[410]

The impression given is that no one was particularly invested in either side of the quarrel other than John and the Pastons, and while others were ready to come down on one of the sides it was not really a pressing matter for them. However, naturally, Margaret was not ready to take no for an answer in this case: 'Notwithstanding I sent him word without that Yelverton had been there in his own person he might not claim the property, and advised him to be aware what return he made that he were not hurt by it, and so he has made no return yet. What he will do I do not know. He is still in this country yet, and shall be this four or five days, but your council thinks it were well done that you get an alliances and a plurias that it might be sent to the sherif, and then he can make no excuse but needs to serve ... it or else to make a return as he will abide by.'[411]

Despite all that had occurred, not everyone had turned against John, even if it is often claimed to be the case in history books. Margaret was obviously insecure about the support she could win and her description of her efforts reflects this: 'I cannot know how the cattle will be gotten without other process be had more than we have yet.' Moreover, she feared that any commissions featuring John would turn men against her family. This fear seemed well-founded: 'Item, on Tuesday next coming shall the sessions of the peace be at Walsingham. What shall be done there I know not yet, for as for any indictments that we should labour against them, it is but vast work, for the sheriff nor the jurors would no thing do against them.'[412]

Margaret concluded the letter on a positive note with a list of men who would work for her husband. However, if either she, her husband, or John were hoping for any final decision during the upcoming commission of the peace, they were to be disappointed. On 18 August, Margaret described in a letter to her husband what had happened. This letter is a font of information, if obviously biased, so that the description is worth quoting in full here, starting with the conclusions she took from it: 'As for the replys, Richard Calle says he has sent you an answer of them and also the copies of them. As for the high sheriff, he demeaned him right well here to me, and he said to me as for the replys he would ask council of learnt men what he might do therein and as largely as he might do there, or in any other matter twitching you, daying himself harmlessly, he would do for you and for yours that he might do.'[413] She goes on to say that she had waited to write her husband: 'I wrote to you not before I did after the sessions was because that Yelverton held sessions at Durham and Walsingham the next week after the assises and to have knowledge what labour was made there, and to have sent you word thereof.'[414] Then she goes into detail of the assizes:

> There was great labour made by the bailiff of Coshay and others for to have indicted your men both at Durham and at Walsingham, but I purveyes a men that here purpose was letted at those two times. I have sent to Sir Thomas Howys yesterday Richard Calle, for the matte of my lady of Bedford, but he might not speak with him nor I have no answer thereof yet, but I shall send to him again this week.
>
> Item, I have done laid the presentation of Drayton, and have presented Sir Thomas Hakon, parson of Felthorp, the which is hold right a good man and well-disposed, and the Duke of Suffolk has laid in another, and there shall be taken an inquisition thereupon, and Master Steven is yours avowed therein.[415]

With this plea sent, the conflict ended for the summer. It is very interesting to note that for all the violence and bribery going on, both John and the Pastons decided to hand their claims to the parson and wait for a decision there, though it would be naive to think either of them would have accepted a decision that ruled against them.

After August 1465, a short period of peace broke out between the two factions, possibly because John, together with his wife, left Suffolk to attend their second great festivity that year, namely the enthronement of Elizabeth's cousin George Neville as Archbishop of York. The celebration, which happened on 22 September, was organised by George's brother Richard Neville, Earl of Warwick, and has since gone down in legend for its grand scale and opulence. In fact, it has sometimes been suggested that Warwick, who was notoriously unhappy with Edward IV's choice of bride, was trying to outshine the king.[416] Acting as steward for the new archbishop during the festivities, with their brother John acting as treasurer, Warwick hosted some of the most important men and women of the realm. The new archbishop himself sat at a place of honour, in the centre of the high table. John was one of the lords temporal who sat on his left, with several lords spiritual, including the Bishop of London, sitting on the new archbishop's right.[417]

As was often the case during such festivities, women were not meant to sit with the men at the highest table. Elizabeth was seated at the first table outside the hall, which was headed by her youngest brother, Richard, Duke of Gloucester. Warwick's daughters Isabel and Anne also sat at this table, as did Elizabeth's aunt, the Countess of Westmoreland, and her cousin by marriage the Countess of Northumberland.[418]

Though the guest list was full of important nobles of the realm, it was not that which saw the festivities written into history. What really caused comment, at the time as well as later, was the luxury of the event. The kitchens, for instance, served up '104 oxen, six wild bulls, 1000 muttons, 400 swans, 304 veal, 2000 pigs, 204 cranes, 400 herons, 2000 chickens, 4000 rabbits, 1200 quails, 1000 capons, 1000 egrets, 200 pheasants, 500 partridges, 104 peacocks, 500 deer, 4000 ducks, 308 pike, twelve purpoises and seals, 4000 cold pastries of vension, 1500 hot pastries of venison, 4000 jellies, 4000 cold baked tarts, 3000 cold baked custards, 2000 hot baked custards, spices, sugered delicates, waifers plenty, 75600 gallons of ale, 25200 gallons of wine and 76 gallons of hippocras'.[419]

Presumably, John, much like all the other visitors, was awed by this showcasing of wealth and taste, and presumably he would have enjoyed the luxuries of the earl's household. However, if Warwick's plan was to win him over to his own faction, in strong opposition to the queen's faction, he was to be disappointed. John, and Elizabeth as well, made a point of getting along well with Warwick, but they committed to his side no more than they committed to the Woodville faction. They proved to be rather good at keeping the balance, possibly because they genuinely had no interest in which faction held more power and was favoured by the king. If their presence at George Neville's enthronement was an attempt to win their favour, it was the only one; neither the Woodville family nor the Earl of Warwick ever tried winning their support again, though they both appeared to be on good terms with them. John simply appeared to have no interest in any sort of partisan politics, setting him apart from almost every other noble at the time.

It would have been late autumn by the time John and Elizabeth returned to Wingfield Castle. Presumably, at least Elizabeth would have been busy with preparing all that needed to be prepared for her confinement. John, however, could not yet quite concentrate solely on such domestic matters, even had he been so inclined to do so. The violent quarrel he had with the Pastons in the summer still required his attention, and around this time his men acted in a shocking manner, as another letter from Margaret Paston, written on 27 October, attests. She wrote that 'Bartholomew White has been strangely entreated, and his brother and others that came to record with him, and they were beaten and put in prison and fouly reviled by Harlston and the bailiff of Ey and others of the Duke of Suffolk's men.'[420] She went on to state that she had been 'at Hellesdon upon Thursday last passed and saw the place there, and in good fauth there will no creature think how foul and cruelly it is arrays but if they saw it. There come much people daily to wonder thereupon both of Norwich and of othere places and they speak shamefully of it.'[421]

This appears to have been something of an exaggeration on Margaret's part – it is recorded that John retained the support of most men from Norwich – but it is obvious that what had been done had turned many against John, which is clearly understandable reading Margaret's whole letter. After assuring her husband that '[t]he duke had better than a thousand pounds that it had never been done' and that her husband 'ha[s] the good will of the people that is so fouly done', she then explains the crimes of John's men:

> [T]hey made your tenants of Hellesdon and Drayton, with others, to help break down the place and the log both, God knows full well against their wills but they dared no other wise do for fear. The duke's men ransacked the church and bore away all the goods that was left there, both of ours and of the tenants, and left not so much but what they stood upon the high altar and ransacked the images and took away such as they might find, and put away the parson out of the church til they had done, and ransacked every man's house in the town five or six times. And the chief masters of robbing were the bailiff of Ey, the bailiff of Stradbroke, Thomas Slyford. And Slyford was the chief robber of the church, and he has most of the robbery next the bailiff of Ey, and as for lead, brass, pewter, iron, [?] and other stuff of the house, men of Coshay and Caveston have it, and that they might not carry have have hewn it asunder in the most despicable wise. If it might be I would some men of worship might be sent from the king to see how it is both there and at the log, before than any snow come, that they may make report of the truth, else it shall no more be seen so plainly as it may be now.

She then went on contradict her own statement that men of Norwich had turned against John by writing that 'the major of Norwich did arrest the bailiff of Normandys, Lovegold, Gregory Cordonere, and

Bartholomew Fuller without any authority save only he says that he has a commandement of the duke to do so, and he will not let them out of prison till he had surety for ache of them in 24 pounds for to answer to such matters as the duke and his council will put against them at any time that they be called, and so will he do to others, as many as he may get, that are you any good will. And also the major would have had them swear that they should never be against the duke nor none of his, which they would not do in now wise.'[422]

It is often assumed that the events of summer 1465, and especially this attack of October 1465, almost wrecked John's reputation.[423] However, not only does this single out the incident in a way is unwarranted considering all the other acts of violence going on at the time, but it is also provably untrue. Yes, the attack was seen as unusually violent even for the time, and even accounting for the natural bias against him in the Paston letters it is clear that these attacks cost John and his case a lot of sympathy. The letters show that this was not because his claim was widely considered to be wrong or that everyone considered it bad for him to take possession of the manor of Drayton by force; in fact, it seems the attack of autumn 1465 was considered unusual simply because it targeted a church. This was a blasphemous attack, and a completely unnecessary act of aggression as well.

Interestingly, as can be seen from Richard Calle and Margaret Paston's letters, John himself was not considered the cause for such violence in the summer, and it seems he was not considered the direct cause for it in autumn either. In fact, Margaret's statement that it would have been better for him had such things never been done in his name suggests that he had lost control of his men. However, it is hard to believe that they had acted completely on their own. Though John might not have given explicit orders to rob people and attack the church, it seems extremely improbable he did not at least know his men intended to intimidate the tenants. A more likely reading of the situation is that he gave an order to that effect, and was later horrified when it escalated as it did. This is an unedifying episode that shows John's worst side: greedy and inclined to violence if necessary.

Whether or not he actually ordered it, John presumably came to regret this attack, though not on moral grounds. With this violence having been done on his behalf, it was hard for him to claim that he was an innocent victim of theft, which according to Margaret Paston's letters might have been feasible in May 1465. Many now considered him the main aggressor.

Interestingly, this was less so during his own lifetime. As Margaret Paston's letters show, even after the attack he received quite some support.[424] At the time, the overreaches and failures of both sides were discussed. However, in the centuries after his death, John has usually been painted as the sole malefactor, with historians such as Henry Napier using this episode as evidence that John was the aggressor at every point.

Even though this is obviously untrue, in the autumn of 1465, John, and perhaps Elizabeth by association, had a hard time in Suffolk due to his actions and those of his men that October. Interestingly, while Margaret Paston's letters make it quite clear that John was supported by both his mother Alice and his wife Elizabeth, Elizabeth was not blamed at all. Since we only know what happened from the point of view of the Pastons, of course, we cannot verify her claims of widespread ill feeling against John in Suffolk.

Life at Wingfield and Ewelme

Perhaps John tried to save face and salvage his reputation after this, for the conflict began to cool. But there is another, rather more sad explanation for his sudden lack of interest in the quarrel. It may well be that in late autumn 1465, John and Elizabeth were distracted by the death of their second daughter. We do not know for certain that she died at this time, only that she died in childhood, either at Ewelme or Wingfield Castle, with the latter being somewhat more likely as the family graves in the church at Ewelme were all marked and survive to this day. If she died at Wingfield, though, it must have been in 1465, as the family moved to Ewelme in late 1466, and her parents' movements from 1466 do not suggest that they went to Wingfield at any point to attend a funeral. If the child died then, it would have been a sad winter for the family, and it might have been a comfort when, in January 1466,[425] Elizabeth gave birth to her fourth child, a second son, whose name we no longer know. His infancy would have been the same as his siblings', and he would have joined his siblings in the nursery.

John Jnr would most likely not have been very affected by the birth of a new sibling, though it might have been the first he would be able to consciously remember in later years. He might have been more shocked at his second sister's death, though if it happened in late 1465 he might still have been slightly too young to understand it. Perhaps a more important change in his life was that at the age of three, he most likely began his first lessons, possibly joining his sister Elizabeth Jnr. Given that both Elizabeth and Alice were able to read and understand English, French and Latin,[426] we know that women's education was important to the family, but we do not actually know if they chose to have their sons and daughters educated together or separately, or if they set John Jnr apart as the heir, giving him a different tutor than his siblings. Common sense suggests that at least during their toddler years, John Jnr and Elizabeth Jnr were educated together, as there would have been no profound differences in what a little boy and a little girl, both meant to be literate and knowledgeable in a range of subjects in later life, would have been taught. The new infant boy and, if she was still alive, their younger sister would still have been too young to have any lessons, and this might have pleased the two toddlers, giving them a feeling of importance.

Whatever their children felt, John and Elizabeth obviously thought that their family was not yet big enough; within a very short time after the birth, Elizabeth conceived again. As sources clearly indicate that the next birth took place in December 1466 or early January 1467 at the latest,[427] it seems that Elizabeth once more conceived before she was even out of confinement. Possibly, even likely, she did not intend to become pregnant again so soon after giving birth, and the conception was an accident. Though it is easy to assume noble births were all planned, this was obviously not always the case. John and Elizabeth were a young, healthy couple, obviously very fond of each other, who enjoyed each other's presence according to our evidence. It is probable that it was nothing deeper than that which made them sleep together so soon after their son's birth, and nothing but chance that made her conceive then. Elizabeth appears to have been a very healthy woman, not too affected by her pregnancies and able to take up her normal life and social obligations again after leaving confinement, showing no ill effects from already being pregnant again.

Such obligations began soon after Elizabeth left confinement again. On 11 February 1466, the king's first legitimate child was born. Celebrations had been planned with the expectation of a healthy son, but the controversial queen instead had a daughter. Several contemporaries expressed happiness at the birth of a healthy princess but also regret that she had not provided a boy to settle the succession. Though England did not observe Salic law, and so women were not barred from inheriting the throne, there was only one precedent of a woman being heir to the throne, and it was not a happy one. Despite this, the king and queen were naturally delighted to have a healthy child, and the planned celebrations went ahead without any changes, the birth being feted as much as it would have been if it had been a boy.

The little girl was baptised, her grandmothers Cecily and Jacquetta and her father's cousin the Earl of Warwick being her godparents.[428] Elizabeth and John were not noted to have been present in the capital during the celebrations after the birth, nor were they recorded as being present at the baptism. Elizabeth may not yet have been churched, and John elected to stay with her and his children instead of going to the capital to attend the celebrations. However, they were present at the churching of the queen some forty days after the princess's birth.

It was a splendid celebration, though one that attracted a lot of criticism at the time and later due to the queen's behaviour. Queen Elizabeth demanded that she be treated in a way that other queens were only treated at their coronations, making the king's sisters and his mother, as well as her own mother, kneel to her for hours while serving her.[429] Naturally, this also included Elizabeth. While some modern writers have claimed that this behaviour was nothing out of the ordinary since it happened at other queens' coronations, this is untrue. A coronation was a once-in-a-lifetime event for a queen, and such behaviour was usually never repeated. That Queen Elizabeth insisted on it, and then on festivities celebrating the birth of a child who did not even settle the succession securely, reflected badly on both her and her husband. It also gave her detractors a lot of ammunition, stoking claims that she and her family were arrogant and wished to humiliate all other nobles in the kingdom,[430] and that Edward IV allowed such behaviour to go unchecked. That the king chose to let his wife debase his mother and sisters like this at her churching lends credence to these accusations. The queen's behaviour even outraged a foreign visitor, Gabriel Tetzel, who described the celebrations as splendid but the behaviour of the queen as arrogant.[431]

It would be interesting to know what Elizabeth thought of her sister-in-law's orders. She showed no sign of resentment, but there is a suggestion that John was unhappy. During the first one and a half years of Queen Elizabeth's queenship, he seemed polite; he was never explicitly rude afterwards, but it is notable that from here on out he appeared to avoid all interaction with her. As John was fairly stubborn, it is not at all unlikely he took affront when his wife, soon after giving birth, was subjected to such humiliating and physically straining orders. Knowing that it was best for them not to be on bad terms with anyone at court, he might very well have been happy for his wife to maintain cordial relations with the queen and her family while himself refusing to do so ever again, thereby making clear his opinion of her. As evidence indicates John and Elizabeth were usually agreed on such matters, it is likely she also took offense but recognised the value of staying on good terms with her sister-in-law and considered herself more equipped for that than her husband. Even John, however, managed not to show any unhappy feelings towards Queen Elizabeth. He and his wife were to attend more court celebrations that year, though none required them to interact with the queen for long.

This rather unedifying spectacle at what was a happy occasion may have had rather more pleasing consequences for John and his wife, as it seems that it inspired a new closeness between Elizabeth and her sister Anne, Duchess of Exeter. Though only five years apart, it is very unlikely the sisters knew each other well growing up as Anne was married to Henry Holland, Duke of Exeter when Elizabeth was only three years old.[432] However, at some point before 1466 they became close, and it may very well be that this was helped somewhat by their shared task of kneeling to the queen at her churching.

Anne's marriage to the Duke of Exeter was not a happy one; her husband was a staunch Lancastrian and was considered an unpleasant man. He was attainted in 1461 when Edward came to the throne, and his lands were granted to Anne, which meant she became a wealthy and independent woman.[433] In 1464, she officially separated from Exeter, which would have given her more freedom than she had as the wife of a controlling man. It is possible that Anne became close to her sister Elizabeth during that time, or that she was supported by Elizabeth and John while she separated from Exeter. However, we only know of a growing affection around September 1466, when Anne made John one of her feoffees.[434] This showed a certain amount of trust, and given that her other feoffees are known to have been close to her it suggests she at least liked John.

Anne's endowment also gave John and Elizabeth much-needed access to more money, which might have been why the wealthy Duchess of Exeter chose to make John a feoffee. John and Elizabeth also built other useful connections, not least through Alice using her connections to the Neville family, but no link was strong enough to compel them to pick a side in any quarrel concerning national politics. John held minor positions like commissions of the peace[435] and was not accused of using them for his own enrichment, except in his constant quarrel with the Paston family. During the course of the Paston feud he was actually accused of meddling in parliamentary elections for personal gain; this would not have been an unusual course to take during such a quarrel, but it is attested by nothing but the Paston letters, and as such cannot really be used as proof that John abused his power to accrue wealth.

Perhaps significantly for John, and definitely for his wife, in the summer of 1466, negotiations were begun for the marriage of Elizabeth's sister Margaret.[436] Margaret was only one year younger than Elizabeth, and the two women had probably spent their childhood together, so it can be assumed they had a connection. Even if they were not close, as a sister of the king Margaret's marriage would have been a great and important event, and naturally John and Elizabeth would have been expected to show an interest. It seems that Elizabeth was at court with John then, but for obvious reasons he received more attention in the sources.

Edward originally decided for his sister to marry Peter, Constable of Portugal. However, Peter died in the summer of 1466, meaning a new prospective groom was needed.[437] He considered the heir of the Duke of Burgundy, Charles, whom history remembers as Charles the Bold;[438] the fact he was available after the death of Charles's wife the year before was surely a relief. As Edward's own marriage had affronted the French king, he hoped to win an ally against France by making an alliance with Burgundy. Burgundy and France were always on difficult terms to say the least, with France considering the rich Burgundian lands a mere province of the French crown and the Burgundian rulers considering themselves an independent duchy.[439] Therefore, an alliance between England and Burgundy served both parties, creating a formidable enemy should France decide to go against either of them. Moreover, since Burgundy was rich and a lot of trade was dependent on them, an alliance was also potentially lucrative for England.

To make arrangements for the match between Charles and Margaret, the Burgundians sent Antoine, the so-called Bastard of Burgundy, half-brother of Margaret's intended.[440] After he was received to great fanfare, he and Edward began working out the details of the marriage. Obviously, Edward could not have done so alone, and his courtiers and advisors would have been present at all meetings in which the marriage was discussed and details negotiated. John appears to have been one of those courtiers, though there is no evidence he got involved in the discussions. However, perhaps because he was Margaret's brother-in-law and as such a member of the extended royal family, he received a big part in the celebrations laid on to honour Antoine.

As Antoine was a well-known and very accomplished jouster,[441] a tournament was arranged in which he was to joust against Anthony Woodville, the queen's oldest brother, himself an accomplished jouster. This was a grand tournament, and Edward saw to it that his family was deeply involved. He decided that John and the king's brother George were to serve the two jousters during the tournament. George, who was a prince, curiously was made to serve not Antoine but Anthony Woodville, who was of much lesser standing. This might not have been a very smart move on Edward's part; unlike John, George was vocally opposed to the queen's family and resented their precedence in many parts of Edward's court,[442] and cannot have been happy to be tasked with serving one of them, even nominally. It is possible this was a deliberate insult by Edward, or, somewhat more likely, a move to show family unity. George never seems to have complained about his part in the tournament, so he might have understood it as that.

John, meanwhile, was assigned to serve Antoine, a source stating that he 'bore the Bastard of Burgundy's helmet before him when he entered the field'.[443] The source goes on to state that 'my said Lord Bastard was always accompanied with the Duke of Suffolk, who very heartily accompanied him'.[444] This suggests that John and Antoine got on very well, spending more time together than necessary. Far from the uncharismatic and deeply disliked duke so often portrayed in modern times, John was clearly capable of being very charming, liked even by distinguished foreign visitors.

Edward's sudden dislike of John after 1464 might have been personal, and the Pastons' was obviously financially motivated. Apart from these two examples, however, John was not at all unpopular, and his time serving Antoine suggests he could be very likeable if he wanted to be. If Edward had appointed George and John not only to introduce Margaret's family but also to subtly humiliate his difficult brother and disliked brother-in-law, he had miscalculated in John's case at least. If anything, John made a new connection with a powerful foreign magnate during the tournament, and it seems that the two remained on friendly terms for the rest of Antoine's life.

After the tournament, Antoine stayed in England as Edward's visitor until the next year, but John and Elizabeth went to Ewelme, where they began to establish their household, moving it away from Wingfield Castle. Why they chose to do this is not known. It has been suggested by several historians, most notably Henry Napier, that the 1465 escalation of his quarrel with the Paston family 'may have influenced the Duke of Suffolk to quit a neighbourhood, where his name, at least, if not he himself personally, was associated with unpleasant transactions'.[445] This motivation cannot be dismissed outright. Though his family only left a year after these 'unpleasant transactions' happened, it is possible, as mentioned above, that John had tried saving his reputation after October 1465 but had found it impossible, finally coming to the conclusion that his interests would be best served if not only he but his entire family, including his children, withdrew themselves from Suffolk for a while.

However, evidence suggests that this is not the most likely theory for why John chose to move his household. For one, if he had concerns for his local reputation and had only chosen to remove his main household from Suffolk in a last attempt to salvage what he could, it makes little sense for Elizabeth to have chosen to stay there to give birth in early 1466. Moreover, if that was the reason for their decision, it seems unlikely it would have come, as it did, after both he and Elizabeth had been absent from Suffolk for several months and thus could not have judged the breakdown of John's reputation in that time.

Perhaps a simpler explanation for their move is that John wished to be close to his mother, whose main manor was Ewelme. Given that the ducal family stayed with her until her death in 1475, after which they decided to go back to using Wingfield Castle as their main residence,[446] this was presumably also the reason they moved to Ewelme. John and Elizabeth had spent a lot of their time with Alice even when they used Wingfield Castle as their main residence, and as can be seen from the Paston letters, she had spent a lot of time with them. Perhaps John decided that as Alice grew older it would be for the best if they stayed near her as much as possible to spare her the strain of travelling when she wished to be near the family. The one flaw in this theory is that Alice seemed to be in perfect health in 1466 and would live another nine years, making such plans superfluous. Even so, she was sixty-two years of age in 1466, a proud age already in the fifteenth century, and possibly John and Elizabeth felt more comfortable knowing they were there should her health deteriorate.

Another possibility is that they simply decided they preferred to stay in Oxfordshire. It was a county in which the Pastons also held a lot of sway, and John may have wished to counteract that. However, it is notable they chose to move into Alice's household at Ewelme, together with their children, rather than into one of their own manors in the county, which suggests that the Pastons were less of a motivation than Alice's well-being.

Whichever their reasons, we know for a fact that John and Elizabeth moved their household and their children's nursery from Wingfield Castle to Ewelme, having many of their possessions brought from Wingfield Castle. An inventory survives from late 1466, including several orders of that kind.[447] Since a cradle was to be prepared for the child Elizabeth was then expecting, along with one that was already in use, we know the children also lived in Ewelme from this point.[448] Probably, for all of them except John Jnr, who had been born in London, it was the first time they left Suffolk.

John Jnr, who was turning four years old when they moved, and his sister Elizabeth Jnr, were probably the only children who truly understood what was happening, and it must have been very exciting for the little boy. However, it seems that he was already expected to represent himself, albeit with the help of his parents. He probably would have accompanied his father on shorter rides through his possessions, being introduced and shown off not only as the Duke of Suffolk's oldest son and heir but also as the king's oldest, and at the time only, nephew. He would also have continued receiving lessons, though perhaps they were now different from those his sister was given, as he learned the skills that would be expected from him in due course as a duke's son and heir. Since he was still too young to leave the nursery, he would still have seen a lot of Elizabeth Jnr and his infant brother. It must have been exciting for them all when his mother had yet another child in December 1466, though it is equally possible John Jnr was uninterested; by now he had four siblings.

Thanks to the inventory from autumn 1466, we have an exact description of how Elizabeth went into confinement, what clothes she brought along and what decorations she chose for her chambers. As Dr Rachel Delman points out in her article 'Gendered viewing, childbirth and female authority in the residence of Alice Chaucer, duchess of Suffolk, at Ewelme, Oxfordshire', Elizabeth chose the items in such a way that it 'befitt[ed] both her status and the new infant's royal blood'.[449] To achieve this, both Elizabeth and her mother-in-law, Alice, had items sent to them from various other manors in their possession. Though the inventory refers to both women as 'my lady',[450] making it rather hard to say which item belonged to whom, inferences can be made from the original locations of the items. The books, clothes and decorations brought from Wingfield Castle to Ewelme were almost certainly Elizabeth's, for instance, while those items brought from London would have belonged to Alice.

Among the first category were clothes brought to Ewelme for the occasion of Elizabeth's confinement. These included a cloak of 'red cloth of gold upon damask, with a frontell of red cloth of gold or damask', a 'beryng mantel of crimson cloth of gold with powdered ermine fur' and a 'cope of red cloth of gold bawdkin with birds, ofrend with russet cloth of gold of damask'.[451] It can be assumed that these were not new items but had been previously used by Elizabeth during her earlier confinements. Other paraphernalia she had brought definitely suggest so, as they included all the items that would be needed for her to hear Mass while in confinement, and those items explicitly included a 'canope for hanging of the pyx, of red and white cloth of gold of bawdkin with birds' that is stated to have been 'broken by my ladie'.[452] Though there is no information supplied as to how Elizabeth managed to break it, this detail clearly shows that the item had been in use before it was brought to Ewelme in 1466.

Whereas such items seem to have been supplied by Elizabeth herself, she apparently gave Alice a lot of advice on how to arrange her chambers for her fifth confinement. From London, explicitly for 'ye tyme of my ladies lying inne', Alice had brought 'a shete of lawne for the gret bed, conteynyng in lengthe iii yerds, one quarter, and in bred 5 hool bred', as well as 'a shete of lawne for the Cowche, conteynyng in length 5 yerds, and in brede 3 hool breds' and a 'head shete of lawne for ye cowche conteynyng in length 3 yerds, and one quarter and half ye nayl, and in brede 2 hool breds'[453] among similar items, clearly intended both for Elizabeth's comfort and pleasant decoration.

Other items were also provided by Alice, such as tapestries to adorn Elizabeth's birthing chamber; some had been made for Alice herself in 1440 and may very well have decorated her own chambers when she gave birth to John. One was a 'long tapyte of aras of dame de honour'.[454] As Delman points out, this could not only have been a generous gesture by Alice towards her daughter-in-law, but also would have served as good advertising for both: 'Such an image [as shown on the tapestry] would have been highly appropriate to the Ewelme celebrations, particularly as Alice and Elizabeth's own reputations and status rested on their production of legitimate offspring. The scene may have also referenced Alice's former position as a dame d'honneur at Margaret of Anjou's court, reminding those present that the duchess was an exemplary model to follow.'[455] Other tapestries chosen to decorate Elizabeth's chambers included one depicting scenes from the life of St Anne, mother of the Virgin Mary. The chambers would have been awe inspiring, clearly signalling to all who saw them the significance of the expectant mother. This must have informed the choice of decorations, with Elizabeth's and possibly Alice's personal taste being just one of the deciding factors after representation, even in such a technically private place.

The same would not have been true of the books Elizabeth chose to have brought for her confinement. Those would have been chosen solely on personal taste, and so they can provide insight into the two women. Naturally, it does not have to be the two women agreed with everything they read; on the contrary, it is highly unlikely they did. They may well have read and discussed various books critically, which was considered intellectually important at the time. The most famous of the books chosen by Elizabeth was Christine de Pisan's *Le Livre de la Cité des Dames*,[456] written some sixty years previously. Penned as a rebuttal of the misogynistic *Lamentationes Matheoli*, written by the clergyman Matthaeus of Boulogne, Pisan's book told the stories of famous women and their contributions to the world as they built a 'city of women'.[457] Even at the time it was much more famous than the work Matthaeus' work, and it has since been called the first truly feminist work. Elizabeth and Alice's choice to study this book presumably means that, even if they disagreed with its premise, they had an interest in the ideas detailed within and the stories of famous women.

Interestingly, perhaps because of Alice's own fame as a powerful woman, and her long widowhood making her independent, it has usually been assumed that the copy brought to Ewelme in 1466 belonged to her.[458] However, this does not seem to have been the case; it was brought from Wingfield Castle together with many of John and Elizabeth's belongings, so it likely belonged to one of them.[459] This, together with Elizabeth's choice to have it brought to her for her confinement, confirms what is already obvious from the way John and Elizabeth ran their household: Elizabeth, like Alice, saw herself as the intellectual equal of any man.

This, of course, does not mean the same thing through a modern lens. Neither John nor Elizabeth nor Alice would have believed that women could do everything men could, and vice versa. Even Christine de Pisan did not express such a view in her book.[460] However, she obviously believed that women's contributions to society were just as important as men's. As William and Alice had clearly believed this as well,[461] it is hardly surprising that John did too. Elizabeth appears to have been raised by women and also shows every sign of sharing the same view.[462] This is not as surprising as it might sound; in fact, there is evidence that it was a widespread belief in the fifteenth century that women, while not being equal to men in everything, were men's equal in importance in the grand scheme of things. It is nonetheless worth noting, as it rather contradicts many modern perceptions about medieval times and it gives an interesting insight into the potential dynamics between John and Elizabeth, with John in no way seeing his wife in any way as his inferior. On the contrary, he had previously shown a tendency to treat her as his equal in a way that *was* rather unusual for the time, such as when he decided she would offer gifts jointly with him at the Salisburys' funeral.[463] Given all this, it seems very unlikely Elizabeth would have agreed to be a passive partner, and evidence bears out that she was not. John, for his part, most probably neither expected nor wanted his wife to be passive.

Another book that was sent for with was the religious work *The Legend of Raggehande [St. Radegunde]*.[464] Notably another book focusing on a woman and as such fitting for the female-only space confinement was meant to be, this choice suggests that religion and theology was an interest of Elizabeth's, one she shared with John, as their inventory of 1466 reveals.

From the items brought to Ewelme for the use of the new baby, conclusions can be made about the care given to its older siblings, John Jnr included. He would have been used to fineries such as head sheets with miniver fur. His nursery was decorated with a tapestry of orstade,[465] and we can reasonably take this as an indication of the generally luxurious settings in which he was raised. This would have been expected for a boy of his standing and parentage, but the constant supply of books around him was more unusual and noteworthy. The fact that *De morali principis institutione*, which Alice had used for John, was not in her possession in 1466 but had been kept by John himself in Wingfield Castle suggests that by this time it was used for John Jnr's education, brought to Ewelme so he could continue his lessons there.[466] Perhaps, as John Jnr grew up, he would have also been instructed using other books. He would have grown up with the knowledge he could be proud not only of his royal heritage but also of his grandmother Alice's grandfather, the famous Geoffrey Chaucer. Apart from the then yet unborn William Shakespeare, Chaucer is perhaps the most famous Anglophone author, and he was very famous in the 1460s already.[467] Certainly John enjoyed his great-grandfather's stories enough to own a tapestry depicting scenes from them,[468] and it stands to reason he would have tried to share this enjoyment with his children.

These were not the only tapestries John owned. Though in large parts concerned with the clothing and items needed for Elizabeth's upcoming confinement, the inventory of 1466 also includes several of John's possessions, brought to him for his use at Ewelme, giving an insight into his own character. Perhaps most notable are the many religious items he owned. Though it was expected of a man of his standing to show at least outward signs of piety, John's collection of religious books and items went beyond lip service. These items included 'a crucifix of Mary and John of silver',[469] 'two silver basins for the altar'[470] and 'a high chalise of silver'[471] among other items made from silver and gold. They also included a 'canopy of red cloth of gold of bawdkin, with alaunts'[472] and other such fineries to be used in their private chapel.

John's book collection also shows his pronounced interest in religion. Among the many books brought from Wingfield Castle to Ewelme were not only those Elizabeth wished to have with her in confinement, and books used for the education of his children, but also some that appear to have been chosen by John for his own pleasure. These included 'a book of English on paper of the pilgrimage, translated by Dan John Lydgate out of French', 'a French book of the tales of philosophers' and 'a French book of temps pastimes containing diverse stories in the same'.[473] All were bound in precious leather, and they were quite obviously prized possessions. That John wished to have them with him, rather than simply kept in one of his manors, indicates he saw them as more than simple status symbols and was actually interested in reading them.

The collection of books indicates that John was a well-educated man with an interest in literature. They also indicate that he was used to having luxuries and fineries around him, an impression that is supported by other items brought to him. For instance, an item mentioned in the inventory is 'a cover in a crossbow of my lord's garnished with gold',[474] indicating that even such items of use were chosen to reflect his status. His chambers were, more generically, filled with items such as 'beds of cloth of gold, blue satin', tapestries depicting things such as 'the fifteen signs of doom' and 'hawking and hunting', and 'cushions of cloth of gold on red satin'.[475]

Whereas the choice of books and religious items as well as the care given to small items such as crossbows is fairly telling, nothing can really be deduced from what decorations John chose for his chambers. They were only what could be expected from a man of his standing. All that can be said about them is that, despite his chronic money trouble, John obviously did not stint on such shows of ducal dignity.

Though his parents would have known that such comforts only hid their constant debts to various merchants as well as others, John Jnr naturally would not have known it. For him, all the luxuries and fineries would have been normal. He, too, probably would have been dressed in only the most expensive of fabrics, especially as he outgrew his toddler clothes. Although he would have been dressed nicely already, his extravagance would only increase as he grew older, and soon there would be a change that would see him stand above his siblings not only due to being the eldest and their father's heir.

He might have already known what was coming by Christmas 1466, around the time his mother gave birth to his fourth sibling, a little girl whom John and Elizabeth chose to name Anne, probably after her aunt, Elizabeth's sister Anne. The name might have been chosen as a sign of gratitude for her making John one of her feoffees in the previous year, to honour her if she was the godmother, or simply because it was a family name. Anne's birth must have been a happy event for John. His third daughter was born healthy, and Elizabeth, too, seems to have survived her fifth birth without any problems. She greeted the new arrival in style; the bearing mantle mentioned above, of blue cloth of gold decorated with lemons, would probably have been the one she wore during her new daughter's baptism and for her churching and purification forty days after the birth.

The Creation of the Earl of Lincoln

Since these occasions would have been public, John Jnr might have seen his mother's clothing and been impressed by it, as its finery surpassed even that which he saw every day. It was clothing for a special occasion, and on seeing it he might have thought of the big day that was approaching in his young life.

If John Jnr did not already know of it, he would soon learn that his uncle, Edward IV, had decided to grant him an earldom. This was a great honour, and would mark the beginning of his career at court. Though only four years of age, Edward favoured him more than he ever did his parents, and would continue to do so for the rest of his life. On 13 March 1467, the ceremony elevating the little boy to an earldom took place. In the presence of John and Elizabeth, Edward IV made John Jnr the Earl of Lincoln and granted him £20 annually from the county of Lincoln to support the honour.[476] At only five years old, John Jnr was among the highest nobles of the realm, not only by birth but also in his own right, and was rich as well. The grant of this honour is recorded in the Calendar of Patent Rolls on 4 July 1468, interestingly stating that the letters patent for it had been lost:

> Exemplification of the tenour of the enrolment of letters patent dated 133 March, 7 Edward IV, creating the king's nephew John son and heir of John duke of Suffolk, earl of Lincoln and granting him and the heirs male of his body 20 l yearly from the issues of the county of Lincoln. These letters have been lost by accident, as Henry Boteler has taken oath in Chancery, and will be surrendered if found.[477]

Nothing is actually recorded of the actual ceremony elevating little John Jnr to this earldom, and if being an earl changed anything in his life immediately afterwards, we do not know of it. The responsibility of the earldom's upkeep would have naturally fallen to his parents at that time. Most likely, however, his sudden rise in status would have been reflected in his lessons; no longer simply a duke's heir, he was now an earl in his own right and would have been taught the upkeep of an earldom with much more immediacy. If he had still shared lessons with Elizabeth Jnr until that time, presumably he no longer did after becoming an earl; at the very least he received more lessons than her.

Most likely, the new earl would also have been shown to his new tenants by his father. This would have kept the little boy and his parents busy, and it might be that this and his own establishment as a local power in Oxfordshire kept John busy during 1467. Not a lot of what he did that year is recorded. He was involved in some commissions of the peace,[478] and it seems he did not regard those appointments as solely nominal. Though appointments of that kind were normal and very common for noblemen and often not only were not actually attended – indeed such roles often overlapped, giving away that they were never intended to be taken literally – John took a different view from most other nobles.

In the four years since he had come of age, John had amply shown that his focus lay not on national politics but instead on regional politics, much more so than was usual for a man of his standing. Presumably, he therefore had more interest than most others in appointments to commissions of the peace and of oyer and terminer, as these kept him abreast of regional affairs as well as helping him establish his position of power. Since he had spent most of his time since attaining his majority in Suffolk and had only arrived in Oxfordshire to make it his family's main home in late 1466, it makes sense such appointments to committees were particularly important to him in 1467. Since neither he nor Elizabeth seem to have been at court that year after their son's elevation to an earldom, John would have had a lot of opportunity to stay with his family. John Jnr would have got many chances to observe his father and learn from him what it meant to be a duke. Of course, we do not know if he chose to personally teach his son anything, but presumably, even if not, he would have closely supervised his children's upbringing, especially that of his heir.

It seems that 1467 was a happy year for John and his family. His eldest had been made an earl, his four surviving children were all thriving and his position in Oxfordshire was growing increasingly secure. Furthermore, at the end of 1467, or in early 1468, Elizabeth became pregnant again. The couple must have been happy about it, but presumably it was no longer a cause for overthrowing their plans. Though she was only twenty-three years old, and John only twenty-five, it was to be their sixth child. For John Jnr, the news of a new sibling cannot have been very exciting as he must have been used to it by now.

However, before the planned arrival of their new family member, another event of more national importance was to draw their attention: the marriage of Elizabeth's younger sister Margaret. Though first discussed in 1466, it had been delayed somewhat by the death of her suitor's father.[479] Her betrothed was now Charles, Duke of Burgundy.

Political Intrigues, Part 2

The new duke, Margaret's prospective husband, did not initially want to follow through with his father's plans. Having Lancastrian blood through his mother, Charles was opposed to the Yorkist government in England, and after his father's death he first chose to wait and see if any other options were available to him.[480] However, his mother Isabella eventually convinced him that it was in his best interest to marry Margaret,[481] and in early 1468 the preparations for the wedding began. It was to take place in the summer of that year, and as Margaret began making her way towards her groom, her departure was marked by many celebrations in England.[482]

Apparently already preparing, Edward IV granted John the lieutenancy of Ireland on 10 March 1468.[483] The appointment was very clearly nominal; John never fulfilled any of the duties connected with it and it seems that neither the king nor anyone else ever expected him to do so. The most likely explanation is that Edward wished for him to be seen as an important man of his government before he took part in the celebrations for Margaret's marriage; no foreign observers should see the king's brother-in-law and think him an unimportant member of the nobility.

The celebrations for Margaret began in June 1468, with her, as a contemporary source puts it, 'riding throughout London behind the Earl of Warwick'.[484] Her doing this was a political decision by Edward IV, to assure every onlooker that there was no rift in the family and that Warwick, who was known to be close to the King of France, supported the marriage. Margaret then stayed with her brother the king and his wife for a short while before riding to catch a ship to Burgundy at Margate.

John was to have a rather important part in the celebrations. Raphael Holinshed, writing around a century after the fact but clearly well-informed on this particular occasion, reports that John was chosen 'with the Duke of Exeter and the Duchesses of Exeter and Suffolk, being both sisters to the Lady Margaret, to attend her till she came to her husband'.[485] The inclusion of the Duke of Exeter, who was long since separated from his wife, is a rather baffling choice, but this too might have been an attempt to present a united front to all foreign observers.

John, and his wife's brother-in-law the Duke of Exeter, were Margaret's closest male relatives on her journey to Burgundy. Though her younger brothers had attended the festivities given for her in England, neither of them actually went with her. Even with those notable absences, her party was a large one, including not only her sisters and brothers-in-law but other important nobles such as the Duchess of Norfolk, Lord Howard and the king's brother-in-law Anthony Woodville, Lord Scales, among others. There were also numerous companions of lower standing, including rich merchants and members of the gentry such as John Paston and his brother.[486]

Though John might not have been very pleased about the Pastons' inclusion in the party, it is a gift for historians, for John Paston wrote letters to his mother about the celebrations. Though some of the less prestigious guests complained about being treated shabbily by the Burgundians during the celebrations, John Paston had no such complaints, describing the duke's court in exaggerated terms as incomparable, stating that he 'heard never of none like to it, save King Arthur's court'.[487] He also stated that the new duchess had been received honourably and there was no cause for complaint, though the main focus of his letter was the tournaments and jousts given to honour the new bride. Paston was obviously delighted by these, but the fact not even he found anything bad to say about John in this situation is rather telling and goes to show that his nemesis comported himself well.

It seems likely that John and John Paston did not see much of one another during these celebrations, and while Paston would doubtlessly have recorded even a hint of a rumour of anything unflattering to John, their experience of the celebrations must have been different. John Paston would have been free to simply enjoy the festivities, which were lavish. However, for John it would have been a rather more familial and personal affair than for most of the others attending the celebrations, if only because of his wife's close connection to the bride. He most likely would also have been closer to the bride and groom than most, and was probably present when Margaret met her future husband's family, her eleven-year-old future stepdaughter Marie and future mother-in-law Isabella. Certainly he was present when Margaret met Charles.[488]

All those meetings went well, but Margaret may very well have been happy to have her sisters and brothers-in-law with her. Though there is no indication what exactly their task was in 'attending' her, assumptions can be made that this meant preparing her for her wedding and giving her advice for married life. John and Elizabeth would have presumably been more suited to the latter task than Anne and her estranged husband the Duke of Exeter. We do not know if either John or the Duke of Exeter, as Margaret's closest male relatives present, had been instructed by Edward to act in his stead and give away the bride in the ceremony; this course of action would have been customary, but in this instance it seems unlikely that customs were followed as it surely would have been noted and Edward most likely would not have wanted either the Duke of Exeter, whose loyalties were at best questionable, or John, whom he apparently disliked, to fulfil such a task.

John and his wife probably enjoyed themselves, but Elizabeth might also felt somewhat sad. Margaret's marriage and consequent move to Burgundy would have meant that she would see less of her sister than she might have in previous years. However, it was a very good match for Margaret, which might have softened such thoughts for Elizabeth and made her happy for her sister's good luck. In any case, the celebrations did not go on as long as had been planned. As John Paston reported to his mother, Duke Charles heard rumours of the French king intending to attack his territories.[489]

Duke Charles was a warlike man, and during the course of their marriage Margaret would not see much of him,[490] though she was to become very close to his daughter.[491] Her relationship to her husband was very different to that which Elizabeth enjoyed with John, but it still seemed a perfectly happy arranged marriage, working as intended. Elizabeth might have worried about her sister so far away, and she kept in contact with Margaret, but her main focus as she and her husband returned home to England would have been her own family and the upcoming birth of a new child.

It was still some months until the birth when they returned, but perhaps Elizabeth was also concerned by what was going on in the kingdom at large by then. Like her husband, her main focus was regional politics, but she would have been personally interested in the widening rift between her brothers Edward and George. Neither John nor Elizabeth had ever shown any sign of wanting to pick sides in the by now escalating conflict, and it is unlikely they did then, though as Elizabeth was later to work to reconcile her brothers it might have hurt her to see them so at odds.

It is very likely Elizabeth's confinement was very similar to her previous one at the end of 1466, though sadly we do not have an inventory so we do not know which, if any, books Elizabeth chose to read and discuss in this new confinement, or if she had different tapestries hung up. Whatever her confinement looked like, and whether or not she was visited by Alice or her mother Cecily, Elizabeth's sixth birth apparently went smoothly. The proud new parents called their new daughter Katherine, perhaps after John's grandmother or after St Katherine, whom they both appeared to particularly revere.

Naturally, little Katherine's birth would have been great tidings for the entire family, but would not have changed much in their everyday life. John Jnr must have been so used to regularly getting new siblings that he presumably did not get overly excited about having another sister, though he might still have been pleased. It is likely, however, that he was more interested in a change in the circumstances of his own life that happened around the time little Katherine was born. Upon turning seven, traditionally, he would have been considered too old to be in the nursery, and it is very likely arrangements for this would have begun several months before his actual birthday. It was typically at that age that the upbringing of boys started including martial arts and therefore became the father or male guardian's responsibility. Though John himself had obviously not experienced it like that himself, as he had been brought up with only his mother as his guardian from the age of seven, there is nothing to suggest he did not want to do things traditionally with his own children, and that means he would have made the arrangements for lessons in martial arts and other typically 'male' tasks for John Jnr in late 1468.

This, of course, does not mean John Jnr would not still have been instructed in other disciplines. On the contrary, he was now old enough to have 'real' lessons, which would have included academic subjects such as mathematics, Latin, French, calligraphy and courtly arts such as conversation and dancing.[492] Seven-year-old Elizabeth Jnr had been mainly instructed alongside John Jnr until this time, and might have left the nursery by the time of Katherine's birth, so she would have registered the change. A child leaving the nursery was considered a main life event, and John and Elizabeth must have been very proud. Indeed, it might have been a welcome distraction from the situation in the kingdom, which was becoming more and more fraught.

A Turbulent Year

The year 1469 was to prove a busy one for John. Very early in the year, his quarrel with the Paston family about the manors, which had calmed down after the death of John Paston Snr in May 1466, flared up again. On 12 March 1469, Margaret Paston wrote to her son to ask him to speak with her 'brother William' to ask him to see to it that 'there may be purveyed be some writing from the king that my lord of Norfolk and his council see of the waste that they done in your lordship and especially at Heynford, for they have felled all the wood and this week they would carry it away, and let run that waters and take all the fish'.[493]

Obviously, Margaret very clearly attributed this attack to the Duke of Norfolk, not to John. However, this has not stopped several historians, including Mary Clive and Paul Murray Kendall, attributing it to John.[494] While this, by Margaret's own words, is untrue, there might be more of a connection between him and this attack than is apparent at first glance. The men most involved in this attack, particularly William Yelverton, were those who had previously been involved with John's men. Moreover, John and the Duke of Norfolk had previously been mentioned as working together to harm the Pastons.[495]

Margaret herself did not miss this connection, and addressed this in her letter, telling her son that 'it is told me that my lady of Suffolk [Alice] has promised you her good will if your bargain of the marriage holds to do as largely as she shall be desired, or largely if there be any appointment taken between you for any matters between her and you'.[496] Here she was referring to the marriage her son was pursuing with one of Queen Elizabeth's cousins, Anne Haute.[497]

Usually, it has been claimed that by 'my lady of Suffolk' Margaret meant John's wife, Elizabeth.[498] However, Margaret's letter makes it very clear that this was not so, as she went on to tell her son his well-wishers 'would advise you to give any money to her to make her refuse or disclaim her title', though she herself did not share this opinion, stating that it seemed to her 'you may well excuse you[rself] by the money that she had last and by the wrongs that were done by her and her men in felling of wood and pulling down your place and lodge at Hellesdon and taking away of the sheep and your father's goods which were taken away at the pulling down of the said place, which well considered she were worthy to recompense you'.[499]

Obviously, none of this could in any way refer to Elizabeth, as unlike Alice she had no title to any of the places in question, nor did she have men of her own to send. It is interesting to see, though, that not only did Margaret admit that several of her son's supporters acknowledged John's family had at least a faint claim to these places but also that she squarely blamed Alice, not John, for what had happened at Hellesdon some years previously. Given that the same men had been involved in the Duke of Norfolk's attack referenced earlier in the letter, she also held this attack against Alice, possibly unfairly. John, however, is not even mentioned in this context.[500]

The difficulties the Pastons faced with the Suffolks were not over. On 3 April 1469, less than a month later, Margaret penned another letter to her son, once more referencing Alice, rather amusingly stating that she was 'at Ewelme in Oxfordshire' at the time of her writing and that it was 'thought by your friends here that it is so that she might be fear[ed] and ought of the way, and then rather feign excuse because of age or sickness if that the King would send for her for your matters'.[501] Since this letter was written on Easter Monday, it stands to reason that John and Elizabeth celebrated Easter together with Alice. Perhaps the quarrel with the Pastons hung heavily over them, but it was to have no lasting consequences for them even if it may have seemed like it would.

In June 1469, the king came to Norwich together with the queen and several of his most important men, among them his brother Richard, Duke of Gloucester. Margaret reported that he, together with his brother the king, would be shown the lodge destroyed by the Duke of Norfolk's men. Even before this happened, Margaret was promised by several of her advisors that they would ask the king 'to speak with the two dukes of Norfolk and Suffolk that they should leave of their titles of such land as was Sir John Falstof's, and if so by that that would do not at the king's request, that then the king should command them to do not waste nor make none assaults nor [?] upon your tenants nor places until such time as the law has determined with you or against you'.[502]

Obviously, despite Margaret's clear bias, it seems that those advising her could not promise that any court would definitely decide in his favour. The titles and possessions of the lands were obviously disputed, despite both Johns asserting that they were both completely right in claiming it. However, independent of from the king's visit, it seems that John had been working on some sort of ceasefire with the Paston family, for Margaret also told her son that one of their men, Jacks Hart, 'shall tell you what language was spoken between the Duke of Suffolk's council and him and me',[503] without clarifying that this referred to any attack or quarrel.

If it was because of these consultations or perhaps the hope that a court would soon decide we do not know, but after June neither John nor the Paston family furthered the quarrel, even though the king did not become involved as Margaret Paston had hoped. That he did not do so is hardly surprising, for that summer the situation between him and his brother George and cousin the Earl of Warwick escalated, taking precedence over any local quarrel he hoped to solve.

Soon after Edward's visit to Norwich, Warwick and George, Duke of Clarence, openly defied the king's orders by going to Calais, where Warwick, as Captain of Calais, was extremely powerful, and there marrying George to Warwick's older daughter, Isabel.[504] Cecily, George's mother and John's mother-in-law, famously went to see her son before he went to Calais,[505] indicating she was aware of his intentions and did not betray them to the king. This has sometimes been taken as evidence that she supported the decision, but of course that is hard to say. All that can be said from her movements is that it is very likely she was aware of what

George and Warwick were planning. As the groom's older sister, perhaps Elizabeth, too, was aware of those plans. Given that she and John would side with Edward IV in the crisis that was to come, perhaps it is more likely neither of them was aware of the plans, and so could not pass them on to Edward even had they wanted to.

Probably at the same time, John and Elizabeth appear to have spent some time together at Ewelme, not busy with either the Paston quarrel or anything that went on in the kingdom. It must have been a relaxing if rather short time for them, and it was around that time that Elizabeth fell pregnant once again. However, this peaceful interlude was not to last long, for at some point at the end of July 1469 Edward IV learnt of the marriage between his younger brother and Warwick's older daughter. He was predictably furious. Declaring that Warwick and George had gone against his will, together with his youngest brother Richard he rode to gather men. John was not involved in this, but even so, he and Elizabeth must have watched the unfolding events in the kingdom with worry.

If they had already sided with Edward and agreed with his actions, worse news was to come for them. The Earl of Warwick and his new son-in-law were prepared for Edward's actions against them, and when they returned to England from Calais they quickly gained the upper hand. Within weeks, the earl and the duke overpowered Edward IV and his forces and took him prisoner. It appears they did not detain Richard, Duke of Gloucester,[506] perhaps because they did not think he was a danger.

In the first weeks of his imprisonment, Edward IV was kept at Warwick Castle, where he was treated honourably, even permitted to go hunting under supervision. However, as time passed, Warwick apparently began to fear that Edward might escape or be freed, and had him brought to Middleham Castle, where he was kept in honourable confinement.[507] While he was imprisoned, the earl and his son-in-law attacked his Woodville in-laws, which might have been their main aim from the first, as both had previously spoken out against them. Queen Elizabeth's father, Richard Woodville, Lord Rivers, and one of his sons, John Woodville, were captured by Warwick's forces, subjected to a mock trial and executed.

Though the same fate would likely have befallen any man of the Woodville family unlucky enough to be captured by Warwick's forces, John Woodville was at particular odds with the Warwick faction due to his controversial marriage to Warwick's aunt, Katherine Neville. This was made in 1465,[508] when John was only nineteen and Katherine was sixty-seven, and it had caused a lot of outrage. It was widely assumed that Katherine herself was against the marriage and that it was only made to increase the Woodvilles' wealth. There is evidence for this; in fact, the marriage was openly planned with Katherine's death in mind. This insulted her nephew Warwick as well as other relatives and turned several of them against Edward – who, despite being Katherine's nephew himself, supported the marriage – but it also insulted several of Warwick's associates and drove them to support him over Edward. The most notable example was Henry FitzHugh, 5th Baron FitzHugh, whose youngest daughter was disadvantaged by some of the illegal arrangements made to enrich John Woodville through the marriage.[509] If not for the Lancastrian side sensing the chance to cause trouble for the Yorkist king and win back the throne, it is likely Warwick would have been able to dictate the terms of Edward's immediate kingship.

However, it was to unfold differently. Being heartened by the dissent in the Yorkist government, several Lancastrian exiles saw the chance to have another go at unseating Edward. Warwick and his faction did not want to support them at this time, so the earl gathered men to fight against them.[510] However, this put Warwick in an impossible situation. Men of a Yorkist persuasion did not want to fight on the orders of a man who had apparently imprisoned the king, and Warwick had to partially free Edward so that he could appear beside him, to make a show of all being well between them.[511] This made men gather to fight for Warwick to defeat the Lancastrian forces, and he had the Lancastrian leaders sent to be executed in Edward's presence. However, in the meantime, Edward had been able to use his freedom to summon nobles to support him. This enabled him to leave Warwick's captivity and ride to London.[512]

On the way there, Edward was joined by the nobles he had sent for. John was among them, and probably rode to meet him from Ewelme, which might mean he only joined with his party shortly before it reached London. Wherever he met him, John rode into London with Edward and his party. As he was, alongside his teenage brother-in-law Richard, of the highest standing after the king, he was mentioned first together with Richard in the sources reporting this, such as a letter to Margaret Paston:

> The King is come to London and there come with him and wide with him the Duke of Gloucester, the Duke of Suffolk, the Earl of Arundel, the Earl of Northumberland, the Earl of Essey, the lods Harry and John of Buckingham, the Lord Dacre, the Lord Chamberlain [William Hastings], the Lord Mountjoy, and many other knights and squires, the mayor of London, twenty-two aldermen in scarlet, and of the craftsmen of the town to the number of two hundred all in blue.[513]

Quite obviously, Edward's entry into the city was meant as a show of his power and popularity, and John may have enjoyed for once being in favour with the king, taking part in such a triumphant royal entry. His status as a duke and the king's brother-in-law means that he presumably had a place of honour in the procession, possible beside or just behind the king. Edward, for his part, may not have enjoyed the fact that his most noble supporter, alongside his brother Richard, was his little-loved brother-in-law, but he could not afford to lose his support, and giving John a position of high honour would have seemed a small price to pay.

John was also present at a council that took place in November 1469, during which Edward issued a general pardon for the events of the summer.[514] He knew that Warwick was too popular for him to punish, and George seemed to have immunity due to being his brother. Perhaps he truly hoped that their failed endeavour had taught them a lesson and they would not act against him again. Certainly he must have hoped so, and it stands to reason that John did too. After the council was over in December 1469, John returned home to his family in Ewelme for the winter.

Upheaval

Despite the fraught situation in the kingdom, it must have been a happy winter for John and his family. He would have been able to see his children often, celebrating milestones in their development. One such would have been John Jnr turning seven that winter, meaning that he, like Elizabeth Jnr, would finally have been old enough to leave the nursery. Perhaps that meant that he once more had at least some lessons together with his older sister. However, it is also possible Elizabeth Jnr and her younger siblings had a different tutor than John Jnr. Though obviously the Suffolks laid a lot of focus and attention on their daughters being educated as well as their sons, the heir was typically considered to be special, needing more education than any sisters or brothers, and the Suffolks might have shared such a viewpoint.

While Elizabeth was in confinement once more, the fragile peace that had lasted through the early part of the winter broke. Warwick and his son-in-law started fomenting rebellion, at first surreptitiously, in such a way their names would not be tied to it, but by mid-March Edward IV clearly realised what they were up to, and tried to warn them off by unofficially referring to them as traitors, and finally by having two of their men executed in front of his army.[515]

It was around this time that Elizabeth gave birth to a boy named Edward. Perhaps they had long decided to call their next son Edward, and it does not mean anything they did so at a time when Edward IV's throne was no longer as stable as it had been in the previous years. However, since Edward was their third son, and they had not named the first two after the king, as would have been common, it seems quite plausible they chose to make a statement signalling their loyalties without being too obvious.[516]

Possibly to indicate his support in other ways, John chose to ride by his brother-in-law's side after his victory of March 1470.[517] However, it appears to have been a very brief show of support, because there is no evidence he remained at his side; he was back in Ewelme, with his wife and newborn son, by April 1470. Edward's victory in the spring of 1470 seemed fairly final at first, and it had the effect of rendering the Earl of Warwick and the Duke of Clarence open traitors. Edward saw to it that positions they had held previously were stripped from them in consequence. The most notable of these positions was the captaincy of Calais, which Edward gave to Lord Wenlock. Warwick's men were left with no choice, but to try and escape Edward's forces, which they did.

In April, Warwick, with his wife, daughters and Clarence, tried escaping to Calais. Warwick's daughter Isabel, Clarence's wife, was heavily pregnant, and went into labour on the ship to Calais. However, Calais, now under the captaincy of Lord Wenlock, refused them entry,[518] only sending some wine for the labouring Duchess of Clarence.[519] However, whether due to the adverse circumstances of the birth or simply due to something going wrong during the pregnancy that could not have been prevented in any case, the duchess gave birth to a stillborn baby, which was buried at sea.[520]

Not wanting to go back to England, where they had burned all bridges, Warwick and Clarence decided to go to France. Knowing that they would not be able to rid England of their enemies in the Woodville faction while Edward was in power, they decided to go over to the Lancastrian side in France, where the erstwhile queen, Margaret of Anjou, had been in exile with her son, once Prince Edward, for the last five years.[521] Warwick chose to make his peace with her, much supported by the French king Louis, known to history as the Spider King.[522] Margaret was less than delighted, as Warwick had been instrumental in ousting her husband Henry VI in the first place, while he had made it no secret he held her personally responsible for his father's death.

However, both recognised they needed each other to achieve their goals, and though Margaret insisted that Warwick kneel to her for fifteen minutes to apologise for acting against her and her husband,[523] eventually they started making plans to oust Edward IV and put Henry back on the throne. One of the details they agreed on was that Margaret's son Edward was to marry Warwick's younger daughter, Anne, to cement their alliance.[524] Of course, they were still at a disadvantage, but Edward IV was losing his secure grip on his throne back in England. His victory in March had no lasting effects for the peace of England or the security of his throne. Warwick was very popular in England while the Woodvilles were rather less so, which led to many siding with Warwick, and at least some of his more high-born supporters must have been in contact while he was still in France, organising from across the Channel.

John cannot have been happy with developments. Though physical fear for his children cannot have motivated John the way such fear for his then yet unborn children may have motivated him in 1461, as one of their uncles would assume an important part in the government even if the Lancastrians were victorious, he might have feared they would be overlooked or even punished for his choice to side with the Yorkists in 1461. Whatever his motivations, he was regarded as supporter of Edward's, if a rather tepid one. However, since most of Edward's actions in 1470 to quell the rebellions were military in nature, John could not become actively involved.

He therefore stayed with his family in Ewelme when, in August 1470,[525] Warwick's brother-in-law Henry FitzHugh, Baron FitzHugh, started a rebellion in the north of the country. FitzHugh was married to Warwick's sister Alice, a strong, powerful woman who has been said to have greatly resembled her brother Warwick. It has often been assumed that it was she who told her husband to revolt, which is possible. However, FitzHugh had originally been a Lancastrian, although he had accepted Edward IV after his victory at Towton. It might therefore have appealed to him in any case to side with Warwick and help the Lancastrian party win back the throne; that, or he too wanted to punish the Woodvilles for what many regarded as the theft of land and titles from more 'deserving' nobles. As mentioned above, in FitzHugh's case, one of the 'more deserving' was his youngest daughter, and her deprivation might have made him angry enough to act against them. Whichever it was, FitzHugh's rebellion was easily defused; Edward, perhaps knowing he could not afford to create more enemies at this point, granted a pardon to FitzHugh and everyone in his household.[526]

Though the rebellion itself did not really pose any danger to Edward, it had forced him north to deal with it, so he was caught in the wrong part of the country when Warwick landed in England shortly afterward. In fact, it has been speculated that this was the whole point of the rebellion;[527] it was simply a diversion. If so, it worked perfectly. On his way to meet Warwick, Edward and his party, which included his brother Richard, Duke of Gloucester, his brother-in-law Anthony Woodville, Lord Rivers, and his chamberlain William Hastings, Baron Hastings,[528] were surprised by a night attack by John Neville, one of Warwick's younger brothers. John Neville had originally been on Edward's side, even going against his brother, but felt poorly rewarded by the king. In fact, in some ways it must have seemed to Neville he was being punished, such as when Edward took his earldom of Northumberland from him to give to his enemy Henry Percy.[529] Though Edward made Neville a marquis in consolation, he did not give him any lands or money to make up for the earldom he lost. It must have seemed like a slap to the face to John Neville.

6

The Lancastrian Readeption

Whether it was because of his scant rewards or something else, John Neville eventually decided to side with his brother Warwick and attacked the king's party.[530] Taken unawares, Edward had no choice but to flee. England had turned against him; his was a panicked flight, he and his men had nothing but the clothes on their backs.[531]

It was Edward's turn to go into exile. He and his comrades took a ship to Burgundy, where they hoped to be greeted by Edward's sister Margaret and other Burgundian nobles they had befriended in the process of her marriage. Edward quite literally had to pay the ship's captain with the expensive fur coat he wore.[532] The journey was apparently choppy, and though they eventually arrived safely in Burgundy, rumours circulated for a while that they had drowned on their way there.

This must have been a tense time for John and Elizabeth. Since the party seeking exile in Burgundy included two of Elizabeth's brothers, she must have been very worried about their fate. Perhaps they initially tried not to think too much about it, focusing on their children and their upbringing instead of what went on in the centre of the government. Even so, they would have learnt that Edward's heavily pregnant wife, Elizabeth Woodville, and their three daughters had fled to sanctuary in Westminster Abbey, that Elizabeth gave birth to a son shortly afterwards, and that Henry VI had been released from confinement in the Tower after five long years and reinstalled on the throne.[533]

It was said at the time that Henry VI barely realised what was happening and that Warwick was the one truly calling the shots,[534] and he certainly got what he wanted. In December 1470, his daughter Anne was married to the Lancastrian Prince of Wales, Edward,[535] meaning she would become queen one day, provided Edward IV could be finally defeated. It was also made law that should Edward and Anne remain childless, George, Duke of Clarence would be the next king.[536] His children with Warwick's other daughter Isabel would be heirs afterward.

In this way, Warwick had made sure that one of his daughters would eventually be queen and one of his grandsons king.

The Rebel King's Brother-in-law

Presumably John was not happy about it, but he kept a low profile. Whatever his feelings, he did not show them in public, with the result that he suffered no losses upon the Lancastrian readeption. He was allowed to stay in all commissions of peace he had been appointed to by Edward IV, and was even granted permission to sit on another one for Oxfordshire.[537] He was also invited to Parliament on 26 November 1470, and since there is no evidence of him being punished for non-attendance, it can be assumed he was present when Parliament took place.

John's apparent compliance with the new regime has caused many historians to accuse him of being a turncoat,[538] though rationally it is hard to see what else he could have done. Openly declaring for the Yorkists would have seen him accused of treason and potentially even executed without helping the Yorkist party at all. Not only would it have been a completely pointless sacrifice on his part, but it would have also meant his young children, the oldest of whom was nine and the youngest not even a year old, would be disinherited and his wife possibly imprisoned as his co-conspirator, especially given that she was the deposed king's sister. Had that happened, his children would have been at the mercy of whoever was granted their wardship. Even if John had wanted to side with the Yorkists openly at that point – which we have no evidence for anyway – such considerations would have counselled against it. Nor have many others been lambasted for making the same choice. Once more, the historical record has John singled out and criticised for a perfectly sensible and understandable course of action.

Moreover, while John tried to remain below the radar for the above reasons, it was recorded, and is borne out by evidence, that Elizabeth, together with her sisters Anne and Margaret and her mother Cecily, worked on reconciling George with his brothers Edward and Richard to get him to stop supporting the Lancastrians and, when the time came, to declare for and fight for Edward.[539] This was successful in the end, though naturally it must have seemed risky at the time. It was treason for Elizabeth, Anne and Cecily to try and convince George to declare against the sitting king, Henry VI. Not only that, but it must have required both subtlety and organisational skill. Letters would have had to be sneaked to and from George, as well as overseas to Edward and Richard. Interestingly, these tasks seem to have been done almost entirely by women: Elizabeth, Anne, Margaret and Cecily, who managed to convince George to prepare to re-join his brothers (and then convince Edward that George meant it), and then his wife, Isabel, Duchess of Clarence, who sent one of her ladies to pass on communications between them.[540]

Possibly these women banked on the fact that they would come under less suspicion than men, but given how often women had been involved at the very least in the conception and the planning of rebellions, if not in the actual fighting, and had been punished for it,[541] this seems unlikely and more like a modern idea than one any woman in the fifteenth century would have had. More likely is that they had more of a stake in it than most men, being closely related to the brothers, and also that even if they were found out their punishment would be less severe than that for any man found to have committed treason. Though women had been attainted before and could lose their possessions,[542] or even be sent to a convent or otherwise embarrassed,[543] it was unheard of for women to be executed for treason.

For Elizabeth, if her actions had been found out by anyone in Henry VI's government, a punishment would have been most likely been very mild. She did not own any lands in her own right, and as a married woman would not have been sent away to a convent without risks the government could not afford. As a result, she could plot and even commit treason with a fair expectation of immunity. However, it is extremely unlikely that John was unaware of his wife's involvement. It would have been all but impossible for her to organise even the effort of contacting all her brothers together with her mother and sister, let alone actually keep up with them in such a way that those currently in power noticed nothing, while also keeping it a secret from John. This is especially so since John and Elizabeth appear to have stayed together at Ewelme for all but a month during the Lancastrian readeption. Perhaps their efforts to be on good terms with both sides during the 1460s paid off now; they do not seem to have been watched, which must have made things much easier. It might even be that because of this Elizabeth was at the centre of the communications on the English side; her sister Anne must have been more closely watched by her husband the Duke of Exeter, and Cecily seems to have been watched as well. Elizabeth had more freedom and could send servants and trusted messengers into Suffolk on pretexts associated with her husband's possessions, and from there to the coast, without arousing any suspicion.

We do not know if John was actively involved in these communications, but seeing as he was never mentioned in any sources as doing so it does not seem to be the case. Though it was technically treason for him to even know of the conspiracy and not tell the government – for which he might even have been executed – it would not have been stupid of him to stay out of it. At least this way he had plausible deniability if his wife's efforts came to light.

The Rebel King's Nephew

It would also be interesting to know what John and Elizabeth's children though of all that was happening. Most of them would have been much too young to even understand the basics of the situation in the kingdom, much less what their mother, aunts and grandmother were doing about it in secret. Only John Jnr, who was by then eight years old, and Elizabeth Jnr, who had just turned nine, would have been old enough to even possibly understand. For obvious reasons, John and Elizabeth would have kept all treasonous activities far away from their children's prying eyes.

However, when their uncle Edward returned to the throne as Edward IV, their mother, aunts and grandmother's actions became well-known enough to be talked about in chronicles.[544] As such, they would have become known to the children, especially as they grew up. This is relevant since it seems John Jnr was impressed by the subtlety his mother and other relatives had shown while working against the sitting king, or, in his father's case, being aware of such activities. John Jnr himself would adopt a similar approach after Henry VII came to the throne one and a half decades after the Lancastrian readeption.[545] Perhaps this was a conscious decision. At eight years old, John Jnr would have been old enough to observe his parents, and even if he did not understand at the time what was happening or what they were doing, he would have been able to remember it as an adult.

The culmination of those efforts happened half a year after Edward and Richard's flight to exile. Margaret, Duchess of Burgundy, had not only helped convince George to return to the Yorkist fold but had also convinced her husband Charles, Duke of Burgundy, who had strong Lancastrian leanings, to give them money and soldiers to help Edward regain the throne.[546] Since no battle could reasonably be fought in midwinter, he spent the next few months planning before taking a ship to England. Not all of his party immediately went with him; his brother Richard arrived somewhat later with another ship carrying men. They were met by supporters in England, which has to mean they had had contacts in England who knew of their imminent arrival. We do not know if these informants were Edward's mother and sisters, but since we do know they had been in contact the whole time, it certainly seems possible, even likely. Edward employed a trick upon landing in England that had first been used by the future Henry IV, claiming he had only returned to claim his dukedom of York.[547]

From Yorkshire, where he had landed and made this claim, Edward marched on, gathering men. On 14 April 1471, having openly reconciled with his brother George – Richard of Gloucester had ridden ahead to meet him[548] – the Yorkist forces, led by Edward, met the Lancastrian forces. It seems there was already trouble on Henry's side even before George abandoned them to support his brothers; Warwick's brother John, whether plagued by bad conscience or just caught unawares, allowed the Yorkist forces to pass without engaging them on their way to meet the Lancastrian troops.[549]

7

Yorkist Victory

With George's declaration for the Yorkists, everything collapsed for the Lancastrians. When the forces did battle Henry's cohort lacked the manpower to hold their own. Already nervous after George's betrayal, and perhaps suspicious of each other, the Lancastrians also had to deal with a blinding fog. Because of this, John Neville's forces confused the Earl of Oxford's banner with that of Edward and attacked his men in a fatal case of friendly fire.[550] This involuntary infighting almost cost the Lancastrians the battle itself. It is hardly surprising the Yorkist forces emerged victorious from the battle, which has gone down in history as the Battle of Barnet. The Lancastrians were not entirely defeated but they suffered many losses, most significantly John Neville and the Earl of Warwick himself, who was supposedly killed trying to escape the battlefield after the battle was lost.[551]

John, once more, did not participate in the battle. As usual, his lack of fighting has been used against him and has contributed to the reputation given to him by historians as a man trimming his sails to the wind and not wanting to commit to any side in a conflict.[552] Once more, this is a baseless accusation. No one at the time said anything of the sort, and the evidence obviously shows he wanted the Yorkists to fight but simply could not do so himself. The nature of his injury or sickness contracted at the Battle of Hexham in 1464 is not, but his and everyone else's actions around him during the Lancastrian readeption obviously show it was understood at the time, and no one expected him to fight. Presumably, he and Elizabeth were eagerly and worriedly waiting for news from the battlefield. The Yorkist triumph at Barnet would have pleased them, though since both George of Clarence and Richard of Gloucester are supposed to have sustained minor injuries during the battle,[553] they, or at the very least Elizabeth, might also have been worried about that.

The Lancastrians were not yet entirely vanquished, and perhaps because of that John did not join Edward when he rode to London to greet his wife, daughters and newborn son,[554] who had spent the last six months in sanctuary. Henry VI was once more captured and confined to the Tower of London,[555] where he had already been held from 1465 to 1470, but everyone knew the conflict was not over. After a few days at London, Edward and his forces began marching again, trying to catch up with Margaret of Anjou, who, together with her son Prince Edward and her daughter-in-law Anne, Warwick's younger daughter, was trying to flee to Wales. It seems her plan was to seek sanctuary with Henry VI's younger half-brother Jasper Tudor, and from there to leave England, perhaps to go into exile in France once more.[556]

However, Edward's forces were faster, and caught up with the remaining Lancastrian forces before they could cross into Wales, where the rugged terrain would have made catching up with them much harder, if not impossible. The two sides engaged in battle once more near the town of Tewkesbury, and once again the Yorkist side emerged victorious, perhaps because some of their best commanders had either fled after the Battle of Barnet, among them John de Vere, Earl of Oxford and his friend William, Viscount Beaumont, or had fallen there, like Warwick and his brother John Neville.[557] It also cannot have helped that the Lancastrian side was far from united after the events before and during the Battle of Barnet. Indeed, this led to violence during the Battle of Tewkesbury, most notably when Edmund Beaufort, Duke of Somerset accused Lord Wenlock of cowardice and murdered him on the battlefield.[558]

This time the Yorkist victory was final, especially since Prince Edward died in the battle.[559] Just seventeen years old, he could have been a thorn in Edward IV's side for a long time had he managed to escape across the Channel, especially if he had sired heirs to carry on his claim. Such children would not only have had his Lancastrian claim but would also have been Warwick's grandchildren, and as such could have profited from his immense popularity. With Prince Edward's death, however, and his father in captivity, this was the end for Lancastrian hopes. Though some Lancastrians were still at large and some managed to flee to exile again, they lacked a figurehead to rally around. As a result, the Yorkist victory was to last – for now.

Profits of Siding with Edward IV

John and Elizabeth must have been happy to hear of Edward's victory. Though they had never significantly profited from Edward's kingship and did not suffer any losses during the Lancastrian readeption, upon Edward's victory they could at least be assured that all three of Elizabeth's brothers were alive and well. Moreover, the future of their children must have seemed safer with Edward on the throne than with any Lancastrian king in charge, no matter how well treated they were while still young.

It is also possible that John hoped that, after he and especially Elizabeth had shown support for Edward during the crisis and helped him regain his throne, Edward would treat them better than he had before the Lancastrian readeption. If so, they were to be disappointed.

While Edward apparently realised he owed them a debt, the reward he gave them was a poisoned chalice. At first, his efforts to deal with the immediate fall-out of the Lancastrian readeption must have seemed quite promising to John, for it seems that Edward granted guardianship of the imprisoned former queen, Margaret of Anjou, to his mother Alice.[560] Certainly, we know that by February 1472 the former queen was imprisoned in Wallingford Castle, of which John still held the constableship. This was an appointment that suggested Edward trusted them, and might have seemed a good omen for the future. It also took the responsibility of Margaret's care from Edward himself, and given that Margaret and Alice had at one time been close, it was in fact a rather uncommonly kind choice for all involved. Possibly, the grant of wardship of Margaret of Anjou was also intended to smooth Alice's feathers, for, as Edward was to acknowledge that year, she was still owed £1,000 promised by Edward's father Richard, Duke of York for Elizabeth's dowry.[561]

Whichever it was, his actions were unusually thoughtful and kind. The actions that followed were not, though it could be argued that they were necessary. Within less than a month of Edward regaining the throne, Henry VI was dead, almost certainly on Edward's orders, though the official cause of death was 'purest melancholy'.[562] With him and his son dead, there was no more obvious focal point for any surviving Lancastrians, and Edward could look to the details of rebuilding his government.

One such detail was looking after the several wardships of young noblemen who were not yet of age and had lost their fathers or guardians either to death or exile in the years 1470 and 1471. Among those wardships was that of the teenage Lord Lovell. Fourteen-year-old Francis, Baron Lovell, son and heir of John, Lord Lovell, his twin sister Joan and seven-year-old sister Frideswide had been in the household of Warwick's sister Alice and her husband Henry, Baron FitzHugh, who had supported Warwick and the Lancastrian readeption for the last two years. Young Lord Lovell had been Warwick's ward before that, and had lived in his household for several years. Warwick had technically held his wardship until his death, whereupon it fell back to the crown.

On 11 July 1471, Edward officially granted this wardship jointly to John and Elizabeth. The barony of Lovell was a rich one, but it was only a generous grant on the face of it, and Edward's announcement that it was given to them in 'special gratitude' might soon have rung rather hollow, if it did not seem downright mocking. As was usual, the grant of wardship included 'all lordships, manors, lands, rents, services and possessions with advowsons, knights' fees, franchises, liberties, warrens, courts leets and other commodities' that had once belonged to John, 8th Baron Lovell and would fall to Francis when he attained his majority, as well as 'the custody and marriage of Francis'. However, it explicitly did not 'extent to any possessions which may afterwards descend to the heir'.[563] Those possessions he still stood to inherit were those of his rich and elderly grandmother Alice, Baroness Deincourt. While this was an important stipulation, it did not mean that the wardship was worthless. However, there was another restriction: despite the fact the grant of wardship included the right to decide his marriage, young Francis was already married to Baron FitzHugh's youngest daughter.

Doubtlessly, this would have been a disappointment for John and Elizabeth as many of the Lovell lands lay in Oxfordshire, especially the ancestral home of the Lovell family, today known as Minster Lovell Hall. Connecting those possessions to their family through a marriage would have been seen as a desirable step for the Suffolks, but one they could not easily take despite holding the Lovell wardship. Moreover, it might have also disappointed them personally; as later events and their later actions show, they would have considered Francis, Lord Lovell, a good match for their oldest daughter, Elizabeth Jnr.

However, even with those restrictions, they might have considered the wardship a valuable asset had Edward not constantly helped himself to its lands to enrich himself, his family and supporters. As it stood, John and Elizabeth probably hardly profited from the wardship after expenses. Even so, it seems they took their responsibility as the teenage lord's guardians seriously. They took him and his sisters into their household, and apparently treated them as their own children rather than like a burden.

It seems John took a particular interest in them and their upbringing, and the Lovell children became close to him. Probably little Frideswide, just old enough to be out of the nursery, was educated by the same tutors employed for the Suffolks' own children. Maybe John Jnr and Elizabeth Jnr were happy to have someone almost their own age to play with, but most likely the arrival of the three Lovells did not affect their lives too much. They were used to having many siblings around them, and even if they did not accept little Frideswide as a foster sibling immediately, they must have done so over the years that were to come.

We do not know what the Suffolks did for the education of the fourteen-year-old baron now in their household or his twin sister. Six years older than John Jnr, it would not have been possible to simply educate them alongside the Suffolks' own children as they would have been far ahead of them. Perhaps most likely is that John and Elizabeth considered the twins as too old to even take formal lessons but encouraged their independent learning of subjects such as mathematics and literature;

they might have instructed them personally in such things as they still considered details worth learning. John, it appears, took young Francis under his wing, instructing him how to manage his lands. Possibly, as he did so, John Jnr was also taken along on some of the rides during which his father taught such skills, which would have given not only Francis but also John Jnr the chance to see such duties in action.

Of course, John Jnr was still only eight years old and probably did not have much in common with the older Francis, but maybe he saw him like an older brother. He would have been at just the right age for him to regard this older boy as interesting and to try and emulate him. However, even if he did not, and hardly saw anything of Francis in those early years, he and his new foster brother would come to share what appears to have been a close bond in the years to come. Francis also seems to have become close to John, apparently seeing a father figure in him despite their age difference of only fourteen years. Perhaps they shared similarities in character that made them respond well to each other, or perhaps Francis made a conscious effort to emulate John.[564] Certainly, he was to have a very similar lifestyle to John in his adult years until circumstances forced a change. John's work as the Lovells' guardian reflects very well on him, suggesting a loving and caring man.

We know less of Elizabeth's relationship with her new wards, but even if she did not form as close a bond with them as John did with Francis it can be assumed that they got along acceptably. Living at Ewelme with the family, the Lovells would naturally also have met Alice, but nothing is known of any relationship they might have built with her. Alice was still living with them and so cannot be forgotten as a part of the family dynamics. Five years of cohabitation had not soured the relationship between her and her son and daughter-in-law; indeed, we actually have good evidence of their relationship in 1471, for it was in that year that she made them a very generous gift:

> to my dere and welbeloved sone John duke of Suffolk and to my Lady Elizabeth his wife suster to our soveraigne lord Kyng Edward the fourthe alle me stuffe of plate of sylver of gilte and of golde. And all my beddys of clothe of gold and of solke and of arras and of tapiserye werke.
>
> And all my tapices of arras and of tapiserye. Excepte the plate and the olde beddes and olde tapices of silke and of tapiserye that dayly serven me.
>
> Which also after my decesse I yeve to my seide sone and my seide lady his wife. To have and to holde to my seide dere and welbeloved sone and to my seide lady his wife and to their chyldyr of their bodyes comyng alle the seide plate beddys and tapices with goddess bblessing and myn for ever.[565]

The language of this grant is completely conventional, but it would be interesting to know what inspired it. All we can say is that the reference to her grandchildren in the grant was not strictly necessary, so it can be assumed that Alice was proud of her grandchildren, six of whom were alive when the grant was made.

Curiously, it was around this time that Alice, rather than John, once more chose to act against the Paston family. Margaret Paston explicitly stated so in a letter written a day after John's twenty-ninth birthday: 'The Duchess of Suffolk and the Duke of Norfolk's council intend verily this term in the beginning to commence again the appell against me and you.'[566] Margaret had not hesitated to state when she considered John to be culpable, so in this case it seems as if he had nothing to do with it. This is important to any study of him as he has often been claimed to have been guilty of working against the Pastons in 1471.

This was not the case. While the quarrel was most definitely not forgotten, it seems as if John laid his focus on other issues first in the years that were to come. The first of these came when, in February 1472, Edward IV affirmed that he and his wife held the Lovell wardship. This apparently inspired them to fight for young Francis's rights and theirs, and they began suing those who held lands that came under Lovell's lordship. At least two such legal actions are recorded by documents still held in the National Archives, for lands and possessions in Staffordshire and Berkshire.[567]

Arguments with the King

Of course, this was not selfless. By holding those lands, the Suffolks themselves received more money from the wardship. However, it was also very helpful for Francis himself, as it meant less trouble for him getting lands that belonged to him by right once he attained his majority. Moreover, there is no evidence either John or Elizabeth ever tried exploiting Francis's possessions for their own gain. While it helped them as much as it helped Francis to sue for his possessions to be held by them, it seems they always tried doing what was best for their ward. This can especially be seen by what they did when Edward reacted to their lawsuits by taking more lands from the Lovell lordship to use for himself.[568] This was very clearly a punishment for John and Elizabeth, as he did not declare those lands forfeit or his own possession but simply that he would hold them until Francis came of age. That he punished his sister and brother-in-law for trying to help their orphaned ward reflects terribly on Edward, though it has rarely, if ever, been addressed.

Edward's actions made it clear to John and Elizabeth they were best off not trying to sue for lands in the Lovell wardship. If they did so, it could actively harm their finances even if it did help Francis in the future.

Despite this, they continued the legal actions.[569] Obviously they cared a lot about being good and fair guardians even to their own disadvantage. In the face of this, it is not surprising young Francis felt he could trust John and that they were to become close. Naturally, this would have also reflected on the whole family. Francis would have had cause to be fond of all of them, even John Jnr, who was of course not involved in any of it. Maybe it helped their friendship in later years, though there is no telling if it was so. Perhaps, as time went on, they simply came to like each other.

John and Elizabeth apparently never tried to annul the marriage between Francis and Anne FitzHugh. This would hardly have been unheard of; John himself was ten years old when his marriage to nine-year-old Margaret Beaufort was annulled, so he could have tried to have the marriage of his ward annulled as well. At that point, due to Francis and his wife Anne's extreme youth, their marriage had naturally not yet been consummated. John and Elizabeth could have tried to secure the alliance to Lord Lovell for their own little daughter, Elizabeth Jnr, only two years younger than Anne FitzHugh. Yet it seems they never tried.

All efforts they made for Francis, even at a disadvantage to themselves, they did only for the good of their young ward. Whatever flaws John had otherwise, he was clearly a very good father and guardian who selflessly acted in the best interests of his children and wards.

However, it was not only bad and frustrating news for John that year. At a meeting of the Order of the Garter in May that year, John was elected to be a member[570] – a great honour which must have pleased him. His mother had been a member for nearly thirty years by that time, and it might have pleased John that, at the age of nearly thirty, so was he. It must have been a happy event for him. While sadly we have no more details of the occasion of his election itself, we know it meant a lot to him as he eventually chose to be buried in his Garter mantle.[571]

This was still far in the future in 1472, and most of his time that year appears to have been spent at Ewelme with his family, taking care of all problems that arose. This included, in 1472, finding a suitable bridegroom and husband for the then sixteen-year-old Joan Lovell, Francis's twin sister.[572] There is an interesting oddity about the arrangements made for her: Francis apparently found it important that his sisters were at least sixteen years of age when they married. While this was completely normal and expected for consummation, it was not so for cohabitation. John and Elizabeth had been living in the same household together at a younger age than that, though they only established their own separate household when they were over sixteen. Perhaps John therefore understood his ward's decision, or else he did not but was happy to defer to him. This is not too significant in the case of Francis's twin sister, Joan, who after all turned sixteen only a little over a year after staying in the Suffolk household, but it had more implications for the younger of Francis's sisters, Frideswide, who was eight years younger than her brother. Following Francis's wishes in this case meant passing up a chance to arrange a marriage for the girl to the benefit of his own family, yet John chose to follow his wishes. This whole arrangement conjures the image of a good, loving family run by a couple who were good, loving guardians.

Joan Lovell's marriage was arranged, however, and the wedding was to go ahead after she turned sixteen, probably at the end of 1472 or the very beginning of 1473. John, possibly helped by Elizabeth, chose a groom from the Stapleton family for Joan. The de la Pole family had long since been connected to the Stapleton family. John's cousin Katherine had married the uncle of the man chosen to marry Joan.[573] It was a suitable match for both, and moreover one that must have seemed personally acceptable for both bride and groom. The groom was not titled but was the oldest son and heir of a rich member of the gentry. Called Brian, he was only four years older than Joan. The wedding might have been celebrated in Ewelme. Most likely, with Joan's brother still a minor, John would have acted in loco parentis at the wedding, walking the bride down the aisle, so to speak, to her new husband. Elizabeth might have acted in the stead of the bride's sadly deceased mother, if only by staying with Joan before the wedding and telling her what would be expected of her afterwards.

Joan naturally left the Suffolk household to live with her husband after she was married, which would have mostly affected her twin brother and younger sister. While she might have been on good terms with both her guardians and their children, she could not have had a lot to do with the latter and had not really stayed in the household long enough to really be very close to John and Elizabeth. John Jnr, however, at ten, might have watched the wedding with interest. Neither he nor any of his siblings were yet married or even promised to anyone, though perhaps by that time John and Elizabeth might have started thinking about it. It may well be that weddings were on their minds, because early 1473 saw the wedding of Elizabeth's youngest brother to Edward of Lancaster's widow Anne Neville, an event that John and Elizabeth, and quite possibly also John Jnr, would have attended.

However, there was a more immediate development for their family: at the same time that John was arranging a marriage for his ward, he and Elizabeth would have received good news of their own. Elizabeth was pregnant with another baby, their eighth. Their lives seem to have been very calm and uneventful at this time, and consequently little is recorded. We do know that John was made High Constable of the University of Oxford in 1472,[574] but what, if anything, he did in his first year in that capacity is not known; he appears to have spent most of his time at Ewelme with his family.

The Calm Years: 1473–1474

Elizabeth's pregnancy appears to have progressed without any problems, and in the spring of 1473 she once more went into confinement, soon afterwards giving birth to a healthy son she and John named Edmund after Elizabeth's brother who had been killed on the same day as her father. Edmund would eventually be his father's heir, and as a result it has often been assumed or even outright claimed as fact that he was his parents' second son.[575] However, this is not true. By the time he was born, Edmund had three older brothers: Edward, who was nearly three years older than him; one boy whose name we no longer know, born at the beginning of 1466 and therefore nearly seven years older than him; and, of course, John Jnr, something over ten years older than little Edmund. His future might have seemed uncertain at the time of his birth; perhaps he was originally destined for the Church, but this is sheerest speculation. Edmund would have been raised with his siblings closest in age in the nursery at Ewelme, though it is possible he would not grow up to know John Jnr and Elizabeth Jnr very well as they were significantly older than he was.

There is very little evidence of what John and his family did during the year of 1473. It seems they mostly stayed at Ewelme, John leaving only occasionally to take part in commissions of the peace in regions where he possessed property. It is possible that it was during this year that he truly started becoming close to his ward, Francis, Lord Lovell, after he returned from a visit to his mother-in-law and his young wife. This would make sense of what would happen in 1474, for it was then that Francis's uncle, William Lovell, Lord Morley, died[576] and was followed to the grave shortly afterwards by his wife Eleanor, Lady Morley.[577] They left two children: Alice, who was around John Jnr's age, and Henry Lovell, newly become Lord Morley, age around ten.[578]

It seems the king kept their wardship to himself, never appointing guardians for them. Francis might by then have become close enough to his guardians to mention his cousins' plight to them. Perhaps John and Elizabeth simply heard of it independently, their wards' relationship with them mere coincidence. Whichever it was, it seems the Suffolks took care of them. Perhaps they even had them brought to their household in Ewelme, but that does not seem likely. Theirs was already an expensive household, and with the king holding the Morleys' wardship, no compensation for their upbringing and education would have been forthcoming. However, it seems John saw to it they were always taken care of according to their status. Though not necessarily as helpful as taking them into his household, this at the very least provided them with a highborn and powerful protector. John did not do this solely out of the goodness of his heart; apparently, he and Elizabeth saw the deaths of

William and Eleanor Lovell as an opportunity for their oldest daughter. This might sound callous, but it was entirely normal. John bought the rights for Henry Lovell's marriage from Edward IV.[579]

Following this, as the first of their children, Elizabeth Jnr, then nearly thirteen years old, was married. Her groom, Henry Lovell, Lord Morley, was some three years her junior.[580] With her marriage, Elizabeth Jnr became Lady Morley. Doubtlessly, the marriage would have been a great event, celebrated in style by the Suffolks. It would be interesting to know if John Jnr, now almost twelve, was involved in the ceremony in some way, perhaps as his new brother-in-law's best man. His feelings can only be guessed at. Though he would have always known his sister would one day be married to someone his parents picked out, he might have been annoyed his own marriage did not take place first.

Even if he was jealous, 1474 seems to have been a very happy year for his parents. At some point during the summer, Elizabeth must have realised she was pregnant again. Perhaps John chose to stay with her during her pregnancy. We know nothing of his movements that year after the summer, or in early 1475, suggesting he did nothing worthy of note. Elizabeth went into confinement in the beginning of 1475 and shortly afterwards gave birth to another healthy boy, who received the somewhat baffling name Humphrey. Though quite a common name at the time, it is unclear why John and Elizabeth chose it for their fifth son. The most logical explanation is that the boy was named after either a saint in thanksgiving or a godfather. If the latter is the case, the godfather's identity is sadly no longer known.

8

Changes

The new year started off happily for John with the birth of his son, and at first it was to stay that way. John Jnr, by now twelve, was starting to be recognised by his uncle Edward IV as a future lord of importance. Though John himself showed no interest in national politics, he must have been proud of his son when, on 14 May 1475, John Jnr was made a Knight of the Bath in St Edward's Chamber at Westminster, as part of the ceremony that elevated his cousins, the king's sons Edward and Richard, to the same honour.[581]

As John Jnr was only twelve years old at the time, his parents or at least his father must have accompanied him to Westminster, though there is no mention made of them in any chronicle written about the event. It must have been a happy occasion, but if John enjoyed himself it was to be his last happy time for a while. Within days of John Jnr's elevation to a Knight of the Bath, probably within a day or two of him and his parents returning to Ewelme, tragedy struck. On 21 May 1475, Alice, then seventy or seventy-one, died.[582]

This was a reasonable age for the time, and she was no doubt regarded as an old lady. Indeed, it seems she did not die suddenly or unexpectedly. In March 1475, she sent an urgent letter to William Stonor, grandson of her late third husband:

> Right trusty and entirely beloved friend, we greet you well, desiring and praying you, all excuses laid apart, that in the moment [?] this letter seen you come to us to Ewelme, for certain great causes concerning our well and pleasure, which at your coming you shall understand more plainly, and thereupon you to depart even at your pleasure, so that you fail not herein at this time, as our perfect trust is in your, and as in greater case we will be glad for you, that knows our lord, who have you ever in governance. Written at Ewelme, the 5 day of March.[583]

We do not know what these 'great causes' were, but they might have had something to do with her will, or arrangements she was making for the event of her death, though we cannot be certain. We know she had time to write an apparently elaborate will before she died, though sadly we no longer have it in its entirety. We only have an excerpt, from a letter John wrote in 1476, quoting a part of it and stating that he 'promised her ladyship to be well willing and helping with all my power, and to be of such demeaning I ensured her upon my truth, and upon a book'.[584]

By this, John meant he swore on the Bible. That he did this before Alice's death also suggests that her death was expected and that she was preparing for it in the months before she died. It is also notable that John's statement suggests she was still lucid enough to understand such details, and perhaps even think of them herself and demand them from him shortly before her death. This means she did not suffer from dementia or any similar illness when she died.

She was unusually lucky in her end; not many lived to over seventy in the fifteenth century and then died peacefully in their beds. Maybe this was a consolation for John, as well as for Elizabeth and Alice's grandchildren. John had been very close to his mother in his thirty-three years of life. Doubtlessly, he was devastated by her death, no matter how expected it had been and how lucky she had been to even reach that age. Elizabeth, too, must have been sad; as we have seen, she was close to her mother-in-law. It also must have been a blow for John Jnr and his siblings. Though, then as now, the death of a grandparent was a fairly common if sad experience, they had been living uncommonly close with her for nearly ten years. Only John Jnr and Elizabeth Jnr might have remembered living in Wingfield Castle in the nursery for the first years of their lives, away from their grandmother, and even that is doubtful. Alice's death must have been a devastating blow for them all, as well as a drastic change to their lives.

Aftermath

Alice was buried not next to her husband in Hull but in Ewelme, at the same church in which her parents had been buried. She was laid to rest beneath a splendid effigy that had already been finished in the years before her death in preparation for the inevitable. Her tomb survives to this day in all its glory, one of the very few of its kind that does. It is a transit tomb, which means on top of it is an effigy representing the deceased in life, while beneath it, somewhat hidden, is a memento mori, a representation of the deceased in death and decay. The effigy of Alice in life is absolutely splendid and might actually reflect her true appearance. Certainly it shows a woman very similar in looks to the man represented by the effigy on John's tomb once it was finished two decades later.

If the effigy is accurate as to her looks, Alice was a pretty woman with a long, thin face and a mischievous smile. Alice's funeral must have been a grand affair, with many notables present. Sadly, however, this too is sheerest guesswork as no documentation about it survives. It is known, however, that John gave the church an intricately worked wooden covering for the font that year in honour of his mother. A replica of this still exists in the church today. There can be no doubt this covering was an expensive gift. Clearly, John was not hesitant to spend a lot of money to commemorate his mother, no matter how bad his finances actually were at that time.

His and Elizabeth's lives changed with Alice's death. In another sign that their household's relocation to Ewelme in 1466 had been because of Alice, they decided to remove their main household to Wingfield Castle after Alice's funeral, the same castle where they had lived from 1461 to 1465.[585] At around the same time they would have made this decision, Elizabeth fell pregnant again. Learning this might have been a consolation for John after the loss of his mother. However, he did not have much time to dwell on his loss, on the ways his life changed because of it or the happy news he was to become a father again. Shortly after Alice died, John found himself for once distracted by matters of state. Edward IV had launched an expedition to invade France and win back all the lands lost by Henry VI.[586]

Invasion of France Postponed

All nobles of age and able to gather men were expected to join Edward in France to start his invasion. He had been given funds for these plans by Parliament in 1472,[587] meaning John must have known of Edward's intention long before the invasion actually happened. He was presumably unhappy with the timing, but he did what was expected of him. Though he could not actively fight himself, he had to gather and equip men to fight, and be present on the train to France. Due to his straitened financial circumstances, he had been instructed to bring 300 archers and 40 men at arms, the same number as the Duke of Norfolk but significantly fewer than the other dukes of the realm.[588]

Once all those men needed for the invasion were mustered, the crowds boarded ships to France with most of the nobility of England. John was present, though John Jnr, despite being an earl, was not, presumably due to his young age. Though it was not unheard of for boys so young to be brought along on a military campaign to observe, in this case it would have been too dangerous; there would have been no way to remove John Jnr safely and securely from danger if a battle went awry. As the king's oldest nephew, John Jnr would have been a valuable hostage for the French. John, who had never shown much interest in fighting even when he had been physically able, was probably glad to know his son was safe with his wife as he went to France under his brother-in-law's command.

This was the first, and only, time after 1464 John was involved in any military action. This could be taken to mean that, in fact, it had only been his wish never to get involved in battle again after his sickness of 1464 that stopped him from fighting, not any lasting physical effects. However, even for the campaign in 1475, with him acting like all other nobles, there are some indications this was not so. First of all, as discussed above, there is his contemporaries' complete acceptance of his not getting involved in any battle after the Battle of Hexham. Other men who did not get involved in battles but had no physical explanation for it, such as Thomas, Baron Stanley, did not get away without any mention of it in sources. Moreover, even Edward, who was happy to punish John for invented digressions, did not seem to consider it a failure on his part that he did not fight for him in 1470/1. It is highly unlikely that John's inaction would have been placidly accepted by Edward and by all contemporary sources if it did not have a solid, unassailable explanation. Most significantly for the campaign of 1475, it does not seem like he was expected to fight in France either. His presence seems to have been expected so he could bring a number of men that would otherwise have been lost to the campaign, or just to show his support for Edward and not risk the French noticing his absence and perceiving disunity among the nobility.

As history records, the invasion petered out before it could start due to a number of factors. Most important were the Duke of Burgundy, Edward's brother-in-law, not turning up to support the English as he had promised,[589] and the French king, Louis XI, offering large bribes to many of the English nobles present.[590] It seems like John was paid little attention by both the French king and his brother-in-law while this happened. When Edward met with the Louis to discuss the terms of a peace treaty between them, which eventually included the betrothal of his oldest daughter Elizabeth and Louis's oldest son, he was accompanied by some of the most important nobles of his realm, identified by Philippe de Commynes as 'Clarence, Hastings, Northumberland, Bishop Rotterham and others'.[591] There are two conspicuous absences in this list: Edward's youngest brother, Richard, Duke of Gloucester, and his brother-in-law John.

Richard of Gloucester famously refused to be present as he disagreed with the peace treaty.[592] This did not escape Louis's notice, and he made an effort to win him over. Commynes stated that he was one of a small group who did not agree with the peace made between Edward and Louis, but 'very soon afterwards the before-mentioned Duke of Gloucester called on the King at Amiens and the King gave him some very fine presents such as plate and horses splendidly caparisoned'.[593] There was no such effort made to include John in the list of men who received 'pensions' from the French king for supporting the peace, which included most important men in the kingdom, nor to win him over like his brother-in-law Richard.

In fact, there is so little recorded about John in connection to this invasion that we do not even have a hint as to what his opinion on it was, if he was happy with the peace brokered by Edward or if he agreed with Richard. We do know, however, that despite being a duke and thus one of the most noble men of the realm, and the king's brother-in-law, and so theoretically one of the most important people present, John did not at all profit from the French king's generosity towards the English nobility. He received no pension, no present, and was not even mentioned by Commynes.[594] Whether this was because he was not considered dangerous, or because he agreed with Richard but was not considered worth winning over, we do not know. Clearly, however, John was not seen as in any way important, either as a fighter who had to be placated or as someone who could change Edward's mind. The only part of the peace treaty relevant for him was Louis's purchase of the custody of Margaret of Anjou, which meant she would no longer be in captivity in John's care once the party returned to England.[595]

Whatever he actually thought of Edward's action that summer, John might have wished that he had been given a 'pension', for some regular extra money coming in would certainly have helped him at that point, and he might have been deflated in addition to being grief-stricken over his mother's death when he returned to his wife and family after the failed invasion was over.

Winter

However, while it must have been a depressing summer and autumn for John, offering a rather painful realisation of his own lack of importance for the kingdom at large, John Jnr must have hoped for the opposite. Even while his parents prepared themselves to continue the life they had lived in rural Suffolk in the early years of their marriage, mostly unconcerned with national politics, John Jnr perhaps hoped that his knighting earlier that year meant he would soon become important at court.

However, if he hoped so, he was doomed to wait for it to happen. His parents showed no more interest in bringing him to court than they had in attending court themselves. Moreover, even had they wanted to do so, the events of 1475 most probably would have prevented them. What with Alice's death and their subsequent move back to Wingfield Castle, John and Elizabeth were busy re-establishing themselves in Suffolk again, carving out a position similar to that they had built in Oxfordshire in the last decade. They also had to deal with the fallout of Alice's death. She had been a rich and significant land owner, and John would have had to establish himself as her heir in all positions, making sure he received all of her inheritance that was his due. He would have had to make sure his mother's will was being followed in all other ways as well. This would have been time consuming as well as emotionally taxing.

Perhaps the prospect of soon becoming a father again would have cheered John and helped him through a doubtlessly difficult time, but at the beginning of 1476, before the anticipated time of birth of the newest addition to their family, he and his wife had to deal with another personal blow when Elizabeth's sister Anne died.[596] Anne had remarried in 1474 to a man of much lower standing than her first husband, the untitled Thomas St Leger, member of the gentry. In January 1476, Anne died in childbirth with their first child, a daughter the grieving father named after her.[597]

It appears to have been a love match between Anne and Thomas, and surely Elizabeth and John would have been sad to know Anne had died so shortly after finding happiness. The one bright spot in their grief would have been that Anne's daughter had survived the birth. As mentioned above, we do not know how close Elizabeth and Anne were, though there is some evidence of at least a cordial relationship.[598] Even if it was distant, however, it would have been sad for John and Elizabeth to learn of her death. Not only was Anne's death a personal blow, it also had financial consequences. Having been one of Anne's feoffees, John lost a source of income with her death.[599] It is easy to imagine that, with their always strained fiscal situation, and yet another baby on the way, this loss would have worried him and his wife. Perhaps, learning of her sister's cause of death, Elizabeth was also more worried about her own upcoming birth. Though the baby she was expecting was already her tenth, and she must have always known of the dangers of childbirth, it is hardly far-fetched to believe it would have been scary to have those dangers affect someone close to her.

In the event, such fears would have been well founded. Unlike her sister, Elizabeth survived her next childbirth, but only barely; though she would suffer from no lasting physical effects, her recovery took several months. But the daughter she bore did not live long. Called Dorothy, she appears to have died either during her birth or immediately afterwards. We only know that she lived long enough to be baptised, which must have been a consolation for her parents in their grief.

Why the name Dorothy was chosen for this unfortunate baby is unknown. It is possible she was born on the feast day of St Dorothy, which takes place on 6 February.[600] If so, the name may have been chosen to honour the day of her birth, or perhaps it was a sadly futile attempt to invoke heavenly help and protection for the child. However, this is by no means certain. Perhaps the child was born on some other day and named after the saint because she was favoured by her mother, father or both. Conversely, the baby might have received her name because of an emergency baptism; in such cases the baby often received the name of any godparent available at short notice, such as the midwife attending the birth or a lady-in-waiting of the labouring mother. Even that does not have to be the case, however. Perhaps little Dorothy simply received her name because her parents liked it.

Whichever it was, the name brought the child no luck, and the year was to continue on rather sad terms. The next recorded event involving the Suffolks was a funeral, namely the reinterment of John's father-in-law Richard, Duke of York and his son Edmund.[601]

9

The Political Development of John, Earl of Lincoln

It was a grand occasion, as much an occasion for Edward to show off his credentials and importance as it was a reinterment of Edward IV's father and brother. The festivities surrounding the event lasted for nine days, starting on 21 July 1476 with the exhumations of the bodies at Pontefract.[602] From there, Richard, Duke of Gloucester led the procession bearing the body to the south as chief mourner. When the procession arrived at Fotheringhay, where they were to be reinterred, it was met by several nobles to be escorted to the church in which the remains were to find their final resting place. John Jnr was among those nobles, as was his uncle George, Duke of Clarence, though John does not seem to have been.[603] Only on the next day did he arrive, together with the queen and her entourage, to take part in the funeral itself.

Interestingly, it seems as if Elizabeth was not present to see her father and brother reburied. She was not among the many ladies of high standing in attendance, which included not only the queen and her two oldest daughters but also Margaret Beaufort, to whom John had been briefly married as a child.[604] This might have been because she was still too weak to travel after the disastrous birth at the beginning of the year, but it is also possible that, like her mother, she simply chose not to be present for reasons unknown.

John does not seem to have actively participated in the funeral, though John Jnr did, laying three cloths of cloth of gold on the coffins of his grandfather and uncle.[605] Quite possibly, he was chosen for this high honour as the oldest grandchild and nephew of the deceased, while his father, despite being of higher standing than him, stayed in the background as he was not so closely related to either of the men being laid to rest.

The funeral was followed by a magnificent feast at Fotheringhay Castle, which almost all English nobility attended.[606] Almost certainly, John and John Jnr were present, though no contemporary source mentions their presence. This is not particularly notable in the case of John, but interesting in the case of his son considering his close relation to the deceased. However, it seems likely that his absence from the sources was not because of any sinister reasons but simply due to his relative youth.

Naturally, we do not know the thoughts of either father or son, but it is hard to believe it was as emotionally taxing for either of them as it was for the king and his younger brothers. John had good reason to dislike his father-in-law, at least, and while John Jnr did not, he had never met either his grandfather or his uncle and therefore cannot have mourned them personally. Most likely, he would have been somewhat sad as it was a sombre occasion, while at the same time excited to once more be prominently involved in a big event. John was probably less interested, and might have been glad when it was over and he could return home to his wife and younger children.

The Suffolk Lifestyle

Once back home, however, John had to deal with another unhappy situation. After five years of living with them, Francis, Lord Lovell, then nearly twenty years of age, left their household to move in with his wife.[607] It must have been a wrench for John and his children, and possibly also Elizabeth, to lose him and his younger sister to another household, after spending so long as their foster father and foster siblings respectively. Perhaps more importantly, however, Lord Lovell's move to his own household meant that while John still held his wardship for another year, he would not have had much access to any of the money. Though it had not been much to begin with, John would not have insisted on keeping the small amount he got from the wardship for himself. He had often shown he was a good guardian, and as such he would have done what was best for his ward.

However, this meant his financial situation was more difficult than ever in the autumn of 1476,[608] and it may have been because of this that once his wife had recovered from her catastrophic birth she went to court. Quite possibly, this was an attempt by her to get some preferential treatment for her family. All we know is that Elizabeth went to court that autumn. A letter from Elizabeth Stonor to her husband, John's nephew, written on 22 October attests to this. In it, Elizabeth Stonor speaks of Elizabeth's visit to court, but also states that she had been 'with my lady of Suffolk at this day hoping that I might have had her at some leisure that I might have spoken to her for the money'.[609] Sadly, the letter does not give any clarity as to whether this is money Elizabeth and John owed the Stonors or vice versa, but it clearly shows that money was an issue for the Suffolks, in one way or another, that October.

Elizabeth Stonor's letter offers more insight, though. It shines a rare light on Elizabeth's movements, her relationship to her family, and the way the Suffolk household was run. Elizabeth Stonor explained to her husband that she had 'been with my lady of Suffolk as on Thursday last was, and waited upon her to my lady the king's mother and hers, by her commandment. And also on Saturday last was I waited upon her there again, and also from then she waited upon my lady her mother, and brought her to Greenwich to the king's good grace and the queen's, and there I saw the meeting between the king and my lady his mother. And truly I thought it was a very good sight.'[610] This suggests that it was considered something of a rarity for either of the women to be at court, and that it was Elizabeth making her mother go there. That Elizabeth Stonor explicitly considered it a 'very good sight' to see mother and son meeting could mean that there were tensions between them that Elizabeth may have wanted to see buried. She wanted peace in her family. Elizabeth was obviously someone who liked being on good terms with everyone, no matter how much she disagreed with them privately.

However, even so, she does not seem to have had much interest in staying long at court, for Elizabeth Stonor goes on to report that her aunt by marriage was 'very busy to make her[self] ready, for she is riding to Canterbury at this same day [of writing]'.[611] Again, no clarification is added for this, or any hint as to why Elizabeth wanted to go to Canterbury. She obviously did not intend to stay there for very long, having told Elizabeth Stonor that she would 'be here again as on Saturday next coming'.[612] Given that she rode from London, where she could have made any purchases she wished, it seems likely that she went to Canterbury for the one attraction it had that London could not offer: the tomb of St Thomas Becket, a very popular saint. As to why Elizabeth wished to see the tomb, if she wanted to pray for his support in something in particular or just wanted to pray, we do not know. However, it is very interesting to note she chose to make the journey very hastily, and without her husband, despite evidence suggesting he was in London with her at the time.

Interestingly, Elizabeth Stonor went on to state that 'my lady of Suffolk is half displeased because that my sister Barantyne is no better arrayed, and likewise my sister Elizabeth. And she says without they be otherwise arrayed, she says, she may not keep them, and she says that my mother and yours should say that you have enough to find my sister Elizabeth with all.'[613] Especially in the light of the money trouble implied in the letter, this is a very interesting insight into the Suffolk household and how it was run. Obviously, the inventory from 1466 gives the right impression. The Suffolks held their household, their personnel and certainly also their children to a high standard and insisted on finery. At the same time, that Elizabeth is claimed to be only 'half displeased' suggests that she was not a strict and unreasonable person, and bolsters the impression of her as a peacemaker at heart, trying to stay on good terms with everyone. It seems that she and John had by then perfected their 'good cop-bad cop' system whereby she tried to reach their mutual goals through gentle means while he, if necessary, was prepared to be less than gentle.

In autumn 1476, however, it does not seem like this is why John did not accompany Elizabeth to court, if indeed she had gone to court to work towards getting preferential treatment. Rather, he does not seem to have gone to court despite being in London because he was rather busy himself, trying to make arrangements for the lands and possessions he had inherited from his mother.

It might be considered rather strange that he did not do so before this time, but this was presumably due to the late date on which he received the writ to enter all possessions she had held 'in dower or otherwise'.[614] Despite Alice having died on 21 May 1475, this writ was only issued to John on 15 August 1476, and it stands to reason his efforts to make arrangements to suit him started only afterwards. We know he was still busy with this in November 1476, for on the 16th of that month he made a deed which he had enrolled at the chancery court:

> To all the men this writing shall come John, Duke of Suffolk, greeting in our Lord. Forasmuch, as the honourable, and my most dread Lady and Mother, Alice, late Duchess of Suffolk, whom God assoil, in her testament amongst other declarations of her last will, did do write one article, under the words that followen: 'Item, I will that mine executors, immediately after my decease, take wholly the issues, revenues, and profits, coming and growing of my manor of Norton-under-Hampden, in the county of Somerset, with the appurtenances, which for the sum of 200 pounds sterling, I purchased of Dame Katherine, the wife late of Sir Miles Stapleton, Knight, now the wife of Sir Richard Harecourt, Knight; of my manor of Cotton Henmales, in the county of Suffolk; of my manors of Newenham Courtney, Swereford, in the county of Oxenford; of my manors of West Wythenham, Buryfeld, Langeley, Bradley, with all the lands and tenements in South Moreton, in the county of Berkshire; of my manors of Hatfield Peverell and Termyns, in the county of Essex, with all and every their appurtenances; and of all other lordships, manors, rents, lands, and tenements, with the appurtenances, which I have at any time purchased, seth the decease of my said worshipful Lord and husband, William, Duke of Suffolk, whom God assoil; paying therewith first my debts, and then all my bequests above specified, that is to say, such of the bequests as I perform not in my life; and thereupon I specially pray, require, and on God's behalf, charge my feoffees of the said manors, lands, and tenements, with the appurtenances, that they peaceably suffer my

executors to take up, and receive all the profits, issues, and revenues, coming and growing, after my decease, of all the said manors, lands, and tenements, with all their appurtenances, in my will afore specified and recited, to the full accomplishment and performing of this my present will and testament, as they will answer afore God at the dreadful day of doom, for to the intent of fulfilling of this present testament and last will I have enfeoffed them, and none otherwise: nevertheless, I will, that all such of my servants as depart from me during my life, have no part of the bequests to them above made.

To the performing of which article, alsowell as of the remnant of her last will, I, the said Duke, promised her Ladyship to be well willing and helping with all my power, and never to let or suffer, nor make to be let any thing thereof, after my power, and to be of such demeaning, I ensured her upon my truth, and upon a book. And now eftesones, I have assured, and promised the same before the King, and before my Lord Cardinal, Archbishop of Canterbury, upon my faith and truth. And, for to encourage and, make the persons which my said Lady hath named to be her executors for to be the more bold, and of the better will to take upon them the administration of her goods, and performing of her last will, I now, by this my deed, bind me in 2000 pounds, to be paid, in case that her executors, which shall take upon them the administration of her goods, be lett, or disturbed by me, or my commandment, for to take, levy, or receive, any party of the revenues of the livelihood especified in the foresaid article, or to administer freely any party thereof, according to my said Lady's last will, declared in the same article. In witness whereof to this writing, I have set my seal, and signed it with mine own hand, the 26th day of November, the 16th year of my Sovereign Lord King Edward the Fourth. And, for the more surety hereof, I will, tha t this my deed be enrolled in the King's Court of his Chancery, and also registered in the Court of my Lord Cardinal, Archbishop of Canterbury. And over this, I require all the feoffees of the foresaid manors, lands, and tenements, that they pay, and peaceably suffer to be paid to the said executors, all the revenues growing of the same, according to my said Lady's will, as they will eschew mine indignation and uttermost displeasure.[615]

This deed was duly enrolled with the note, 'Be it remembered, that the aforesaid Duke came into the Chancery of the King ' at Westminster on the 3rd day of December in the present year, and recognised the writing aforesaid, and all the contents of it, in the form aforesaid.'[616]

Sadly, this is the only part of Alice's will that has survived in any form. Her inquisitions post-mortem and her dealings with feoffees in life gives an idea of how rich she was,[617] so we know that John would have inherited a sizeable number of manors and lands, and therefore also a sizeable annual income. However, sadly we have no idea how much of it she left directly to John and how many of her lands she left enfeoffed. Nor do we know what personal items she left to him or her grandchildren.

While this is something that can no longer be found out (unless a copy of her entire will is found), John's deed certainly shows up an oddity concerning her last will: he had sworn 'upon my truth, and upon a book' that he would 'be well willing and helping with all my power, and never to let or suffer, nor make to be let any thing thereof, after my power, and to be of such demeaning'.[618] This rather sounds as if there had been strife between mother and son before Alice's death, making Alice doubt that John would fulfil the terms of her will if he was not compelled in this way.

This is possible, but there is no other evidence for it. John spoke of his mother with obvious affection in this letter, and though it could be argued this was standard language, not actually indicative of anyone's feelings, there is other evidence that John's relationship with his mother was good, and in fact uncommonly close, all his life until her death. More likely is that by necessitating this step Alice and John circumvented any claim of John falsifying her wishes to suit himself and his own benefit, and prevented anyone who might feel disadvantaged by her will from claiming it was done by John for ulterior motives. By entering a bond of the massive sum of £2,000, he clearly showed that it would disadvantage him to go against his mother's wishes, and it gave the feoffees a chance to air any grievances. John was, therefore, as secure as he could be in his actions regarding his mother's will.

Family Troubles

John might have been happy about the smooth transaction of entering this deed, and somewhat hopeful about entering into his mother's inheritance, but any happy mood was not to last. At the end of the year, another blow for him and his family was to fall. Another family member, namely the wife of Elizabeth's brother George, Duke of Clarence, died; she was soon followed by her and George's infant son, Richard.[619] This would have been sad news for the Suffolk family, even if they apparently had not known the Duchess of Clarence well. They must still have been sorry for her and also for her grieving widower and now half-orphaned children. Elizabeth's brother, George, did not take the death of his wife well, which would have been concerning for her and for John. His behaviour was becoming increasingly erratic.[620]

When Elizabeth and John's brother-in-law, Charles, Duke of Burgundy, died on 5 January 1477,[621] his daughter Marie became Duchess of Burgundy. This meant she needed a husband, and George apparently suggested marrying her himself.[622] Supposedly, his sister Margaret, Marie's stepmother, supported her brother in this, and perhaps Elizabeth herself agreed. History books often present George marrying Marie as a stupid idea, supported by no one but the smitten older sister Margaret, but if Margaret ever supported the idea of such a match, she would have been extremely unlikely to do so simply from fond feelings for her brother. Margaret was a shrewd politician,[623] perhaps more so than anyone else in her family, though neither Elizabeth nor Anne ever had a chance to show their mettle as politicians. As it stands, Margaret would not have acted simply out of personal feelings, and if she actually did support George's suit for Marie, she would have done so knowing George could offer her stepdaughter and the duchy of Burgundy something valuable. That might even have been thought to be the crown of England; through her paternal grandmother, Marie had inherited a Lancastrian claim to the English throne.[624] Together with George's Yorkist claim, they might have been a danger to Edward, and it is most likely because of this that Edward refused to even countenance such a match at the time.

Naturally, George was naturally not the only one to make a bid for Marie's hand. Marie was a great prospect, duchess in her own right of the richest dukedom in Europe. Of course, hers was not an easy position despite this and any prospective husband of hers would know that it would come with complications. There is no reason to assume George was unaware of this, though it is often claimed he was not. Edward, too, must have been aware of the advantages and disadvantages any future husband of Marie's would have, and he offered his own candidate for Marie's hand: his brother-in-law Anthony Woodville, Lord Rivers.[625] However, Anthony was objectively a far worse candidate than George. He did not have royal blood to speak of, nor would he really bring any useful connections to Marie and Burgundy. If George, Duke of Clarence, was an unsuitable candidate to marry the Duchess of Burgundy, Anthony Woodville, Lord Rivers, was an even more unsuitable one, though in both cases, it could be argued the men only wanted to marry Marie for their own benefit. Even so, George had more to offer than Edward's candidate at least, and it seems that for once, Edward did not judge him.

The problem does not seem to have been that George wanted to marry Marie of Burgundy in itself but, as alluded to above, what such a marriage would entail.[626] As Marie of Burgundy's husband and Duke of Burgundy in his wife's right, George would have had access to a lot of power and to untold riches, and that, in addition with Marie's Lancastrian claim, caused rumours to float around. These were either stoked by the King of France to sow division in England, or simply picked up by him and passed on to Edward, particularly the one that George meant to use his new-found riches and power to make himself King of England.[627] Whether or not this rumour was true, it spread, and John and Elizabeth must have heard it too. Given how they had reacted eight years earlier, when George had first gone against Edward, it can be assumed they were against any such plans he might have had. However, by 1477 the situation in the kingdom had changed a bit, and perhaps they too had slowly turned against Edward, as many were starting to do, though they were not ready to personally act against him. Perhaps John and Elizabeth considered the rumours to be false, and therefore did not spend any time worrying how to react to such plans. At worst, the rumours would have been very alarming for the Suffolks, but worse was to come.

As the year went on, George's unpredictability intensified.[628] His intention to marry Marie of Burgundy might have seemed unwise to Edward, but it was understandable; his actions later that year were less so. He began claiming that his wife and baby son had been poisoned,[629] and, without the king's permission, he staged a trial for those he held to be responsible for the alleged crime and condemned them to death for it.[630] It has historically been agreed upon that the Duchess of Clarence and her infant son died of natural causes, and the idea they had been poisoned came from the imagination of an increasingly unhinged widower[631] or a calculating man who was planning a grab for power.[632] The latter theory assumes that these executions were George's way of showing to his brother that he considered himself king and did not need his permission to hold trials, and hence what he did was at best self-justice and at worst murder.

We cannot know what John and Elizabeth's opinions on all this were, but we cannot be certain they necessarily disagreed with George, at least with his claims if not with his methods. John Jnr, who was to turn fifteen in 1477, probably also had an opinion on the situation, as he was by then definitely old enough to understand and make deductions from what he was told. As none of them ever acted against Edward, it might be assumed they disagreed with George. However, John and Elizabeth had shown before that whatever their opinion on the events in the centre of the government they preferred to keep their heads down, and John Jnr would go on to show that he was extremely good at disassembling, so their inaction cannot really be used to make any deductions about their feelings.

However, there is no evidence anyone in the Suffolk family was ever close to George, so it is more likely they sided with Edward, and while not wishing George ill, they wanted him to return to Edward's fold once more. But that was not to be. The situation between Edward and George rapidly escalated. Edward, presumably as a warning to George after his unlawful execution of two people for the murder of his wife and son, had three of George's associates tortured and executed.[633] This has usually been portrayed as a reasonable act by Edward in the centuries since,[634] but it was rather brutal and, in any case, was hardly likely to defuse the situation between him and his brother. Perhaps it was even calculated to make George overplay his hand and act in such a way Edward would look reasonable whatever he chose to do against his brother. Certainly, Edward's youngest brother Richard appeared to think so, and would consider Edward's eventual, final, decision unlawful.

This does not have to mean he agreed with George and his actions, and even if he did this does not mean that John, Elizabeth or John Jnr did. As it was, perhaps their focus, or at least the focus of John and Elizabeth, was elsewhere and they simply hoped for the best and did not get involved. Perhaps they considered it more prudent not to do so, or, in the face of their own troubles in recent years, they were not ready for the concern of becoming involved in the controversy surrounding their brother and brother-in-law. In the span of two years, John had lost his mother, two sisters-in-law and a baby shortly after birth; it is hardly surprising neither he nor his wife seemed to show much of an interest in what was going on between Edward IV and his brother George. It might have simply seemed too much for them.

If so, they were among the only nobles who did not show much of an interest in that particular conflict. The whole kingdom appeared transfixed by it, and no one but the two brothers got in any way involved. There was no obvious, open picking of any sides, though all of them must have had an opinion. It was hard to avoid doing so, for both George and Edward aggressively carried out their conflict in front of everyone.[635] It would have been hard for them not to have everyone interested in it, but both their actions appeared calculated to draw as much attention as possible.

After Edward had three of his men tortured and killed, George reacted by openly interrupting a meeting of the royal council to protest Edward's actions and read out a plea of their innocence.[636] This was seen at the time as extremely foolish at the very least, and it has been perceived similarly in the centuries since.[637] Certainly, it did nothing to defuse the situation, any more than Edward's torture and execution of the three men had done, though it seems doubtful anything could have calmed the situation at that time, and quite possibly neither of the brothers wanted things to settle down anyway.

Some saw George's behaviour as calculated disrespect, and some historians share this opinion to this day.[638] Others, at the time as well as today, have expressed the opinion that George became mentally unstable after the death of his wife. We do not know which, if either, of these interpretations is true, though his family, apart from Edward, seemed to believe the latter theory.[639] This may be because they knew him best, and therefore could judge his behaviour well, though it might equally have been wishful thinking, a preferable theory to their son and brother wishing to unseat and presumably kill their other son and brother.

Whatever exactly was going on, there is evidence George was frightened of Edward, and not just for his own life. Apparently he attempted to have his son smuggled out of England to his birthplace, Ireland,[640] and it has been assumed that George was particularly popular there and therefore trusted the Irish lords to keep his son safe. While this may or may not be true, Edward, and especially his wife Queen Elizabeth, were not popular in Ireland, apparently having been involved in the death of Thomas FitzGerald, Earl of Desmond.[641] Perhaps this, more than any personal popularity, made George choose Ireland as a refuge for his son. However, it was not to be. George's attempt to smuggle out his son was a failure, and the three-year-old Edward remained in England, though in modern times this has been questioned.[642] There is a theory that little Edward was substituted with a lowborn boy, and that this decoy was intercepted and brought back to England while George's real son arrived safely in Ireland.[643] However, that seems more than a little unlikely, as will be detailed later.[644] In any case, Edward grew tired of his brother's behaviour and had him arrested in July 1477.

Though there was a short hearing, there was no date given for a trial, and apparently it was widely assumed that George never would sit trial.[645] John and John Jnr may very well have believed the same, though perhaps they were more jaded. As Edward's brother-in-law and nephew, they knew Edward better than most others, and especially John had often encountered his rather cruel side. Perhaps, they were among the very few who suspected that George would die on Edward's orders, sooner or later.

Something else rather interesting happened in the autumn of 1477, at least for John: his long-term enemy John Paston, son of the father with the same name who died in May 1466, made a will. There is nothing very unusual or interesting in that by itself, but it is highly significant that, after all these years of enmity, sometimes escalating into violence, John Paston mentioned John in his will: 'To the extent that I have disclosed but onto few persons concerning the few farm that is paid t[...]o the Duke of Suffolk...'[646] Sadly, the will is badly damaged and no more of the sentence concerning John can be read, but it is curious Paston included something about payments to John that he had rarely told anyone in life. It seems extremely unlikely it was something unflattering to John or damaging to his claim, as without a doubt John Paston would have had that widely publicised. Perhaps, when Paston died shortly afterwards, John heard of his inclusion, but it is doubtful this would have meant anything to him unless it came with some sort of concession from the Paston family, which it did not. However, John Paston's death would cause more trouble for John and for his family in the year to come.

The family church of St Mary the Virgin in Ewelme, where family members including Alice Chaucer, her parents and almost certainly one of John's daughters are buried. The almshouses, which were endowed by John's parents, can be seen on the right.(Courtesy of Poliphilo under Creative Commons)

The gatehouse of Wingfield Castle, ancestral home of the Suffolks. John Jnr as well as several of his siblings were born there, and the family lived in the manor from 1461 to 1466 and from 1475 to John's death in 1492.

A.D. 1478, 20 May.

J. Whetley to Sir John Paston.

[From Paston MSS. B.M.]

To the ryght worsh[yp]full Sir John Paston, Knyght, loged at the sygne off the George at Powlys Wharff, in London, be thys delyvered in hast.

LEAS it your meastershep to understond the dealyng of every thyng, the wych I was charged with at my departyng frome your measterchep.

Fyrst, your suppena to Denton was delyvered by me on Trenite Sondaye, in hys parych cherch, at Matens tyme, be ffor the substans of the parych; and as for Drayton wod, it is not all down yet, but it drawes fast toward. I have the names of all the mynestres off and in that wod, and more schall know or I come, yf ther be any more dealyng, &c.

And as for Haylysdon, my Lord of Suffolk was ther on Wedensday in Whytson Weke, and ther dined, and drew a stew and toke gret plente of fych; yet hath he left you a pyke or ij., agayn ye come, the wych wold be gret comford to all your frendes, and dyscomford to your enmys; for at hys beyng ther that daye ther was never no man that playd Herrod in Corpus Crysty [1] play better and more agreable to hys pageaunt then he dud. But ye schall understond that it was after none, and the weder hot, and he so feble for sekenes that hys legges wold not bere hyme, but ther was ij. men had gret payn to kepe hym on hys fete; and ther ye were juged. Som sayd "Sley;" some sayd "Put hym in preson." And forth com my lord, and he wold met you with a spere, and have none other mendes for the troble at ye have put hym to but your hart blod, and that will he gayt with hys owen handes; for and ye have Haylesdon and Dreton, ye schall have hys lyff with it. And so he comford your enmys with that word that thay have dealed and dealeth with the wod, and most pryncepall nowe is Nycolesse Ovye. For as for Ferrer,[2] the Meare, he delys not with owt it be under covert; for it is sayd that he be soght my lord that he myght have other sygnementes for hys money that he had payd, for playnly he wold deall no mor with the wod. And so my lord hath set in the Bayly of Cossay, and all is doon in hys name; and as for hys servauntes, thay dayly thret my measter your brother and me to slay for comyng of ther lordes ground, and thay say that we made an entre; and thay beth answerd as ye comaunded me, for many a gret chalaunge make thay to Mester John, both Measter Wodhowse, Wysman, with other dyveres that I know not ther names; but he holdeth hys own that thay gayt no grownd of hym. And thys he lettes thaym knowe that if thay bete hym or any of hys, thay schall aby vj. for on, and so thay deall not but with ther tonges; and as yet, syth Ferrer was at

The 1479 Paston Letter in which John Whetley describes John, 2nd Duke of Suffolk, making death threats towards John Paston while suffering from food poisoning after eating fish John Paston had stored in the manor of Hellesdon. This was only one of many clashes between John and his rivals in the Paston family, if a particularly notable one.

Richard, Duke of York, John's father-in-law. Richard was considered a likely candidate to have ordered the murder of John's father William de la Pole, 1st Duke of Suffolk, and it seems as if John believed this to be true. Despite supporting Richard's son Edward in his bid to become king, he never supported Richard. (Courtesy of the British Library)

Cecily Neville, wife of Richard, Duke of York, mother of Elizabeth, Duchess of Suffolk and her siblings, mother-in-law of John, 2nd Duke of Suffolk and John Jnr's grandmother.

Edward IV, brother-in-law and uncle respectively of John and John Jnr. While Edward kept John and Elizabeth at arm's length, he was supportive of John Jnr.

Elizabeth Woodville, whom Edward IV married in secret. The Suffolk family was among the few nobles who were neutral on this controversial queen and neither supported nor opposed her and her family, despite some slights done to them.

Margaret of York, wife and later widow of Charles, Duke of Burgundy. She was the sister-in-law and aunt respectively of John and John Jnr. While about her relationship, if any, to John nothing is known, she and John Jnr organised the 1487 rebellion against Henry VII together.

Charles 'the Bold', Duke of Burgundy, brother-in-law to John's wife Elizabeth, and uncle by marriage to John Jnr. John and Elizabeth were guests of honour at his marriage to Margaret, Elizabeth's younger sister. (Courtesy of the Gemaldgalerie)

The Old Gaol in Hexham, which already existed in 1464. John might have seen this building, as he participated in the Battle of Hexham in that year. This involvement was the last battle he ever fought, most likely because he was critically injured during it.

The Tower of London, where John Jnr's most famous cousins, the so-called 'Princes in the Tower', are last known to have stayed. According to many theories, they were murdered there by their and John Jnr's uncle, Richard III, shortly after his accession to the throne. Both John and John Jnr, and even Elizabeth, appeared unbothered by such theories. (Courtesy of Charlie Marshall under Creative Commons)

Richard III, who showed John Jnr much favour. After the death of Richard's only legitimate son, John Jnr was his heir presumptive. (Courtesy of the Rijksmuseum)

Above left: An early sketch of Sandal Castle in Wakefield, West Yorkshire. Alongside Sheriff Hutton, a headquarter of the Council of the North, of which John Jnr was president from 1484 until Richard's death in 1485.

Left: The ruins of Sandal Castle today. John Jnr had Sandal Castle furnished with a new bakehouse and a brewhouse to his specifications when he and his brother-in-law Henry Lovell, Lord Morley, resided there to run the Council of the North. (Courtesy of Tim Green under Creative Commons)

Sheriff Hutton Castle in North Yorkshire, the second headquarters of the Council of the North. (Courtesy of Bulphan under Creative Commons)

Above: Bosworth, site of the famous battle where Richard III was deposed by Henry Tudor. After his death, Henry took the throne as Henry VII though by law, Richard's death made John Jnr king.

Right: Richard III's usurper, Henry VII. John Jnr was one of the very few people Henry trusted completely, giving him important tasks and honours. John Jnr acted the part of his friend while plotting against him for nearly two years before openly declaring against Henry.

This page: The site of the Battle of Stoke Field in 1487, where John (Jnr), Earl of Lincoln was killed on 16 June 1487, in rebellion against Henry VII. John Jnr was one of the instigators of this rebellion. In whose name it happened is still debated, with the traditional story being that it was done in the name of Edward, Earl of Warwick.

The tomb effigies of John's grandparents Michael de la Pole, 2nd Earl of Suffolk and Katherine de Stafford at St Andrew's Church in Wingfield. Michael died of dysentery during the Siege of Harfleur in 1415. The death of his oldest son, Michael Jnr, shortly afterwards during the Battle of Agincourt saw John's father William inherit the family title. (Courtesy of Eebahgum under Creative Commons)

The tomb effigy of Alice Chaucer, mother and grandmother respectively of John and John Jnr. Alice was very close to her son's family and they lived in her household from 1466 until her death in 1475. (Courtesy of Simon Cope under Creative Commons)

Above and below: The almshouses at Ewelme, built by John's parents Alice and William, then Earl and Countess of Suffolk. At the end of 1486, John Jnr took out a loan of £20 from there to help his brewing rebellion. (Courtesy of John Salmon under Creative Commons)

Right: The font at the church of St Mary the Virgin, Ewelme. It is a reproduction of one given to the church by John in 1475, in the memory of his mother Alice after her death.

Below: The Chapel of St John within the church of St Mary the Virgin, Ewelme. Alice's tomb can be seen on the left. Her parents, John's grandparents Thomas and Maud Chaucer, are also buried in this church.

St Andrew's Church in Wingfield, in which several de la Pole family graves are to be found. (Courtesy of Brokentaco under Creative Commons)

The tomb effigies of John, 2nd Duke of Suffolk and his wife Elizabeth at St Andrew's Church. Despite not being an ardent fighter, and an injury preventing him from taking part in warfare after 1464, John's effigies shows him in armour. His wife Elizabeth is shown in her widow's weeds. (Courtesy of Deben Dave under Creative Commons)

1478

The year 1478 actually started with a happy event in which John Jnr was to take a significant part: the wedding of the king's second son, Richard of Shrewsbury, who was then four years old, to the five-year-old Duchess of Norfolk, Anne Mowbray. The event took place on 15 January,[647] with a lot of splendour that even at the time seemed rather incongruous to many, with Edward's brother still in the Tower, ostensibly awaiting execution. It might be that these circumstances actually explain the sumptuousness of the wedding; it was put on as a counter event, a distraction from the bad news that had reflected rather badly on him.

Interestingly, the king decided to include John Jnr prominently in the proceedings, alongside his favoured Woodville in-laws and his youngest brother, Richard of Gloucester. John Jnr's inclusion in it is as telling as his parents' exclusion and absence from it. Quite obviously, when including his family, Edward saw no reason to include his sister Elizabeth and her husband, who were, after all, the youthful groom's aunt and uncle. As we know from eyewitness evidence that some of their servants were present, it stands to reason that so were they, though apparently they made no lasting impression on anyone there, and were not at all involved in any of the proceedings.

They might, however, have been proud of their son's inclusion in the events. '[M]y lord the noble Count of Lincoln' led the little bride into St Stephen's Chapel in Westminster Palace, holding her left hand, while the groom's maternal uncle Anthony Woodville, Lord Rivers, held her right hand.[648] Given how much Edward favoured his Woodville relations, and how much he disadvantaged John Jnr's parents, his inclusion in the ceremony in what was obviously a position of honour is rather startling. No chronicler found anything wrong with the way John Jnr performed his duties then, and Edward appeared pleased with him as well.

After the wedding ceremony, a great feast took place in Westminster Palace, where 'appurtances to matrimonial feasts' were served.[649] It may have been during these festivities that John Paston the younger, the same one who had made his will in autumn 1477, spoke with some of John's servants in such a way that made him decide to write to his brother. This he did six days after Richard of Shrewsbury and Anne Mowbray's wedding, stating that he had 'comment with divers folks of the Duke of Suffolk now this Christmas and since then, which let me in secret wise have knowledge, like as I write onto you, that he must make a shift for money, and that in all haste. Wherefore, sir, at the reverence of God, let it not be lacksaid [?], but with effect applied now while he is in London, and my lady his wife also, for I ascertain you that 100 mark will do more now in their need than you shall paradventure [?] do with two hundred marks in time coming and this season not be taken.'[650]

Sadly, Paston does not add why John was in such need of money so suddenly. However, he added a very interesting stipulation for his brother that is rather telling about John: 'And always find the mean that my lady of Suffolk and Sir R. Chamberlain may be your guide in this matter, for as for my lord he needed not to be moved with it til it should be as good as ready to the sealing.'[651] This is a rare insight into the sort of money trouble John occasionally faced, which was so bad in the winter of 1477 that he was apparently not only ready to sell valuables, in this case a ring, but to sell them beneath their worth.

Obviously, John Paston did not expect the Suffolks' trouble to last indefinitely, which opens the question why they needed money so urgently at that time and could not wait it out. They were constantly in debt but they were hardly the only nobles in this situation, and it is unlikely an merchants would have denied them something they needed, even if they had no money to give at the moment of purchase. Two possibilities arise: either they needed to purchase something at that moment, or they had promised to pay something back at the time and knew they would not get the money from Alice's inheritance quickly enough to pay. The former is somewhat more likely, possibly in connection with the latter, though not definitely so, as if there had been no pressure they would not have gone to such extremes. This, of course, means that they needed something so urgently they were forced to sell valuables to get it, and from someone who was not ready to give it to them on credit.

Even such things as services by a physician, whose attentions could obviously not be postponed, would most likely have been available to a royal duchess and duke on credit. So it cannot have been that one of their children was sick that put them in this dire situation. Nor was it that Edward demanded money from them. While this would have put them in a situation of having to get the money immediately, evidence rather points to the contrary; Edward actually saw to it that some of their debts were paid with his own funds that summer.[652] Perhaps this means that he was owing them an amount that they urgently needed for something else, but that very thing remains lost to history, a puzzle that can no longer be solved.

It is interesting that this letter, too, very much supports the idea of Elizabeth being the one less stubborn and more amenable to reason than her husband, and treats it as fact that John was willing to listen to his wife even when she made a decision he was expected to dispute. John Paston clearly seemed to think that she was one of the few who could reason with him and change his mind. Even the Pastons, then, who were hostile to John, considered him putty in his wife's hands, ready to accept her actions even if they went against his wishes. The letter clearly assumes, from previous knowledge, that John gave Elizabeth complete control over their finances and did not want to restrict her in any way or, as was more common, provide her with her own income. Theirs was obviously an equal partnership.

What Elizabeth decided on, in this case, if she had the nerve to demand more money for their ring or agreed with the unfavourable terms suggested to the Pastons, we sadly do not know. However, there is an indication that the Suffolks' jewel was sold not to the Pastons but instead pledged to Edward IV.[653] It is naturally possible that these were two different jewels, but perhaps somewhat far-fetched. We do not know whether they got enough money to cover their need at that time through their pledging this jewel to Edward, but it does seem likely, as there is no further indication of financial need in any source.

Any negotiations Elizabeth made with the Pastons, and possibly her husband, would have happened at an extremely tense time for her, for on 8 February, while she was in London with her husband and their oldest son, her brother George was tried for treason.[654] Apparently, all nobles who were of age and could make it were present for this trial. Richard, Duke of Gloucester, was definitely there, watching his two brothers as defendant and accuser. The trial was such a big event that John Jnr, newly turned fifteen but considered an adult in many ways, was surely present with his father. Presumably, it would have been a sad occasion for them both, though each proved time and again that they were good at hiding their real feelings. Perhaps, despite George being their brother-in-law and uncle respectively, they shared a feeling expressed often at the time[655] and in the centuries since: that George brought his fate on himself. However, they also might have considered Edward's reaction unforgivable. We do not know; it was reported at the time that Edward completely took over the part as accuser during the trial, letting no one speak but George, who acted alone as his own defender.

Not surprisingly, all chroniclers' focus was only on the king and his brothers. John and John Jnr, despite their own close relation to accuser and accused, managed to stay beneath the radar. This might be in part because, while it is possible George sometimes visited his sister Elizabeth and her family, and Elizabeth had obviously wanted for him to become reconciled with his brothers during the Lancastrian readeption, there is much less evidence for Elizabeth and John having a good relationship – or indeed any relationship – with George than with any other of her siblings, including the rather obscure Anne. As such, while doubtlessly a jarring event for both Johns, not least due to their knowledge of the pain the proceedings would cause their wife and mother, it may not have been personally as hurtful to them as it was for Richard of Gloucester.

The trial ended predictably, with George being found guilty of treason. An Act of Attainder was passed against George. It was rather vague and has since baffled many historians. Perhaps it stumped John, who must have been there in Parliament when it was passed, as while many of George's previous crimes were listed it only enumerated vague claims of 'acting against the king and his oldest son' as his reason for actually being attainted.[656] However, maybe John took it as Edward simply wishing to be rid of George and wanting a pretext. Several people at the time thought so. However, despite the fact that a death sentence for George was passed, he was not immediately executed. Instead he was imprisoned again,[657] and there seems to have been an expectation that he would not actually be executed, his sentence commuted to imprisonment.[658]

This was not to come true. Ten days after the trial, Parliament requested Edward go ahead with the execution and the king complied with this request. However, even at the time this was seen as a sort of ploy to take responsibility away from Edward.[659] Perhaps this was needed. Edward actually going through with having his brother executed caused rather a stir. Though he was not the first English king to face a rebellion by his brother, he was the first English king to have such a brother executed. His family was extremely unhappy with this. It is well known that Richard of Gloucester regarded his brother's execution as 'murder by colour of the law'.[660] It is also well known that Richard protested against his brother's execution at the time, and pleaded for his life with Edward.[661] He does not seem to have been the only one who did so; it was said at the time that George's whole family did.[662] This would have meant his sister Margaret, by then Dowager Duchess of Burgundy, and his mother Cecily, as well as Elizabeth, once more back in her role as peacemaker. This time, however, they were unsuccessful.

We do not know if the characterisation of George's family refers to only the immediate family or his wider circle. If the latter, it might very well have included John and John Jnr, potentially even Elizabeth Jnr. John might have tried, but he might also very well have figured, if he cared enough, that any petition he made for George's life was as likely to harm George's case as to help it. John Jnr, however, whom Edward obviously liked, presumably would have attempted pleading for his uncle, if he cared enough about him to want to do so. Frustratingly, we just do not know. Whether the two Johns tried pleading for their brother-in-law and uncle or not, all those who did struggled in vain. George's execution went ahead on 18 February 1478; he was twenty-eight years old. There is actually no description of the execution, only the record that it was done in private, supposedly to spare his and Edward's mother, Cecily, more heartbreak. There are later rumours that he was drowned in a butt of malmsey wine, and it is possible that this is true. If so, it almost certainly was not the mocking gesture it is sometimes claimed to have been in the time since but either George's own choice of death or simply the easiest way for all involved.

John and Elizabeth, like Cecily, do not appear to have attended George's funeral, which Edward had Richard arrange and preside over.[663] Cecily might not have been able to stand it, while Elizabeth and John either felt the same or saw no point in it. John Jnr might not have felt it suitable to go either. Conversely, he might have attended; his movements at that time are far less certain than his parents', and it is possible that he was present at the funeral Richard organised, in a similar position to the one he had held at the reinterment of his grandfather and uncle. If he did go it would have been because he wanted to, not because Edward ordered it. There would have been no reason for him to do so in any case. It would not have been an honourable occasion, a moment for John Jnr to shine, nor would Edward have had cause, as he apparently thought he had with Richard, to give an order making clear he expected him to clean up after the king.

If John Jnr was actually present at George's funeral, it was a decision he made by himself. It is possible he did so, as there are almost no records about the occasion, and if he did he might have attended instead of his mother, or to offer moral support to his uncle Richard. Equally possible is that he instead chose to go to Wingfield Castle, the family's main home, to stay with his younger siblings, as either then or shortly afterwards his parents decided to go to Oxfordshire where, soon afterwards, John's quarrel with the Paston family flared up again.

More Trouble with the Pastons

We do not know why it started again. There had been no difficulties between John's family and the Pastons since 1472, when Alice had been accused of trying to one-up the Pastons.[664] Maybe the resumption of hostilities was due to the fact that John Paston had clearly tried to take advantage of John's need to strike an unfavourable deal with him, but it was more likely because of the death of the elder John Paston that the quarrel flared up again that year.

We do not know who started it this time. Even the Paston letters we have about it give no hint, simply taking as granted that the recipients of the letters were aware of all that had gone before the moment of writing. In the first of these letters, dated to 13 May 1478, John Paston tells his mother that he has 'most needs be here [in Suffolk] this next term' because of 'such causes as are now beginning between my lord of Suffolk and me for the manners of Hellesdon, Drayton, etc.'[665] He does not explain this any further, which gives the distinct impression of him wanting to prevent John from using rumours of his impending death to push through his own claim to the manors.

John Paston was not wrong to worry, as proven by a letter sent only a week after he said this. Written by John Whetley, it is an interesting and in fact rather entertaining missive that not only throws light on John's actions concerning those controversial manors that year but also his attitude during the quarrel. Whetley, who obviously sided with the Pastons, described an incident that took place at the manor of Hellesdon in the week between 13 May and 20 May and which he personally witnessed:

> To the Right Worshipful Sir John Paston, Knight, lodged at the sign of the George, at Paul's Wharf in London – be this delivered in haste.
>
> Please it your Mastership to understand the dealing of every thing, the which I was charged with, at my departing from your

Mastership. First, your subpoena to Denton was delivered by me on Trinity Sunday in his parish church at matins time before the substance of the parish: and as for Drayton wood, it is not all down yet, but it draws fast towards. I have the names of all the ministers of and in that wood, and more shall know, ere I come, if there be any more dealing.

And as for Hellesdon, my Lord of Suffolk was there on Wednesday in Whitsunweek, and there dined, and drew a stew, and took great plenty of fish. Yet hath he left you a pike or two, again ye come, the which would be great comfort to all your friends, and discomfort to your enemies, for at his being there that day, there was never no man that played Herod in Corpus Christi play better, and more agreeable to his pageant, than he did.

But ye shall understand that it was afternoon, and the weather hot, and he so feeble for sickness, that his legs would not bear him, but there were two men had great pain to keep him on his feet. And there ye were judged, some said, 'Slay', some said 'Put him in prison' and forth come my Lord, and he would meet you with a spear, and have none other mends for that trouble that ye have put him to, but your heart's blood, and that he will get, and with his own hands, for and ye have Hellesdon and Drayton, ye shall have his life with it. And so he comforted your enemies with that word, that they who have dealed, and deal with the wood, and most principal now is Nicholas Ovy, for as for Farrer, the Mayor, he deals not, without it be under court: for it is said that he besought my Lord that he might have other assignments for his money that he had paid, for plainly he would deal no more with the wood.

And so my Lord hath set in the bailiff of Cossey, and all is done in his name; and as for his servants, they daily threat my master your brother and me to slay, for coming on their Lord's ground, and they say that we made adventure, and they be answered, as ye commanded me, for many a great challenge make they to Master John, both Master Wodehouse, Wiseman, with other divers that I know not their names, but he holdeth his own, that they get no ground of him.

And this he lets them know, that if they beat him, or any of his, they shall abide six for one, and so they deal not but with their tongues; and as yet, since Farrer was at London, there passes not three acres of wood down, but they carry fast for fear of rain.

Moreover, my Lord of Suffolk is removed into Suffolk, the morrow after that he had been at Hellesdon; and my Lady purposed to remove after on this day Corpus Christi even, by the grace of Jesu, who preserve you ever in worship.[666]

Though it is interesting to see that Whetley admits to the Pastons doing what they had accused John of doing in 1465 – taking wood from the lands of Drayton without any official permission, and enjoying as little local support for it as John supposedly had in 1465 – the main focus of the letter is very clearly on John's actions in Hellesdon on 'Wednesday in Whitsun week'.

We do not know if the actions as described in the letter were common for John or not, though the letter seems to suggest that they were not. Whetley clearly frames the events of that day as something special and noteworthy. Though very obviously Whetley writes with the conviction that the manors and lands of Drayton and Hellesdon belonged to the Paston family, it is notable that two years after the events described in the letter John possessed both securely enough to enfeoff them.[667] Since there is no evidence that a legal change of possession took place between 1478 and 1480 even though the matter was once more submitted to a supposedly independent judge, presumably John, Duke of Suffolk had legal possession of them in Whitsun week 1478, though at least Hellesdon was obviously held by John Paston in practice. This shows that, despite what the letter writer implies, John Paston was not the innocent victim of John's unexplained and sudden aggression in this.

This is another example of a Paston letter being taken at face value by historians and used against John without an attempt to examine the circumstances of the occasion. Naturally, John himself was no innocent in this. However, it is interesting to note that though he had already showed he had no compunction about sending men to take manors he considered rightfully his, in this instance he decided against it, instead choosing the rather harmless, if passive-aggressive course of simply inconveniencing the Paston family by turning up to eat some of their food. All that came later seems to have been exacerbated by John's sickness that day.

Perhaps John chose this course of action thinking of his reputation, given how it had suffered in 1465,[668] but his actions on the day Whetley reports were at best bravado, his threats obviously empty, and there was no real danger to Paston. If anything, John's decision to show up that day at a manor held by Paston but claimed by him, to do nothing but eat Paston's fish and make empty threats, shows a streak of mischief in his character.

Apparently, his intention on that day in 1478 was to show to Paston he did not accept his possession of the manor of Hellesdon and to cause some minor inconvenience to him by eating most of his fish. It is interesting, too, that Whetley stresses John's appetite, explicitly saying he ate 'a great many' of fish and barely leaving any for Paston should he soon come to the manor he had appropriated from John. Obviously, the writer's intention was to make John look like a glutton, so his statement concerning John's eating may have been somewhat exaggerated. It is, however, unlikely to have been completely invented, as it was a private letter in which such an invention would be rather useless as slander, especially since it was something Paston could have easily verified with his servants. John eating so many fish solely to make sure Paston had few left to eat himself throws an entertaining, if not exactly flattering, light on John's character.

The next bit of the letter is somewhat more enlightening as to the whole situation between John and the Pastons, though it raises questions too. Apparently, after having eaten, John and his men began condemning Paston. Whetley frames this in such a way to make it sound like it was John's only reason to go to the manor in the first place, which is certainly possible. However, since he also states that John was very sick then, this whole episode can be seen in a different light as well. Whetley treats John's sickness rather matter-of-factly, as if expecting Paston to make sense of its sudden mention without any explanation, or to have knowledge of it already.

Despite John's sinister accusations that Paston tried to murder him, this does not have to be suspicious. At the time, letters were usually carried by messengers and it is possible that even this conversational letter was brought to John Paston by someone who gave him more details to supplement it. However, historians are sadly not furnished with extra information. It is also possible that whatever severe but apparently short illness John had that day had already been reported to Paston independently, and Whetley was aware of any rumours about it. Since he does not seem to have had any idea that Paston had heard of anything else that happened in Hellesdon on the day John visited, this seems less likely than him being informed by a messenger carrying the letter.

John's sickness seems to have come on rather suddenly. According to Whetley it only came on after John ate the pike, and the implication is that it was caused or at least exacerbated by the afternoon's heat. Whetley does not spell this out, but it is unlikely John would have gone to challenge, or even just annoy, Paston or his men while so sick that 'his legs would not bear him'. Moreover, his words and those of his men as reported by Whetley suggest they made out Paston as the party responsible for John's sickness. After being stricken with it, John made his empty threat of wanting to kill Paston. This was clearly bombast, and not even taken seriously by the letter writer, who obviously disliked John. Obviously, however, he did not make this threat out of nowhere, but instead because he considered himself, or at least claimed to consider himself, under threat by Paston, accusing him of not only wanting to take his manors from him – surely an accusation that John Paston had also already openly levelled against John several times – but also of wanting to kill him, to have 'his life with [them]'. John at the very least framed his threat in such a way that he made it a reaction to a danger from Paston, not unprovoked aggression. It has never been thought by anyone he actually meant this accusation literally, though this is not at all impossible. In fact, some of the evidence indicates so.

For one, it appears to have been a singular outburst, one he never repeated that we know of and which he and Paston never addressed again. If it had been part of a campaign to intimidate Paston, or even a mutual act of aggression, it stands to reason he would have at the very least spoken about it again, or Paston would have used it against him. Moreover, the behaviour of John's men is also notable. Whetley explicitly says that they started 'judging' Paston. He does not say what for, but the men's proposed punishments for Paston were rather extreme. Though putting him in prison might have been considered a reasonable punishment at the time for stealing manors from a duke, 'slaying' would not be. It has to be noted that a lord's servants often got heavily involved in his quarrels, sometimes more so than the lord or lady themselves, and as such John's men could have got carried away and suggested punishments for Paston that did not suit his purported crime. Even so, it is interesting the letter writer apparently connects the servants' words with John's sickness and John's own outburst as the culmination of the servants' 'judgement'. Whetley never actually says what Paston was 'judged' for.

When writing about John, Duke of Suffolk and the Pastons, one is naturally always tempted to think anything that went on between them was connected to their quarrel about their manors, but this is never actually said in the letter and the context suggests otherwise. The most likely version of the events, as described in Whetley's letter, is that having eaten 'a great plenty' of fish, John became suddenly and unexpectedly violently ill, and he and his men blamed John Paston for this, perhaps suspecting Paston's men of having poisoned John's fish. It seems unlikely that there was any truth at all in such a suspicion, and John never appears to have repeated it, perhaps realising he had overreacted after he had recovered or consulted a doctor. The true nature of his illness is unclear. While intense, it was apparently not at all serious, for within a day of getting ill John could travel again. Elizabeth, who had apparently stayed with him in Oxfordshire, travelled back to Suffolk shortly after him, and it is unlikely she would have wanted to let him travel alone, with only some servants, if he had not already recovered or was at the very least much better.

This suggests he either contracted a light summer flu or had some sort of stomach trouble as a result of eating the fish. The latter is likely if, as seems to be suggested by Whetley, the fish was stored for John Paston and not freshly caught, particularly since the weather was explicitly said to be very hot that day, which would have sped up and exacerbated any possible spoiling of food. John becoming ill of food poisoning after eating fish stored by Paston's servants might also explain why neither he nor John Paston ever addressed this unedifying episode again. John might have realised, once he became aware of what really had ailed him, that he had acted out in a way that did not reflect well on him, while Paston might have realised how John had come to the conclusion he wanted to hurt him, and that for his part, even unintentionally, having indirectly served the king's brother-in-law a meal that made him sick would not reflect well on him.

Despite the dramatics in the scene described in the letter, it never seems to have had any consequences for John and Paston's quarrel. It does, however, throw an interesting light on John's character, showing that he could be mischievous, and also had a rather frightening temper. While his streak of troublemaking is found in much of what we know of him, his temper was apparently less often so visible, and seems to have been more bluster than anything else. The fact that John insisted on standing up to utter his empty threats even while his legs would not support him also shows his stubbornness, which is one of his most notable character traits.

Traditionally, it is claimed that Elizabeth and John's second youngest son, William, was born that year,[669] but her movements show this cannot be true, and there are several sources attesting to the fact that William must have been born after the year 1478.[670] In fact, Elizabeth was not pregnant that year and would not fall pregnant until the next year.

Most of the summer and autumn 1478 seems to have been uneventful for the family, with John trying to settle both his debts and his quarrel with the Paston family. Despite the dramatics of his actions in May, neither he nor the Pastons really did much about it that year, apparently trying to solve it legally, as can be deduced from a letter sent by John Paston on 25 August that year in which he asked his namesake brother to 'take heed less that the Duke of Suffolk's council play therewith now at the vacation of the benefice as they did with the benefice of Drayton, which by the help of Master John Salett and Donne, his men, there was a quest made by the said Donne that found that the Duke of Suffolk was very patron, which was false yet they did it before an evidence'.[671] Apparently, despite John Paston quite naturally disagreeing with such findings, John had by that time found enough convincing evidence that the manors were his by right, forcing the Paston family onto the defensive. Whether or not anything else was found for or against John by any court that year we do not know, and he does not seem to have been very concerned with it.

It is possible that the sudden favour of the courts was due to an equally sudden favour by the king: in 1478 John once more received the Lieutenancy of Ireland.[672] However, once more this seems to have been a nominal post. John never actually acted in this capacity. Perhaps due to her husband's sudden rise in favour, Elizabeth too received an honour in 1478. Together with her niece, the king's oldest daughter, and some other ladies, she became a Lady of the Garter that year.[673] She must have been pleased about this, but it did not mean she and her husband spent more time at court than they had in previous years. Instead, she and John apparently enjoyed a fairly quiet life with their children at Wingfield Castle for the rest of the year.

We do not know, of course, if John Jnr was actually present then. Aged nearly sixteen then, he may very well have visited friends or relatives at that time, though his parents' castle at Wingfield remained his main home and it would stay that way all his life.

Roles in Edward IV's Later Government

Whatever John Jnr and his parents were doing at the time, it seems to have excited no notice. The next year began as calmly for them as 1478 had ended, with John and Elizabeth, and quite possibly John Jnr, spending time in Suffolk. The first half of the year must have been very uneventful, though it was at some point during this time that Elizabeth became pregnant with her and John's eleventh child.

In the summer of 1479, John was stripped of the Lieutenancy of Ireland,[674] which he had only been granted the year before, when Edward granted it to his younger son, Richard of Shrewsbury. This cannot have affected John's life very much, though it is possible he was annoyed by having been granted something for so short a time. Most likely he was actually pleased; perhaps to soften the blow of taking the lieutenancy from him, Edward granted John something else: the stewardship of the University of Oxford.[675]

As John was very interested in books and scholarship, this grant may have pleased him more than the Lieutenancy of Ireland. Certainly, it was a grant that was much more than nominal, and the events of a year later would show that he was respected and considered important at the university. It seems that John used this unexpected rise in royal favour to decide his quarrel with the Paston family in his favour once and for all. This can be seen as using an unfair advantage, but it was the sort of behaviour that was completely normal at the time and can hardly have come as a surprise to the Paston family. John seems to have been secure in holding the advantage, choosing not to send any men or threaten or cajole Paston in any way. Instead, he took the matter to court once more, where Paston seemed to think he had a fair chance of winning the case. On 29 October of that year, he reported to his mother that he 'rode beyond Donstaple and there spoke with one off my chief witness, which promised me to take labour and get my writings touching this matter between me and the Duke of Suffolk'.[676]

John Paston died shortly afterwards, but since neither he, in the short time he had left, nor his brother of the same name, ever expressed any belief that the judge deciding the case had rigged it in John's favour, it seems that John's eventual victory was all above board. It is, of course, possible that the judge was not bribed or threatened but nonetheless saw it as the smartest choice to decide the case in favour of the king's brother-in-law, who was suddenly rising at court.

This newfound prosperity did not see John at court more than in the previous years, but instead he was involved in those parts of court life that he liked. One such part was the Order of the Garter. Interestingly, though John had been a Knight of the Garter since 1472, he did not show any interest in it until Elizabeth too was a member. Once that happened, with Elizabeth he petitioned for them to be given a licence to give gifts to St George's Chapel in Windsor. They received a grant for this in December 1479.[677]

The reason for John's sudden rise in the king's favour is unknown, but it coincided with his son John Jnr's own ascent and was quite possibly influenced by it. If so, it would be an interesting reflection on John Jnr's personality. It is known Edward liked him, and we know John Jnr was to become friends with his youngest uncle, Richard of Gloucester. There was absolutely nothing speaking against such a friendship, but later Lancastrians would also seem to be friendly with John Jnr. Obviously, he was possessed of a rare charm, an ability to make everyone like him, and it is at the very least possible he used this charm to make Edward favour his parents.

Lincoln's Marriage

John Jnr's charm did not just cause Edward to favour his parents, but also to treat John Jnr himself. At the end of 1479, the king decided to arrange his marriage to Margaret FitzAlan, granddaughter of the Earl of Arundel.[678] Perhaps he felt that he could find a better match for his oldest nephew than the boy's parents could, though his choice of bride for John Jnr does not suggest so. Perhaps he simply considered the couple a good match; Margaret was his wife's niece. The most likely version is that Edward found the marriage a convenient way of bringing John Jnr into his circle.

It is interesting to note, however, that John and Elizabeth had apparently not made any efforts to find a wife for their son before Edward did. Though John Jnr had turned eighteen at the end of 1479, there is no hint they had attempted to arrange a suitable match for him or even put their feelers out. In fact, they seemed rather remiss on finding any spouses for their children.

At the end of 1479, of their nine living children only Elizabeth Jnr was married and there appear to have been absolutely no efforts made on their part to find suitable spouses for the others. This was extremely unusual, and we do not have an explanation for it. Perhaps John took after his father in that way; William had spent well over a decade as an earl, under rather dangerous circumstances, without thinking of getting married and fathering an heir, and while he had made suitable arrangements for John as a child he had not been in any hurry to marry him until he feared for his life. Maybe John had a similarly cavalier attitude towards marriages, and while he seized the chance to make a good marriage for his children when the opportunity arose, he did not go out of his way to seek such opportunities. If so, Elizabeth must have agreed with him, as she was perfectly capable of making herself heard and putting her foot down when she wanted.

Perhaps, having such an unusual attitude, they were happy for Edward to have found a bride for their son and heir, freeing them of the responsibility of eventually having to do it. We cannot know. Similarly, we can only wonder at John Jnr's thoughts. That he had to marry someone who was chosen for him is unlikely to have bothered him, as he would have expected that. However, he might have had his own feelings about the match made for him. At the very least, John Jnr was not one of the few who protested against his arranged marriage, though he may have been one of the doubtlessly far longer list of people who privately disagreed with the choice made for them. Perhaps most likely, he simply accepted his upcoming marriage for what it was: an inevitable match in which he had no choice, of which he had to make the best. Conversely, he might have been happy to finally be married, as it meant security for his future in at least one way.

His bride was the oldest daughter of Thomas FitzAlan, heir to the Earl of Arundel, and Margaret Woodville, sister of Queen Elizabeth.[679]. Thomas FitzAlan and Margaret Woodville had only been married in 1465, so even if their daughter Margaret was conceived immediately after their wedding she cannot have been much older than thirteen years of age when she married John Jnr. In fact, she was probably much younger; traditionally, the birthdate for her next oldest brother is given as sometime in 1475 and that of Margaret as sometime in 1473. This might actually have been the earliest possible birth year for her, as her mother might have been considered too young for childbirth before that. However, Margaret Woodville's birthdate is also disputed, so nothing can be said with certainty. Since there is absolutely no evidence John Jnr and his wife Margaret ever shared a household, it is very probable she had not yet reached the age of sixteen when their marriage was curtailed in 1487, and was therefore no older than eight when she married John Jnr.

It was, of course, not at all uncommon for even marriages with such a significant age gap to be made in the fifteenth century, though it is possible John Jnr would have preferred to be married to a woman his age, not to a little girl with whom he would not be able to have children before his late twenties at the earliest. Most likely, however, he considered it a good match. Despite her lower status as the granddaughter of an earl, he cannot have expected to be married to any woman of higher rank, as almost all dukes' daughters were too closely related to him to be considered suitable spouses. Moreover, the FitzAlan family was rich,[680] which meant that Margaret could expect a good inheritance one day, plus she presumably brought a large dowry, though sadly we have no confirmation on this point.

Given his parents' chronic money troubles, John may have appreciated this aspect of his marriage. Moreover, while the wedding in 1480 meant he had a wife in word alone for over a decade, this did not mean he would have had to live without female company or even children until his wife was old enough to live with him and become his wife in deed as well as word. It was perfectly acceptable for men to have mistresses and illegitimate children, even when they had an adult wife. There would have been absolutely nothing wrong with John Jnr having one or even several mistresses and fathering bastards, but if he ever did we have no knowledge of it. Perhaps he had little interest in it, or perhaps he was simply discreet, not flaunting such behaviour the way his uncle Edward did. Once more, it is an aspect of John Jnr's life that remains a mystery to us.

The wedding was arranged and went ahead, probably in early 1480. It might have taken place at court, or at his parents' palace of Wingfield Castle. The king might have been present of at the very least sent a gift. If the king visited it, it was an uncharacteristically low-profile visit. The ceremony must have been at least somewhat grand; after all, it was the wedding of a duke's oldest son and heir, who was moreover the king's oldest and very favoured nephew. The details, however, have to be left to our imagination, as no source survives to shine any light on it. What is known is that John endowed his son and new daughter-in-law with some lands, passing on as the latter's jointure the manors of Hellesdon, Drayton, Bacton by Bromeholme, the hundred of Shropham, Tolthorp, Hurtes, Bedklyng, Ketylberston, Dagworth Sorrellys and Howesin Alderton.[681] It was a very generous grant, worth £124 annually,[682] which indicates the importance John assigned to his heir's marriage and shows that John, despite fighting so much for his possessions, obviously had no problem granting them and passing them on to his son.

It was also a rather clever grant. By including the manors of Hellesdon and Drayton in it, he made sure Paston would not be able to try to claim them. Should he try to do so after they had been granted to John Jnr and his youthful wife, he would not only go against the king's favoured nephew but also against a niece of the notoriously clannish Queen Elizabeth. By making this grant, John effectively put the manors forever out of Paston's reach – a subtle act that would have doubtlessly found the approval of all those on his side in this quarrel.

It does not seem as if the fact that he was a married man after 1480 changed anything in John Jnr's life except to make him somewhat richer. Little Margaret was not, as sometimes happened, moved into the household of her new parents-in-law. Why this was decided against is not known, but it may have been due to the Suffolks' straitened financial situation. Perhaps they did not think they would be able to give her the upbringing to suit her status as an earl's wife and granddaughter and future duchess, having enough trouble providing such an environment for their own children. Whatever the reason, once the actual wedding was over, life went on as usual for the Suffolk family.

John Jnr might not often have thought about the fact he was a married man, as it was a fact that had no impact on him. In recent years it has sometimes been claimed that not only did he live together with his wife Margaret in their own household, for which we have no evidence, but that they actually had one[683] or even two children who predeceased their father. These children have variously been claimed to have been two boys called Edward and Edmund, a single boy who was called Edward,[684] or a boy and a girl called Edward and Margaret – but they are mythical. There is no trace of evidence of any such child ever existing, and until the early twentieth century no one claimed they existed.

The wedding aside, the year 1480 seems to have been a good year for the family, and very calm. After the trying and difficult years that had preceded it, this must have been a relief. Even if they had not intended and perhaps not even wanted it, their son's wedding must have been a cause for celebration, something cheerful and happy after so much bad news.

10

Suffolk's Role in Noble Society, 1480s

John and Elizabeth appear to have made arrangements for the future of another of their children, though this did not involve a wedding. On the contrary, they planned to have their third son, Edward, given to the Church. This was quite normal for younger sons of nobles, who did not stand to inherit anything of their parents' lands, but that Edward was chosen as the first of the Suffolk children to go down this route clears up some misconceptions about the family. Since it was Edmund who eventually was John's heir, it is often assumed that he was John and Elizabeth's second son. This is obviously untrue, as several contemporary sources exist to make it pretty clear that Edward was born in 1470[685] and Edmund at the beginning of 1473.[686] However, it also makes something else obvious: Edward was also not John and Elizabeth's second son.

While it was entirely common for younger sons of nobles to be given a position within the Church, it was extremely uncommon, if not unheard of, for second sons to do so when their older brother did not have any children yet. The concept of one heir and one spare was too well-established, and even when the heir, like John Jnr, was already old enough to no longer be at risk from the catastrophically high child mortality rate, the danger of something happening to him was too high to risk allowing the spare to become a clergyman. Even in the case of the Suffolks, who had more sons, this could have caused trouble, as in the event of John Jnr's death it would have meant that Edward, had he been the second son, was heir while unable to take up the duties it entailed. Even in the event of his titles passing on to his next-youngest brother, this could still have caused trouble as this brother would not have been the legal heir.

This means that, clearly, the Suffolks must have had a son born between John Jnr and Edward, and still alive in 1479. Sadly, though this boy must have been in his teens by then, and presumably died only several years later, we know almost nothing about him, not even his name. Interestingly, John and Elizabeth apparently considered it more important to make arrangements for their third son to join the Church than to arrange a good marriage for this second son. There is another oddity with Edward being given to the Church as he was a scholar at Oxford University. He is a rather obscure boy, who sadly would go on to die in his teens, and as such is often confused with his younger brother Edmund.[687] This confusion has caused rather widespread claims that Edmund was educated at Oxford University, which is untrue; that was Edward. Though other sons of John and Elizabeth would eventually also become clergymen and scholars,[688] Edmund was never among them.

Edward was clearly prepared for a life in the Church before 1480, as we know from a letter the University of Oxford wrote to the Bishop of Salisbury, probably in the summer of that year, asking him to send Edward to be further educated at their institution:

> Experience shows that nothing is so effectual in preserving the state, and nothing renders it more illustrious, than high birth and virtuous character united. Since, therefore, the University has been the means of educating many of noble lineage, we may reasonably congratulate ourselves upon our honourable office; and in your own instance, were there no others, the antiquity of your family, the rectitude of your whole life, and your singular prudence in affairs of state, would furnish us sufficient reason for this boast. Such, moreover, is your influence, that it is in your power to procure for us the unexampled honour of having entrusted to our charge the education of the son of the Duke of Suffolk, whose earlier years have been spent under your careful training in virtue and knowledge. We earnestly beg that you will do this, and suffer us to complete the work you have so far accomplished.[689]

This clearly suggests that Edward had been living in the Bishop of Salisbury's household, but sadly this is the only indication we have of such an arrangement, so nothing more can be said about his placement there, neither when it happened nor why John and Elizabeth chose Salisbury for their son's education.

Naturally, as the university did not decide to beg the king for his nephew's presence based on the ten-year-old's merits as a scholar, it seems they gained something from Edward de la Pole arriving as one of their pupils. Quite obviously, the real reasons would have been Edward's connections. He was the king's nephew, and he was the son of the university's steward. Both of these reasons would probably have been important to the university but, given the timing of when they started to request Edward's presence, it is not hard to see a connection to John becoming steward. Quite possibly, the university hoped to flatter him and thereby encourage him to either do more for them or to keep doing the good work already did.

It is also possible that John had made arrangements for his son's further education that included more funding for him and the university, and the latter was eager to receive such an endowment. Though, as repeatedly mentioned above, the Suffolks usually lacked money, John had shown that despite this he did not skimp where his children were concerned. John Jnr had received a big boon for his marriage, and there is no cause to believe either John or Elizabeth would not have been equally generous when making arrangements for their younger children. Certainly, whatever the exact motivations, it seems as if educating young Edward was important to the university, for they sent their plea not only to the bishop who was Edward's guardian but also to the king:

> That we enjoy your protection in those days of constant troubles to the Church, is in the highest advantageous both to our reputation and ease, and already the effect has been wonderful in every branch of study; so that you are now adding to the renown of your arms the glory of being a Christian king. And in the education you think it behoves you to provide not only for your own illustrious children, but also for others nearly related to you, we see a farther proof of the respect you entertain for our studies; for it is plain that you desire them to be imbued with the same affection for us as that you feel yourself.
>
> But to have the education of your nephew, the Lord Edward Pole, intended for the active service of the priesthood in the militant Church, would be the most signal token of your peculiar favour. The lord of Lords and king of Kings from all nations of the world selected the Jews to be his people, and sent His only begotten son to be incarnate of that chosen race; and in like manner you have made us, of all your realm, the particular object of your care; to whom then, rather than to ourselves, could you better commit the education of this adopted child of God? Grant us then, we pray, this great favour, and confirm the expectation your previous interest in us has raised in our hearts; and be assured that your own honour, no less than our prosperity, will feel the impulse. If, as we read, the Cesars reckoned painted statues in the heathen temples a means of securing the worthless glory of this world, how much more glorious will it be for you to have as it were a living likeness of yourself placed here in the capitol of virtue and knowledge, to the honour of the true God.[690]

Just why such a letter was sent to Edward IV – who does not seem to have had anything to do with the decisions made for Edward de la Pole so far – and not to John or Elizabeth is unknown. Perhaps the university thought that Edward would be able to convince both the Bishop of Salisbury and the boy's parents if either of them hesitated, or they hoped that the king would take an interest in his namesake nephew attending the university and reward them for educating him.

Their pleas were successful. Edward was eventually sent to Oxford University, but it was to take a while between their first letters and the decision being made. The reason for that may be the obvious one: the Bishop of Salisbury would not have made such a decision without consulting John and Elizabeth, and at the time of the letter Elizabeth was probably already in confinement waiting to give birth to her eleventh child. If so, this would have at the very least slowed any arrangements she and John made with the Bishop of Salisbury for their son's future, if not outright stopped them for a while.

Traditionally, it is claimed that the baby Elizabeth bore in 1480 was her last son, Richard de la Pole. This is untrue. Again, there is no contemporary evidence for the claim, and in fact contemporary evidence contradicts it, showing he and his next older brother were both born after 1480.[691] The baby Elizabeth gave birth to in 1480 in fact seems to have been the rather elusive Geoffrey de la Pole. Unlike the last, this birth went as expected and both mother and son survived healthily. It is sometimes claimed that Geoffrey died in infancy,[692] but there is evidence he survived and, like his brother Edward, became a scholar and a clergyman, albeit a very obscure one. He was named after his famous forebear, his father's great-grandfather Geoffrey. Possibly, his grandmother Cecily acted as his godmother, or one of his siblings stood as his godparent.

The birth would without a doubt have been a very happy occasion for John and Elizabeth, and another might have soon followed. In 1480, their daughter Elizabeth Jnr and her husband both became old enough to establish their own household. However, there is no evidence they ever did so, and it may be that, like John and Elizabeth had done with Alice, Elizabeth Jnr and Henry decided to live in her parents' household. This is purest speculation, but with no evidence of the young couple having a household of their own it is certainly reasonable.

All this would have been enough to keep John and Elizabeth busy that year, but there has been a suggestion made in recent years that John was also once more busy that year with his incessant quarrels for possessions, namely because his mother-in-law Cecily received a petition that there had been 'injuries done'[693] against the city of Norwich, and she was to bring a remedy against them.[694] Despite the fact that this petition against Cecily neither details what those injuries were nor names or hints at the perpetrators, it is sometimes assumed John was the culprit.[695] This is possible, but he never before nor afterwards ever had any quarrel with the City of Norwich and there is no evidence he had one then. The suggestion seems to be based mainly on the fact that in 1481 two tenants in Norwich credibly accused him of having ejected them from a manor he claimed for himself.[696]

Again, this is possible, but hardly the only, or even the most likely, explanation for the 'injuries', as it stands to reason that his culpability would have at least been indicated had he been involved. The fact that Cecily was the one who was asked to 'remedy' the injuries, sometimes taken as indicative of John being the one who had caused them,[697] is also not very telling. Cecily was, after all, not only Duke John's mother-in-law but also the king's mother and held many lands, and as such could have had the power to deal with any sort of injuries to the city. So while it is not impossible at all that in 1480 John stretched to Norwich in his everlasting quest to claw back all the money and possessions he considered owed to him, on the whole it seems rather unlikely.

However, in 1480, John and Elizabeth did something that was to become controversial in later years, although it wasn't at the time: they granted a chapel to Elizabeth's mother, Cecily.[698] Such grants were not uncommon, but their son Edmund would later claim that Edward IV had forced his parents to do it.[699] By the time Edmund made the claim, both his father and his grandmother Cecily were dead, though his mother was still alive and did not contradict her son. However, this does not have to mean she agreed. Perhaps she simply wanted to keep the chapel out of the new king's hands and thought the best way to do so was to let Edmund claim she and John had been forced to relinquish it in the first place.

It is, however, also possible that they were in fact forced to do so. Edward IV still appeared to favour the couple then, granting them another licence to make a gift to St George's Chapel in Windsor,[700] but even so it was very much Edward IV's style to give something to someone by taking it away from someone else. If this was the case, it did not weaken the apparently cordial relationship between Cecily and her daughter and son-in-law. Apparently, in summer 1480, she visited them for a while from her nearby manor,[701] and she might have been present when her grandson was born.

Towards the end of the year, after Elizabeth left confinement and any property quarrels were solved for the time being, the arrangement for Edward de la Pole to go to Oxford University finally went through. Though Salisbury had apparently secured John and Elizabeth's agreement fairly soon after the first letter was sent to him,[702] arrangements stalled for a while after that, and the university was apparently rather nervous about the possibility of either his guardian or his parents deciding against his going there after all:

> Your constant good offices are more than we can repay, and we most heartily rejoice at your exalted position, by which alone without your noble birth you stand superior to all other distinguished men of these days. We know that you desire our prosperity, but you can hardly imagine how great has lately been our anxiety. You say

> (to quote the words of your elegant epistle) 'it shall not be long before I come to lay that noble child in his mother's lap', but we are weary with longing for your arrival and our old troubles seem to break out afresh. No greater honour could be done to us than to place the King's nephew Edward Pole in our charge, and your own name will at the same time be made immortal.[703]

One of the arrangements that had to be made before Edward was sent to university seems to have been choosing another noble boy to join him there and to keep him company. The boy chosen for this, possibly by his parents or by the king, was James Stanley,[704] second surviving son of Thomas, Baron Stanley and his first wife Eleanor Neville. Edward and James were related through their mothers, but it is doubtful they had a lot in common. James was around six years older than Edward, and presumably neither the ten-year-old nor the sixteen-year-old found each other particularly interesting. That James was chosen to be Edward's friend rather than another noble boy closer in age might point to the actual reason for James's presence; though it was claimed that he was to attend the university to be a friend to Edward,[705] presumably he was more meant to keep an eye on him and be some sort of mentor. After all, he was old enough to serve in such a capacity and young enough to be someone Edward felt he could approach.

Once this was decided on, and all other arrangements made, the Bishop of Salisbury brought his young ward to the university, quite possibly accompanied by his parents. Going by the eagerness the university had showed to have him as their student, he would have been received with honour. Surely John was proud of his son, going to university to start his own life at such a young age. It would, however, not have changed much about his own life, since Edward had not been living in his and Elizabeth's household at that point. If he wanted to visit his son he could ride to see him at Oxford University just as well as he could have before at the Bishop of Salisbury's household.

Lincoln's Political Involvement

However, while Edward's new vocation did not change anything in his parents' life, John Jnr's latest moves probably did. By autumn 1480, John Jnr seems to have spent more and more time away from Wingfield Castle establishing himself at court. In November 1480, shortly after Edward de la Pole had started his new life at Oxford University, Edward IV's youngest child, a daughter called Bridget, was born,[706] and shortly afterwards she was baptised in a great ceremony. Her grandmother Cecily, who was also John Jnr's grandmother, was one of her godmothers, her oldest sister Elizabeth was her second godmother, while the Bishop of Winchester stood as godfather.[707] Though not given such a vital part, John still had an important spot in the baptism ceremony:

> First, about a hundred torches, borne by Knights, Esquires, and other honest persons, and my Lord Maltravers bear the basin, having a towel about his neck, in like wise the Earl of Northumberland a taper unlight, and the Earl of Lincoln the salt, and the canopy borne by three Knights and one Baron.[708]

This, once more, was a position of honour. There is no telling what exactly John Jnr thought, but at the tender age of eighteen he was already a vital part of his uncle's court in a way his parents never had been. Notably, they were not present at the baptism of their niece Bridget, and presumably had neither been invited nor had any interest in attending. Maybe John Jnr attended the Christmas festivities at court after his young cousin's baptism, but if so he was not mentioned. Since he, unlike his parents, was usually mentioned in sources when he was present at court, it stands to reason he was not there. Presumably, he attended the Christmas festivities put on by his parents.

He might have been at court more often in 1481, but very notably he was absent from his uncle's most important concern that year: the war against Scotland.[709] This was led by Richard, Duke of Gloucester, in Edward's name, while Edward himself was staying in London due to being too unwell to fight, though he was not actually sick.[710] The campaign was designed to once and for all end the quarrels and skirmishes that had dogged the Anglo-Scottish border for years.[711] Many nobles were involved, such as John, Lord Howard, and Edward Woodville, one of the queen's brothers, but none of the Suffolk family were. John, of course, could not fight, but John Jnr's absence is somewhat inexplicable. He was nearly nineteen, older than his father had been when he had become involved in the so-called Wars of the Roses. He would have been old enough to fight, but he did not; stranger still, no one seems to have commented on his absence. The Scottish campaigns were quite important to English politics, and many if not most nobles of the right age and condition took part. However, John Jnr, who satisfied both criteria, does not seem to have been considered. He sat out the campaigns in both 1481 and 1482.

Possibly, he chose to stay at court with his uncle Edward, and some other nobles like William, Lord Hastings. However, it is worth noting that no one ever accused John Jnr of cowardice, and he would not prove wary of getting involved in battles in the future. Perhaps he simply did not want to fight; as he was to show, he was very good at doing only what he wanted to do. But even if so, it is remarkable that no one ever commented on his absence. His erstwhile foster brother Francis Lovell, himself not a very notable or famous man at the time, expressed fear that if he did not show due enthusiasm for fighting he would be branded a coward.[712] No one ever expressed any such thoughts about John Jnr. This was perhaps because John Jnr, though of higher standing than his former foster brother, did not yet have his own household, nor had he attained his majority yet.

For his father, the usual explanation held; he was not physically able to fight and no one expected him to. He seemed to lead a fairly calm life that year. As mentioned above, he ejected two tenants from a manor near Norwich, though little other information survives about the incident and it does not seem to have affected John's standing very much.[713] Though he may have been involved in other quarrels about possessions, or else have ridden out to see his lands in that year, possibly with Elizabeth, it seems he spent most of the first two-thirds of the year at Wingfield Castle. During that time, Elizabeth became pregnant for the twelfth time.

A bit of evidence exists, though, that while John Jnr did not join in the Scottish campaigns he was at his uncle's court at the time, together with his parents. This evidence is found in a document describing a visit Edward IV made with several of his courtiers to Oxford University on 22 September 1481:

> On the 22nd of September 1481, Waynflete, Bishop of Winchester, set out for Woodstock, where King Edward, of his own accord, and of his special favour, promised to visit his new College [Magdalen College] in the evening, and to pass the night there; which pleased the founder in a very high degree. After sunset, he entered the parish of St Giles's with a multitude of men, innumerable torches burning before him. The Chancellor, Mr Lion Woodville, brother to the Queen, with the masters regent and non-regent, received him honourably without the University and escorted him to Magdalen College. He was there received in like manner, and introduced by Waynflete, the President, and Scholars, in procession. With him came the Bishops of Chichester, Ely, and Rochester, the Earl of Lincoln, Lord High [Steward], Lord Stanley, Lord Dacres of Sussex, Sir Thomas Barowyg, Knight, and many other nobles, who all met with an honourable reception from the founder, and passed the night in the college.[714]

Though only John Jnr is mentioned by title, John was still high steward at the time of the visit so we know he was also present; nevertheless it is interesting that his high title and standing as the king's brother-in-law were not considered as important as his being high steward.

Elizabeth, too, was present, being stated to have been accompanied 'with a considerable retinue'.[715] She and the other ladies present, including the queen herself, were greeted graciously by the university, plied with gifts of gloves and wine.[716] However, it seems that none of the women joined the men when they attended public debates among the scholars; perhaps some unspoken rule prevented them.

Almost certainly, the three of them would have used their time at Oxford University to see their son and brother Edward, and ask him how he was. Any meeting cannot have been very long, for as the account makes clear, the king and all those with him left the university again after a single night spent there. If John Jnr was sad he could not see his brother for longer, another event was planned at court that surely would have taken his mind from this when his aunt Margaret, Dowager Duchess of Burgundy, came to visit the English court.[717]

It was not solely a family visit or a social visit, rather inspired by her wish to ask for help in her difficult political situation in Burgundy. Once more, France was threatening the small but rich duchy, and Margaret wanted to ask for English help.[718] Even so, her family was eager to see her. Edward IV arranged a great celebration for his younger sister's arrival,[719] at which her other brother Richard was no doubt present, as were Elizabeth and John, along with the newly seasoned courtier John Jnr. Perhaps John and Elizabeth brought a few of their younger children as well, those old enough to attend court to meet their aunt; if so it would have been for Margaret's benefit and not the children's, as it is unlikely any of them would have been able to remember Margaret from before her marriage. Indeed, even John Jnr may not have remembered her. Though he was already six years old when she married, he might not have seen all that much of her while she was still unmarried and living in England. However, he met her in late 1481, and perhaps they made an impression on each other. Several years later, fate was to throw them together.

Neither of them could have known this at the time, and it is entirely likely that during the visit their conversation did not surpass one of polite interest. Margaret would have presumably had more to talk about with Elizabeth and John, with whom she appears to have been on good terms before she married. She seems to have stayed friends with Elizabeth; we know less about her and John's feelings about one another, but there was never a hint of any sort of trouble between them before she married and there is no reason why John should not have been happy to see his sister-in-law again in 1481.

Margaret did not get what she wanted from Edward due to his contract with the French king.[720] He did not want to lose a steady source of income and the prospective alliance of his daughter to the French dauphin by siding with Burgundy and attacking France.[721] However, despite this, Margaret's trip to England was not completely in vain. She received a little bit of help from some courtiers and nobles, independently of Edward. Most notably, Edward's lord chamberlain William, Lord Hastings agreed to go against Edward's decision and follow his own interests by sending Margaret some troops.[722] It was presumably better than nothing, though less than what she would have hoped for when she came to England. At the very least, she might have been glad to have seen her family again, and her family to see her, since a lot had changed since she had last seen most of them.

After Margaret had left England again, it seems that John and Elizabeth left court and that John Jnr joined them to celebrate Christmas in Wingfield Castle. That he chose to do this when he could have spent Christmas at court once more shows the strength of his relationship with his parents. Perhaps he was also present in the manor when his mother, probably at the beginning of the year 1482, gave birth to his eleventh sibling. It must have been almost routine for everyone involved, but like his father and mother, doubtlessly John Jnr was happy when his mother gave birth to a healthy son, whom his parents chose to call William after his grandfather.[723]

It is sometimes speculated that William was not the second youngest but the youngest, his brother Richard being older than him.[724] This theory is based on the fact that after all the non-clergy sons but Richard and William had died, it was Richard and not William who was considered by European leaders to be the Duke of Suffolk.[725] However, the birth order of the brothers is certain, and the reason why William was never considered rightful Duke of Suffolk seems to have involved wider circumstances rather than seniority.[726]

Once more, it seems the family spent most of the year in Suffolk, John Jnr as well as his parents. He apparently managed once more to keep out of the continuing Scottish campaign without anyone lambasting him for it. At least in the early part of the year, he was also not with Edward, who went to Fotheringhay to give his brother Richard, Duke of Gloucester, instructions for those campaigns.[727] However, when he was at court he might have been told by his uncle of the letters he had had from Oxford University regarding his brother Edward, letters which doubtlessly would have pleased him and his parents when they heard of them. One of those letters mentions Edward in passing as 'Lord Edward Pole, your nephew, a youth endowed by nature with the highest gifts of intellect and heart'.[728] Another letter was more detailed, assuring Edward IV that his namesake nephew was 'a youth whose virtues are as lofty as his rank[.] From the first he has exhibited talents superior to those of his companions, and yet withal such is his modesty and politeness that his conduct is admired by all.'[729] It would have been obvious to his parents and brother, as well as to the king, that this letter contained heavy flattery and that it would not have been possible for the university to report that Edward was remarkably talentless, but since the letter was unprompted it probably would have pleased them as it suggested that he was finding his way at university and enjoying his life there.

Apart from cheering young Edward's family, it also seemed to have its intended effect on his uncle, who chose to favour his namesake nephew by petitioning the pope to grant him a bishopric once he was fourteen.[730] This was a rather great sign of favour, as certainly such a grant would have cost money, and might have sweetened John and Elizabeth towards him. Of course, this still would not have been completely selfless as it served any king to have bishops in his country well-disposed (and indebted) to him.

Both the recipient of the letter, Edward IV, and John Jnr would most likely have not dwelled for long on the praise for Edward de la Pole. While both were surely pleased, they had different issues on their mind. For Edward IV, this was the development of the military campaign against Scotland, which ended that summer with victory for his forces as they took Edinburgh[731] without much of a fight, leaving him in a position to dictate terms of peace to the Scottish king.

John Jnr, meanwhile, probably had his own future on his mind in 1482, for in that year he turned twenty and would have started to prepare for reaching his majority the next year. Though, as he was not a duke yet and was lucky enough for his father to still be alive, he might still have looked forward to it. There was the promise of many lands,[732] leading to a sizable income.[733]

Despite this upcoming milestone, John Jnr was too young to attend Parliament that year. John, however, was summoned and perhaps he and Elizabeth joined Edward IV at court for Christmas that year before Parliament assembled. Before he could do so, he had to settle some local matters, however. Perhaps the grants to John Jnr put his father in a rather difficult financial situation, or something else did. We do not know for certain, but we do know that by 4 December 1482 John was hurting for money, and writing letters to see to it he would get some that was due to him:

> Thomas Geffrey, I will, and charge you, that you deliver unto my trusty servant, Robert Restold, the whole farm of my manor of Maundevill, of the year last past ended at Michaelmas; and this bill, of my own hand, shall be to you sufficient discharge against me, and my heirs.
>
> Written at Westhorp, the 4th day of December, in the 22nd year of King Edward the 4th.[734]

However, despite such letters, it seems that this issue was not completely settled in December 1482, possibly because other matters distracted John that month, such as a visit from John, Lord Howard around the same time. Lord Howard stayed with John and Elizabeth for three days,[735] after which it seems that they all went to court together to attend the Christmas celebration.

It was an especially great celebration, with most nobles present. John and Elizabeth had more reason than usual to attend these festivities, which might be why they spent the holidays at court for once. During the festivities, the so-called heroes of the Scottish campaigns were praised openly.[736] These men included not only Thomas, Baron Stanley and John, Lord Howard, but first and foremost Richard, Duke of Gloucester.[737] Elizabeth might have wanted to be present to see her youngest brother celebrated, but this was probably not the main reason she and her husband chose to stay at court then. During the celebration, another event took place: the elevation of their erstwhile ward Francis, Baron Lovell, to a viscountcy.[738] This must have pleased especially John, who had built a close relationship with Francis when he had been his ward, though in itself that too might not have constituted enough reason for them to attend court just to witness the elevation. However, Francis's sponsors for his elevation were not only his wife's older brother Richard, Baron FitzHugh but also his younger cousin, Henry Lovell, Baron Morley.[739] Henry was, of course, Elizabeth Jnr's husband. It seems probable she was at court with him, which might have been the main reason that her parents came as well.

The good mood at court during the Christmas festivities was not to last, though. Bad news was to hit the court: the French king, Louis, though reported to be ailing, had made a deal with Burgundy following the death of Marie, Duchess of Burgundy, in the spring that year.[740] From the Burgundian side, it was a mixture of good and bad news; from the French side, it was simply good. Marie's widower, Maximilian, the future Holy Roman Emperor Maximilian I, had agreed to betroth his young daughter to the French dauphin,[741] which ended any immediate hostilities between the duchy and France, but would give their eventual children a claim to the throne. It was what was best for both France and Burgundy at the time,[742] but it was bad news for England, as it meant that the French dauphin's engagement to Edward IV's oldest daughter, Elizabeth, was annulled.[743] So was the entire Treaty of Piquenique,[744] which had not only stipulated this engagement but also the yearly payments for Edward and several important English nobles, which Richard, Duke of Gloucester had so disliked.

Due to this development, hostilities with France seemed likely once more. Since John had not received any annuity from the French crown, the loss of these bribes would not have made any difference to him personally, and since he was unable to fight he would not have had to fear losing his life in an upcoming conflict in France as his grandfather and several of his uncles had. He might, however, have feared for the lives of several of his sons, of whom at least John Jnr and his second son were old enough to get involved in any conflict.

John Jnr's thoughts are harder to guess, but it can be said that he was clearly not a warmonger – if he had been, he would have gotten involved in the Scottish campaigns – but nonetheless was perfectly prepared to fight once he considered it the right thing to do. His feelings about a possible upcoming conflict with France would therefore have depended on whether or not he considered it justified. Presumably, if he shared the feelings of most of his contemporaries, he would have considered it righteous, but there is no way of telling. Such personal feelings were no doubt discussed, *sotto voce*, while Parliament sat through January and February 1483.

John attended Parliament, and perhaps John Jnr and Elizabeth stayed with him during that time. As usual, John and Elizabeth left court to go back to Wingfield Castle when Parliament had closed, and possibly Elizabeth had already gone there before. Whenever they left, it was to be the last time they saw Edward IV. Within six weeks of Parliament closing, the king was dead.

11

Change of Kings

Edward's death was sudden and shocking.[745] Though his health had not been perfect, and in modern times he is often speculated to have had a minor heart attack after learning that Louis of France had broken the Treaty of Piquenique,[746] he was still only forty years old and had showed no signs of being badly ill. His cause of death remains unclear; all that we know is that he became sick after a fishing trip on the Thames at the end of March, and despite initially recovering enough to dine together with his wife and some of his children after a couple of days, the illness suddenly became worse and he died within a week.[747] With physicians unable to identify his cause of death,[748] rumours naturally began to spread. Some people suspected he had been poisoned by a French agent. In France, rumours circulated that the shock of the broken treaty had killed him. Doubtlessly, there were more rumours, and in modern times it has even sometimes been speculated that his wife's family, the Woodvilles, had him poisoned.[749] There is no more evidence for this than there is for any contemporary speculation, and perhaps the most likely theory of Edward's death is the one that was most widespread at the time: he burned himself out, 'like a candle burning on both ends'.[750]

Suffolk's Part in the Succession Crisis

John Jnr seems to have been present in the capital when his uncle died,[751] though apparently not at his deathbed. His parents and siblings must have heard of the king's death within only a few days of it happening, possibly thanks to John Jnr sending a messenger, but none of them came to London to take part in the king's funeral.[752]

This is rather baffling, as on the face of it there was nothing to stop them attending. Maybe something had happened within their own family that saw them stay home, but we have no record of it. It is sometimes pointed out that Edward's own mother, Cecily, also did not attend the funeral,[753] and that in her case and his sister Elizabeth's it might have been that they could not stand the thought of seeing Edward buried. However, while this is conceivable for Cecily, it seems rather unlikely for Elizabeth. It was especially harsh of John not to attend. While it might very well have been a blow for him and his wife to hear of Edward's death, neither of them had been particularly close to him, so attending his funeral would not have been emotionally unbearable. However, it seems that it was not a decision they made because of any lack of feeling for Edward. Though there was no indication at the time, later events were to show that it was probably due to an emergency in their family that they did not come.

Such an emergency is not explicitly mentioned in any source, perhaps due to them not being major players; indeed, their absence from Edward's funeral was never commented on in any contemporary source. It could be argued that this was because no one from his close family except John Jnr attended the funeral at all. Richard, Duke of Gloucester had not been informed of the king's death by the dowager queen,[754] and by the time he got word of it, supposedly from William, Baron Hastings sending a messenger to inform him,[755] it was too late for him to reach London in time for the funeral. Edward IV's oldest son and heir, recognised as Edward V after his father's death, was still in his own household in Ludlow, waiting for his uncle and guardian Anthony Woodville, Lord Rivers, to gather men in his name to go to the capital[756] and would not have been able to reach London in time either. Perhaps because it was already a custom, as it was in later years, for dowager queens not to attend a king's funeral, and vice versa, Elizabeth Woodville did not attend the funeral either; nor did her children, perhaps thinking that doing so without their mother was not suitable.

However, though none of the rest of his family was present, John Jnr played a rather vital part in the funeral, acting as chief mourner.[757] This was a position of high honour, but it does not necessarily reflect any particular trust in him or any indication of his high standing at court; the only other person who could have done it in his stead would have been Richard, Duke of Gloucester, and he was unavailable. Nonetheless he appears to have acquitted himself with gravitas and dignity.[758] There was some talk of him crying during the parade, but this, of course, was standard language. It does not have to mean he actually shed tears, and if he did it might have been only because he considered it appropriate for his position. Since John Jnr was to later show great talent as an actor, it is very hard to judge his feelings from such actions. However, Edward IV had always favoured John Jnr and treated him well; even if he resented the king's treatment of his parents, it is likely the young man felt at least some sadness for his late uncle.

John Jnr's role as chief mourner did not simply require him to lead the funeral procession and to break the first stave on Edward's grave.[759]

It also fell to him to deal with any organisational problems, which he apparently did very well. One such hiccough that is recorded is that there was a quarrel of precedence between William Berkeley and the Earl of Arundel, the grandfather of John Jnr's young wife Margaret.[760] Apparently, John Jnr either had his mother's gift for peacemaking or a lot of natural authority or both, for his ruling was accepted without any grumbling.[761]

John Jnr likely stayed in the capital after the funeral, expecting the arrival of his young cousin, the new king, from Ludlow, and his uncle Richard, Duke of Gloucester, from Yorkshire.[762] However, things were not destined to go smoothly and the situation soon escalated. John Jnr would have been in the best position to watch it develop, and was perhaps one of the very few people who had enough information to judge the events with something approaching reasonable accuracy. Naturally, this does not have to mean that he lacked bias. It is notable that John Jnr obviously used a rare and useful gift he had to make everyone like him. He was one very few notable courtiers at Edward IV's court who was not associated with either of the pro- or anti-Woodville factions who held power there. In fact, neither of these factions ever had a single bad word to say about him in the sources.

Having crossed paths, Richard, Duke of Gloucester and Edward V soon ran into trouble. Richard had arranged for Edward's maternal uncle and guardian Anthony, Lord Rivers to meet with their party at Northampton. However, when Richard arrived at the meeting point with another of the new king's uncles, Henry, Duke of Buckingham, it seems they found only Anthony, who claimed that Edward V had ridden ahead with his men due to fear there would not be enough accommodation for his retinue once his uncles arrived.[763] We do not actually know all this for a fact, only rumours that were reported at the time and the end results of it all. However, John Jnr, possibly still in the capital, and John, who was definitely at Wingfield Castle, would have been in the same situation of only hearing rumours.

They would soon have heard it reported that Richard had arrested not only Lord Rivers but also the king's older half-brother Richard Grey and his chamberlain Thomas Vaughan.[764] The charge on which he arrested them was plotting to waylay Richard and Henry to kill them or prevent them reaching the capital.[765] The charge was believed by many, but disbelieved by just as many. Though for obvious reasons historians in the intervening centuries have dismissed the charge without even examining it,[766] modern-day historians have, on the whole, taken it more seriously.[767]

Presumably, at the time, people would have engaged with it. John Jnr might have asked himself the same questions everyone else asked themselves, and which have been asked by historians who have not outright dismissed the charge: why would the three arrested men do what they had been charged with, and conversely why might Richard of Gloucester and Henry of Buckingham invent such charges?

Surely John Jnr, who had been somewhat privy to the workings of the government immediately following Edward's death and funeral, would have also asked himself the reasons for the Woodvilles' strange behaviour recently. For example, something that supposedly happened – and had led to uproar, with William, Baron Hastings, being outraged at the suggestion – was that the dowager queen had wanted to have her son accompanied by 5,000 armed men on his way to London.[768] Though he might have needed more than the number of men brought by his uncle Richard of Gloucester, who was accompanied by three hundred unarmed men clad in mourning,[769] there was absolutely no need for 5,000 armed men, and Baron Hastings threatened to withdraw to Calais with all his men if the dowager queen insisted on it.[770] Even the 2,000 men Edward V eventually set off with were considered far too many by most.[771] This might have made it easier for John Jnr to believe that Edward V's guardians had in fact carried themselves with sinister designs and Richard of Gloucester and Henry of Buckingham had been correct.

Some other details might also have suggested that to him, including rumours that Richard and Henry had interrupted the king and his party at dawn, apparently intending to leave without waiting for them as Lord Rivers had claimed they would,[772] and musings on how strange it was that that Edward V supposedly thought Northampton – a great city in which many nobles had townhouses, and which had seen many historic events and housed Parliaments – was too small to accommodate both the king and his uncles. This, of course, is only the version given by Domenico Mancini in his famous report that was finished in 1483, and the Great Chronicle of London. Even if it is true in its essentials, doubtlessly other versions would have been told in London and the rest of the country as well, and there is absolutely no telling what John or John Jnr believed or why.

However, quite possibly, they hardly had time to think about it, especially if John Jnr was still in the capital at that time, as events were to spiral quickly after that. Though there was no chance of making Edward V's coronation happen on 4 May, the strangely early date scheduled by the dowager queen, the new king and his uncles soon arrived in London and were greeted by the city aldermen and nobles.[773] If he was in the capital then, John Jnr was surely among them.

However, while every effort was made to give this was ceremony sufficient gravity, there were two problems which rather put a dampener on it. For one, neither the king's mother nor his siblings were present; upon hearing that her brother, second-oldest son and Thomas Vaughan had been arrested, the dowager queen fled to sanctuary with all her daughters and the king's younger brother,[774] rather baffling people, including the young king when he heard of it.[775] Additionally, Edward

V's procession was followed by four carts of weapons, with criers announcing that these weapons had been kept by the Woodville family and their supporters outside the city to attack Richard of Gloucester and Henry of Buckingham once they arrived.[776]

This latter story is feasible, though Mancini claimed that these weapons had been stockpiled before the gates of the City of London for use against the Scots.[777] It has been suggested that this is rather unlikely, as London is rather far away from Scotland and it would have made no sense to stash weapons there – even less so since the Scots were considered defeated for the time being in summer 1482[778] – but this version must have been popular in London for Mancini to include it in his report.

This is one aspect in which John Jnr must have been absolutely sure of the truth; he had been involved enough in the government to know if weapons had been stockpiled for use against Scotland, and if so where they had been stored. But, as mentioned above, this does not have to mean he was actually unbiased, simply that he knew the truth. Perhaps, like William Hastings, he simply sided against the Woodvilles and had no interest in defending them with the truth. It has to be pointed out, however, that we do not actually know where John Jnr was in the weeks that followed. He did not seem to be involved when the regency council took up its work. There are a lot of rumours also about this regency council, and what it did at first.[779]

As had apparently been stipulated by Edward IV in his will, Richard of Gloucester was confirmed as lord protector – this is one of the few actions that appeared to be uncontroversial among the council's members. We do not know the identities of every member of the council, but we do know some Henry, Duke of Buckingham; Thomas, Baron Stanley; John, Lord Howard; John Morton, Bishop of Ely; and William, Baron Hastings. Neither John nor John Jnr ever claimed to have been members, and there is no evidence they were. Though John Jnr was the recipient of some grants and made a member of several commissions,[780] this does not have to mean he was physically present in London then. His father had regularly been given such positions in commissions in the last twenty years without ever seeming to participate in any but a few regional ones. Such grants were often purely nominal.

Though it is perhaps somewhat unlikely that John Jnr would have left London when the regency council started up its work had he stayed there after Edward's funeral, it is possible he left London immediately after the funeral due to the same family emergency that had compelled his parents to stop attending Edward IV's funeral. This was the death of John Jnr's next oldest brother. It is actually not known exactly when this boy died, only that it must have been between 1480 and spring 1483. There is no indication for any sort of mourning going on in the family in 1481 or 1482, so perhaps the most likely is that he died around the same time as his uncle Edward, which might explain why John and Elizabeth chose not to go to Edward's funeral, and possibly also why John Jnr was not mentioned in any of what went on in London after his uncle's funeral; he might have gone home to Wingfield immediately after it was over. If his brother was already sick by then, it would explain why his parents did not want to leave him to go to Edward IV's funeral, quite naturally considering it more important to stay with their sick or already dying son than to attend the king's funeral. John Jnr would at the very least have wanted to be present when his brother was buried.

However, even such a horrid blow was hardly uncommon at the time, and life had to go on. Perhaps it was something that helped take their minds off this recent death when they went to London at the end of May or early June to, as they would have thought, attend the coronation of their nephew and cousin. Presumably, they believed the information they had received that the coronation for the new king had been scheduled, or they believed that, as was initially claimed after the regency council took up its work, it would take place on 24 June.[781]

At first, all appeared to go smoothly. Richard, Duke of Gloucester sent a letter to York on 5 June, which indicated he expected his nephew's coronation and his first years of kingship would go well under his protectorship. Though it has been mostly ignored by commenters, whether due to bias or hindsight, Richard and the regency council also made concrete plans for the coronation, ordering clothes for the young king and even having coins minted with Edward V on them. Apparently thinking that the coronation was near, several wives of men on the regency council arrived in London, most notably the protector's wife Anne. So did several nobles who were not on the regency council.[782] It seems likely that John, Elizabeth, John Jnr and Edmund also arrived in London at that time, perhaps also accompanied by Elizabeth Jnr and Anne. Neither John nor John Jnr had anything to do with what was to follow. Once more, they would have presumably only have heard of it through rumours, putting the two Johns in a very similar situation to us today. Naturally, unlike us, they would have been able to quiz those who had actually been present, if they were interested in doing so.

Shortly after they arrived, trouble started in the capital. On 8 June, Richard of Gloucester and the members of the regency council were supposedly informed of something that changed everything.[783] This was when Richard was told by Robert Stillington, Bishop of Bath and Wells, that Edward IV's secret marriage to Elizabeth Woodville had not been his first marriage; he had apparently made another secret marriage, sometimes said to have been officiated over by Stillington himself.[784] This previously unknown secret marriage was meant to have taken place in 1461, the supposed bride being Lady Eleanor Talbot.[785] If this was true, it would mean that Elizabeth Woodville was never truly Edward's wife, and that her children with him were illegitimate, meaning Edward V was not the rightful king. In fact, if it was correct, Richard of Gloucester himself should be king.

Naturally, because of how he died and what happened afterwards, it has often been claimed in subsequent centuries that Richard himself fabricated the story.[786] Others strenuously argue against that.[787] There is some evidence for it being true,[788] but we probably will never know for certain. However, even if the claims were false, Richard might not have been responsible and he might have genuinely believed them.[789] Many others certainly did.[790]

The day after this news was put about, a letter from one Simon Stallingsworth was sent in which he explains that 'all the lords temporal and spiritual'[791] were also present and would have heard, if Richard did not tell them before, of this supposed pre-contract. If Richard invented the story of the pre-contract, or it was invented for him, it is unlikely he would have told either John or John Jnr. Like most others, they were left to work out for themselves what they thought of the new information and whether they should believe it. Apparently they either believed in it or thought it was better for them and for the kingdom if Richard became king instead of young Edward. Such sentiments seem to have been shared by most of the lords, and Stallingsworth's report that there were 'a lot of words against the coronation'[792] soon became truth. Edward V was considered the rightful king no longer.

Not everyone accepted this; there were voices against it, and some protests as well. They might have been made because the protesters believed Edward V was in fact the true heir to the throne, the rightful king. They might also have been made because the protesters did not like the thought of Richard being in power, rightful or not. Both would be perfectly likely motives, and perhaps it was a mixture of both.

The most famous protesters to actively work against Richard were William, Baron Hastings, John Morton, Bishop of Ely and several others of lesser standing.[793] Even in sources written in Tudor times it was claimed they were plotting against Richard, and doing so before the pre-contract, which they always claimed was fabricated, became public.[794] As such, their plotting may not have solely been because of Richard's sudden grab for power; perhaps Richard was seen as a danger to these men even as mere protector.

Certainly, Richard was openly afraid for his life, and not only his, after the pre-contract became widely known. Only a day afterwards, on 10 June, he wrote a rather panicked letter to York[795] stating that Elizabeth Woodville and her supporters wanted to harm or kill him and his supporters, and on 11 June he wrote another letter to his cousin, Lord Neville, asking for help in both.[796] Whatever one thinks of Richard, it is hard to deny the letters conveyed real panic. It is not quite clear who Richard was afraid of other than Elizabeth Woodville, and who else he feared for. Though he said that the queen wanted to harm 'the old royal blood of the realm',[797] there were not too many royals of this old blood present in the capital apart from himself and Henry, Duke of Buckingham, who was his first cousin once removed. John Jnr, his younger brother

Edmund, his sisters if they were present and his mother were perhaps the most royal personages then present in London after Richard himself, but there is no indication any of them was meant in Richard's letter. John Jnr was not mentioned in any source connected with the succession crisis, nor was his father or anyone else from their family, not even when the situation escalated on 13 June 1483.[798]

On this day, perhaps the most famous event of the succession crisis took place. The treason – or, as has often been claimed, invented treason – of William Hastings and his co-conspirators was discovered. This was supposedly an attempt to kill Richard and those closest to him.[799] However, the plan was betrayed to Richard[800] and he reacted to it immediately. Contrary to later propagandists and historians,[801] Richard was not actually prepared for any conflict and had only sent for armed men a few days before;[802] they had not yet arrived in London, so he needed help. Most other nobles in the capital had men with them, though we do not actually know if this was true for John or John Jnr. If they did, it was probably not the number of men Richard needed to engage with the men on Hastings's side. Nor do we know if either John or John Jnr would have been prepared to offer their men to Richard. John Jnr might have been prepared to do fight, since he was later to show closeness to Richard, but in this particular case he might just as well have wanted to sit it out. The father and son who did help Richard and offer their men to him were John, Lord Howard and his son Thomas.[803] John Howard had enough men to help take up arms against Hastings's men, and Thomas Howard, a seasoned fighter, actually helped lead them.[804]

What supposedly happened was that Richard, having been told of Hastings and his co-conspirators' treason, confronted them with it at the next meeting of the regency council, which took place on Friday 13 June 1483.[805] In response, Hastings, who had come to the meeting armed, attacked Richard,[806] who called for help. The Howard men then came in to disarm Hastings, arrest him and his co-conspirators and defuse the situation.[807]

There is a suggestion that Hastings was given a short trial under the Law of Arms.[808] In any case, he was executed on the same day,[809] which naturally has commanded all conversation about this day's events. Most historians in the intervening centuries have swallowed later Tudor propaganda about Richard randomly and unlawfully murdering people who stood in his way, while at the same time insisting that Hastings did not actually plot against Richard.[810] Some of the few historians who did not do so have pointed out that Richard's actions may very well have been the equivalent of self-defence.[811] More recently, it has been more accepted that Hastings did actually receive a trial under the Law of Arms; what this entailed is detailed by Annette Carson.[812] This squares with the evidence we actually have for the situation on 13 June, including the fact that evidence was shown to the city fathers.[813] This, of course, does not have to mean such evidence was not fabricated, and that Hastings's execution and the arrest of the others was righteous; it does, however, mean it was legal.

Domenico Mancini, the best source we have for these proceedings, reports that many people disbelieved Richard's claims,[814] but he also states that the town criers instructed by Richard to explain the situation effectively dispelled any panic there had been in the city.[815] This has to mean that many people believed Richard's actions were rightful, even if Mancini was not among their number.

It can reasonably be assumed that John and John Jnr at the very least supported Richard's actions. If he was not already so, John Jnr was about to become close to his uncle Richard, which might account for his support. Meanwhile, John himself was never to show any particular closeness to Richard, though they also did not seem to have any problems with one another. He was, however, close to John, Lord Howard,[816] who was closely involved in the events of the succession crisis and a strong supporter of Richard's, which suggests that at the very least that John was not repulsed by what was unfolding.

With Hastings's arrest and execution, and the arrest of his co-conspirators, who included Hastings's secretary and Edward's erstwhile mistress Elizabeth Shore,[817] the greatest trouble in the capital had been quelled. Arrangements were soon being made for Richard to take the throne. Though none of the Suffolks were noted to have been involved in any of the lead-up throughout June, it is reasonable to assume they were at the very least present when a sermon was preached to the masses in London stating why Richard was rightful king, and also when Henry, Duke of Buckingham gave a speech outlining these claims,[818] and when, finally, the kingship was formally offered to Richard in his mother's townhouse.[819]

Suffolk's in Richard III's Government

It may even have been quite a happy occasion for the family, and perhaps they hoped for preferment from Richard they had never got from Edward, or, in the case of John Jnr, for a continuance of the preferment shown to him by Edward. John Jnr was not to be disappointed if he held such hopes; he was favoured by his uncle Richard even more than he was by his uncle Edward.

His parents, John and Elizabeth, were not quite so lucky. Though Richard did not ever disadvantage them in the way Edward often had, he also gave them no special favour. However, he was to take special care of their children, even more so than Edward had done. Also, they at least had important parts in the coronation that was planned after Richard had officially taken the throne on 26 June 1483, although they do not seem to have been at all involved in the preparations.

Unlike during Edward's reign, John was to find several of his close associates in position of power in Richard's government. Perhaps the most notable instance of this, in the very beginning of Richard's reign, before even the coronation, was the elevation of his closest friend to the position of lord chamberlain. Richard's closest friend was Lord Francis Lovell,[820] John's former ward and John Jnr's former foster brother. The two young men appear to have been close, and it might have paid for John to not only have his brother-in-law, one better disposed towards him than Edward had been, as king but his foster son and others who were close to him in positions of power.

The first sign of favour by Richard towards the family was his decision to include their son Edmund, who was only ten years of age, in the list of men and boys who were to be knighted on the day before his coronation.[821] It was normal before coronations for a number of young men to be knighted, and so naturally Edmund was not the only one singled out for such an honour. However, even so, his inclusion was a sign of favour, and had he not been related to the king it seems very likely he would not have been knighted at such a young age.

Edmund's inclusion in the number of boys and men to be knighted before Richard's execution also shows that his older brother, the one older than Edward but younger than John Jnr, must have definitely been dead by then. Much as he must have been alive when Edward started living at Oxford University, as a spare would never have been made a member of the clergy, Edmund would never have been given the honour of being knighted in such a ceremony if he had an older brother without a knighthood.

Edmund would have gone through the same ceremony Richard himself had gone through at a slightly younger age before Edward's coronation. There would have been a ceremony that lasted a day and ended with the new king ceremoniously conferring the honour of a knighthood on his young nephew and his companions. Presumably, John and Elizabeth would have been proud, and John Jnr quite possibly as well, though they had to prepare for more important tasks in the coronation itself. All three of them had been granted clothing, or fabric for clothing, the same as almost everyone included in the coronation received – Francis Lovell being the one notable exception.

For Elizabeth, who was in the queen's train the night before the coronation, this meant she received two fine dresses, one of red silk and white damask, one of blue velvet and red silk.[822] The latter dress was worn by her, and all other ladies in the queen's train, in the queen's procession the night before the coronation, while the red and white dress was meant for the actual coronation ceremony.[823] The men received three ells of red fabric each, meaning that John and John Jnr, much like most of the other men, would have matched during the ceremonies.[824] This choice of dresses and fabric for the men was not made by Richard; it was very common for coronations and had been used by most of his predecessors for nearly a century.[825] Since it was the first double coronation since 1308, when Edward II and his queen Isabella had been crowned together, several aspects of the ceremony were different than they were during Edward IV's coronation and would be during Henry VII's. For one, it was, by necessity, a bigger, grander affair, as not only one but two people were being crowned.

Richard's coronation went down in history as a particularly well-attended one,[826] and both the actual ceremony and the following festivities are quite well recorded. Elizabeth, Duchess of Suffolk got a position of honour in the procession of the queen into Westminster Abbey, where the coronation took place.[827] She walked directly behind the queen and Lady Margaret, Baroness Stanley, who had the honour of carrying the queen's train.[828] Elizabeth led the procession behind her.[829] Her husband and oldest son were both in the king's procession. John, in fact, held the same position he had performed in Elizabeth's coronation, carrying the sceptre.[830] It was therefore not a position of honour explicitly chosen as a sign of affection, favour or gratitude by the new king, but it was a position of honour nonetheless, and John might have enjoyed filling it.

For John Jnr, it was of course his first participation in a coronation, as he had not yet been born when his uncle Edward had been crowned, and had been only two years old when Queen Elizabeth had been crowned. He, too, was given a position of honour by the new king, but one that reflected his station in life as an earl, a duke's heir and the king's nephew; it was nothing personal. He carried the 'ball and cross, signifying the monarchy'.[831] As Peter Hammond and Anne Sutton point out in their book *The Coronation of Richard III: The Extant Documents*, both Johns received the positions that were their due, not only because of their close familial relationship to the king but because they were political powers that were needed.[832]

The coronation appears to have been a happy occasion. After the ceremony was done, a banquet took place. Once the participants had some time for themselves, John, Elizabeth and John Jnr all received positions due to their standing as well, sitting at the same table as the king and queen. There is no mention of Edmund in any source, so it might be he was deemed too young to participate in the banquet.

The banquet, much as the coronation ceremony before that, went according to tradition, as it had for countless other coronations before and would for many afterwards. Naturally, there was a lot of standing on ceremony involved, but there is no reason to believe that the Suffolks had anything but a pleasant time.

12

Lincoln in Richard III's Government

After the coronation was over, the new king, together with his queen and most of his nobles, retired to the palace of Westminster for two weeks. The Suffolks joined him there as well, presumably together with Edmund, though only his parents and John Jnr are explicitly mentioned by sources. This stay at Westminster was as informal as a royal court ever got, and while the king made some grants and could not forsake matters of state, no official duties were performed. If John Jnr had not been close to his uncle before that time, he seems to have become so during the summer of 1483. They were certainly close in age, much closer than John Jnr had been with Edward, which might have helped them form a friendly relationship very quickly. In fact, John Jnr was closer in age to his uncle Richard than he was to many of his siblings, the age gap between being the same as between John Jnr and his brother Edward. Richard certainly seemed to like John Jnr, but he was not alone in that. Nearly everyone liked John Jnr; he had no enemies during all his time at the courts of Richard III and Henry VII.

As for John Jnr's feelings for Richard, those are harder to guess at. As time passed, his actions certainly suggest he came to like him, but it is perfectly possible that he originally started having no strong feelings of either sort for his uncle, simply seeing his accession as a good opportunity to carve out a place as a very important man at court. Being just about to come of age, it is possible that John Jnr considered his time had come for a bigger, more important part in national politics and wanted to make sure it happened by befriending his uncle. However, this is not too likely. While John Jnr did not share his father's distaste for national politics, he also never showed any eagerness to be involved, and if this was his intention when Richard ascended the throne he was extremely subtle about it.

Whatever his motivation, John Jnr chose to stay with his uncle, who, after two weeks of staying at Westminster, went on his first royal progress through the country. He was one of the very few men who stayed with Richard during the entire progress, his erstwhile foster brother being one of the others. His parents were not. Though they appear to have joined Richard on the very first leg of the journey, which was more than they ever did for Edward, they did not stay long. However, during that fairly short time they appeared to do some rather successful networking at the new court. Moreover, it seems that their most dire money problems were either over, or at the very least delayed, at that moment in time. From summer 1483, during the time of the progress, a mention of a gift from John to John Howard, newly made Duke of Norfolk, survives: a gift of a horse.[833]

John and John Howard were in fact on friendly terms before that; as mentioned above, in Howard's household accounts a visit to the Suffolk household in December is mentioned. It seems like John was eager to continue this friendly association. This could have been out of simple friendship, but perhaps there was also a wish to keep up a friendship with someone who had become very important in the new government. In any case, it appeared to work. The two men remained close.

After making this gift to Lord Howard, it seems like John, Elizabeth and young Edmund left the royal procession, going back to Suffolk. Though a different brother of Elizabeth's now sat on the throne, and they could hope for better treatment from him than they had had from Edward, and though they were now more connected with important men in the government than they had been before, it does not seem like they wanted to change their lifestyle much. Indeed, nothing much changed in their lives while Richard was king, though John found himself involved in government actions slightly more often than during Edward's time.[834] A lot was to change for John Jnr, though, who had never held such a position at Edward's court as he was to hold at Richard's. He soon became a fixture, staying at his uncle's side throughout his first royal progress.

The progress appears to have been a success for the king and something of a celebration for all those around him. As they made their way through England, Richard was famously praised by Thomas Langton as the best king he could imagine, a godsend.[835] Famously, he also stated that Richard was becoming rather more sensuous, though he did not consider this to detract from the praise he had heaped on him.[836] Though this was about Richard directly, and not specified, it certainly suggests he was not the strict, nearly Puritan, presence he has so often been depicted as since, and presumably this reflects the mood of the court, which would have been very good during the royal progress.

From Westminster, the court first went to Windsor, where John Jnr's parents and younger brother appear to have left court. The queen decided to stay at Windsor for a while on her own for reasons unknown,[837] and after two days at Windsor the court went on without her. It is not known why she stayed behind, though perhaps it was to wait for the Spanish ambassador.[838] Since she does not seem to have been much of a presence at court, it is likely her absence would not have put a dampener on the mood of the courtiers as they progressed to Reading, where they stayed another two days before going to Oxford, where Richard had apparently chosen to go for his own pleasure, to visit the university and listen to some disputations.[839]

They were greeted by the chancellor of the university, and by Lionel Woodville, who was president. As one of the nobles of highest standing at Richard's court, John Jnr was the first lord temporal of the king's entourage listed in the report the university wrote for their annals about the visit:

> On the twenty-second day of July, Lord William Waynflete; Bishop of Winchester, revered in Christ the holy father and lord, founder of the college, came to Oxford, and supervised the state of his college and the buildings of the same, and also to respectfully receive the illustrious lord King Richard the Third in its often-named college, making [his way] towards Woodstock.
>
> On the twenty-fourth day of the month, the illustrious lord King Richard the Third was respectfully received at first out[side] the university by the chancellor of the university and by counsilors and non-counsilors. After the respectful reception and the procession into the college of the blessed Mary Magdalen by the said lord founder and by the president and scholars, they spent the night there and the day after, which was the day of St Jacob [James] the Apostel, and the day of St Anne, mother of Mary, until after breakfast, with many spiritual and temporal lords and other nobles, as befitted them.
>
> At the same time as the king, there came to the college the lord bishop of Durham, the lord bishop of Worcester, the lord bishop of St Asaph and master Thomas Langton, bishop-elect of St David's, his lordship the earl of Lincoln, the lord steward the earl of Surrey, the lord chamberlain, lord of Lovell, lord Stanley, lord Audeley, lord Becham, lord Richard Radclyff knight, and several other nobles, who stayed the night in the college, and our lord founder received them with honour.
>
> On the twenty-fifth of the month, commanded and desired by the lord king, there were made in the great hall of the college two disputations; the first being in moral philosophy by master Thomas Kerver, opposing one of the students of the same college. Then, there was another solemn disputation, theological, in the presence of the king, by master John Taylour, professor of sacred theology, and the master William Grocyn answering. All of whom were honourably and greatly rewarded by the lord king, namely,

the doctor of theology, with a buck and a hundred shillings, his responder [opponent] with a buck and five marks, the master who disputed in philosophy with one buck and five marks, and the student responding with one buck and forty shillings. Moreover, the noble king gave the president and scholars two bucks with five marks for wine, etc.

May the king live eternally.[840]

Sadly, the report makes no mention what any of the nobles accompanying Richard did when he was listening to disputations. Perhaps John Jnr, who had grown up in a household that very much valued scholarship and the written word, joined his uncle. However, unlike for his father, mother, and in fact his uncle Richard, there is no indication that John Jnr was at all interested in scholarship. Whether or not he joined him, it stands to reason he would have found time to visit his younger brother Edward, who by that time had been at Oxford University for nearly three years. Sadly, this might have been the last time the two brothers ever saw each other.

From Oxford, the royal progress went on to Woodstock, though the king rode back to Oxford on the evening of their arrival for reasons unknown. He may or may not have taken John Jnr with him, but afterwards the latter was definitely at his side in Woodstock, from where the court went to Minster Lovell Hall, the home of the king's lord chamberlain. Though a small village even then, John Jnr might very well have visited it before when going to visit his former foster brother. It was a very peaceful village, and the lord chamberlain's ancestral manor was beautiful. Richard chose to stay there for four days, which was longer than he had stayed in any town on the way there.

Perhaps the stay there was intended to be something of a breather, but news was to arrive that threatened the tranquil Oxfordshire sojourn. There was trouble in the capital; someone was apparently trying to kidnap John Jnr's famous cousins, the former Edward V and his younger brother Richard, who are known to history as the Princes in the Tower. Richard reacted to this attempt immediately, writing a letter to the Bishop of Lincoln, instructing him to 'make our letters of commissions to such persons as by you and our council shall be adviced for to sit upon them'.[841]

Recently, it has been suggested that with this letter he gave orders for the two boys' murder,[842] but for all the mystery surrounding their fate we know this to be factually untrue. The erstwhile princes were still seen alive by the end of August 1483,[843] a month after the letter was written. In fact, there is even some debate whether the letter was really about an attempt to kidnap them at all; some have suggested it was in fact about an attempt to smuggle some of their sisters out of sanctuary, an idea that is suggested by the Crowland Chronicle.[844] At the very least this must have occurred to the king as a possibility; he made arrangements against such an endeavour, positioning armed guards around Westminster Abbey.[845]

However, even such events do not seem to have much disturbed the festive attitude at court. From Minster Lovell, the court went on to Gloucester, and from there to Tewkesbury,[846] where the new king, possibly accompanied by his oldest nephew, visited the graves of his brother George and sister-in-law Isabel, and paid some debts his brother had left behind.[847] On this progress, the king naturally did not only display himself; matters of state still had to be addressed. On 14 August 1483, Richard, among other things, granted the constableship of Wallingford Castle to his lord chamberlain.[848] John Jnr might not have been very pleased by this, and certainly his father would not have been once he heard of it. The grant included all the privileges associated with the constableship, and by passing them to Francis Lovell the king actively took them from John, who had held them since 1471.

Both the men had a family claim to the constableship of Wallingford Castle, as both their ancestors had held it and these offices at various times, but there is no telling why Richard suddenly decided to take them from John and give them to Francis, other than an inclination to give his lord chamberlain whatever he wanted. John might have been hurt by the transfer, and perhaps more so by it being taken by his former ward, whom he had treated extremely well. However, it seems to have caused no trouble between John and Francis. John lacked his son's subtlety and very much showed when he was displeased, especially where possessions were concerned, so their continued good relationship presumably means John did not carry a grudge about it.

It is, in fact, perfectly possible that there was an arrangement between John and his former ward that might explain the grant. It is also possible Francis asked for the grant on the strength of the constableship of Wallingford once belonging to his grandfather without asking John about it beforehand or making an arrangement for it but that John, despite presumably not being pleased, understood the struggle for possessions only too well and therefore did not resent him. Whichever it was, it is clear that John, though greedy for possessions like any noble, was not the horrible man that is so often depicted, downright obsessed with amassing as many possessions as he could. The news of this loss also did not turn John against his brother-in-law Richard.

After the court left Tewkesbury and John Jnr's relatives' tombs behind, the progress went on to Worcester and from there to Warwick. The court stayed there for a bit longer as the queen arrived to join the progress again, re-joining her husband and bringing with her the Spanish ambassador.[849] The chronicler John Rous described the meeting with this ambassador, stating that 'there were then at Warwick with the king the prelates of Worcester, Coventry, Lichfield, Durham, and the bishop of St Asaph, the Duke of Albany, brother of the Scottish king, the Earl of

Huntingdon, John Earl of Lincoln, and the lords Stanley, Dudley, Morley, Scrope and Francis Lord Lovell, chamberlain of the king, and William Hussy, main justiciar of England, and many other lords'.[850] Obviously, Rous did not consider John Jnr to be any more important than any of the other lords he mentioned, giving the impression he was simply one of the many men whom Richard consulted on the proposals brought by the ambassador, which according to Rous included a proposal of marriage between Richard's only legitimate son, Prince Edward, and one of the Spanish monarchs' daughters.[851]

Whether John Jnr would have had a lot to say about the discussions is doubtful given that he had not been involved in national politics long enough to really have a firm grasp of foreign affairs. For the same reason, it is doubtful if any thoughts he expressed on the subject would have been taken very seriously by the king or anyone else. However, it is notable that by now he was considered important enough to include in such discussions. John Jnr appears to have been satisfied with that for the time being. He seemed perfectly cheerful, and was included in court functions as the court went on from Warwick to Coventry, then to Leicester, Nottingham Castle, Pontefract Castle and finally York, where great festivities were to take place. John Jnr figured prominently in the entertainments, yet did not draw much attention from any chronicler.

John Jnr participated in Richard's triumphant entry into the City of York. The king, his queen and his only legitimate son, who had arrived from his nursery at Middleham Castle for the occasion, entered the city to the great delight of many watching inhabitants. The York Civic Records describe the occasion in detail, stating that a delegation of the city's aldermen met the party immediately outside the city and then progressed into York, where they were greeted by 'persons of every occupation',[852] dressed finely as they went through the streets to reach the archbishop's palace, where they were to stay during their visit. Along the way, three pageants were staged for them, and the king and queen were presented with generous gifts of money and plate. Those attending are said to have been, apart from the king himself, 'the Queen and the Prince, and many other magnates, both spiritual and temporal, including five bishops, those of Durham, Worcester, St. Asaph's, Carlisle and St. David's, the Earls of Northumberland, Surrey and Lincoln, Lords Lovell, FitzHugh, Stanley, Strange, Lisle and Greystoke and many others'.[853] Clearly John Jnr was important enough to be noted, perhaps more because of his title and connections than anything else, but no more important than any other nobles. This was the case for the majority of the time in York; he was there, but did not stick out.

Two further big events took place during this time. The king and queen had a church service during which they were greeted as was their due, though for some reason there was no anthem sung for the queen.[854] An even more notable event that took place during that time was the investiture of John Jnr's cousin, Richard's legitimate son Edward, as Prince of Wales.[855] It was a grand celebration, so great that rumours started that Richard had celebrated a second coronation in York.[856] Though naturally this was provably untrue, it might have been a rumour that caused unrest in the southern parts of the country, in which it was already rumoured with concern that due to Richard's previous close association with the north of the country he would favour those parts and they would be disadvantaged.[857] This might have actually contributed to the trouble that was to happen a month after little Prince Edward's investiture, but at the time no one at the royal court yet knew of it.

Richard spared no expense for his son's investiture. The Spanish ambassador, who was still with the court, was knighted by Richard as part of the festivities. So was the young prince's half-brother, Richard's illegitimate son John, and his nephew, George of Clarence's son, little Edward, Earl of Warwick.[858] The investiture is also described in great detail in the York Civic Records. Again, John Jnr attended the ceremony.[859] He might have enjoyed it, as it was a grand celebration, though he hardly knew his young cousin. Even if he was not very interested in the child, the celebration once more showed Richard's great popularity in York.

John Jnr was probably not well acquainted with Yorkshire then, as few of his family's holdings were there, and he himself held only one manor and some lands there of comparatively little worth. It seems likely, therefore, that he would not have been very interested in this part of the country before 1483. However, even at this early time in Richard's reign, the king might have informed his oldest nephew that his future plans for him would involve him mainly staying in the northern parts of England, serving in a council he intended to set up under the nominal presidency of his young son.[860] Though this council was only officially created half a year later, it must have been planned for longer, and perhaps in autumn 1483 Richard was already making sure John Jnr knew of his future task, and John Jnr busy preparing himself for it.

However, the time to calmly do so would not last for much longer. After Prince Edward's investiture, Richard as well as his queen and his son stayed in York a bit longer. Richard granted a tax exemption to the city, and was celebrated wherever he went. It was a very successful visit, and not only Richard but his whole court, including John Jnr, must have felt happy and hopeful for the future when he finally left the town at the beginning of October. At least Richard's actions suggest so, and it is reasonable to assume John Jnr felt the same. By this time, he definitely appears to have become close to his uncle, and he was with him in the town of Lincoln, close to some of his own possessions, when the king learnt of the brewing rebellion[861] and moreover, of the betrayal of Henry, Duke of Buckingham, who had supported Richard during the succession crisis and had been so rewarded by Richard.[862]

The Rebellion of 1483

The rebellion was mainly by disaffected southerners and Woodville supporters, as well as some Lancastrian exiles seeing a chance to finally come back to England.[863] It has been blown out of proportion in the centuries since, but there can be no doubt it was considered rather dangerous at the time. Richard immediately did what he could to counteract it, sending various supporters to gather men and prepare to fight. One of them was his brother-in-law, John, who rose to the occasion as best he could, sending off letters to order men to assemble. One of them, to John Paston of all people, actually still survives:

> Our said most dread Sovereign Lord, as a Christian Prince, his said enemies and rebels to resist, has assigned and commanded us to do all manner and others defensible able to labour, as well archers as hobbellers, to come before us, and charge them armed, and arrayed every man after his degree and power, to attend upon his person, and upon us, to do him service, in defence, as well of the church as of the said nobles and subjects of this ' realm, against his said enemies and rebels. We therefore will, and, in our said Sovereign Lord's name, straitly charge and command you, that in all possible haste ye do this to be proclaimed. And that all manner men able to do the King service, as all Knights, Esquires, and Gentlemen, as townships and hundreds, as well within franchises and liberties as without, within the counties of Suffolk and Norfolk; and that they be charged to be ready at all times, upon an hour's warning, and ordered according to the last commission afore this, to attend upon his Grace, and upon us, to do him service, whensoever they shall be commanded: not failing hereof, as ye will answer at your peril.
>
> Given at Long Stretton [in Norfolk] the 20th day of October. And furthermore, that ye give credence unto our servant this bringer, as this same day we received the King's commission at 4 after noon.
>
> Suffolk, your friend.[864]

This shows that John, once more going against the reputation he has been given by historians, was perfectly willing to take a role in conflicts to see them resolved for the side he picked. As usual, his capabilities were limited; he could only gather a finite number of men due to his difficult financial situation, and he could not fight himself. However, this was known to Richard and he only expected John to do what he could. In this, he was not disappointed.

John Jnr also appears to have helped; certainly, he was later rewarded for helping to suppress the rebellion. What exactly he did we do not know, but it seems reasonable to assume he offered military assistance of some sort. This would have been the first time John Jnr was ever involved in any military operation at all, and though it ended without actual fighting, it must have been a special experience for him. The rebellion seemed to seal the close relationship between John Jnr and Richard, perhaps because it showed to Richard that he could completely trust his oldest nephew even in a crisis. The young man had supported his uncle in the face of nasty rumours flying around about him, most concerning the fate of John Jnr's famous cousins, 'the Princes in the Tower'.

It has since become accepted that the rebellion started because of a popular conviction that Richard had ordered the two boys killed,[865] but whatever actually happened to them this is not true. We actually know for a fact that the rebellion was first planned when the boys were provably still alive and seen in the Tower.[866] In fact, the Crowland Chronicle, written very early in the reign of Henry VII, in the spring of 1486, claimed that the rumours were started by the rebels explicitly to turn people against Richard.[867]

What actually happened to the boys remains a mystery. Perhaps John Jnr did not know either. Though it seems logical to assume he knew something – and if he did, so did his parents – we cannot actually know for certain that this was the case. Whatever he knew, he clearly chose to remain loyal to his uncle. If he even believed it was possible Richard had killed his cousins, this decision would make him look both cold-hearted and reckless, as it might have put himself in danger as a focal point of rebellion. But neither he nor his father, who had shown a tendency to be very kind to children and teenagers, nor Elizabeth, who was explicitly a peacemaker, in any way distanced themselves from Richard. However, this is of course a rather vague claim of the strength of characters of people so long dead, and not solid evidence as to what happened to the boys.

Whatever the Suffolks thought, believed or knew, they remained very loyal to Richard. In fact, John Jnr ever became closer to his uncle. For John Jnr, November 1483 must have been an exciting, significant month. It was then, after the rebellion had petered out, he went to court with Richard. Despite the fact the rebellion had eventually failed without causing much harm, it had stirred up enough trouble to require some cleaning up. John Jnr was on several commissions to find and arrest rebels.[868] We do not know if any of them were successful, but it is possible that it was his actions in these commissions that later saw him rewarded. However, the rewards were rather substantial, including the lucrative manors of Wodehay, Westbury and Roos, so there might have been more going on.[869]

John Jnr did not only receive those manors. While the rebellion was still ongoing, he had reached his majority – though, as he was not a duke yet and was lucky enough to have a living father, he might still have looked forward to it. John appeared to consider it an important milestone. It was almost certainly at that time that he granted John Jnr 60 acres of meadow in the parish of the More, as well as the manors of Fyfield, Long Wittenham, Eaton, Frylsham, Garford, Streteley, Burfelde, Garsyngton, Nethernhall and Grymston, which were in the counties of Essex and Oxfordshire. John also granted him the tenements and lands of Brokdisshe. All in all, these grants had an income of £147 annually, meaning that John Jnr's wealth at least kept pace with his growing responsibilities. He did not, however, receive a summons to Parliament in January 1483, possibly because his birthday had been too shortly before the invitations went out.

Maybe he did not have the time to think about it very long, for there was a lot to be done in the aftermath of the rebellion. As the dust settled, Lady Margaret Stanley, who had carried the queen's train at her coronation, was outed as one of the main instigators of the rebellion.

When she was punished, John Jnr was one of the main benefactors of her confiscated wealth.[870] He was to receive a large part of it, explicitly lands worth £334, 2s *5d* annually.[871] However, he was not to receive it immediately. Famously, her husband Thomas, Baron Stanley was to hold her lands and possessions during his lifetime,[872] and John Jnr was to receive those of her lands granted to him after Stanley's death. Such an arrangement was not uncommon, and John Jnr did not have to cope with being given only empty or at least cheap promises as a reward for his services; in recompense, John received the sizable sum of £176 13*s* 4*d* annually until such a time that the Beaufort lands would fall to him from the Duchy of Cornwall.[873]

John Jnr was a rich man from then on, though he does not appear to have shown very much interest in his newly acquired possessions, never being recorded to have ridden out to see the lands. It is of course possible he did so, but any such visit must have been brief, for we know his whereabouts for the majority of 1484. In this lack of interest he showed a similarity to his former foster brother, Francis Lovell, who equally received sizeable grants of lands in reward for his support during the 1483, and who never ventured out to them. Though in Francis's case a lack of travelling seems to have been because of some unspecified illness, it is still interesting to note the similarity, which might have been the result of influence from John and Elizabeth.

Perhaps it was a certain similarity to his best friend that also made Richard warm to John Jnr. Whatever it was, they were definitely close by December 1483 despite the fact John Jnr did not receive a summons to Parliament. It may be that in this month, too, after the first fallout from the rebellion had been dealt with, he rode home to see his family, especially his siblings whom he had not seen for nearly a year, and his parents, whom he had not seen for nearly half a year. However, it is also possible his parents came to celebrate Christmas at court, though that would have been out of character. We do not know much of the festivities at court that Christmas, but it seems to have been a massive celebration. Richard ran up £1,200 worth of debts, and pawned some plates to the City of London to pay for it.[874]

The king had clearly decided to celebrate Christmas in style, perhaps even purchasing jewels for the occasion as on 9 December he gave a safe conduct to a jeweller on the condition he himself got the first pick of his wares.[875] There would have been mummeries, songs and minstrels, but also a focus on the religious part of the celebration. Such a focus might have delighted the very pious John and Elizabeth, if indeed they were present, though what John Jnr thought is less easy to guess. We do not even know if he was present. If not, we know he returned to the capital soon after Christmas with his father, who was to attend his uncle Richard's first – and, as history was to show, only – parliament.[876] It was a very good one, and has been praised ever since, even during times when he was deeply unpopular. The Victorian Lord Campbell called it 'the best Parliament for common people since Henry II',[877] who had reigned some three hundred years before Richard. There was a similar comment made in Tudor times to Cardinal Wolsey.[878]

Many measures were enacted for the good of the commoners, such as forbidding people to sell anything with cloud on title (a disputed claim) and reforming the bail system.[879] A rather more xenophobic measure, which was greeted by English merchants, basically stripped Italian merchants of most of their rights as businessmen.[880] All in all, it was a parliament with which the English people were happy, which was surely all that counted for an English king. John did not get involved at all in legislation; most probably, he would not have particularly cared, as he had never shown the slightest interest in any lawmaking in the previous parliaments he had attended.

John was considering his own ideas when the parliament ended. On its last day, 20 February 1484, he was granted a licence to found a 'fraternity or gild' together with the Bishop of Lincoln and his former ward Francis Lovell. Called the 'Fraternity of the Holy Cross of Abendon', it was the renewal of an older foundation and was to have 'twelve masters, secular persons or other of either sex', with its primary purpose 'the repair of the highway leading from Abendon to Dorchester, co[unt] Oxford'. John's position in this was fairly conventional. His greatest input was in the 'thirteen poor men and women and two chaplains' who were to 'celebrate divine service daily' not only for 'the good estate of the king and his consort Anne, queen of England, and his first-born son Edward, prince of Wales' but also for 'the said founders and brethren and sisters of the gild and for their souls after death and the souls of the king's father Richard, late duke of York, William, late duke of Suffolk, and William Lovell, late of Lovell, knight'.[881] This was a perfectly standard request, and going by the belief system of the time it would have reflected well on his own soul as well as helping his father's.

Presumably, these arrangements were made while they were all still in London, during or after Parliament. The arrangements were only made official after Parliament ended on 20 February, but it stands to reason they would have been discussed before that day. It is interesting to note that John was more involved in such actions during Richard's reign than he had been during Edward's reign or would be during Henry VII's.

After Parliament closed, a triumphant if brief period of rule began for Richard. Shortly after Parliament ended, he was to score another victory. There is some indication John was still present, and John Jnr definitely was, when Richard received the news that, allowing for some assurances, the erstwhile queen Elizabeth had declared she was ready to come out of sanctuary with her daughters, where she had been since late April 1483. Though certain anti-Ricardian historians have since insisted that Elizabeth Woodville had no choice but to leave sanctuary[882] despite her dictating the terms of her emergence,[883] this is not so. When Richard agreed to openly swear an oath to her safety he had been prepared to swear since May 1483,[884] he was being gracious. While it was somewhat embarrassing for him to have his former sister-in-law and his nieces in sanctuary, ostensibly hiding from him, it was hardly a pressing issue. It had not detracted at all from his triumphant reception during his first royal progress the year before, for instance. Richard could have waited her out if she had attached conditions he did not want to fulfil; Elizabeth had no way to put any pressure on him.

In any event, the deal was sealed between them. In a grand show, Richard, in royal regalia, swore an oath that included details such as the dowry he would give his nieces when they were old enough to be married.[885] In return, Elizabeth Woodville, then officially called Lady Grey due to her marriage to Sir John Grey before she met Edward, swore fealty to him together with her daughters.[886] This spectacle played out before many lords spiritual and temporal,[887] including both Johns. As with almost anything Richard did, this has been read differently by historians than it was by his contemporaries. Whereas many of the former have taken it as an admission of weakness and guilt in various matters,[888] contemporaries saw it more as gesture of peace, showing the king was intent on establishing harmony and showing family unity. What both Johns thought of it all we do not know, but unlike many others in Richard's government they had never been on bad terms with Elizabeth Woodville or any of her relations, and so they might have been happy to see her back at liberty from her self-imposed sanctuary, at least officially on good terms with king and government.

The emergence of Elizabeth and her daughters was to have direct effects on John Jnr soon. The younger daughters were sent to the royal nursery at Sheriff Hutton, while the two oldest – Elizabeth and Cecily – might have immediately gone to serve as the queen's ladies-in-waiting, but there is no certainty on this point. Their whereabouts at that time cannot be ascertained.

With his duties done, John went back to his wife and family in Suffolk, while John Jnr travelled with his uncle as the court went on progress once more. Presumably, it was already planned then that he would stay in the north of the country once the court had arrived there, and take over government work there for his uncle, probably as assistance for his little cousin Edward, Prince of Wales. He was set to become a power in the north, the way Richard himself had been when his brother had been king. Richard being a regional power there had been very helpful for stabilising Edward IV's rule, and perhaps Richard thought it would be good if he did something similar during his own reign. Since he was extremely popular in the north, it could also be that in this way Richard intended to make sure northerners knew he had not forgotten them and their concerns even though as king he had the whole country to safeguard.

Whichever it was, John Jnr would have prepared for new tasks as the court set off on progress by a similar route to the year before with some additional stops this time. It seems the king and his court travelled from Westminster, stopping at Canterbury to make offerings at the tomb of St Thomas Becket, to Cambridge and its university rather than Oxford as the year before, then to Minster Lovell and finally to Nottingham Castle, where the court stayed in April.[889]

The stay at Nottingham was somewhat longer than any other stop, presumably because it was a very central place where Richard could best arrange to meet ambassadors and see to coastal defences. This occupied him for a while in April 1484,[890] and it was there that, shortly before Easter, he and the court received news of his only legitimate son and heir's sudden death.[891] Though in later years it was often claimed that the child was always sickly,[892] there is no evidence for this. In fact, the only quasi-contemporary source reporting little Edward's death, the Crowland Chronicle, written two years after it happened, stated that he died after being 'seized with an illness of but short duration',[893] suggesting it was unexpected. It would have been devastating for his parents, and the Crowland Chronicle states that they were 'in a state almost bordering on madness, by reason of their sudden grief'.[894]

Though John Jnr presumably did not know his cousin well, he must have felt sad about his death, and also sorry for his grief-stricken aunt and uncle. Though he had no children himself and therefore could not understand their pain from personal experience, he had lost several siblings in infancy and had seen his parents lose children, and may therefore have felt a sort of kinship for them in their recorded grief. He hardly would have been the only one; many of those at court would have been able to empathise with the bereaved parents from personal experience. John and Elizabeth probably heard the news a while after it happened, as the unfortunate boy died during Holy Week, possibly on Maundy Thursday.[895]

John and Elizabeth would have sent their condolences to the king and queen. However, they were likely also aware what the news meant for their own oldest son. Prince Edward had been King Richard's only legitimate child, and with his death the question of the succession arose. Though the king and queen were still young enough to have more children, the immediate succession was still a pressing matter.

Heir to the Throne

It is usually claimed that Richard had to make a decision between John Jnr and his brother George's son Edward, Earl of Warwick.[896] However, this choice never existed. Little Edward, Earl of Warwick, was debarred from inheriting the throne due to his father's attainder, a fact explicitly mentioned in Richard's Titulus Regius, the legal document explaining his right to the throne.[897] This was important because if Warwick had not been debarred he would have been in line to the throne before Richard himself as his older brother's son. It has often been pointed out that attainders could be lifted, and they frequently were, but this overlooks that such actions tended to specifically exclude any right to inherit the throne. More importantly, such an argument overlooks the fact that Richard would be deposing himself if he followed this course of action.

John Jnr had no such problems. He was legitimately next in line, as his mother was Richard's older sister and he was her oldest son. The English system was such that sons inherited before daughters even if the daughters were older, but daughters were not excluded from inheriting and could pass any claims they had to their own sons. This meant that despite Richard being younger than Elizabeth, Duchess of Suffolk, he was entitled to inherit before the claim passed to her and her sons, but they were next in line after him.

Moreover, John Jnr was an adult man of nearly twenty-three years old in early 1484. His cousin Edward, Earl of Warwick, was nearly eleven years old.[898] As such, John Jnr would have been the better choice in any case; if something happened to their uncle, John Jnr could have immediately taken over as king by himself while little Warwick would have needed a lord protector for several years, a situation that did not have happy associations in England and has sometimes been claimed to be the reason, rather than the debated legitimacy of Edward IV's heirs, why Richard took the throne, even among historians sympathetic to him.

John Jnr, then, was heir presumptive by law. There were no legal impediments against him taking the throne should the occasion arise, the law did not have to be changed for him to become heir, and he was an adult and as such better suited to rule. All this should be enough to make it perfectly clear that John Jnr was heir presumptive to the throne after his cousin Edward's death, even without taking into account Richard's own actions, which confirm this.[899]

The confusion about Richard's heir after his son died may come from the claim made by later sources, written during Tudor times, that little Warwick was heir.[900] These sources had obvious motivations for manufacturing this notion. Henry VII would have the little Earl of Warwick locked up in the Tower of London immediately after becoming king,[901] so he was no danger to the regime. However, he absolutely adored John Jnr[902] and did not act in such a way to defuse any danger coming from him, even though John Jnr had several brothers, all of whom disliked Henry and his son and successor, and rebelled against them at various times.[903] It was therefore in the interests of the Tudor dynasty, and therefore all sources written to flatter them, not to draw any attention to the Suffolk boys as Richard's rightful heirs. It made much more sense to claim as her presumptive a boy who could be of no trouble since he was firmly under Henry VII's control.

John Jnr did not seem to give himself any airs about his new position as heir presumptive. Richard gave him the honours associated with it piecemeal, being too busy to spend a lot of time on the matter in the immediate aftermath of his son's passing. Due to the time when poor Prince Edward died, his parents could not be at his funeral, which appears to have been organised with aplomb by Richard's lord chamberlain despite the difficulties.

After less than two weeks, the court left Nottingham Castle for York. This rather contradicts the statement by the Crowland Chronicle that the king and queen were at Nottingham Castle for 'a long while ... in a state almost bordering on madness' because of their grief, though of course the latter statement is not tied to any locality and would have held true even in York. In fact, it seems that the queen did not accompany the king to York, perhaps too stricken by grief to be able to go on while Richard, whatever his feelings, had no choice but to keep up with his work as king. John Jnr was with him, doubtlessly preparing for his new tasks, which had grown more numerous and more important than had originally been planned. However, before he could take up work in the newly formed Council of the North there was another duty to fulfil.

Perhaps the court first went to visit the young prince's grave. It has sometimes been speculated that he was buried in York Minster, and if so such a visit is certainly possible. If he was buried elsewhere, such as Middleham Castle or Sheriff Hutton, the court could not have gone there before they were in York, where they met with ambassador Nicholas von Popplau.[904] Popplau's report of his meeting with Richard is one of the best descriptions of the king we have. An ambassador to the Holy Roman Emperor, Popplau had no reason to be biased either against or for Richard, and therefore his report presumably reflects reality as he saw it. He was very impressed with Richard, to the extent of sadly hardly giving any thought to his courtiers; none of them are mentioned by name, but it is almost definite that he refers to John Jnr.

At one point of his report, invited to a banquet by Richard, Popplau reports that the king offered him to sit between two of his 'blood friends',[905] by which he meant two friends of Richard's who were also his relatives. Apart from John Jnr, there were not any close blood relatives of the king at court, though Popplau appears to have meant both John Jnr, who was Richard's nephew, and his lord chamberlain, Francis Lovell, who was his cousin by marriage and usually addressed thusly by Richard. Of course, it makes sense that John Jnr, newly heir presumptive, would be employed by Richard to entertain ambassadors, but it also illustrates just how important John Jnr had become through this sudden elevation. Despite being the king's oldest and closest nephew, he had been just another noble at court in 1483, worth noting but not dwelling upon. This had changed by May 1484. Richard had also granted John Jnr some more manors in April of that year while at Nottingham, so John Jnr's wealth continued to grow with his importance.

At the same time that his son was entertaining ambassadors after having suddenly become a person of national interest and importance, John was dealing with more normal and commonplace problems. On 1 May 1484, he wrote a letter showing that despite his son's sudden rise to importance he was still struggling with money problems, and chose to settle the problem he had first raised in December 1482:

> The Duke of Suffolk, to Thomas Jeffreys, farmer, of Maudevill's, greeting.
>
> We will, and straitly charge you, that ye content, and pay unto the bringer hereof, for money employed in your household, three pounds, thirteen shillings, and four pence, for such stuff as we our own person have promised, and not to be failed, upon our worship.
>
> Of the which sum of 73 shillings and 4 pence, so by you contented and paid, we will, and also straitly charge our auditors for the time being, by virtue of this our writing, signed with our hand, to make you due and plain allowance at your next account.
>
> At Wingfield, the first day of May, in the first year of King Richard the III.
>
> Suffolk, and fail not on pain of losing your farm.[906]

There is no record to say whether or not Jeffreys did as he was commanded and if John's problems were settled. However, it seems so, since there is no indication of the trouble continuing.

If John's life hadn't changed much despite recent developments, John Jnr's naturally had, and he must have been watched closely at court. After Popplau left, another court event took place that was clearly meant to be joyous, though with Prince Edward's recent death it might have been rather subdued. This was the wedding of the king's illegitimate daughter, Katherine, to the Earl of Huntingdon.[907] Richard had already ordered fine clothes for the occasion before his son's death.[908] John Jnr's young cousins Edward, Earl of Warwick, and Margaret were given splendid clothing; John Jnr was not, but neither were any other adult courtiers. He would have been old enough to make his own arrangements. It is not known if John Jnr had ever met Katherine before, but even if not he would have been conscientious in carrying out any tasks given to him, as he always was.

After this event, John Jnr left court and his independent work for his uncle began. He was appointed to watch the royal nursery at Sheriff Hutton[909] along with his brother-in-law, Henry, Lord Morley, who was also set to help him with the newly formed Council of the North.[910] Both men were to see to it that John Jnr's various cousins were brought up and educated according to their status and were not exposed to what could be considered bad influences.

Perhaps an indication that Cecily and Elizabeth, the two oldest of Edward IV's children, were there at the time when John Jnr took over this duty is that there was a stipulation that 'no boys'[911] were to enter the household until John Jnr and Lord Morley had both granted their permission. There would have been no reason to make any such rule unless some teenage girls were in the household. This was, however, a secondary role to the two men's work running the newly formed Council of the North from nearby Sandal Castle.

The Council of the North was officially founded on 24 July 1484.[912] Its main task was to oversee concerns of the common people in the north of the country, and it was presumably based on Edward IV's Council of the Marches of Wales.[913] John Jnr presided over it, but several historians, Peter Hammond among them, have suggested that the original plan had been for Prince Edward to be the council's nominal president, with John Jnr doing the actual work for him until he was old enough to do it himself.[914] As president of the council his exact tasks are not known, though the ordinances passed for the council give a good idea:

> These articles following be ordained and established by the king's grace to be used & executed by my lord of Lincoln and the lords and other of his council in the north parties for his surety & wealth of the inhabitants of the same.
>
> First the king will that no lord no other person appointed to be one of his council for favour, affection, hate, malice or mad do not speak in the council otherwise than the king's laws & good conscience shall require, but be indifferent and no wise partial. As for his wit & reason will give him in all manners matters that shall be ministered before them.
>
> Item, that if there be any matter in the said council moved which touches any lord or other person of the said council, then that the same lord or person in no wise to sit or remain in the said council during the time of the examination & ordering of the said matter unless he be called, and that he obey and be endured therein by the remnant of the said council.
>
> Item that no manner matter of great weight or substance be ordered or determined within the said council unless that two of these that is to say with our nephew be at the same, and they to be commissioners of our peace throughout those parts.
>
> Item that the said council be wholly if it may be once in the quarter of the year at the least at York to here examine & order all bills of complaints & other there before them to be showed and more often if the case require.
>
> Item that the said council have authority and power to order and direct all riots, forcible entries, distress, takings, variances, debattes & other misbehaviours against our laws & peace committed and done in the said parts. And if any such be that the in no wise can thoroughly order, then to refer it to us, and thereof certify us in all goodly hate thereafter.

Item, the said council in no wise determine matter of land without the assent of the parties.

Item that our said council for great riots done & committed in the great lordships or otherwise by any person, commit the said person to ward in one of our castles near where the said riot is committed. For we will that all our castles be our jail, and if no such castle be near, then the next common jail.

Item we will that our said council incontinent after that they have knowledge of any assemblies or gatherings made contrary to our laws & peace provide to resist, withstand & punish the same in the beginning according to their demerites without further defering or putting it in respect.

Item that all letters & writings made by our said council to be made for the due executing of the premises be made in our name, and the same to be endorsed with the hand of our nephew of Lincoln made underneath by those words: per consilium regis.

Item that one sufficient person be appointed to make out the said letters and writings and the same be put in registry from time to time, and on the same our said nephew and such other with him of our said council then being present set their hand and a seal to be provided for the sealing of the said letters & writings.

Item, we will & straitly charge all & singularly our officers, true liegemen & subjects in these north parts to be at all times obeying to the commandments of our said council in our name and duly execute the same as they and every of them will eschew our great displeasure and indignation.

Memorandum that the king's grace before his departing do name the lords & others that shall be of his council in these parts to assist and attend to that behalf upon his nephew of Lincoln.

Item memorandum that the king name certain learned men to be attending here, so that one always at the least be present, and at the meeting at York to be all there.

Item that the king grant a commission to my lord of Lincoln and others of the council according to the effect of the premises.[915]

These ordinances clearly show that John Jnr was to preside over the council but it is not made explicit, rather his privileges and duties are simply enumerated. The fact that Richard stipulated that John Jnr would need to be present at any matter 'of great weight or substance' obviously shows his importance, while the fact that he was to be accompanied by at least two other men has sometimes been taken as a nod towards his inexperience.[916] However, such an acknowledgement of inexperience was not carried through in all of the ordinances drawn up for the council, making it more likely that this stipulation was simply a measure to avoid claims of John Jnr acting in his own interest that might expose the council's work to criticism. Most of the ordinances show Richard's complete trust in his nephew, and the fact that he was given the authority to sign letters of the council '*per consilium regis*', without even consulting Richard beforehand, was a startling gesture to a young earl who had only attained his majority less than a year before.

We do not know the identity of every member of the council. Henry Percy, Earl of Northumberland, was one of them, as were Richard, Baron FitzHugh and Francis, Viscount Lovell. Not all of them stayed in the north with John Jnr at all times, but one lord who did was his brother-in-law, Henry Lovell, Lord Morley, who was explicitly mentioned together with John Jnr in the ordinances made for the everyday running of the households at Sandal Castle and Sheriff Hutton.[917]

This was important government work, but at the same time it was also a huge honour for John Jnr's entire family. Naturally, with John Jnr being the heir presumptive to the throne, the family had already risen to unlikely heights; John and Elizabeth were suddenly and unexpectedly the parents of the heir to the throne, and their not-quite-twelve-year-old son Edmund, due to his older brother Edward being a man of the Church, was second in line. They probably didn't let themselves believe this would last, but even if John Jnr was bumped down the line of succession by the birth of a new heir it would have been hard to see how John Jnr would ever be anything but an extremely important man in Richard's government. The same went for his brother-in-law, Lord Morley. Though he was nowhere near as important as John Jnr, he was obviously trusted by the king and his job on the Council of the North was an important one. If he comported himself well, he too could probably have expected a position of honour and importance for the rest of Richard's reign, and his wife, John Jnr's sister Elizabeth Jnr, could become an important lady.

The family was to be honoured even more by Richard contacting the Vatican about his nephew Edward being raised to a bishopric. This might be seen as simply a continuation of something his brother had already planned, but Richard had more plans for his sister's family. Having defeated the Scots only in 1482, Richard decided on making a new peace treaty with them.[918] The old one, arranged by Edward after Richard's victory in 1482, had obviously become defunct with Edward's children being declared illegitimate, as the treaty had included the erstwhile Princess Cecily being contracted to marry the Scottish heir to the throne. This could no longer happen, but both Richard and the Scottish king were eager to make a new agreement. A Scottish delegation was to arrive at Nottingham in the summer of 1484 for this purpose. It was to be a great meeting, a show of unity between the two countries. It is well possible that Richard considered it particularly important to have peaceful relations to other countries since his own position had become rather less secure without an heir of his body. He and Queen Anne must have naturally still been trying to conceive another heir, but perhaps Richard was becoming rather worried after nearly four months with no sign of a new pregnancy. It is possible that he therefore chose to give John Jnr several of the posts previously held by his son, such as the Lieutenancy of Ireland.[919] Either way, it definitely made John Jnr secure in his position as heir presumptive.

The meeting with the Scots was described by Paul Murray Kendall, who stated that 'the greatest powers of [Richard's] kingdom'[920] attended the assembly, including 'Norfolk, Northumberland, and Stanley, Chancellor Russel, the Earls of Shrewsbury and Nottingham, the Bishops of St Asaph and Worcester, Sir Robert Percy, Comptroller of his Household, his councillors William Catesby and Sir Richard Ratcliffe, and the Chief Justices Bryan and Hussee. Beyond them in ranks stood the Knights and Esquires of the King's Body and the royal henchmen, captained by Sir James Tyrell.'[921] Notably, no mention is made of John, Elizabeth or John Jnr. This is particularly interesting because the new treaty was to affect their family immensely. Among the matters settled therein was that the Scottish crown prince, James, would one day marry Anne de la Pole, John's seventeen-year-old daughter.[922] It is interesting that she was not yet married or promised to anyone at the time, once more suggesting that John and Elizabeth were not overly interested in making such matches, happy to let the king do it for them.

Given this match, it is strange that Anne's parents were not present to see the treaty made. Of course, this arrangement had to have been discussed with them, and perhaps they were simply missed in the roundup of the English and Scottish delegations. However, as they then became the prospective parents-in-law of the future Scottish king, this is more than unlikely. Similarly, they were surely interested in attending a meeting so important for their daughter's future. Something must have stopped them, though we do not know what. Why John Jnr was not present, however, is obvious: he was busy with the Council of the North. Furthermore, while he presumably would have been happy for his sister, he did not have much of a personal interest in seeing the treaty signed.

Whyever John and Elizabeth were not present, and wherever they were, they must have been pleased about the developments for their family if perhaps also somewhat apprehensive as well. Their oldest son might one day be English king. Their daughter Anne was contracted to become Scottish queen consort one day. Even their son Edward was looking towards a glittering future as an important magnate of the Church. It was a spectacular rise for a family that four generations ago had boasted only merchants without title.

While his parents continued seeing to their regional concerns, John Jnr was slowly establishing himself in his high position. As he spent more and more time at Sheriff Hutton and Sandal Castle, he began making his mark on them, giving orders to alter the places to suit his needs. In a specific case in October 1484, his need was stated by the receiver of Wakefield, one John Woodruff, who spoke about a request 'to cause a bakhouse & a brewhouse to be belded within the Castelle of Sandale by thadvise of Thearl of Lincolne and other the Kinges Counselle lieng there'.[923] Apparently, he did not consider the existing bakery and brewery good enough. Though at first this makes him sound somewhat like a spoiled brat demanding better quality than could reasonably be delivered and not being satisfied with what everyone else ate and drank, this is probably not what happened in this specific case. Presumably, the bakery and brewery were not equipped to deal with producing as much as was needed for a bustling centre of the government, and as such John Jnr took measures to remedy the situation.

It is interesting that such spending was allowed, as the ordinances for the council explicitly limited John Jnr's expenditures. For example, it was stipulated that while the costs for riding out would be covered by funds for the council in case he had to ride to a meeting, he would have to pay for himself if he went hunting or otherwise 'disported' himself.[924] This, too, suggests that the addition of a new bakery and brewery to Sandal Castle was not simply due to John Jnr being dissatisfied with the quality of what the existing ones produced but was considered important to the smooth work of the Council of the North.

However, this stipulation also throws an interesting light on John Jnr. It may very well be that it was only a standard prevention, but it is somewhat jarring in the light of the rest of the guidelines for the running of the household. These still exist, giving a good idea of what John Jnr's days serving as president of the Council of the North would have looked like, while also giving the impression that John Jnr may have been a bit of a reckless spender:

> This is the ordinance made by the king's good grace for such number of persons as shall be in the north as the king's household and to begin the 24 day of July anno 1484.
>
> First that the hours of God's service, diet, going to bed and rising and also shetting of the yeates, to be at reasonable time & hours convenient.
>
> Item that monthly the Treasurer and Comptroller show the expense to one of the council or two the which shall appoint themselves monthly through the year.
>
> Item that if any person offend in breaking of any of the said ordinance or of any other made by the council to punish or expel the offenders after their discretions out of the said house according to their demerits.
>
> Item my lord of Lincoln and my lord Morley to be at one breakfast, the children together at one breakfast, such as present of the council at one breakfast. And also that the household go to dinner at farthest by eleven of the clock on the fleshday [not Friday] etc.

Item the treasurer to have the keys of the yates from the time of the dinner and super begin till the end of the same.

Item that stuff of household be purveyed and provided for a quarter of a year before the hand etc.

Item the costs of my lord of Lincoln when he rides to sessions or to any meeting appointed by the council the treasurer to pay for meat & drink.

Item, at all other ridings, huntings and disportes, my said lord to bear his own costs and charges.

Item that no deliveries of bread, wine nor ale be had but such as be measurable and convenient, and that pot of delivery exceed measure of a potelle, but only to my lord and the children, etc

Item that no boys be in household but such as be admitted by the council etc

Item that every man that is at day wages be at their check and those that be at standing wages without check etc

Item that no servant depart without assent of the treasurer upon pain of losing his service.

Item that no breakfasts be had in the house but such as be assigned etc

Item that convenient fare be ordained for the household servants and strangers to fare better than other etc.[925]

It seems these ordinances were honoured; at least, there is no record of any breach. John Jnr seemed to do his job well, and probably due to this he became more and more a man of importance whom people recognised. Richard supported and in fact explicitly promoted this. When there was a minor riot in York on 4 October that year, the city elders wrote to the king to ask what he wished to be done to the imprisoned ringleaders. Richard responded not only to the elders, with whom he was rather unhappy for having let it happen, but also to the disgruntled citizens at large, asking them why they had not taken their concerns to him or his nephew, the Earl of Lincoln.[926] This suggests once more that he saw John Jnr as his deputy in Yorkshire, and expected him to deal with all that happened there.

Obviously, he had made this clear to others. Upon hearing of the riot, Henry Percy, Earl of Northumberland, wrote a letter to the mayor of York telling him that the correct cause of action for him would have been to contact either him or John Jnr, who had been present in Yorkshire during the 'great riot' and was therefore perfectly capable to deal with it.[927] Upon such reprimands, the city elders of York did as told and contacted John Jnr, who seems to have ably defused the situation. At the very least, the mayor was pleased, and to thank John Jnr for being kind to the city in this matter he and five of the other city elders wrote to Sandal Castle on 15 November.[928]

In only a short time, then, John Jnr had established himself well in the north, showing every sign of stepping into Richard's shoes and one day being able to take over the part Richard had played when Edward had been king.

While John Jnr made his position in the north more stable and secure, his father was asked to sit on a jury for treason, together with many other nobles such as John Howard, Duke of Norfolk, his former ward Francis Lovell and others.[929] The charge was that the accused had written to Lady Stanley's son, Henry Tudor, in France and asked him to invade England and take the throne.[930] This was doubtlessly treason, but the accused was to become rather more famous in the centuries that were to follow for having written a mocking rhyme about the king and three of his councillors: his lawyer, William Catesby; an associate, Sir Richard Ratcliffe; and his lord chamberlain, Francis Lovell.[931] ('The Catte, the Ratte, and Lovell Our Dogge, ruleth all England under the Hogge.') However, despite the fame of his disrespectful ditty, William Collyngbourne was not executed for this. He was not even arrested for it, though when he was eventually arrested for treason and accused of that, this rhyme was mentioned in the accusation.[932]

The verdict can have been in no doubt, and in November 1484 John and the other nobles declared Collyngbourne guilty, which meant that he, being a commoner, was condemned to suffer the cruel fate of hanging, drawing and quartering. It is probably true that not even those making such decisions took any joy in it, but it was the law of the time and it was followed. We do not actually know if John stayed in London afterwards or headed back to Suffolk.

John Jnr was still in Yorkshire and had not been one of the men asked to sit on this particular jury; he might not even have been present at the Christmas festivities that were to follow. Presumably, neither were John and Elizabeth, as usual preferring to stay at Wingfield Castle in Suffolk. If so, they missed out because the festivities that year were to go down in history. Though it might be argued that John Jnr's presence as Richard's heir presumptive would have been needed to show unity to every observer speaking of the festivities, his movements definitely suggest he was not present either, and so does the fact that he is not mentioned in any of the sources about the Christmas festivities.

The person attracting most rumours and mentions during these festivities was John Jnr's cousin Elizabeth, oldest daughter of Edward IV, whom history remembers as Elizabeth of York. She served in Queen Anne's household as lady-in-waiting[933] and attracted a lot of attention, wearing similar clothes to the queen during court games.[934] Though the Crowland Chronicle stated that the Christmas celebrations were conducted with 'all due solemnity', the very same source later lamented that 'too much attention was paid to frivolities'.[935] Elizabeth of York found herself in the middle of those frivolities, and soon rumours began to circulate that Richard intended to marry her, that he had even made her pregnant.[936] Those rumours were obviously nonsense, and easy to disprove, but they were to hound Richard for a while yet. However, Richard was starting to plan a new marriage for himself around that time; either his wife was already so sick that she was not expected to live much longer,[937] or he was intending to divorce her.[938]

However, all this might have first become known to John Jnr after the Christmas celebrations. It might have surprised him to hear the rumours while in Yorkshire but perhaps, knowing them to be untrue, he did not really give them much thought. Since the rumours were to persist, it is well possible that even John and Elizabeth heard of them in Suffolk, but they probably paid the tales no mind; these would not have been the first absurd rumours they had ever heard from a royal court in their lives. For their part they seem to have been in a good place in their life; all of their quarrels for possessions were solved to their satisfaction. They had many healthy children, whose futures seemed bright and secure. Though they did not attend Richard's wild and infamous Christmas festivities at court, it seems they had their own sort of fun in December 1484; it must have been around Christmas that Elizabeth became pregnant again, for the last time. She was forty years old, her husband forty-two. It would be their thirteenth child, but there is no reason why they should not have been pleased by the news when Elizabeth could be certain of the pregnancy a couple of months later.

In all probability, John Jnr too was happy when he heard the news. However, he would have probably been too busy to be concerned with what went on at court. Richard put ever more trust in him, perhaps because he was comporting himself well, or perhaps as a sweetener for the prospective loss of his position as heir presumptive arising from any new marriage for the king. Such plans might have been in motion even before Christmas 1484, as we have documents from Portuguese archives dating to January 1485 showing that Richard had put his feelers out for a marriage between himself and the Portuguese king's sister, Joanna of Aviz, an impressive lady around his age.

John Jnr might have approved of this choice of new wife for his uncle and new queen, or perhaps he was saddened by the suffering of Queen Anne. The latter is a reasonable assumption, as surely he would have felt sorry for a woman only five years his senior who was terminally ill, but there is no evidence the two had even a passing acquaintance beyond what would be expected of them. Whatever he felt, if he was present at court at all for the festivities then he was soon gone again. It seems more likely that he stayed in Yorkshire the whole time. On 17 December he was still there, receiving a letter from the mayor of York, who asked him what to do with a counterfeiter called John Stafford.[939] The next day, John Jnr responded by saying the man should be sent to him.[940] This was done, though what John Jnr did with the man is not known. He must have been lenient, for counterfeiting was a crime punishable by death yet no execution is recorded for the time.

On 8 December, John Jnr was appointed to a commission of array for the North Riding of Yorkshire,[941] and on 5 February 1485 to a commission of the peace for Norfolk and the West Riding of Yorkshire.[942] These appointments appear to have been nominal, as he seems to have spent his time in Sandal Castle. He would have heard of all that was happening at court, but it does not seem to have affected him. He would have heard of the death of the queen, and quite possibly Richard would have sent a messenger to inform him that just a week afterwards he had made an official proposal for Joanna of Aviz's hand.

However, even a day before the queen died, when the tidings must have been expected, John Jnr was writing a letter to the mayor of York about the city's boundary inspections, of which he had been informed.[943] Clearly, if the expected death of Queen Anne personally affected him, he did not show any sign of it. Interestingly, neither did he show any sign of being affected by what went on after she had died. Famously, two weeks after Queen Anne's death and shortly after her funeral, her widower made an announcement that all rumours about him wanting to marry his niece Elizabeth of York were wrong and spread with malicious intent, and that all rumours about him being happy about Anne's death or even having harmed her were wrong; he was, he said, sad about her death.[944] The king claimed the rumour had been spread by his 'French enemies' to torpedo his plans for a new marriage,[945] so the denial was clearly intended to reassure the Portuguese of his sincerity. Orders went out that anyone caught spreading such rumours was to be imprisoned until the source could be found.[946] Orders to that effect were also given in York, but there is no record of anyone being arrested for the offence.

John Jnr did not seem touched by the rumours, and never had anything to do with counteracting them. In fact, sadly very little is known about his last months as president of the Council of the North. No more letters survive after March 1485, though it known that he must have ridden to Sheriff Hutton in early May 1485.[947] He was there with his young cousin Edward, Earl of Warwick, when the mayor of York and some aldermen asked for a criminal imprisoned there to be sent to the City of York to receive his punishment.

Bosworth and Demotion

Though there is no evidence he was involved in any preparations, John Jnr would have heard about the looming invasion planned by Henry Tudor. His task was not to raise men for Richard; on the contrary, the only event of note in his life at this time is that his cousin Elizabeth was sent to the royal nursery in Sheriff Hutton, over which John Jnr still presided. He travelled to see Richard in late July 1485,[948] and was present when Thomas Barowe arrived in the king's presence to give him the great seal.[949] The task given to John Jnr by his uncle in the face of the invasion was to stay at Sheriff Hutton, not Sandal Castle, and pay attention to his cousins, a task that has sometimes caused people to speculate he had been employed with some secret mission. This will be examined in due course.[950] It has also sometimes been postulated that he did in fact fight at Bosworth,[951] but in the face of his movements after the battle this is extremely unlikely. It seems that he returned to Sheriff Hutton after meeting his uncle in early August, and was there when the Battle of Bosworth took place.

John, meanwhile, appears to have been asked to raise men, but there is some doubt whether he did so. It might not actually be surprising if he did not; as he could not fight, he had not raised men for Edward in 1471 either.[952] Moreover, two things happened in John's life in early August 1485 that were rather more immediate than raising men and were extremely emotionally taxing for him. First, at the beginning of August, Elizabeth went into confinement in expectation of the birth of their thirteenth child. It was around this time that it became known that Henry Tudor's fleet had evaded a blockade and landed in Milford Haven in Wales.[953] Naturally, his wife's confinement should not have stopped John from doing providing men. However, he received a second piece of news at just that time that would have driven all other thoughts from his mind. His son Edward had died, apparently unexpectedly, at Oxford University. He was just fifteen.[954]

John could not hope for Elizabeth's support in making the necessary arrangements in the wake of such news. Probably her confinement would have worried him as well; in addition to his grief for his son, he might have feared that telling her could harm her and their unborn child. He must have been grief-stricken and terribly worried as he made his way to Oxford University to attend his son's funeral. He can hardly be faulted if, under the circumstances, he did not think of his brother-in-law's upcoming fight for the throne.

Despite this, however, his inaction has been variously spun by historians, who inevitably came to the conclusion that he either stayed on the fence[955] or abandoned Richard, whom he hated.[956] There is evidence against this, and such assumptions do not take into account his background and circumstances at the time, nor his family. Even had John hated his brother-in-law Richard, he would not have deliberately forsaken him, especially given that a Tudor victory would have seen his daughter Anne and oldest son demoted and removed from the succession to the thrones of Scotland and England. As usual, hatred of Richard, John or both has affected many historians when it comes to this matter. John must have hoped for his brother-in-law to win. However, after riding back from his son's funeral in Oxford to be with his family in Suffolk, he could have done nothing but wait for news.

It would have been similar for John Jnr. He, too, must have been hit by the news of his brother Edward's death, and quite possibly he too worried for the health of his mother and unborn sibling, but he could not ride to be present at his brother's funeral nor to be with his mother and younger siblings at Wingfield. He had to wait where he was, in Sheriff Hutton, for the outcome of the battle, praying for his uncle's victory. Sadly, his hopes and prayers were in vain. As history records, Richard III lost the battle and his life at Bosworth Field on 22 August 1485. On that date, John Jnr became *de jure* King of England. At the same time, he looked to a future in which he would lose almost all of the importance he had enjoyed in the last few years.

13

The Suffolks under Henry VII

The news of Richard's death in battle would have had unhappy and far-reaching consequences for John Jnr. For one, with Richard dead he was, by law, King of England. In practice, of course, this meant nothing, as his kingship did not rest on any authority but a law that would be changed soon. Henry Tudor was the new king.

Even so, the fact that he was technically king must have occurred to John Jnr when he heard of his uncle's death. At the time it cannot have been a comforting thought; on the contrary, he would have feared for his life. Even leaving aside the fact that his claim to the throne was much stronger than Henry Tudor's, he had been a man of much importance in Richard's reign and might have expected to be punished for that alone. In addition, he probably grieved for the uncle he had served so diligently, the uncle who had been called his friend by an unbiased commenter.

Sometimes, it is assumed that even with all this going on John Jnr was endeavouring to fulfil a secret mission given to him by his uncle in case he did not survive the battle. Rumour had it that he was tasked with sending Edward, Earl of Warwick, out of the country and putting a commoner boy in his place.[957] There is nothing by way of evidence that this happened, save for a claim in 1487 that he and some others rose up to put him on the throne.[958] However, as will be detailed below, whether they actually did rebel for little Warwick is disputed, and even if they did it does not at all have to mean they had the real Warwick in their care.

There has also sometimes been an assumption that the so-called 'Princes in the Tower', John Jnr's famous cousins, were in the royal nursery at Sheriff Hutton, being two of the 'children'[959] mentioned in the ordinances for the Council of the North, and they were the ones he hurriedly smuggled away after hearing of his uncle's defeat and death. Since, by definition, the mystery of what happened to those boys is still unsolved, such a claim must remain speculation. The evidence for this idea will be discussed below as well.[960]

Whatever John Jnr did after hearing of his uncle Richard's defeat and death, he must have done it quickly, and soon he and his cousins would have been left with nothing to do but await the nest move of the new king, Henry VII.

Suffolk's Reaction to Henry VII

John and Elizabeth must have heard of Richard's defeat and death fairly soon after it happened as well. It must have been a blow for them, even though they were not as close to him as their son had been. It was not just about Richard either, though Elizabeth, at the very least, probably mourned her younger brother; they too must have also feared his defeat meant their son might be in danger. They would definitely have known that he would never have a chance of becoming king while Henry ruled, and their daughter Anne would never be the Scottish queen consort.

As usual, they did not openly do anything to go against the sitting king. However, they made their feelings about Richard's death and Henry VII's accession clear in another way. When Elizabeth gave birth to a healthy baby boy within a few weeks of her brother's death, she and John chose to name this son Richard. This was, quite obviously, a statement, even more blatant than naming a son Edward had been in 1470. Then it had been a gesture in support of the sitting king. When Richard de la Pole received his name, it was a statement in support of a defeated king and against his usurper. Since it was a family name for Elizabeth, there was nothing Henry VII could have done about it even had he wanted to.

There is no evidence he was bothered, though. Henry had bigger problems at the time than what the Duke and Duchess of Suffolk named their thirteenth child. Most likely he did not hear of it at the time, and if he ever found out before Richard was an adult, he might not even have known the child's exact age. It was a very typical, subtle gesture by John and Elizabeth. It made very clear their opinion to all who cared to look, without being so blatant that it would risk endangering them or their family.

Interestingly, in recent years there has been a question about Richard de la Pole's paternity. A theory has gained some traction that he was not the youngest son of John and Elizabeth but in fact John Jnr's illegitimate son, passed off as theirs by John and Elizabeth after John Jnr's later death.[961] This is meant to have been intended to spare the boy the disadvantages of being a rebel's son, and the supposed evidence is that he, rather than his older brother William, was addressed as 'Duke of Suffolk' by several European rulers during the 1510s and 1520s.[962] However, this can be debunked. For one, Richard being born in 1485 means that in case of him being illegitimate, he would have spent two years being known as that before John Jnr became a rebel. Too many people would have known this and his real identity would never have been kept a secret. Moreover, as an illegitimate son, he would have stood to inherit nothing, meaning his father's rebel status would not have caused him much harm. In this case, John and Elizabeth could have simply raised him as their illegitimate grandson without having to pretend he was their son. It is a known fact that Richard de la Pole was born in 1485 to John, Duke of Suffolk and his wife Elizabeth, as their thirteenth and final child.

While John, perhaps with the excuse of awaiting the impending birth of the said Richard, did not come to see the new king in London, Henry sent men to Sheriff Hutton to have John Jnr and all his cousins brough to the capital. John Jnr must at the very least have been apprehensive about what was to happen, but perhaps he needn't have been. Even if John Jnr feared some sort of punishment for being Richard's loyal subject, he must have known that he would not be in any physical danger; even if Henry had been minded to have him punished or executed on trumped-up charges – though there is no evidence to suggest this – it would have solved none of his problems. Five of John Jnr's brothers were still alive then, and his claims to the throne would have just passed to them. However, Henry must have been aware of the fact that as Richard's heir the young man was a focal point for rebellion.

It was presumably with this in mind, and in the hope of stopping anyone so minded from trying to rise in John Jnr's name, that immediately after Bosworth the king had it announced that John Jnr had fallen in battle together with his uncle.[963] While the list of the fallen included some genuine mistakes, such as Francis, Lord Lovell,[964] John Jnr's inclusion in the list of casualties must have been a piece of deliberate misdirection. Unlike Lovell, he had not been at the place of the battle, nor even near it. The fact he was expected to be in Sheriff Hutton with his cousins after the battle, and was found there,[965] attests to it. There is no chance his name was included by accident, or that anyone could have genuinely thought that he actually had died in the battle. Presumably, Henry VII's plan was to have John Jnr safely in his custody by the time anyone found out that he was still alive.

Though several Yorkists were imprisoned by Henry – among them Thomas Howard, Earl of Surrey, son of John Howard, Duke of Norfolk; and Henry Percy, Earl of Northumberland[966] – he must have known there was no way he could imprison John Jnr. The imprisonment of Howard on the bogus charge of having committed treason against Henry before he was even king caused enough trouble for the new king, and John Jnr had done nothing that could be passed off as a crime even under Henry's illegal standards of treason.

Henry probably intended to keep a close watch on John Jnr once he was at court and to have him swear fealty, but things didn't go to plan. John Jnr's gift for making people like him appears to have helped him immensely in this case. Henry VII seems to have taken to him immediately when he arrived at his court. While John Jnr's young cousin Edward, Earl of Warwick, was imprisoned,[967] there were no serious repercussions for John Jnr. He was stripped of the presidency of the Council of the North, the Lieutenancy of Ireland and several of the manors that had been given to him by Richard, but this cannot truly be counted as punishment as Henry could hardly have been expected to leave his supporters and his mother attainted so John Jnr could keep their manors and lands, nor to leave Richard's effective deputy in charge of the north.

In fact, rather amazingly, Henry instantly began favouring John Jnr. Most notably, he made the rather baffling decision not to make the erstwhile Ricardian swear fealty to him. This led to the rather absurd situation of the *de jure* king being at the court of the *de facto* king without the latter having taken any steps to make sure the former accepted or even recognised him as king. Henry VII soon came to view John Jnr as his friend, perhaps even as his closest friend.

It was during this time that John Jnr really showed an amazing talent for acting and disassembling. As early as Christmas 1485, his actions show that he must have secretly loathed Henry with a passion.[968] He spent well over a year at his court actively plotting the king's overthrow and death, all the while staying close to Henry physically and being considered one of his closest and most loyal men. He was not just seen that way by the smitten king himself; nobody at court seemed to suspect him of plotting against Henry.

Perhaps because he knew the value of treating the Yorkists well, or perhaps out of his affection for John Jnr, Henry treated the Suffolks with preference. Naturally, some of their higher offices were taken from them. However, apart from the repercussions for Anne, whose future was completely changed, this mostly concerned John Jnr, as he had held the highest and most important jobs after becoming Richard's heir. It would not have come as a surprise to anyone that his job as the president of the Council of the North was taken from him,[969] along with all posts associated with that role. As mentioned above, other lands that Richard had granted him were taken when the attainders against Lancastrians were lifted, but Henry tried his best to recompense the Suffolks for that. With John Jnr's erstwhile foster brother, Francis Lovell, refusing to accept Henry as king and therefore being stripped of his lands and possessions, Henry VII gave the constableship of Wallingford Castle back to John. Some of the lands in Oxfordshire previously held by the viscount were also passed to John.[970] John Jnr, meanwhile, seems to have even gained some more manors under Henry, namely Friskney, Deptford, West Greenwich, Ravensbury, Hat Peverell, Termyns, Suthwold, Datyngton and Donyngton, Serjante, the messuages, tenements and lands of East Greenwich, tenements, land, meadow, pasture and a mill in Ravensbury, Micham, Marteyn and Merdon, as well as eleven tenements in London and 'a Chief Place sette in the parish of Seynt Laurence Pultney'.[971]

When Henry's coronation took place, both Johns were included in a position of honour. During the procession a day before the actual coronation ceremony, John Jnr was given the signal honour of being one of the two earls preceding the new king himself, with the earls of Derby and Nottingham walking before John Jnr and the Earl of Oxford,[972] one of Henry's staunchest and most important supporters. John, meanwhile, walked directly behind the king together with the king's uncle Jasper Tudor, who had been made Duke of Bedford.[973]

During the actual ceremony, John once more found himself in the same position he had occupied for the coronation of Richard and Elizabeth, carrying the golden sceptre signifying peace.[974] John Jnr, too, was in a similar position to the one he had been in during Richard's coronation, carrying the 'ball and cross, signifying the monarchy'.[975] While John, by that time, might have been considered something of a fixture in his position, for John Jnr his inclusion in such a place of honour was rather more of a statement. While he had been in a position that suited his standing at Richard's coronation, it had still been one that reflected his being the king's oldest nephew. This was to be expected at Richard's coronation, but not so much at Henry's. There would have been other earls more suitable, perhaps, for that honour from a Lancastrian point of view.

He and his father, despite presumably being less than happy with Henry being king, certainly went through the motions of loyalty, though only as far as it suited them. When Henry made John and several other nobles swear to abolish their own private armies of retainers, John duly swore to do so but made no move to actually follow through with it.[976] Despite this, Henry did not punish him, showing that he appeared to like him, or at least did not consider him dangerous. The same held true for John Jnr, whom Henry chose to keep around at court, apparently not thinking that John might resent him for taking his titles.

However, John Jnr's loss of positions put Henry in some difficulties. For instance, Henry had given the presidency of the Council of the North to Richard, Baron FitzHugh, a decision that was to prove less than ideal. Richard III had been very popular in the north, particularly in Yorkshire, and inevitably unrest erupted there after his death. In fact, this went so far that some rebels invited Scottish forces to invade and force Henry off the throne. Baron FitzHugh utterly failed to thwart the Scots and bring the northerners to heel, and there are suggestions that this was deliberate on his part. Though nothing could ever be proved, he was stripped of the presidency in December 1485. Henry Percy, Earl of Northumberland, was released from prison and given FitzHugh's job. However, he also failed to get a grip on the situation.

The men of the north of England cruelly displayed how they would not make peace with the new king. There was a very brutal attack on one of the Earl of Northumberland's men, his 'servant Robert Robinson, bailiff of [Northumberland's] lordship of Ulvyngton',[977] during which a Yorkist called John Eglesfield 'beat and sore wounded in peril of death'[978] poor Robert without anybody intervening, which shows the strength of the feeling against anyone even vaguely associated with Henry. While this would have worried Henry, by November 1485 he must have at least believed he had the Suffolk family firmly on his side. After his coronation, his first parliament was called and everyone was to swear fealty to him.[979] This was mostly asked of men loyal to Henry for whom it was only a formality, such as his uncle Jasper Tudor, newly made Duke of Bedford, and the Earl of Oxford. Very tellingly, John and John Jnr were included.[980]

After more than two months of Henry being on the throne, John and John Jnr finally had to swear fealty. In those months, John Jnr had obviously wrapped Henry securely around his little finger. Perhaps due to this, Parliament treated him and his family particularly leniently. Though harsh measures were enacted against many Yorkists, even predating his reign by a day so that all those who had fought against him could be called traitors, this harshness did not extend in any way to John or John Jnr. In fact, Henry even made sure to state in the Act of Resumption, annulling all grants made by Richard, that John was exempt.[981]

Henry clearly was secure in his support from the two Johns. The elder was made a trier of petitions for 'Gascony and the other lands and possessions overseas', together with the Archbishop of York, the bishops of Winchester, Exeter and Norwich, the earls of Nottingham, Derby and Devon, the abbots of St Albans and Chichester and along with Lord Fitzwalter, Lord Dudley, Sir Thomas Brian and Sir Guy Fairfax,[982]while John Jnr was made a trier of petitions for England, Scotland and Wales alongside the Archbishop of Canterbury, the bishops of Lincoln and Ely, the abbots of Westminster, Abingdon and Gloucester, Henry's strongest supporters the Duke of Bedford and the earls of Oxford and Arundel, plus several lesser barons and knights.[983]

Parliament concluded before Christmas. John Jnr, however, may very well have spent Christmas at court with Henry, or gone to see his mother and newest brother once Parliament was concluded. The former is somewhat more likely, since it was Henry's policy to always keep him around. It has usually been speculated this was because Henry, who did not trust him, wanted to keep an eye on him,[984] but this is unlikely. Henry did not manage to even realise John Jnr so much as resented him, much less suspected he was working against him. If he did indeed keep John hr close because he wanted to keep an eye on him, he did a remarkably poor job of it. Perhaps more likely is that Henry considered John Jnr a good friend and liked having him at court, with the added bonus of hopefully showing their closeness to any dissatisfied Yorkists. He was mistaken if he thought this was successful, however; there was a riot in Parliament in December 1485 caused by his bad treatment of Yorkists, particularly his predating of his reign.[985]

The Rebellion of 1486

John and John Jnr had nothing to complain about, though. Henry treated them extremely well, though it stands to reason that, as always before, John elected not to spend Christmas at court. He might, however, have come back to court only a month later, when Henry VII married his niece, Elizabeth of York, on 18 January 1486.[986] If John was there, which seems likely, his wife probably accompanied him. She appeared to be on good terms with her niece and might have wanted to be there for her wedding, even if it was to a man she had every reason to hate.

There is no indication that any of the Suffolks played a part in the ceremony or the festivities that followed, but very few details are known about this event in any case. However, we do know that John Jnr was already actively plotting Henry's overthrow and death. He did not let anything on, obviously playing his part well even while he was in contact with his erstwhile foster brother Francis Lovell about helping him in a rebellion against the new king.

Francis Lovell had taken Richard's death badly. He had refused to accept Henry VII as king,[987] declining even to swear with crossed fingers as John Jnr had. Most of all, he wanted revenge for Richard. Naturally, any such plans were complicated by his refusal to even pretend to accept Henry. He had been attainted, putting him in danger of being captured and executed if any of Henry's men caught him. At the beginning of 1486, though stripped of his considerable wealth, he was still safe in St John's Abbey in Colchester, which had extended rights of sanctuary that meant he did not have to leave after forty days.[988] In fact, this was presumably why he chose Colchester. He was not the first Yorkist to have done so; John, Lord Howard had done the same during the Lancastrian readeption of 1470/1, which might have been how Francis had learned of it.[989] However, the abbey had two more perks.

First of all, the abbot of Colchester, Walter Stansted, was a staunch Yorkist. He was the perfect man to help Francis with his plans for rebellion.[990] The second perk was that the abbey was close to Wingfield Castle and several Suffolk possessions. Maybe Francis figured this would be helpful for him as well, or perhaps he simply wanted the option of a visit from the closest thing he had to a father. We actually do not know if John ever went to see Francis, but it is at the very least possible, if not even likely. John Jnr, too, might have gone to visit him, but only if he ever left court during that time, which does not seem to have been the case. More likely, he was put into contact with Francis and his co-conspirator, the brothers Humphrey and Thomas Stafford,[991] who had fled to sanctuary with him, by servants of his parents who sympathised with his goal of unseating Henry. There must have been many; despite what later propaganda claimed or what is even still stated in modern history books, Henry VII's accession was not greeted with universal jubilation; on the contrary, there were pockets of dissent everywhere. Perhaps John

Jnr would have been more aware of this than Francis, removed as he was from wider events.

John Jnr's information from court would have been extremely valuable for a planned rebellion. Even so, it must have been he who sought contact with Francis at this time and not the other way around. John Jnr had more to lose, but if Francis refused collaboration with him he could hardly betray John Jnr to anyone for having plotted treason. Presumably, John Jnr would have contacted Francis after he heard about many men being recruited for rebellion.[992] John Jnr would have only needed to signal that he was ready to help. To have actively sought out this rebellion to offer his assistance suggests that John Jnr must have utterly loathed Henry.

We do not know if John knew of his son's plans. It is usually roundly assumed that he did not,[993] and it is certainly possible that John Jnr preferred for his parents not to know, protecting them in case he was discovered. It is by no means certain, however. As detailed above, John Jnr's actions would have relied heavily on local knowledge and the information and help of trusted servants, and it is perfectly possible that even if John Jnr did not actually tell his parents his plans they understood what was going on. John is usually not considered to be the rebellious type, but he had shown some form in the past. He had been perfectly happy to have his wife working against the government in 1470/1 during the Lancastrian readeption,[994] and he had already showed he did not particularly support Henry VII. Nor, as time would show, did he really have any respect for him. It is therefore perfectly possible he knew, or at the very least suspected, what his oldest son was doing.

Typically, John does not seem to have come along when Henry VII started his first progress in spring 1486. John Jnr did, though, riding alongside Henry; all the while, he was trying to ensure that the king would never make it back to the capital. This must have taken a certain amount of coldness, but John Jnr apparently never forgave Henry for killing his uncle, whom he had liked, and treating his corpse so terribly afterwards that it was even mentioned with disgust by chroniclers active during his reign and the reigns of his descendants. The fact that Henry had clearly begun a massive propaganda campaign to blacken Richard's name could not have helped, nor could the legal trickery employed to declare Yorkists traitors after the fact.[995] Whatever it was that most upset John Jnr, he wanted revenge, and being close to Henry did not weaken his resolve.

Even before the progress started, Henry was facing several troubling incidents. One of them was in Wales, and Jasper Tudor, Duke of Bedford, had headed there to quell it as described in a letter to Sir Robert Plumpton dating from 15 February 1486.[996] This must have given the rebels hope; one of his foremost commanders was out of the picture. However, it would almost certainly also have made Henry more alert. Nevertheless,

John Jnr still made sure to help Francis's rebellion; indeed, it must have been his assistance that prevented the revolt from failing before it had even started. A man who was privy to Francis's plans, Sir Hugh Convey, told Henry of them and later reported:

> That time my Lord Lovell lay in Colchester a trusty friend of mine came to me and showed me in counsel the day and time of his departing, and his purpose. I was sworn to him that I should never utter this to man living to his hurt, but yet forthwith afterwards, because of mine allegiance, I came to Sir Reynold Bray and showed him all as is above, and forthwith he said that Master Bray showed the same unto the King's [*sic*].
>
> Whereupon I was brought before his Highness, and I affirmed all to be true as my said friend had showed; and the King said that it could not be so, and reasoned with me always to the contrary of my sayings. At last he asked what he was that told me this tale of his departing. I prayed his Highness to pardon me, for I said that I was sworn to him that I should never utter him, to be drawn with wild horses; wherewith the King was angry and displeased with me for my good will.[997]

This shows that there was some very detailed information about Francis's intentions circulating, and once Henry realised it was serious he would have sought the man's capture the moment he left sanctuary. Since Francis was not actually captured despite this, it has to mean he either planted false information to confuse the king or, more likely, was informed by a sympathiser that his plans had been leaked, enabling him to change tack. The informant can only have been John Jnr, as no one else at court is known to have been involved in the rebellions, or at least no evidence for their involvement survives.

It might also explain why John Jnr chose to stay so close to Henry VII at court. Of course, it was a good way to hide his intentions, but by spring 1486 Henry trusted him in any case, and being so close to him must have made it harder to hide communications with rebels. In some ways, it would have been easier for him to pretend a disinterest in national politics such as he had actually displayed until he became Richard's heir presumptive. However, being so close to Henry gave him access to privileged information that would have helped in plotting a rebellion. He also managed to completely win Henry's trust, something which is shown by the fact that they set out on the progress together.

The new, as yet uncrowned, queen did not join on the progress. It has sometimes been claimed this was because she was newly pregnant, though she can hardly have been certain of it yet. A more popular and also more likely theory is that Henry wanted to be alone on the progress to show himself off as monarch in his own right, without drawing attention to his wife and her claim, which was regarded by many as far superior, especially after Henry's first parliament had overturned Richard's Titulus Regius, his claim to the throne that had declared Edward IV's children illegitimate. However, if this was why he did not want his wife to join on his progress it is rather strange that he was perfectly happy with John Jnr going with him. Even if Henry considered Richard's claim to the throne to be factually fabricated, he would have known that not everyone shared that opinion. John Jnr's presence at his progress may very well have reminded disaffected men and women of his claim. Despite this, Henry appeared to have no apprehensions about having John Jnr riding alongside him.

Always a showman, John Jnr did not let the opportunity slide. Whether this was simply in his nature or if his intention was to nettle Henry, a report exists stating that he rode a white horse with a saddle inlaid with gold and silver[998] – not in itself an attack on Henry, but he would have looked flashier than the king himself. Yet, again, Henry failed to rise to the bait, if indeed a bait it was. As they started on progress, he only began trusting John Jnr more. It seems John Jnr did a very good job of charming Henry.

The royal progress in early 1486 seems to have been closely modelled after Richard's successful progress of 1483, starting in Westminster then going north with John Jnr at his side. On 11 March, while on the way to Cambridge, Henry made John the head of a party including 'Thomas, earl of Derby, John, viscount of Welles, George Stanley of Straunge, knight' as well as some lesser men, to 'deliver the goal of the town of Cambridge of William Hill, selater, and William King, wever, both of Cambridge, prisoners therein'.[999] The selection suggests these were men Henry trusted, and he clearly counted John Jnr among them and did not shy away from giving him responsibility. Apparently, he did not at all suspect that John Jnr might do something to help these prisoners. His trust was not misplaced; John Jnr did nothing of the sort, probably because they were not traitors but simply criminals.

Henry heard of the rebellion fairly soon into his progress, while celebrating Easter in Lincoln on 26/27 March.[1000] According to Polydore Vergil, he did not take the threat seriously at first, but, perhaps informed by spies that the situation was starting to become dangerous, soon changed his mind. On 4 April, he appointed 'Thomas, earl of Derby, George, Lord of Strange, William Stanley, knight, the king's chamberlain, William Gryfuth, chamberlain of North Wales, Richard Harper, Andrew Dymmok and John Luthrington' to a commission to raise men 'in the counties of Chester and Flint, and in North Wales'.[1001] In the following days he issued similar orders to other nobles, including his uncle Jasper, Duke of Bedford, who raised 3,000 men.[1002] How many were raised in all is unknown. During the Buckingham Rebellion, Thomas Stanley had raised some 10,000 men; perhaps it was a similar number this time.[1003]

Curiously, neither John nor John Jnr were asked to raise men to counteract the rebellion. Perhaps Henry had suddenly developed trust issues towards them, but if so they were not to last. More likely is that he knew John would not be able to raise very many men as he had never been able to do so, and as for John Jnr he simply wanted to keep him close. The Crowland Chronicle claims that many of the men raised were unarmed, 'seemingly rather to pacify than to exasperate a hostile population'.[1004] As the Chronicle was written at the time of the rebellion this could very well be true, and it would not have been a stupid move; anything more punitive could have looked unnecessarily belligerent, and being supported by unarmed men could have allowed him to look harmless while still having men ready to fight if necessary.

In spite of these preparations, the rebellion was becoming more and more threatening. Rumours were started, whether by the rebels of simple hearsay, perhaps encouraged by the chaos of the rebellion, that Edward, Earl of Warwick had been freed from the Tower of London and was with Francis Lovell.[1005] Another rumour was put about that Francis had captured Henry VII.[1006] Such notions sound preposterous with hindsight, but they were taken seriously by many at the time. The idea that Henry VII had been captured was used by Thomas and Humphrey Stafford to encourage men to 'assist in the destruction of Henry VII'[1007] – a rather strange claim, given that they had only gained entrance to the city of Worcester in late March by claiming that Henry had given them a pardon.[1008] This, perhaps more than any other incident during the rebellion, shows very well the conflicting information circulating in spring 1486.

John Jnr would naturally not have been involved in causing such rumours, and at Henry's side he would have had difficulties stoking them. Perhaps he had men instructed all over the country to do so, but we do not know. Most likely, John Jnr was playing at being Henry VII's devoted friend, fulfilling orders he gave him until either Francis and the brothers Stafford had raised a sufficient army to attack Henry or else until they had reached the north of the country, where Francis was fomenting the biggest part of the rebellion and where Richard III had been most popular.

If John Jnr hoped for an army to be raised against Henry and attack him during their progress, he was to be disappointed. Much like the Buckingham Rebellion three years earlier, this rebellion quickly fizzled out with no bloodshed. Vergil claims that this was achieved because the Duke of Bedford, having gathered his men 'immediately ordered his heralds to offer impunity to all who had thrown down their weapons'.[1009] If so, he either made this announcement without clearing it with his nephew or Henry agreed to it and then went back on his word, as there were trials and executions for rebellions in April and May 1486. However, it is more likely that neither Bedford nor Henry himself went back on their word and that Vergil, writing over twenty years after the fact, sought to deliberately minimise the threat of the rebellion by taking the fact that some pardons were granted[1010] and using it as evidence that all those involved received pardons. It could be argued that Vergil truly believed this was what happened, since it is not an account that flatters Henry, arguing as it does that the rebellion was not very dangerous but that Henry was nonetheless afraid of it. His account also makes Henry look rather slow on the uptake, so it was unlikely to have been written to please him.

However, even so, Vergil's account overlooks almost a month of threats and consequences. While the plan to gather an army led by Francis Lovell had collapsed by mid-April, it did not spell the end of the rebellion. Soon afterwards, Francis had new plans. It appears there was some attempt, probably modelled after Jack Cade's rebellion in 1450 and the FitzHugh rebellion in 1470,[1011] to put forward a strawman rebel, given the typical name of Robin of Redesdale. There is no evidence this got beyond the planning phase, though John Jnr would later turn out to have been involved; in May 1487, after John Jnr had left Henry's court and openly declared for his enemies, a York resident named James Taite who housed John Jnr and his entourage when he arrived in York would state that during his stay there John Jnr met with two men 'who dwelt around Middleham', invited them to come to his quarters and discussed openly joining the planned rebellion. Taite would later claim to have heard John Jnr discuss using his house as a starting point for the rebellion, saying that 'here is a good gate for us to Robin of Redesdale over the walls'.[1012]

That Taite had such exact knowledge of John Jnr's actions suggests that either he was in on the plans himself or John Jnr was remarkably careless while plotting treason. The former is suggested by the fact that Taite only revealed this knowledge after being caught and interrogated in May 1487 for saying that John Jnr 'wold give the king's grace a breakfast [his just deserts]',[1013] clearly showing he sympathised with him. Making himself out to have been a bystander could have been an attempt to lessen his punishment. If not, and he was speaking the exact truth, it makes it clear that John Jnr was a rather reckless man, either secure in not being caught or, quite possibly, in Henry not believing evidence against him. Henry's reaction in 1487, when John Jnr actually did leave court to declare for his enemies, suggests that if John Jnr did expect Henry to believe his innocence, he was not completely wrong.[1014] However, John Jnr and his co-conspirators' plans never came to fruition.

This does not mean the danger was over for Henry VII. Perhaps not trusting any plans John Jnr was making, or perhaps simply unwilling to wait, Francis Lovell decided to either kidnap or kill Henry as his party approached York.[1015] This plan was catastrophically underdeveloped, failing to take into account details John Jnr would have known and should have been able to pass on, and therefore must have been developed on the spur of the moment by Francis and some of his remaining men, without involvement by John Jnr. Even so, it came close to succeeding[1016] and Henry, not unreasonably, was said to be 'affected by great fear'[1017] when he reached York 'since he had no army, no weaponry with which to arm his followers, and no place where he could enlist soldiers at that time, in a city which was hostile, in whose mind the memory of Richard's name remained fresh'.[1018]

This may have been written with hindsight, though it is possible Henry correctly guessed that even the failure of this attempt did not yet mean the end of the rebellion. Francis apparently contacted John Jnr again after this failure, probably realising it was not possible otherwise to develop a plan that had a chance of succeeding. John Jnr would have been able to pass on all that Henry had planned: the festivities for 22 April once he had arrived in York[1019] and the St George's Day festivities a day later.[1020] It was to be a lavish show for Henry,[1021] and it seems that this time John Jnr passed on all pertinent information to the rebels. Quite possibly, he was also the one who found men in York prepared to help with the attempt to kill Henry during the St George's Day festivities.

Though it is not known exactly what was planned in case this attempt succeeded, it is reasonable to assume that the rebels counted on the support of the citizens in thwarting any attempts at revenge by Henry's men. However, what they intended to do once this first danger was over is unknown, as there was no real figurehead for the rebellion. Its main goal seems to have been to unseat and kill Henry. It has sometimes been speculated, then and since, that Edward, Earl of Warwick was the intended new king should the overthrow of Henry take place.[1022] Certainly, that was the implication behind rumours about him being freed from the Tower of London.

However, for Warwick, the same issues that would have prevented him from being Richard's heir still held true. While him preceding Richard in the line of succession if his father's attainder was overturned was no longer a problem, the attainder itself still was. So was the fact that he was only young, twelve to be precise, and as such not really a prospective king who could deal with coming to the throne after the previous king was assassinated to put him there. Much more likely is that the plan was for John Jnr to take over as king after Henry was killed, but, with him still being at Henry's court, this could not be openly announced as it would endanger his life.

Henry definitely suspected nothing, and the attempt on his life appears to have come as a surprise to him. The Crowland Chronicle reports that while Henry was 'devoutly intent upon the festival of St George, he was nearly taken by the cunning of the enemy'.[1023] Sadly, it gives no details as to how this attempt happened, but again it can be assumed that the idea was to seize Henry, carry him away from his enemies and either kill him on the spot or declare John Jnr king and have him give orders for Henry's execution for regicide.

As history records, it did not come that. The plan was foiled by the Earl of Northumberland, who 'prudently hastening to meet these first [stirrings], had some of the instigators of this rising hanged on the gallows'.[1024] This failure, narrow though it was, was fatal to the rebellion. Most likely, the Crowland Chronicle exaggerated Northumberland's part; while he probably caught the rebels, he did not have the authority to order executions. Naturally, in case of an emergency such rules could have been relaxed, but with Henry being present this would not have been necessary. What most likely happened was that Northumberland found out what the rebels were planning and captured them before the plan could come off, then they were led before the king, questioned and executed. They might have faced a short trial, but if so no indication of it has survived.

Interestingly, none of the men who were caught betrayed the whereabouts of Francis Lovell before their execution, nor stated that John Jnr had been involved in the planning of the attack. This indicates that Northumberland's discovery of the plot was in fact mere coincidence, and that he had no deeper knowledge of it. However, it is possible that he was contacted by the rebels, perhaps in the hopes of winning him over; after all, Northumberland had reason to resent Henry. This would explain him knowing who was guilty of crimes worthy of a death sentence. If so, he did not know of John Jnr's involvement, which suggests that the rebels had tightened their ship and kept John Jnr out of the loop, perhaps to protect him.

However he came to his knowledge of the rebellion, Northumberland would not be the last to miss John Jnr's part in it. His involvement has often been overlooked. This is partly because of how well he kept his own involvement hidden from his Henry and his government, but the greater reason is that the rebellion itself gets very little coverage in history books, and when it is mentioned at all it is brushed aside as a footnote, not a conspiracy that penetrated government circles.[1025]

Henry was never any the wiser as to John Jnr's involvement. On the contrary, he appeared to consider John Jnr one of his core supporters. As the rebellion fizzled out after the failure to kill him in York, Henry made him a member of several commissions to 'enquire of all treasons, felonies and conspiracies'[1026] as well as 'to hear and determine the same', in 'the county of Hereford', 'the counties of Warwick and Worcester' and 'the city and suburbs of London'.[1027] John Jnr was one of the very few men, including John de Vere, Earl of Oxford, and the king's uncle Jasper, Duke of Bedford, who was a member of all these commissions, which were dated from 3 May to 5 July 1486.[1028]

As John Jnr, as well as Bedford, were at Henry's court during all this time, they could not have done such enquiring as was expected of them in person. This would not have been difficult for the commissioners to work with, as the commissions overlapped and they would hardly have been expected to be in all those places at once. However, pretending to fulfil the task to Henry's satisfaction without anyone suspecting him of anything, while at the same time trying to work in the rebels' favour, would have been a tightrope act for John Jnr. It seems he rose to it. The commissions he worked in found enough rebels for Henry to be certain they did their work well, while never finding anyone who would have been able to give away the whereabouts of Francis Lovell or to implicate John Jnr.

Notably, many of those rebels found and tried received a pardon.[1029] It might very well be that John Jnr influenced Henry to be lenient; certainly, his generosity then was in stark contrast to his harshness immediately after the Battle of Bosworth. A notable exception to this was the treatment meted out to Francis's co-conspirator Humphrey Stafford. After their rebellion had failed, he and his brother Thomas had sought sanctuary again in the church of Abingdon, closely connected to John. Henry VII chose to break sanctuary and have them pulled out. While Thomas Stafford was pardoned, Humphrey was condemned to death and died by hanging, drawing and quartering.[1030] The breaking of sanctuary caused quite some trouble for the king, requiring him to bribe the pope to retroactively allow the act.[1031] It also did not help his popularity, and therefore it might have been easy for John Jnr to convince him it was in his interest to show leniency to more minor rebels.

Amazingly, John Jnr still got closer to Henry. However, his father kept well away. Both John and Elizabeth paid lip service to notions of loyalty when it was asked of them, but they went to court voluntarily even less often than they had done under Edward IV and Richard III. John Jnr must have been in contact with them, but he does not seem to have spent any time with them that year.

In early September, John Jnr travelled to Winchester with the court, where his cousin Elizabeth was to give birth to her and Henry's first child. Henry had chosen Winchester for symbolic reasons for the birth, signifying his supposed connection to King Arthur, whom he claimed as his ancestor. John Jnr joined the court there, while John and Elizabeth once more did not. They were not present when Queen Elizabeth gave birth, nor at the baptism of her healthy son, who was named Arthur after Henry's supposed ancestor. John Jnr, once more, was given a position of honour in this ceremony:

> The Marquis of Dorset and the Earl of Lincoln, gave assistance to my lady Cecily, the Queen's eldest sister, who bore the Prince, wrapped in a mantle of crimson cloth of gold, furred with ermine, with a train, which was borne by m lady Marquis of Dorset, and Sir John Cheney supported the middle of the same; and afterwards the Marquis of Dorset, the Earl of Lincoln, and the Lord Strange, served Queen Elizabeth (the queen mother) of towel and water; and Sir Roger Coton served the other gossips.[1032]

Quite interestingly, John Jnr was the only person given such a position who was not closely related to the baby. Along with the child's grandmother, aunt and uncles (by marriage), his first cousin once removed seems a pretty weak connection. Why Henry chose to include him so prominently we do not actually know. Perhaps he simply did so because he really liked him, though this was unlike Henry. Maybe it was another attempt to show a strong connection with a reformed Yorkist. Whatever the reason, John Jnr was once again treated with honour.

The court stayed in Winchester until Queen Elizabeth was churched, after which time they left for Greenwich. John Jnr, once more, was noted to have 'attended the court to Greenwich, where they kept the solemn feast of All Hallows. [1 November]'.[1033] After the festival of All Hallows, it seems John Jnr left court for the first time since he had met Henry. This is especially notable because even Henry's uncle Jasper had left court more often. It has been claimed that this was because Henry did not trust John Jnr to leave court, but this is obviously untrue as he had trusted him with sensitive tasks all year.

14

The Simnel Rebellion

John Jnr used the time away from court to take out a loan of £20 from the almshouse in Ewelme.[1034] Probably he passed this money on to the abbot of Abingdon to support Yorkist allies abroad, most likely in Burgundy and Ireland. A report of this is found in the State Papers of Henry VII, though it was only discovered later, after John Jnr had openly declared for the rebels.[1035]

The money borrowed from Ewelme was supposedly taken abroad by a servant of the Abbot of Abingdon,[1036] who was himself very supportive of the Yorkist cause and had connections with Francis Lovell. In fact, the whole town of Abingdon had close ties with both him and the Suffolk family; not only John and John Jnr but also Francis Lovell belonged to the Fraternity of the Holy Cross, founded there.[1037] As such, John Jnr interacting with the abbey would not have aroused any suspicion. If Henry VII had him watched after he left court, of which there is no evidence, he would not have found any indication of wrongdoing in John Jnr visiting the almshouse at Ewelme and being in contact with Abingdon Abbey.

John Jnr must have kept his other preparations for a new rebellion similarly concealed. This would not always have been as easy, for he would have needed to keep in contact with his aunt Margaret, the dowager Duchess of Burgundy, and with Francis Lovell, the most hunted rebel in all of England. We do not know when the planning started, but it must have been well before November 1486 if John Jnr was already making such concrete plans as loaning money for it then.

While John and Francis may have stayed in contact in some way since the failed rebellion of the spring, less is known about how either he or Francis made contact with Margaret. John Jnr can barely have known her, having met only once since he had been six years old. Francis definitely did not know her. This opens up an intriguing possibility: that it was John Jnr's mother, Elizabeth, who put them in contact. There is, however, no evidence for that, simply an assumption of her being the obvious person to do so. We do not even know if John and Elizabeth were aware of their son's actions. It seems somewhat unlikely that they were not, given that he needed to use family connections to contact his fellow rebels and make preparations for the next planned rebellion by winter 1486, but we cannot know for certain. At the very least, John and Elizabeth had plausible deniability.

John Jnr might have spent Christmas at his parents' household in Suffolk, as there is no record of him being at court for Christmas that year. By January 1487, however, news about a new rebellion began to spread. On 24 January 1487, the Earl of Oxford wrote a letter to John Paston, reproaching him for apparently accidentally passing on wrong information about Francis Lovell's whereabouts and stating that 'the king had knowledge thereof more than a seven-night passed. And for such names as you have sent, supposing them to be gone with the lord Lovell, they be yet in England, for he is departing with fourteen persons and no more.'[1038] Oxford seems to have been mistaken about what he said he knew, but it shows that at the very least it was known by then that trouble was once more afoot, and that Burgundy would be involved. There was no connection made to John Jnr, however; he kept his head down splendidly.

Perhaps it was once more his doing that Francis was warned about his plans and whereabouts being discovered, but in this case we have no indication it was so. Maybe by this time Francis had simply found a way to pass on wrong information, probably through his wife Anne, who was the Earl of Oxford's niece by marriage. In any case, by that time at the latest Henry VII started making arrangements to deal with the upcoming rebellion. On 2 February, a meeting started at Sheen to discuss how to deal with it. It seems that John travelled to be present.[1039] John and John Jnr both appear to have attended the meeting at Sheen without becoming involved. Maybe Elizabeth accompanied her husband. If not, Christmas 1486 was the last time John Jnr ever saw his mother. It seems that he was present only for the first few days and then left to take a ship to Burgundy.

There is some debate as to whether his departure happened in early February or only after the end of Henry's council. Later sources, written during the reign of Henry VIII and his children, suggest that it was only after the council was ended, and that he was explicitly present during several of the measures Henry VII undertook to counteract the upcoming rebellion.[1040] However, curiously, they also insist that John Jnr was the one who took a lowborn pretender to Burgundy to claim he was Edward, Earl of Warwick.[1041] The curious effect of this is that traditional sources have John Jnr bringing a pretender to Burgundy in early February – early enough to make Henry VII react – and at the same time they have him present at Henry VII's court during some of these reactions. Obviously this cannot be true, and the way the rebellion progressed from February onwards suggests that John Jnr left court in early to mid-February to go to Burgundy.

The traditional story postulates that John Jnr left court in early February, taking with him a lowborn boy from Oxford called Lambert Simnel, whom the rebels passed off as Edward, Earl of Warwick.[1042] Whether or not it is true that the pretender claimed this, it is definitely known that Henry VII's government reacted to the pretender's existence by asserting this in mid-February.[1043] It stands to reason that John Jnr indeed left England in February and did not wait until March. His attainder was later dated to 9 March,[1044] but this is much more likely to have been the date Henry received confirmation he was in Burgundy rather than the date he left court.

Suffolk's Reaction

Since John was present when his son left, it is all but impossible to believe he did not know what his son was planning. At the very least, he must have had a suspicion; he cannot have been oblivious to his son leaving court, and even if he did not ask him why, he must have known that it was not to simply go home. Since the two had always showed every sign of being close, it is more than possible that John Jnr told his father where he was going and what he was doing if John did not already know beforehand. John Jnr would have said goodbye to his father, perhaps emotionally, knowing there was a chance he would never see him again.

While John Jnr made his way to a port to catch a ship to Burgundy, a lot would have depended on him not being caught on the way. Doubtlessly, he would have made arrangements and enlisted helpers. Some of his parents' possessions were on the Suffolk coast, and some of those areas had been hotbeds of unrest since Henry VII's accession. It seems likely John Jnr left England from there. Still, while he could have hidden with sympathisers had Henry sent men to find him, it would have been easier for him if Henry did not yet know that he had abandoned him. Perhaps he invented a cover story for leaving, which might also explain his late attainder.

John would have had to pretend a lot during that time. He seems to have done so well; indeed, the usually paranoid Henry never believed he was in any way connected to his son's rebellion.[1045] While as yet unaware, or perhaps in denial, about John Jnr having betrayed him, Henry otherwise did all he could to counteract the rebellion. Most notably, at his council at Sheen, his mother-in-law Elizabeth Woodville was stripped of all her belongings and banished to the monastery of Bermondsey, apparently 'by thadvise of the lords and other nobles of our counsaille for diverse consideracions vs and theym moeuying'.[1046] Not surprisingly, this move caused 'much wondering'[1047] and has, especially in modern history books, often been taken to mean Henry VII at the very least suspected her of being involved in the rebellion.[1048]

Though it is sometimes claimed that Woodville herself chose this move,[1049] it stands to reason that this is untrue. Her making such a decision would not have required 'thadvise of the lords and other nobles of our counsaille', nor would such a decision have been ignored by men such as Polydore Vergil, writing for Henry in later years, who offered the rather flimsy excuse that Henry simply mistrusted Elizabeth because she had made peace with Richard three years earlier.[1050] It might very well be argued that Henry simply disliked Elizabeth and did not want to have to pay for her, but even so, such a decision could have been postponed until after the rebellion was dealt with. The fact that her banishment to the monastery of Bermondsey was decided on during the council which had explicitly met to decide how to deal with the upcoming rebellion suggests that she was at the very least suspected of being involved in some way. The fact that her son, Thomas Grey, Marquis of Dorset, who had been trusted enough to sit on commissions to find and judge traitors in 1486, was also imprisoned at the time suggests the same.[1051]

If Elizabeth was actually involved, she and John Jnr might have been working together. Perhaps it would have helped that he had never taken any side in the factional conflicts at Edward's court, allowing a certain trust and a basis for them to work together that might not have been there for many others.

Another precaution taken by the council was to counteract any claims by the rebels of having Edward, Earl of Warwick with them by having the real Warwick brought from the Tower of London and paraded through London to show him off to the population. This took place on 17 February, and after the parade the eleven-year-old was lodged at Sheen for the rest of the time the council sat there, afterwards being returned to the Tower of London.

One account written over half a century after the fact, and since often taken at face value, states that during that time John Jnr was still present at Henry's court and 'daily spake with him'[1052]. However, in the context it clearly was meant to show John Jnr knew the figurehead he was rising for was not actually Warwick, exposing him as a liar and a malcontent unconcerned with the facts. This attempt to make John Jnr and his co-conspirators out as liars is another point of interest. After all, it suggests that having Edward, Earl of Warwick might not have been what the rebels actually claimed. Though it has long been accepted that the rebellion was in Warwick's name, and that the pretender was in fact a lowborn boy from Oxford, sometimes said to have been a baker's son or a shoemaker's son, and schooled to impersonate Warwick, there is no such certainty in contemporary sources. Nor can any evidence for it be found in the rebels' actions.

As has been pointed out above, the traditional story has some obvious holes and contradictions, not least that it would require John Jnr to be in two places at once. Even allowing for him to have left court immediately after Henry's council at Sheen started, with the pretender in his company as traditionally claimed, the timeline does not fit. Since Henry's council first assembled on 2 February, John Jnr would have to have left court, arrived in Burgundy, presented the pretender as Edward, Earl of Warwick, seen him accepted and proclaimed as such and prompted a reaction from Henry within a space of two weeks at the most. Whoever the pretender was, and whoever he claimed to be, he must have been in Burgundy before John Jnr arrived there.

This is supported by several sources. As early as 24 June 1486, Margaret, dowager Duchess of Burgundy, was recorded to have given a present of wine to a boy who was recorded in her accounts as Edward, son of the Duke of Clarence.[1053] This opens the possibility of the boy in Henry's care not actually being the real Edward, Earl of Warwick but a substitute, brought to court by John Jnr after having sent his real cousin abroad as soon as he heard of their uncle Richard's defeat. This theory has become popular in recent years[1054] but it has some obvious holes. Apart from the problems with Warwick becoming king, such as that he was barred from the throne and that even if his attainder was lifted it would expose him to attacks, the very fact of Henry holding a substitute claiming to be him would have thrown a question mark over his very identity. While John Jnr and others who had been closely acquainted with him over the years might have been able to ascertain the true Warwick, the vast majority of people would not.

Moreover, there is no reason why John Jnr, about whose identity there was no doubt and who was an adult who had been Richard's heir presumptive and whose claim to the throne was spotless, would ignore all this to rise for a teenage boy whose identity would be questioned as much as his claim to the throne should the rebellion succeed, and who would therefore be much less likely to hold onto the throne. Despite several respected historians such as Dr John Ashdown-Hill[1055] arguing for this scenario, it seems rather unlikely. Even less likely is that John Jnr, who already had a claim superior to Warwick's, would rise for a boy claiming to be Warwick despite knowing him to be a lowborn boy with no claim at all.

However, another theory exists that has become more popular in recent years: that the boy the rebels rose for was in fact one of John Jnr's cousins called Edward; not the little Earl of Warwick, but instead the erstwhile Edward V.[1056] Due to centuries' worth of claims that Edward V and his brother were murdered in the Tower of London in 1483, this theory seems rather less likely at first. However, it remains a fact that we just do not know what happened to the boys, and if he was indeed the boy in whose name the rebellion of 1487 happened it would answer some previously unanswered questions.

The theory is that either Richard sent his nephews abroad to his sister Margaret in Burgundy after taking the throne or that they lived under John Jnr's watchful eye in Sandal Castle as two of the 'children'[1057] whose care is mentioned in the ordinances for the Council of the North, and were sent to Burgundy after Richard's death. Upon Edward V turning sixteen, at which age he was old enough to fight in battle and take the throne without needing a lord protector to rule in his name, Margaret organised a rebellion for him to take back the throne he had briefly held in 1483. While it might sound far-fetched to modern readers, it would have seemed less so in 1487, when the myth of Richard's evil had not yet taken root and Edward being murdered by his uncle was simply one rumour among many. Nor is it a theory that should be dismissed outright, as there are tantalising hints pointing towards it in several sources.

The theory is explained in full detail by Matthew Lewis in his book *The Survival of the Princes in the Tower*[1058] and by Gordon Smith in his article about the rebellion.[1059] These two works explain that there are several sources – including the chronicle by Bernard André, who was close to Henry – which state that the pretender of 1487 did not claim to be Edward, Earl of Warwick, but instead one of Edward IV's sons. Moreover, while traditionally it is claimed that the boy in whose name the rebels rose was a child of ten,[1060] not all contemporary sources agreed on it, and the boy was variously claimed to be ten, twelve or fifteen years of age.[1061] The latter, of course, was Edward V's age in late 1486.[1062]

If so, the theory is that Henry VII had Edward, Earl of Warwick paraded through London not to show that he was in his care and counteract any claim to the contrary by the rebels but instead to confuse the population, trying to make them think that the pretender was claiming to be Edward, Earl of Warwick[1063] and not Edward V. Even if Henry VII had believed this to be untrue, it would have been much harder to disprove than that he was Warwick, and would have raised too many uncomfortable questions the king would not have been able to answer.[1064] Moreover, it would have drawn attention to the fact that by overturning Titulus Regius, Henry had made Edward and his brother legitimate again and given them a claim far above his own.[1065]

Whether this was a problem Henry actually had to deal with in 1487, he would certainly have been busy in the spring of 1487. It seems that by 9 March, shortly after the council at Sheen was finished, he either learnt of John Jnr arriving at his aunt Margaret's court in Burgundy or he accepted that the man he had regarded as his friend had betrayed him. It was to 9 March that John Jnr's attainder was later dated, which has to mean the date had some significance.

Such a realisation would have stung Henry, but he had no time to dwell on feelings. Instead, he started making arrangements to stop the rebels before they could land in England and to find all supporters they had in England. Henry saw to it this was done by forming several commissions of array. Curiously, two of those commissions, formed on 7 April, prominently included John, together with John de Vere, Earl of Oxford and several untitled knights. Since those commissions were meant to 'cause to be repaired and well guarded the beacons on the seacoast for forewarning the people ... of the coming of the king's enemies'[1066] in Suffolk and Norfolk, it might well be that Henry feared that if John was not involved the men of those counties would simply ignore his orders. Even so, John's inclusion and the complete lack of suspicion with which Henry treated him is notable. Henry never seemed to suspect John of being in any way involved in his son's rebellion, or even to have known of it before he left court.

While Henry made these arrangements, the rebels prepared to legitimise their claim and invade. If John Jnr truly arrived in Burgundy at the beginning of March, he spent around two months there, presumably getting to know his aunt Margaret more closely and discussing with her the finer details of the rebellion. Curiously, while other rebels, such as Francis Lovell, were mentioned in passing in all sources discussing the rebellion, both contemporary and later as well as English and French, it was John Jnr who was regarded as the main instigator.[1067] This might be because he was more involved in the exact planning of the details, but this is guesswork. It might also be because he was the most highborn of the English rebels, and therefore the most notable to chroniclers.

Preparation for Battle and Lincoln's Death

The plans for the rebellion make it clear that, though historically it has been regarded as something of a damp squib, it was to be quite dangerous for Henry. Margaret's stepson-in-law, Maximilian, King of the Romans, organised for Swiss and German mercenaries to support the rebels. At the same time, messages would have been sent to Ireland to ensure support there. This would not have been too difficult, as Ireland had traditionally supported the Yorkist side in the Wars of the Roses and did so in 1487.

Once all these details were settled, the rebels, including the young pretender, took ship from Burgundy to Ireland, arriving in mid-May.[1068] Their presence there was not just to inspire Irishmen to join their cause and to meet with Irish nobles like the Earl of Kildare, who supported them;[1069] the young pretender's legitimacy depended on something else: he was to be crowned King Edward in Dublin Cathedral.

As the rebels and the pretender only arrived in mid-May, arrangements for this ceremony must have been made before their arrival, for after roughly a week in Ireland the pretender's coronation took place. It is not actually known whether he was crowned as Edward V or Edward VI.[1070] Like with his age and his supposed identity, no certainty exists in any sources, and all physical evidence that could answer the question has been lost. His regnal number might very well also solve the question of who the boy was or pretended to be. All we can say with any certainty is that on 24 May 1487, the rebels' claimant was crowned as King Edward.

The coronation was a singular event in English history, marking the first and only time a pretender was crowned while the king he challenged still sat on the throne he claimed. It is, in itself, also a piece of evidence pointing towards the claimant being someone of real royal blood. Though it was not a coronation in Westminster Abbey, as was traditional for English kings, it was a solemn ceremony attended by several bishops and two archbishops, and as such not easily dismissed by pious medieval men and women. After the coronation was performed and the pretender crowned and anointed, it would have been impossible to disregard this and give the throne to a different person, like John Jnr, if the rebellion was successful. Whoever was crowned must have been considered worthy of this honour by those organising the coronation.

Sadly, we know little about the ceremony itself, only that it seems to have been a grand affair. The French chronicler Jean Molinet, writing some years after the events he described, stated that it was attended by the German and Swiss mercenaries, who 'arrived in Ireland where they found [the claimant], together with the earls of Lincoln and Guldar [Kildare] and the nobles of the country, who, with the agreement of all of the people, did crown him King of England with two archbishops and twelve bishops'.[1071] Though Molinet is shaky on details and, as in this case, gets the sequence of events wrong, claiming that the mercenaries arrived after John Jnr and the nobles accompanying him, it is interesting that he considered the coronation to have been such a great event. It could well be that this was due to his own bias, as his chronicle made it clear he considered the rebels to be in the right, referring to the claimant, whom he took to be Edward, Earl of Warwick, as 'King Edward' repeatedly while calling Henry VII 'the count of Richmond'.[1072] However, the impression of the coronation as a great affair is given reflected by other sources, even Polydore Vergil, who does not mention the coronation in itself but states that the pretender was feted and treated like a real royal.

Though few details have survived of the coronation itself, what has survived suggests it was modelled very closely after the ceremony for crowning English kings used during the preceding centuries. As Dr John Ashdown-Hill points out, it would have been easy for Margaret, dowager Duchess of Burgundy, to find such items as were needed for it, such as a ring and spurs.[1073] The rebels sourced a crown from a statue of the Virgin Mary.[1074] What part John Jnr took we do not know. A fairly recent story claims that the Archbishop of Armagh 'refused to take part in the ceremony or give it his blessing'[1075] because he had been 'warned by a letter from Morton that Simnel was a fraud'[1076] and that 'the infuriated Lord Lincoln [John Jnr] had to be restrained from knocking him down',[1077] but this story originates in the late twentieth century and seems to muddle events before and during the coronation. Though the archbishop, who was close to John Morton, Bishop of Ely, one of Henry's closest men, claimed later to have refused to take part in the coronation, he did not claim that John Jnr tried to physically attack him but instead that he threatened repercussions on him and was pacified by the Earl of Kildare. While this may very well be true, it is nowhere near the same as John Jnr threatening physical violence on the archbishop during the actual coronation ceremony.

Once the coronation was done, the newly crowned pretender was carried to Dublin Castle on the shoulders of strong men to show him off to the population and win their hearts.[1078] According to Molinet, this was successful, and in fact it seems that all Ireland save for the city of Waterford chose to accept the young pretender as King of England. After a coronation banquet in Dublin Castle, about which we sadly know nothing but that it took place, the rebels went to Drogheda the next day,[1079] where a parliament took place in the claimant's name. Even coins were minted. Again, this shows that whoever the claimant was it would have been all but impossible to have him set aside and swapped with either the real Earl of Warwick or even John Jnr himself should the rebellion succeed.

We do not know John Jnr's part in the parliament that followed. However, it stands to reason that he was involved in organising supporters and planning their invasion of England. This is supported by Molinet's claim that 'many lords of the surroundings put themselves under [the pretender's] authority'[1080] after the coronation. Possibly, they also sent messages to England to warn supporters of their upcoming invasion. Certainly when they landed in England, on 4 June, several of their supporters awaited them. It seems likely that Anne Lovell had instructed them to wait, having been informed by her husband that they would land.[1081]

Having landed, John Jnr set off with most of the men that had been gathered while Francis went to attack the Earl of Oxford and won a skirmish against him on 10 June,[1082] doubtlessly giving the rebels hope. John Jnr, a man whom everyone liked, tried winning more support, for example at York, but in this, perhaps with the town fearing repercussions, he failed. On 16 June 1487, his forces having met up with Francis's once more, the two rallied and engaged the royal host in a fight. It was John Jnr's first actual taste of fighting. It was also to be his last.

The battle was long, lasting nearly three hours, and hung in the balance several times before finally swinging in favour of the royal forces. When the dust settled afterwards, John Jnr was dead.

We do not know how he died. The commonly accepted version holds that he died in battle.[1083] All sources, even those hostile to the rebels, agree he was a good and courageous fighter; another legend stated that he was mortally wounded during the battle and was found afterwards lying under a tree by royal forces, who staked him through the heart.[1084] All we know for sure is that on 16 June 1487, John de la Pole, Earl of Lincoln, breathed his last.

15

Suffolk's Last Years

Several sources claim that Henry VII was both sad and angry about John Jnr's death.[1085] He had apparently given orders for John Jnr not to be harmed if at all possible,[1086] something that is stated by Bernard André, who was at his court and therefore in a position to know, as well as by other government-approved sources.[1087] Because of this, it is often claimed that Henry was unsure who the pretender had really been and wanted John Jnr taken alive so he could question him about his motives and the identity of the pretender.[1088] However, none of this is suggested by any sources written within a century or so of his death by people who could have known those who had fought in the battle or known Henry or John Jnr. On the contrary, Polydore Vergil explicitly writes that Henry's men did their best to kill John Jnr for fear that Henry would not only pardon him should he survive but once more give him a position of high honour in his government, enabling him to wreak more havoc.[1089] None of this can be ascertained, but what we know of Henry's attitude towards John Jnr in the two years he knew him suggests it is far from impossible.

It is not known where John Jnr was buried. The most likely version is that he was buried with the other fatalities on the battlefield,[1090] but it is possible that Henry allowed John and Elizabeth to have him quietly and privately buried somewhere.

John and Elizabeth's reaction to their oldest son's death is not recorded. They must have known that it was a possibility he would die as a consequence of his rebellion, but even so it would have been a blow for them. In fact, it would later be claimed, for example by the Tudor chronicler Camden, that John eventually died of grief. Though that seems unlikely, as he did not die for another five years, the claim is rather random and unnecessary for any point Camden wanted to make, suggesting John's grief for his son was noted and potentially even considered excessive by contemporaries. If so, however, no contemporary made a note of it, and John was still expected to fulfil all his duties to the king. In November 1487 he was summoned to Parliament; this would have been painful for him, as it was during this session that John Jnr's attainder was passed.

Whatever his thoughts and feelings, John apparently kept them hidden from Henry, or else Henry sympathised with him. Whichever it was, Henry did not hold John Jnr's rebellion against the father, nor did he seem to have ever suspected him of having supported it. When John Jnr's attainder was passed, Henry added a codicil:

> [p]rovided always that this act of attainder made in this present parliament against John, late earl of Lincoln, shall not extend or be prejudicial to John, duke of Suffolk, during his life with regard to the manors or lordships of Hellesdon, Drayton, Burgh next Aylsham, East Ruston, Bacton and Broomholm, with the annuity belonging to them, the hundred of Shropham in the county of Norfolk, the manors and lordships of Kettlebaston, Hurts [Hall], Blickling and Dagworth in the county of Suffolk, and the castle, manor and lordship of Donnington with the appurtenances in the county of Berkshire, or any of the aforesaid castle, lordships, manors and hundred, or of any part or member of them. And it is also ordained and enacted by the said authority that the said John, duke of Suffolk, shall have, hold and enjoy the aforesaid castle, manors or lordships of Hellesdon, Drayton, Burgh next Aylesham, East Ruston, Bacton and Broomholm, with the aforesaid annuity, and the said hundred of Shropham, the said manors or lordships of Kettlebaston, Hurts [Hall], Blickling, Dagworth and the said manor and lordship of Donnington, and all of them, with the appurtenances, during the life of the said duke, notwithstanding the said act of attainder, or any other act made or to be made, in any way; saving to each person and persons, other than the said earl of Lincoln and his heirs, all such right, title, entry and interest as they, or any of them, had or should have had in any of the things stated if the said act or acts, or any of them, or anything contained in them, or any of them, had never been had or made.[1091]

In short, John was not to be hurt in any way by his son's attainder, and the possessions he had granted to John Jnr were even to fall back to him until his own death, when they would revert to the Crown. This was a very generous act on Henry VII's part as these possessions were worth more £100 annually,[1092] and it definitely suggests that Henry still considered John to be one of his closest men. This is particularly interesting as John's behaviour towards him was not any different than his behaviour towards Richard or Edward had been. He acted loyally but showed no interest in government work or anything Henry did.

However, while it seems logical that staying at court must have been painful for him at least for a while after John Jnr's death, John did not have a choice in 1487 and had to stay after Parliament ended in

November 1487, for shortly afterwards the coronation of John's niece Elizabeth, Henry VII's wife, took place. John and Elizabeth were both involved in the ceremonies.

On 26 November, the day before the actual ceremony took place, John rode in a position of honour in the queen's procession from the Tower of London to Westminster, leading it. Elizabeth sat in the second chariot following the queen,[1093] also a position of honour but one that was owed to her due to her high standing as duchess of the realm and the queen's aunt. It seems the two of them fulfilled their tasks well, without drawing any comment. During the coronation ceremony, John once more bore the sceptre.[1094] Though it was a position of high honour, it is likely that no one commented on this despite John Jnr's recent rebellion because of the fact that John had held this position in the previous three coronations and was probably considered a fixture by then. That Elizabeth was not, despite being in a position of honour during the banquet held for the queen, is less surprising as women were generally exempted from responsibility when their male relatives committed treason.

Perhaps to show that he and Elizabeth supported Henry, John chose to stay at court for Christmas festivities. He was named as being in close attendance upon the king until Twelfth Night, when it was noted that 'the king went to the even-song in his surcoat outward, and on the morrow, at matins time, the Duke of Suffolk followed in the procession next unto the King, and accompanied the Lord D'Aubigny, one of the ambassador of France'.[1095] It seems John was employed by Henry to entertain the French ambassador, which he seems to have done without provoking any comment.

1488–1492

John is often criticised for keeping a good relationship with the king after his son's death, most notably by Henry Napier,[1096] but it is hard to see what else he could have done. He still had a large family to protect, after all, and it must have been with this in mind that he remained close to Henry and did not show any unhappy feelings he had towards him. However, this does not mean he was happy to do whatever Henry wanted. In the spring of 1488, John attended the king's Easter festivities,[1097] once more in a position of honour. However, when Henry asked him to be present at the Garter celebrations later that year, in November 1488, John declined. He did not do so for personal reasons, but instead gave Henry the rather snarky reply that the celebrations were not grand enough to for him to attend.[1098] What Henry made of that is sadly not recorded, though it seems he did not carry a grudge about it. Clearly, it appears that John, like his oldest son, had a way of firmly wrapping Henry around his little finger.

Though John, after making his excuses for the Garter festivities in November 1488, no longer spent as much time at court as he had after John Jnr's rebellion and death, Henry continued favouring him. John appears to have been relieved about this and did nothing to turn Henry against him, but he continued to show little to no interest in life at court or the person of the king after that date.

The year 1488 seems to have been a fairly calm one for John and Elizabeth, spent mostly at Wingfield Castle. They likely tried to keep their lives as private as possible, with the result that little is known about what they did there. John did not attend court at Christmas 1488, or for any of the festivities that followed. Probably, he simply spent his time with his family, watching over the upbringing of the younger children and making sure that his son's rebellion did not damage his position as regional power in Suffolk. However, in these last years of his life, ever since John Jnr's death, no quarrels about possessions are recorded for him. He kept a very low profile.

Perhaps it was this that eventually gave rise to the rumour of him dying of a broken heart, and perhaps his sudden reluctance to fight for what he considered his possessions was in fact due to his oldest son's death. However, given the readiness with which he served Henry to secure a future for himself, his wife and his remaining children, this seems somewhat unlikely. The snark with which he answered Henry when asked to do something he did not want to do also speaks against any sort of depression or disinterest in life since the death of his oldest son.

It seems more likely that, though only in his mid-forties, John's health was deteriorating. It is known that he was ailing in the last year of his life, and quite possibly whatever illness he had then started earlier, making him unable or unwilling to do more than was necessary. Such an idea is supported by what little we actually know of his actions. On 3 March 1489, a note was recorded in the Calendar of Patent Rolls stating that 'the king had been informed of the Duke's intention to surrender the Letters Patent' of the constableship of Wallingford 'into Chancery to be cancelled, and that he had surrendered the same'.[1099] Given the vigour with which he had previously fought for every possession and honour he considered his due, this definitely suggests that he felt unable to fulfil the task.

In 1489, John and his wife, and especially their daughter Elizabeth Jnr, had to deal with another blow: on 13 June that year, Elizabeth Jnr's husband Henry Lovell, Lord Morley, died in the Battle of Dixmude in present-day Belgium. Though Elizabeth Jnr had apparently never left her parents' household, and Henry's death therefore would not have changed her circumstances of life a great deal, it must have been sad for her and for her parents. It is sometimes claimed that Elizabeth Jnr herself died in the same year, but this is untrue. Her gravestone states that she died at the age of fifty-two, surviving both her parents.

However, it seems that their son-in-law's death made John and Elizabeth think about prospects for their other children. Though they had always been rather remiss with arranging marriages for them, they appear to have decided in 1489, perhaps with John already being unwell, that it would be best to see to it that their son Edmund, aged sixteen and now John's heir, was suitably married. The bride they chose for him was Anne Scrope, daughter of the Baron Scrope who had been a close ally of Richard III.[1100] She was around Edmund's age, but very little is known about their marriage. It may very well be that Edmund left his parents' household after his wedding, which seems to have taken place in 1490, but it cannot be said with any certainty. It does seem, however, that John did not live long enough to see the birth of their daughter, his only legitimate grandchild.

Though Edmund's marriage remained the only one John and Elizabeth arranged, they also saw to the futures of some of their other children. Most notably, in 1490, their daughter Anne, then already twenty-four years of age, joined a convent at Syon.[1101] Perhaps at the same time, the fifteen-year-old Humphrey also entered a monastery, in which he was to live a calm and very low-profile life.

It may have calmed John to have secured the future for at least some of his children, for by 1491 he seems to have become seriously ill. Perhaps expecting to die soon, he also tried his best to maintain good relations with Henry VII, perhaps hoping to see to it that he would extend the kindness he had shown him to his children. In 1491, he allowed Henry and his queen to stay at his manor of Ewelme for a month. However, despite what is sometimes claimed,[1102] he did not stay there himself when the royal couple visited. Though only forty-eight years old, John no longer travelled then, spending all his time at Wingfield Castle with Elizabeth and their youngest children. Though it is sometimes claimed he died that year, this is known to be untrue.

The last mention of John alive is found in the Calendar of Patent Rolls on 15 May 1492,[1103] when he was named as a justice of the peace for Oxfordshire. It seems that despite being sick at that time and obviously preparing for his death, he was expected to live a little longer. Perhaps Henry simply did not know the extent of John's illness, or else his condition suddenly worsened.

Within a week of being made a justice of the peace, John de la Pole, Duke of Suffolk, was dead. His exact date of death is not known, but it must have been between 16 and 21 May 1492.[1104] He seems to have died peacefully in his bed, surrounded by his children, with his loving wife at his side. His turbulent life had a peaceful end.

16

Life after Suffolk

John was buried in the family church in Wingfield in his Garter clothing.[1105] It seems to have been a quiet funeral, not a grand affair as the burials of nobles sometimes were.

Henry VII showed all the signs of being sad about his death, but he was not to show John's family the same kindness he had shown John after his oldest son's death. With his death, all the possessions that John Jnr had held during his lifetime fell to Henry VII,[1106] meaning Edmund inherited a rather depleted dukedom. This was something he must have expected, but presumably he did not expect what Henry did next, which was to demote him from duke to earl on the grounds that he lacked sufficient funds to support a dukedom. Though this was technically correct, it had held true for John all during his life, and Edmund seems to have taken it as a sign by the king to show him his place and warn him not to act above his station.

If that was Henry's aim, it failed. One after another, the whole family turned against him. In the year after John's death, his widow Elizabeth went to Burgundy to visit her sister Margaret. This could have been seen as an affront against Henry in itself, given the part Margaret had played in 1487, but it was made worse by the fact that in 1493[1107] Margaret was plotting another rebellion against Henry. It would have been impossible for Elizabeth to visit her without knowing this, and it made a pretty clear statement.

In consequence, Henry had Elizabeth watched but never acted against her. When first her son Edmund and then her son Richard started acting against him, however, eventually fleeing to Burgundy, where they announced that Edmund was the rightful King of England,[1108] Henry declared them traitors.[1109] He also had their brother William, who had stayed at his court and who was not involved in any rebellion, imprisoned in the Tower of London;[1110] he would remain there until his death. William de la Pole holds the sad distinction of having the longest stay as a prisoner in the Tower of London in its long, bloody history.[1111]

Both Edmund and Richard were to keep trying to win the throne in their names until they died. Elizabeth, however, was to know nothing of it. In early 1503, she died at the age of fifty-eight. She was buried next to John in the family church at Wingfield. Their tomb and their effigies still exist today. They lie together for eternity, near the manor where they spent so many years together with all the tragedy and happiness that entailed. The tranquillity of their resting place is just what John would have wanted.

Notes

1. Ed. Edward A Bond, Thomas de Burton, *Chronica Monasterii de Melsa, a Fundatione Usque ad Annum 1396, Auctore Thoma de Burton, Abbate. Accedit Continuatio ad Annum 1406* (London: Longmans, Green, Reader and Dyer, 1868.) p. 48
2. ibid
3. Ed. Gwilym Dodd, Douglas Biggs: *Henry IV, The Establishment of the Regime, 1399-1406* (York: York Medieval Press, 2003) p. 132
4. Chris Given-Wilson, *Henry IV* (New Haven and London: Yale University Press, 2016) pp. 43-47
5. J. L. Kirby, 'Inquisitions Post Mortem, Henry V, Entries 800-851', in *Calendar of Inquisitions Post Mortem: Volume 20, Henry V* (London, 1995), pp. 248-272. *British History Online* http://www.british-history.ac.uk/inquis-post-mortem/vol20/pp248-272 [accessed 7 June 2020]
6. ibid
7. ibid
8. ibid
9. Nicholas Orme, *Medieval Children* (New Haven and London: Yale University Press, 2001). pp. 35–43
10. He is mentioned as earl in the Calendar of Patent Rolls, Richard II, Volume VI, AD 1396–1399, p. 464
11. Chris Given-Wilson, *Henry IV* pp. 138–157
12. ibid
13. ibid
14. For an overview on Henry IV's reign and the rebellions he faced, see: Ed. Gwilym Dodd, Douglas Biggs, The Reign of Henry IV: Rebellion and Survival, 1403-1413 (York: York Medieval Press, 2008)
15. ibid
16. He is referred to as earl in: Calendar of Patent Rolls, Henry IV, Volume II, AD 1401–1405. p. 128

17. Henry Alfred Napier: *Historical Notices of the Parishes of Swyncombe and Ewelme in the County of Oxfordshire* (Oxford: James Wright, Printer to the University, 1863.) pp. 37/8
18. Chris Given-Wilson, *Henry IV* p. 508
19. Calendar of Patent Rolls, Henry IV, Volume II, AD 1401–1405. p. 331
20. Chris Given-Wilson, *Henry IV* p. 508
21. ibid, pp. 513–526
22. For his policies against rebellions, see: Ed. Gwilym Dodd, Douglas Biggs, *The Reign of Henry IV: Rebellion and Survival, 1403-1413* (York: York Medieval Press, 2008)
23. Henry V's policies are explained in: Ian Mortimer, *Henry V: The Warrior King of 1415* (New York City: Rosetta Books, 2009, 2013)
24. 'Henry V: November 1414', in *Parliament Rolls of Medieval England*, ed. Chris Given-Wilson, Paul Brand, Seymour Phillips, Mark Ormrod, Geoffrey Martin, Anne Curry and Rosemary Horrox (Woodbridge, 2005), *British History Online* http://www.british-history.ac.uk/no-series/parliament-rolls-medieval/november-1414 [accessed 7 June 2020].
25. This is explained in: Ian Mortimer, *Henry V: The Warrior King of 1415* (New York City: Rosetta Books, 2009, 2013)
26. ibid
27. Anne Curry, *Guide to the Hundred Years' War* (New York: Palgrave Macmillan, 2003.)
28. ibid
29. 'Henry V: November 1414', in *Parliament Rolls of Medieval England.*
30. ibid
31. Susan Curran, *The English Friend* (Norwich: Lasse Press, 2011.) Position 759
32. 'Henry V: November 1415', in *Parliament Rolls of Medieval England*, ed. Chris Given-Wilson, Paul Brand, Seymour Phillips, Mark Ormrod, Geoffrey Martin, Anne Curry and Rosemary Horrox (Woodbridge, 2005), *British History Online* http://www.british-history.ac.uk/no-series/parliament-rolls-medieval/november-1415 [accessed 7 June 2020].
33. ibid
34. Ian Mortimer, *Henry V: The Warrior King of 1415* (New York City: RosettaBooks, 2009, 2013) 'August'
35. ibid
36. ibid
37. ibid
38. In his own words: 'Henry VI: November 1449', in *Parliament Rolls of Medieval England*, ed. Chris Given-Wilson, Paul Brand, Seymour Phillips, Mark Ormrod, Geoffrey Martin, Anne Curry and Rosemary Horrox (Woodbridge, 2005), *British History*

Online http://www.british-history.ac.uk/no-series/parliament-rolls-medieval/november-1449 [accessed 7 June 2020].
39. ibid
40. Ian Mortimer, *Henry V* 'September'
41. In his own words: 'Henry VI: November 1449', in *Parliament Rolls of Medieval England*
42. ibid
43. Ian Mortimer, 1415: *Henry V's Year of Glory* (London: Random House, 2009) pp. 388-464
44. The most famous example is Laurence Olivier's film adaption of the play, produced during WW2.
45. Ian Mortimer, 1415 pp. 388-464
46. ibid
47. ibid
48. Ian Mortimer, 1415 p. 1
49. Ed. J. L. Kirby, Janet Stevenson, *Calendar of Inquisitions Post-Mortem and other Analogous Documents preserved in the Public Record Office XXI:6–10 Henry V (1418–1422)* (Woodbridge: Boydell Press, 2002) p. 85
50. ibid
51. ibid
52. His movements in the years after he inherited his earldom are detailed in Susan Curran, *The English Friend* (Norwich: Lasse Press, 2011.)
53. Ed. J. L. Kirby, Janet Stevenson, *Calendar of Inquisitions Post-Mortem and other Analogous Documents preserved in the Public Record Office XXI:6–10 Henry V (1418–1422)* (Woodbridge: Boydell Press, 2002) p. 85
54. For Henry's actions immediately following the battle, see: Ian Mortimer, 1415 'November'
55. Ian Mortimer, 1415 p. 371
56. The timing of the taking of Caen coincides almost exactly with the William's Proof of Age, J. L. Kirby, 'Inquisitions Post Mortem, Henry V, Entries 800-851', in *Calendar of Inquisitions Post Mortem: Volume 20, Henry V* (London, 1995), pp. 248-272. *British History Online* http://www.british-history.ac.uk/inquis-post-mortem/vol20/pp248-272 [accessed 7 June 2020]
57. Ian Mortimer, 1415 p. 414
58. ibid, p. 371
59. ibid, 'November'
60. ibid
61. ibid, p. 517
62. ibid
63. Bertram Wolffe, *Henry VI* (New Haven and London: Yale University Press, 1981) p. 70
64. ibid

65. In his own words: 'Henry VI: November 1449', in *Parliament Rolls of Medieval England*
66. Helen Castor, *Joan of Arc. A history* (London: Faber and Faber Ltd, 2014) 'This War, Accursed of God'
67. ibid
68. ibid
69. ibid
70. In his own words: 'Henry VI: November 1449', in *Parliament Rolls of Medieval England*
71. ibid
72. ibid
73. Lauren Johnson, *Shadow King. The Life and Death of Henry VI* (London: Head of Zeus Ltd, 2019) 'That Divine King your Father'
74. Helen Castor, *Joan of Arc. A history* (London: Faber and Faber Ltd, 2014) 'This War, Accursed of God'
75. Lauren Johnson, *Shadow King. The Life and Death of Henry VI* (London: Head of Zeus Ltd, 2019) p. 28
76. ibid, pp. 28-9
77. ibid, pp. 28-30
78. In his own words: 'Henry VI: November 1449', in *Parliament Rolls of Medieval England*
79. Susan Curran, *The English Friend* (Norwich: Lasse Press, 2011.) Position 3153
80. See below, Chapter 2.5
81. In his own words: 'Henry VI: November 1449', in *Parliament Rolls of Medieval England*
82. See below, chapter 1.
83. See below, introduction.
84. ibid
85. In his own words: 'Henry VI: November 1449', in *Parliament Rolls of Medieval England.*
86. For a history on her, see: Helen Castor, *Joan of Arc. A history* (London: Faber and Faber Ltd, 2014)
87. ibid
88. ibid
89. In William's own words: 'Henry VI: November 1449', in *Parliament Rolls of Medieval England*
90. ibid
91. ibid
92. ibid
93. It has sometimes been questioned if she actually was his granddaughter, but there can be no doubt. See, for example: Marion Turner, *Chaucer: A European Life* (Woodstock: Princeton University Press, 2019) pp. 507/8
94. J. S. Roskell, 'Thomas Chaucer of Ewelme', in *Parl. and Pol. in Late Med. Eng.* iii. 151-91

95. Henry Alfred Napier, *Historical Notices of the Parishes of Swyncombe and Ewelme in the County of Oxfordshire* (Oxford: James Wright, Printer to the University, 1863.) pp. 21, 41/2
96. J. S. Roskell,'Thomas Chaucer of Ewelme', in *Parl. and Pol. in Late Med. Eng.* iii. 151-91
97. ibid
98. Marjorie Anderson, *Alice Chaucer and Her Husbands*, PMLA Vol. 60, No. 1 (Mar., 1945), pp. 24-47 p. 26
99. ibid
100. Ed. Thomas Stapleton, *De Antiquis Legibus Liber. Cronica Maiorum et Vicecomitum Londoniarum et quedam, que contigebant temporibis illis ab anno MCLXXVIII; cum appendice* (London: Camden Society, 1846), pp. clvi/clvii
101. Marjorie Anderson, *Alice Chaucer and Her Husbands*, PMLA Vol. 60, No. 1 (Mar., 1945), pp. 24-47 p. 26
102. ibid, p. 27
103. ibid, pp. 28-9
104. ibid
105. Piers de Fenin, *Mémoires de Pierre de Fenin comprenant le récit des événements: qui se sont passés en France et en Bourgogne sous les règnes de Charles VI et Charles VII, 1407-1427* (Histoire) pp. 224-239
106. ibid
107. ibid
108. ibid
109. Henry Alfred Napier, *Historical Notices of the Parishes of Swyncombe and Ewelme in the County of Oxfordshire* (Oxford: James Wright, Printer to the University, 1863) pp. 35/6
110. Susan Curran, *The English Friend* (Norwich: Lasse Press, 2011) Position 3384
111. ibid
112. Marjorie Anderson, *Alice Chaucer and Her Husbands*, PMLA Vol. 60, No. 1 (Mar., 1945), pp. 24-47 p. 30
113. Susan Curran, *The English Friend* (Norwich: Lasse Press, 2011), Positions 3399-3414
114. ibid
115. In William's own words: 'Henry VI: November 1449', in *Parliament Rolls of Medieval England.*
116. The National Archives Currency Converter
117. In William's own words: 'Henry VI: November 1449', in *Parliament Rolls of Medieval England.*
118. Calendar of Patent Rolls, Henry VI, Volume II, p. 86
119. Susan Curran, *The English Friend* (Norwich: Lasse Press, 2011) Positions 3427-3440
120. Marjorie Anderson, *Alice Chaucer and Her Husbands*, PMLA Vol. 60, No. 1 (Mar., 1945), pp. 24-47 p. 29

121. In William's own words: 'Henry VI: November 1449', in *Parliament Rolls of Medieval England.*
122. ibid
123. Marjorie Anderson, *Alice Chaucer and Her Husbands*, PMLA Vol. 60, No. 1 (Mar., 1945), pp. 24-47 p. 31
124. Chancery Inquisitions Post Mortem, Henry VI, File 70, No.35
125. John Goodall: *God's House at Ewelme: Life, Devotion and Architecture in a Fifteenth-Century Almshouse* (London: Taylor & Francis, 2017) p. 23
126. Susan Curran, *The English Friend* (Norwich: Lasse Press, 2011) Positions 3606
127. Ed. Charles Lethbridge Kingsford, *The Stonor letters and papers, 1290–1483* (London: Offices of the Society, 1919) p. xxiii
128. Rachel M. Delman, *Gendered viewing, childbirth and female authority in the residence of Alice Chaucer, duchess of Suffolk, at Ewelme, Oxfordshire* (2019) https://www.tandfonline.com/doi/full/10.1080/03044181.2019.1593619
129. John A. A. Goodall, *God's House at Ewelme, Oxfordshire: Life, Devotion and Architecture in a Fifteenth-Century Almshouse* (Aldershot: Ashgate, 2001), 281–91
130. Susan Curran, *The English Friend* (Norwich: Lasse Press, 2011) Positions 481
131. ibid
132. ibid
133. ibid
134. Rachel M. Delman, *Gendered viewing, childbirth and female authority in the residence of Alice Chaucer, duchess of Suffolk, at Ewelme, Oxfordshire* (2019) https://www.tandfonline.com/doi/full/10.1080/03044181.2019.1593619
135. ibid
136. ibid
137. John A. A. Goodall, *God's House at Ewelme, Oxfordshire: Life, Devotion and Architecture in a Fifteenth-Century Almshouse* (Aldershot: Ashgate, 2001), 281–91
138. Nicholas Orme, *Medieval Children* (New Haven and London: Yale University Press, 2001). pp. 35–43
139. ibid
140. Calendar of Patent Rolls, Henry VI, Volume IV, AD 1441–1446, p. 319
141. Nicholas Orme, *Medieval Children* (New Haven and London: Yale University Press, 2001). pp. 35–43
142. ibid
143. Josephine Wilkinson, *Richard the Young King to Be* (Stroud: Amberley Publishing, 2014) p. 56
144. A good explanation of father's parts in their children's upbringing is found in Nicholas Orme, *Medieval Children* (New Haven and London: Yale University Press, 2001)

145. For an overview of his jobs: Calendar of Patent Rolls, Henry VI, Volume IV, AD 1441–1446, also: Lauren Johnson, *Shadow King. The Life and Death of Henry VI* (London: Head of Zeus Ltd, 2019)
146. Josephine Wilkinson, *The Princes in the Tower* (Stroud: Amberley Publishing, 2013) pp. 14/5
147. ibid
148. ibid, p. 13
149. See below, footnote 165
150. Lauren Johnson, *Shadow King. The Life and Death of Henry VI* (London: Head of Zeus Ltd, 2019), chapter 14
151. ibid
152. ibid
153. ibid
154. ibid
155. Ed. Thomas Basin and Charles Samaran, *Histoire de Charles VII: Tome Premier, 1407–1444* (Paris: Les Classiques de l'Histoire de France Au Moyen Age. Volume 15, 1933)
156. ibid
157. This was, in fact, one of the charges against William in 1450: In William's own words: 'Henry VI: November 1449', in *Parliament Rolls of Medieval England.*
158. ibid
159. ibid
160. ibid
161. Nicola Tallis: *Uncrowned Queen: The Fateful Life of Margaret Beaufort, Tudor Matriarch* (London: Michael O'Mara Books Limited, 2019)
162. H. T. Riley, *Ingulph's Chronicle of the Abbey of Croyland* (London: George Bell and Sons, 1908) p. 399
163. In William's own words: 'Henry VI: November 1449', in *Parliament Rolls of Medieval England.*
164. Nicola Tallis: *Uncrowned Queen: The Fateful Life of Margaret Beaufort, Tudor Matriarch* (London: Michael O'Mara Books Limited, 2019)
165. S. Bentley, *Excerpta Historica or Illustrations of English history* (London, 1831) p. 4
166. In William's own words: 'Henry VI: November 1449', in *Parliament Rolls of Medieval England.*
167. John Fisher, *Mornyng Rememberance*, p. 2
168. Michael K. Jones, Malcolm G. Underwood, *The King's Mother. Lady Margaret Beaufort, Countess of Richmond and Derby* (New York: Cambridge University Press, 1992.) p. 37
169. He is referred to as marquis in the Calendar of Patent Rolls, Henry VI,IV, AD 1441-1446, p. 409
170. Lauren Johnson, *Shadow King. The Life and Death of Henry VI* (London: Head of Zeus Ltd, 2019), chapter 14

171. ibid
172. Calendar of Patent Rolls, Henry VI, Volume IV, AD 1441–1446, p. 319
173. Lauren Johnson, *Shadow King. The Life and Death of Henry VI* (London: Head of Zeus Ltd, 2019), chapter 14
174. ibid
175. ibid
176. ibid
177. Henry Alfred Napier: *Historical Notices of the Parishes of Swyncombe and Ewelme in the County of Oxfordshire* (Oxford: James Wright, Printer to the University, 1863.) p. 61
178. ibid
179. Susan Curran, *The English Friend* (Norwich: Lasse Press, 2011.) Position 5334
180. ibid
181. Calendar of Patent Rolls, Henry VI, Volume V, AD 11446-1452 p. 133
182. ibid
183. In William's own words: 'Henry VI: November 1449', in *Parliament Rolls of Medieval England.*
184. K. L. Clark, *The Nevills of Middleham: England's Most Powerful Family in the Wars of the Roses* (Stroud: The History Press, 2016) p. 97
185. Henry Alfred Napier, *Historical Notices of the Parishes of Swyncombe and Ewelme in the County of Oxfordshire* (Oxford: James Wright, Printer to the University, 1863) pp. 69-71
186. ibid
187. In William's own words: 'Henry VI: November 1449', in *Parliament Rolls of Medieval England.*
188. ibid
189. see: Lauren Johnson, *Shadow King. The Life and Death of Henry VI* (London: Head of Zeus Ltd, 2019)
190. This is the whole subject of Alex Brayson, *Deficit Finance During the Early Majority of Henry VI of England, 1436–1444. The 'Crisis' of the Medieval English 'Tax State'* (2019)
191. ibid
192. K. L. Clark, *The Nevills of Middleham: England's Most Powerful Family in the Wars of the Roses* (Stroud: The History Press, 2016) pp. 49/50
193. ibid pp. 57/8
194. ibid
195. ibid
196. ibid
197. He is mentioned as a duke in Calendar of Patent Rolls, Henry VI, Volume V, AD 1446-1452
198. Testament of William de la Pole, Duke of Suffolk, quoted in: Henry Alfred Napier: *Historical Notices of the Parishes of Swyncombe*

and Ewelme in the County of Oxfordshire (Oxford: James Wright, Printer to the University, 1863.) p. 82

199. Susan Curran, *The English Friend* (Norwich: Lasse Press, 2011) Position 992
200. Henry Alfred Napier: *Historical Notices of the Parishes of Swyncombe and Ewelme in the County of Oxfordshire* (Oxford: James Wright, Printer to the University, 1863) pp. 84-7
201. ibid
202. Susan Curran, *The English Friend* (Norwich: Lasse Press, 2011) Position 5902
203. See below, Chapter 3.1
204. K. L. Clark, *The Nevills of Middleham: England's Most Powerful Family in the Wars of the Roses* (Stroud: The History Press, 2016) p. 97
205. Susan Curran, *The English Friend* (Norwich: Lasse Press, 2011.) Position 5902
206. In William's own words: 'Henry VI: November 1449', in *Parliament Rolls of Medieval England.*
207. Nicola Tallis: *Uncrowned Queen: The Fateful Life of Margaret Beaufort, Tudor Matriarch* (London: Michael O'Mara Books Limited, 2019)
208. In William's own words: 'Henry VI: November 1449', in *Parliament Rolls of Medieval England.*
209. Nicola Tallis: *Uncrowned Queen: The Fateful Life of Margaret Beaufort, Tudor Matriarch* (London: Michael O'Mara Books Limited, 2019) Positions 668-713
210. 9 January being the date when William's treasurer was killed, 28 January the day William was arrested
211. Calendar of Papal Registers, X, pp. 471-4
212. Nicola Tallis: *Uncrowned Queen: The Fateful Life of Margaret Beaufort, Tudor Matriarch* (London: Michael O'Mara Books Limited, 2019)
213. 'Henry VI: November 1449', in *Parliament Rolls of Medieval England.*
214. ibid
215. ibid
216. ibid
217. ibid
218. ibid
219. ibid
220. ibid
221. ibid
222. Matthew Lewis, *Richard, Duke of York: King by Right* (Stroud: Amberley Publishing, 2016) position 2678
223. ibid
224. ibid, Position 5393

225. Letter quoted in Henry Alfred Napier: *Historical Notices of the Parishes of Swyncombe and Ewelme in the County of Oxfordshire* (Oxford: James Wright, Printer to the University, 1863) pp. 88/9
226. ibid
227. Matthew Lewis, *Richard, Duke of York: King by Right* (Stroud: Amberley Publishing, 2016) position 2697
228. James Gairdner, *The Paston Letters, AD 1422–1509. Volume I. New Complete Library Edition* (London: Chatto & Windus, Exeter: James G. Commin, 1904) pp. 124/5
229. ibid, pp. 124-126
230. Matthew Lewis, *Richard, Duke of York: King by Right* (Stroud: Amberley Publishing, 2016) position 2697
231. James Gairdner, *The Paston Letters, AD 1422–1509. Volume I* pp. 124/5
232. ibid
233. ibid, p. 126
234. Nicola Tallis: *Uncrowned Queen: The Fateful Life of Margaret Beaufort, Tudor Matriarch* (London: Michael O'Mara Books Limited, 2019) Positions 990-1004
235. Typical example: Henry Alfred Napier: *Historical Notices of the Parishes of Swyncombe and Ewelme in the County of Oxfordshire* (Oxford: James Wright, Printer to the University, 1863)
236. ibid, p. 103, quoting a grant to Alice by the queen, stating which manors and lands she immediately got.
237. See below, chapter 2.
238. Matthew Lewis, *Richard, Duke of York: King by Right* (Stroud: Amberley Publishing, 2016) position 2738–3235
239. ibid
240. ibid, position 3107
241. ibid
242. See: Lauren Johnson, *Shadow King. The Life and Death of Henry VI* (London: Head of Zeus Ltd, 2019)
243. ibid
244. Henry Alfred Napier: *Historical Notices of the Parishes of Swyncombe and Ewelme in the County of Oxfordshire* (Oxford: James Wright, Printer to the University, 1863) pp. 91/2
245. Peter Spring: *Sir John Tiptoft: 'Butcher of England': Earl of Worcester, Edward IV's Enforcer and Humanist Scholar* (Barnsley: Pen & Sword Military, 2018)
246. 'Henry VI: November 1450', in *Parliament Rolls of Medieval England*, ed. Chris Given-Wilson, Paul Brand, Seymour Phillips, Mark Ormrod, Geoffrey Martin, Anne Curry and Rosemary Horrox (Woodbridge, 2005), *British History Online* http://www.british-history.ac.uk/no-series/parliament-rolls-medieval/november-1450 [accessed 10 June 2020].

247. ibid
248. ibid
249. ibid
250. Michael Hicks, *'Pole, John de la, second duke of Suffolk'*, Oxford Dictionary of National Biography (Oxford University Press, 2004)
251. Calendar of Papal Registers, X, pp. 471-4
252. ibid
253. ibid
254. Rachel M. Delman, Gendered viewing, childbirth and female authority in the residence of Alice Chaucer, duchess of Suffolk, at Ewelme, Oxfordshire (2018) https://www.tandfonline.com/doi/full/10.1080/03044181.2019.1593619?fbclid=IwAR3zANh8h84dUUpkqdX6R6_qz4DJ8v1TrljoQn22_vr_ffyFz43MqeGVdCw&
255. The Ewelme Inventory, quoted in Henry Alfred Napier: *Historical Notices of the Parishes of Swyncombe and Ewelme in the County of Oxfordshire* (Oxford: James Wright, Printer to the University, 1863) pp. 125-129
256. See below, chapter 5
257. Matthew Lewis, *Richard, Duke of York: King by Right* (Stroud: Amberley Publishing, 2016) position 3311
258. Nicola Tallis, *Uncrowned Queen: The Fateful Life of Margaret Beaufort, Tudor Matriarch* (London: Michael O'Mara Books Limited, 2019) Positions 1703
259. John Fisher, *Mornyng Rememberance*, p. 2
260. H. T. Riley, *Ingulph's Chronicle* p. 400
261. Matthew Lewis, *Richard, Duke of York: King by Right* (Stroud: Amberley Publishing, 2016) position 3687
262. ibid, positions 3687-5393
263. Rachel M. Delman, Gendered viewing, childbirth and female authority in the residence of Alice Chaucer, duchess of Suffolk, at Ewelme, Oxfordshire (2018) https://www.tandfonline.com/doi/full/10.1080/03044181.2019.1593619?fbclid=IwAR3zANh8h84dUUpk qdX6R6_qz4DJ8v1TrljoQn22_vr_ffyFz43MqeGVdCw&
264. Matthew Lewis, *Richard, Duke of York: King by Righ*t (Stroud: Amberley Publishing, 2016) position 4029
265. Calendar of the Patent Rolls, Henry VI, Volume VI, AD 1452-1460, p. 370
266. *Sequitur generacio illustrissimi principis Ricardi, Ducis Eboraci & c ex serenissima principissa, uxore sua, Caecilia. T. Hearne, Liber Niger Scaccarii nec non Wilhelmi Worcestrii Annales Rerum Angelicarum, Volume 2* (London: 1774), p. 525
267. 'Deeds: A.6301–A.6400', in *A Descriptive Catalogue of Ancient Deeds: Volume* 4, ed. H C Maxwell Lyte (London, 1902), pp. 22-34.

British History Online http://www.british-history.ac.uk/ancient-deeds/vol4/pp22-34 [accessed 10 June 2020].
268. James Gairdner, *The Paston Letters, AD 1422–1509. Volume III. New Complete Library Edition* (London: Chatto & Windus, Exeter: James G. Commin, 1904) p. 226
269. John Ashdown-Hill, *Cecily Neville, Mother of Richard III* (Yorkshire-Philadelphia: Pen & Sword, 2018) Position 622-630
270. ibid
271. See below, chapter 5
272. See below, chapter 10
273. Ed Alison Hanham, John Benet's Chronicle, 1399-1462 An English Translation with New Introduction (New York: Palgrave Macmillian, 2018)
274. Calendar of Patent Rolls, Henry VI, Colume 6, AD 1452-1460
275. Michael Hicks, 'Pole, John de la, second duke of Suffolk', *Oxford Dictionary of National Biography* (Oxford University Press, 2004)
276. Matthew Lewis, *Richard, Duke of York: King by Right* (Stroud: Amberley Publishing, 2016) position 4530–4590
277. See below, chapter 5
278. See below, chapter 5
279. See in: Ed. Charles Lethbridge Kingsford, The Stonor letters and papers, 1290–1483 Vol. III (London: Offices of the Society, 1919)
280. See the entire discussion about this in
281. See: James Gairdner, *The Paston Letters, AD 1422–1509. Volumes I & II*
282. James Gairdner, *The Paston Letters, AD 1422–1509. Volume Iii*
283. See below, chapter 10
284. Matthew Lewis, *Richard, Duke of York: King by Right* (Stroud: Amberley Publishing, 2016) position 4918
285. James Gairdner, *The Paston Letters, AD 1422–1509. Volume III* p. 226
286. ibid, pp. 227-230
287. ibid
288. Matthew Lewis, *Richard, Duke of York: King by Right* (Stroud: Amberley Publishing, 2016) position 5393
289. ibid, position 5205
290. Ed. John Silvester Davies, *An English chronicle of the reigns of Richard II, Henry IV, Henry V, and Henry VI written before the year 1471; with an appendix, containing the 18th and 19th years of Richard II and the Parliament at Bury St. Edmund's, 25th Henry VI and supplementary additions from the Cotton. ms. chronicle called 'Eulogium'* (London: Camden Society, 1856)
291. Matthew Lewis, *Richard, Duke of York: King by Right* (Stroud: Amberley Publishing, 2016) position 5065
292. Mary Clive, *This Son of York. A biography of Edward IV* (London: Macmillan London Ltd, 1973). pp. 56–61

293. ibid, p. 55
294. Ed. John Silvester Davies, An English chronicle of the reigns of Richard II, Henry IV, Henry V, and Henry VI written before the year 1471; with an appendix, containing the 18th and 19th years of Richard II and the Parliament at Bury St. Edmund's, 25th Henry VI and supplementary additions from the Cotton. ms. chronicle called 'Eulogium' (London: Camden Society, 1856)
295. 'Brief notes of occurrences under Henry VI and Edward IV', in *Three Fifteenth-Century Chronicles with Historical Memoranda by John Stowe*, ed. James Gairdner (London, 1880), pp. 148-163. *British History Online* http://www.british-history.ac.uk/camden-record-soc/vol28/pp148-163 [accessed 11 June 2020].
296. ibid
297. Calendar of Patent Rolls, Edward IV, Henry VI, Richard III, Volume I, AD 1461-1485, p. 261
298. ibid
299. ibid
300. 'Brief notes of occurrences under Henry VI and Edward IV', in *Three Fifteenth-Century Chronicles with Historical Memoranda by John Stowe*, ed. James Gairdner (London, 1880), pp. 148-163. *British History Online* http://www.british-history.ac.uk/camden-record-soc/vol28/pp148-163 [accessed 11 June 2020]
301. James Gairdner, *The Paston Letters, AD 1422–1509. Volume VI* p. 72
302. The Ewelme Inventory
303. ibid
304. ibid
305. ibid
306. ibid
307. 'Edward IV: November 1461', in *Parliament Rolls of Medieval England*, ed. Chris Given-Wilson, Paul Brand, Seymour Phillips, Mark Ormrod, Geoffrey Martin, Anne Curry and Rosemary Horrox (Woodbridge, 2005), *British History Online* http://www.british-history.ac.uk/no-series/parliament-rolls-medieval/november-1461 [accessed 11 June 2020].
308. Rachel M. Delman, Gendered viewing, childbirth and female authority in the residence of Alice Chaucer, duchess of Suffolk, at Ewelme, Oxfordshire (2018) https://www.tandfonline.com/doi/full/10.1080/03044181.2019.1593619?fbclid=IwAR3zANh8h84dUUpkqdX6R6_qz4DJ8v1TrljoQn22_vr_ffyFz43MqeGVdCw&
309. See below, chapter 4
310. ibid
311. James Gairdner, *The Paston Letters, AD 1422–1509. Volume I–VI. New Complete Library Edition* (London: Chatto & Windus, Exeter: James G. Commin, 1904)

312. James Gairdner, *The Paston Letters, AD 1422–1509. Volume III.* pp. 271/2
313. See the books brought for their education: Rachel M. Delman, Gendered viewing, childbirth and female authority in the residence of Alice Chaucer, duchess of Suffolk, at Ewelme, Oxfordshire (2018) https://www.tandfonline.com/doi/full/10.1080/03044181.2019.1593619?fbclid=IwAR3zANh8h84dUUpkqdX6R6_qz4DJ8v1TrljoQn22_vr_ffyFz43MqeGVdCw&
314. James Gairdner, *The Paston Letters, AD 1422–1509. Volume IV* pp. 65/6
315. ibid
316. ibid
317. Rowland's Historical and Genealogical Account of the noble family of Neville, quoted in: Henry Alfred Napier: *Historical Notices of the Parishes of Swyncombe and Ewelme in the County of Oxfordshire* (Oxford: James Wright, Printer to the University, 1863) pp. 110-112
318. ibid
319. ibid
320. ibid
321. Calendar of Patent Rolls, Edward IV, Henry VI, Richard III, Volume I, AD 1461-1485, p. 264
322. ibid
323. See below, chapter 4
324. Mary Clive, *This Son of York. A biography of Edward IV* (London: Macmillan London Ltd, 1973) pp. 89-99
325. ibid
326. ibid
327. ibid
328. James Gairdner, *The Paston Letters, AD 1422–1509. Volume VI. New Complete Library Edition* (London: Chatto & Windus, Exeter: James G. Commin, 1904) pp. 105-107
329. Mary Clive, *This Son of York. A biography of Edward IV* (London: Macmillan London Ltd, 1973) pp. 89-99
330. ibid
331. ibid
332. ibid
333. James Gairdner, *The Paston Letters, AD 1422–1509. Volume VI* pp. 105-107
334. ibid
335. For example: Dr Anthony Corbet, *Edward IV, England's Forgotten Warrior King. His Life, His People and His Legacy* (Bloomington: iUniverse, 2015) p. 248
336. Ed. Charles Lethbridge Kingsford, *The Stonor letters and papers, 1290–1483, Volume I* (London: Offices of the Society, 1919), pp. 116/7

337. Mary Clive, *This Son of York. A biography of Edward IV* (London: Macmillan London Ltd, 1973) p. 107
338. ibid, p. 102
339. ibid, pp. 100-113
340. Annette Carson, *Richard III, The Maligned King* (Stroud: The History Press, 2008) p. 24
341. Mary Clive, *This Son of York. A biography of Edward IV* (London: Macmillan London Ltd, 1973) p. 107
342. ibid
343. Annette Carson, *Richard III, The Maligned King* (Stroud: The History Press, 2008) p. 24
344. See: Peter W. Hammond, Anne F. Sutton, *The Coronation of Richard III: The Extant Documents* (Middlesbrough: A Sutton Publishing, 1984) for what lands were granted to Elizabeth.
345. Calendar of Patent Rolls, Edward IV, Henry VI, Richard III, Volume I, AD 1461-1485, p. 435
346. Michael Hicks, *'Pole, John de la, second duke of Suffolk'*, Oxford Dictionary of National Biography (Oxford University Press, 2004)
347. Desmond Seward, *The Last White Rose* (London: Constable, 2010), pp. 24/5
348. Ed. Charles Lethbridge Kingsford, *The Stonor letters and papers Volume I* pp. 116/7
349. ibid
350. ibid, p. 116
351. ibid
352. See below, chapter 5
353. See below, chapter 5
354. The Ewelme Inventory
355. Josephine Wilkinson, *Richard the Young King to Be* (Stroud: Amberley Publishing, 2014) p. 65
356. See below, chapter 10
357. Ed G. Smith, *The Coronation of Elizabeth Wydeville* (London, 1935), pp. 17/8
358. ibid
359. James Gairdner, *The Paston Letters, AD 1422–1509. Volume VI* pp. 129/30
360. ibid
361. ibid
362. ibid, pp. 131-133
363. For example: Henry Alfred Napier: *Historical Notices of the Parishes of Swyncombe and Ewelme in the County of Oxfordshire* (Oxford: James Wright, Printer to the University, 1863) pp. 37/8
364. James Gairdner, *The Paston Letters, AD 1422–1509. Volume VI* pp. 136-140
365. ibid
366. ibid

367. ibid
368. ibid
369. ibid
370. ibid, pp. 145/6
371. ibid, pp. 147-150
372. ibid
373. ibid
374. ibid
375. ibid
376. ibid
377. ibid
378. ibid
379. ibid, pp. 156-159
380. ibid
381. ibid
382. ibid
383. ibid, pp. 159/60
384. ibid
385. ibid
386. ibid, pp. 160-162
387. ibid
388. ibid
389. ibid
390. ibid
391. ibid, pp. 162-164
392. ibid, pp. 164-166
393. ibid
394. ibid
395. ibid
396. ibid
397. ibid
398. ibid
399. ibid, p. 208
400. ibid
401. ibid, pp. 173/4
402. ibid
403. ibid
404. ibid
405. See, for example: Paul Murray Kendall, *Richard the Third* (London: George Allan & Unwin, 1955–1956), p. 73
406. James Gairdner, *The Paston Letters, AD 1422–1509. Volume VI* pp. 173/
407. ibid
408. ibid
409. ibid

410. ibid
411. ibid
412. ibid
413. ibid, pp. 179-181
414. ibid
415. ibid
416. Leland's Collectana, Volume VI (London: 1770), pp. 2-14
417. ibid
418. ibid
419. ibid
420. James Gairdner, *The Paston Letters, AD 1422–1509. Volume VI* pp. 206/7
421. ibid
422. ibid
423. See, for example: Henry Alfred Napier: *Historical Notices of the Parishes of Swyncombe and Ewelme in the County of Oxfordshire* (Oxford: James Wright, Printer to the University, 1863) p. 119
424. ames Gairdner, *The Paston Letters, AD 1422–1509. Volume VI. New Complete Library Edition* (London: Chatto & Windus, Exeter: James G. Commin, 1904), also below.
425. See below
426. The Ewelme Inventory
427. ibid
428. K. L. Clark, *The Nevills of Middleham: England's Most Powerful Family in the Wars of the Roses* (Stroud: The History Press, 2016), p. 295
429. Ed. Malcolm Letts,The Travels of Leo of Rozmital through Germany, Flanders, England, France, Spain, Portugal and Italy 1465-1467 (London: Hakluyt Society, 2017), pp. 44-49
430. John Ashdown Hill, *Elizabeth Widville, Lady Grey: Edward IV's Chief Mistress and the 'Pink Queen'* (Barnsley: Pen&Sword, 2019), position 1453
431. Ed. Malcolm Letts,The Travels of Leo of Rozmital through Germany, Flanders, England, France, Spain, Portugal and Italy 1465-1467 (London: Hakluyt Society, 2017), pp. 44-49
432. Matthew Lewis, *Richard III: Loyalty Binds Me* (Stroud: Amberley Publishing, 2018) p. 33
433. 'Edward IV: November 1461', in *Parliament Rolls of Medieval England*, ed. Chris Given-Wilson, Paul Brand, Seymour Phillips, Mark Ormrod, Geoffrey Martin, Anne Curry and Rosemary Horrox (Woodbridge, 2005), *British History Online* http://www.british-history.ac.uk/no-series/parliament-rolls-medieval/november-1461 [accessed 13 June 2020].
434. *Calendar of Close Rolls, Edward IV: Volume 1, 1461-1468*, ed. W H B Bird and K H Ledward (London, 1949), *British History*

Online http://www.british-history.ac.uk/cal-close-rolls/edw4/vol1 [accessed 13 June 2020].

435. Calendar of Patent Rolls, Edward IV, Henry VI, Richard III, Volume I, AD 1461-1485
436. Henry Alfred Napier: *Historical Notices of the Parishes of Swyncombe and Ewelme in the County of Oxfordshire* (Oxford: James Wright, Printer to the University, 1863) p. 118-121
437. Mary Clive, *This Son of York. A biography of Edward IV* (London: Macmillan London Ltd, 1973). p. 96
438. Luc Hommel: *Marguerite D'York ou La Duchesse Junon* (Paris: Librairie Hachette, 1959) pp. 76-93
439. Luc Hommel: *Marguerite D'York ou La Duchesse Junon* (Paris: Librairie Hachette, 1959) pp. 76-93
440. Henry Alfred Napier: *Historical Notices of the Parishes of Swyncombe and Ewelme in the County of Oxfordshire* (Oxford: James Wright, Printer to the University, 1863) pp. 120-124
441. ibid, p. 120
442. Ed. C. A. J. Armstrong, *The Usurpation of Richard III by Dominic Mancini*
443. Henry Alfred Napier: *Historical Notices of the Parishes of Swyncombe and Ewelme in the County of Oxfordshire* (Oxford: James Wright, Printer to the University, 1863) p. 121
444. ibid
445. Henry Alfred Napier: *Historical Notices of the Parishes of Swyncombe and Ewelme in the County of Oxfordshire* (Oxford: James Wright, Printer to the University, 1863) p. 119
446. See below, chapter 8
447. The Ewelme Inventory
448. ibid
449. Rachel M. Delman, *Gendered viewing, childbirth and female authority in the residence of Alice Chaucer, duchess of Suffolk, at Ewelme, Oxfordshire* (2019) https://www.tandfonline.com/doi/full/10.1080/03044181.2019.1593619
450. The Ewelme Inventory
451. ibid
452. ibid
453. ibid
454. ibid
455. Rachel M. Delman, *Gendered viewing, childbirth and female authority in the residence of Alice Chaucer, duchess of Suffolk, at Ewelme, Oxfordshire* (2019) https://www.tandfonline.com/doi/full/10.1080/03044181.2019.1593619
456. The Ewelme Inventory
457. Ute Gerhard: *Geschlechterstreit und Aufklärung*. In: dies (Hrsg.): *Frauenbewegung und Feminismus. Eine Geschichte seit 1789*. 2. Auflage (München: C.H.Beck, 2012) p. 11

458. Rachel M. Delman, Gendered viewing, childbirth and female authority in the residence of Alice Chaucer, duchess of Suffolk, at Ewelme, Oxfordshire (2018) https://www.tandfonline.com/doi/full/10.1080/03044181.2019.1593619?fbclid=IwAR3zANh8h84dUUpkqdX6R6_qz4DJ8v1TrljoQn22_vr_ffyFz43MqeGVdCw&
459. The Ewelme Inventory, quoted in Henry Alfred Napier: *Historical Notices of the Parishes of Swyncombe and Ewelme in the County of Oxfordshire* (Oxford: James Wright, Printer to the University, 1863., pp. 125-129
460. Christine de Pizan. *Das Buch von der Stadt der Frauen* (München: Deutscher Taschenbuch Verlag, 1995)
461. See above, introduction
462. See: John Ashdown-Hill, *Cecily Neville, Mother of Richard III* (Yorkshire-Philadelphia: Pen & Sword, 2018)
463. See above, chapter 4
464. The Ewelme Inventory
465. ibid
466. ibid
467. Marion Turner, *Chaucer: A European Life* (Woodstock: Princeton University Press, 2019)
468. The Ewelme Inventory
469. ibid
470. ibid
471. ibid
472. ibid
473. ibid
474. ibid
475. ibid
476. Calendar of Patent Rolls, Edward IV, Henry VI, Richard III, Volume I, AD 1461-1485, Volume II, p. 96
477. ibid
478. ibid, pp. 753
479. Luc Hommel: *Marguerite D'York ou La Duchesse Junon* (Paris: Librairie Hachette, 1959) pp. 26/7
480. ibid
481. ibid
482. ibid, pp. 37-52
483. Mary Clive, *This Son of York. A biography of Edward IV* (London: Macmillan London Ltd, 1973). pp. 126-128
484. Quoted in: Mary Clive, *This Son of York. A biography of Edward IV* (London: Macmillan London Ltd, 1973). p. 126
485. Raphael Holinshed, Chronicles of England, Scotland and Ireland (1577)
486. ibid
487. James Gairdner, *The Paston Letters, AD 1422–1509. Volume IV* pp. 297/8

488. Mary Clive, *This Son of York. A biography of Edward IV* (London: Macmillan London Ltd, 1973). p. 126
489. Luc Hommel: *Marguerite D'York ou La Duchesse Junon* (Paris: Librairie Hachette, 1959) pp. 47-51
490. ibid, p. 76-93
491. ibid
492. Paul Murray Kendall, *Richard the Third* (London: George Allan & Unwin, 1955–1956) p. 51
493. James Gairdner, *The Paston Letters, AD 1422–1509. Volume V* pp. 10-12
494. Paul Murray Kendall, *Richard the Third* p. 73
495. James Gairdner, *The Paston Letters, AD 1422–1509. Volume III*
496. James Gairdner, *The Paston Letters, AD 1422–1509. Volume V* pp. 10-12
497. ibid
498. ibid
499. ibid
500. ibid
501. James Gairdner, *The Paston Letters, AD 1422–1509. Volume V* pp. 14-17
502. ibid, pp. 30-33
503. ibid
504. John Ashdown-Hill, *The Third Plantagenet* (Stroud: The History Press, 2014) pp. 99-112
505. ibid
506. P. W. Hammond, *The Battles of Barnet and Tewkesbury* (Gloucester: Alan Sutton, 1990) pp. 8/9
507. ibid. p. 8-10
508. Charles Ross, *Edward IV* (New Haven and London: Yale University Press, 1974) p. 93
509. For the Arrangements made: ibid
510. P. W. Hammond, *The Battles of Barnet and Tewkesbury* (Gloucester: Alan Sutton, 1990) p. 11
511. ibid
512. ibid
513. James Gairdner, *The Paston Letters, AD 1422–1509. Volume II* p. 389
514. *Calendar of Close Rolls, Edward IV: Volume 2, 1468-1476*, ed. W H B Bird and K H Ledward (London, 1953), *British History Online* http://www.british-history.ac.uk/cal-close-rolls/edw4/vol2 [accessed 14 June 2020].
515. P. W. Hammond, *The Battles of Barnet and Tewkesbury* (Gloucester: Alan Sutton, 1990) p. 14
516. Edward's age is given in: 'Vatican Regesta 677: 1476-1484', in *Calendar of Papal Registers Relating To Great Britain and Ireland: Volume 13, 1471-1484*, ed. J A Twemlow (London, 1955),

pp. 274-277. *British History Online* http://www.british-history.ac.uk/cal-papal-registers/brit-ie/vol13/pp274-277 [accessed 14 June 2020].

517. P. W. Hammond, *The Battles of Barnet and Tewkesbury* (Gloucester: Alan Sutton, 1990) pp. 19/20
518. ibid
519. ibid
520. ibid
521. ibid, p. 25
522. ibid
523. ibid, p. 27
524. ibid
525. Anthony J. Pollard, *Lord FitzHugh's Rising in 1470* (Bulletin of the Institute of Historical Research, 1979)
526. Calendar of Patent Rolls, Edward IV, Henry VI. AD 1467-1477 p. 215
527. Anthony J. Pollard, *Lord FitzHugh's Rising in 1470* (Bulletin of the Institute of Historical Research, 1979)
528. P. W. Hammond, *The Battles of Barnet and Tewkesbury* (Gloucester: Alan Sutton, 1990) p. 36
529. ibid
530. ibid
531. A. P. R. Obermann, H. Schoorl, 'Koning Edward IV van Engeland op Texel', *Holland*, Volume 13 (1981) p. 13
532. ibid
533. James Gairdner, *The Paston Letters, AD 1422–1509. Volume II* p. 412
534. P. W. Hammond, *The Battles of Barnet and Tewkesbury* (Gloucester: Alan Sutton, 1990) p. 42
535. ibid, p. 29
536. ibid, p. 46
537. *Calendar of Close Rolls, Edward IV: Volume 2, 1468-1476*, ed. W H B Bird and K H Ledward (London, 1953), *British History Online* http://www.british-history.ac.uk/cal-close-rolls/edw4/vol2 [accessed 14 June 2020].
538. For example: Matthew Lewis, *Richard III: Loyalty Binds Me* (Stroud: Amberley Publishing, 2018) p. 156 and Michael Hicks, 'Pole, John de la, second duke of Suffolk', Oxford Dictionary of National Biography (Oxford University Press, 2004)
539. Ed. John Bruce, *Historie of the Arrivall of Edward IV in England and the Finall Recouerye of his Kingdomes from Henry VI AD M.CCCC.LXXI* (London: John Bower Nichols and Son, 1838) p. 10
540. Ed. Andrew R. Scoble, Esq., *The Memoirs of Philippe de Commines, Lord of Argenton, containing the histories of Louis XI and Charles VIII Kings of France and of Charles the Bold, Duke*

of Burgundy. To which is added the scandalous chronicle, or secret history of Louis XI, by Jean de Troyes (London: George Bell and Sons, 1877) pp. 184/5

541. For example Alice Montacute, see: Matthew Lewis, *Richard III: Loyalty Binds Me* (Stroud: Amberley Publishing, 2018) p. 59
542. ibid
543. As happened to Elizabeth Shore, for example
544. Ed. John Bruce, *Historie of the Arrivall of Edward IV in England and the Finall Recouerye of his Kingdomes from Henry VI AD M.CCCC.LXXI* (London: John Bower Nichols and Son, 1838) p. 10
545. See below, chapter 13
546. Luc Hommel: *Marguerite D'York ou La Duchesse Junon* (Paris: Librairie Hachette, 1959) pp. 69-71
547. Ed. John Bruce, *Historie of the Arrivall of Edward IV in England and the Finall Recouerye of his Kingdomes from Henry VI AD M.CCCC.LXXI* (London: John Bower Nichols and Son, 1838) p. 5
548. ibid, pp. 10/1
549. ibid, p. 6
550. P. W. Hammond, *The Battles of Barnet and Tewkesbury* (Gloucester: Alan Sutton, 1990) pp. 76/7
551. ibid, pp. 77/8
552. For example: Matthew Lewis, *Richard III: Loyalty Binds Me* (Stroud: Amberley Publishing, 2018) p. 156 and Michael Hicks, 'Pole, John de la, second duke of Suffolk', Oxford Dictionary of National Biography (Oxford University Press, 2004)
553. For example: Matthew Lewis, *Richard III: Loyalty Binds Me* (Stroud: Amberley Publishing, 2018) p. 169, John Ashdown-Hill, *The Third Plantagenet* (Stroud: The History Press, 2014) pp. 123/4
554. Ed. John Bruce, *Historie of the Arrivall of Edward IV in England and the Finall Recouerye of his Kingdomes from Henry VI AD M.CCCC.LXXI* (London: John Bower Nichols and Son, 1838) pp. 15/6
555. ibid
556. P. W. Hammond, *The Battles of Barnet and Tewkesbury* (Gloucester: Alan Sutton, 1990) pp. 82-6
557. See above.
558. ibid, p. 95 (nach unten zu Tewkesbury)
559. P. W. Hammond, *The Battles of Barnet and Tewkesbury* (Gloucester: Alan Sutton, 1990) p. 97
560. James Gairdner, *The Paston Letters, AD 1422–1509. Volume V* p. 131
561. P.R.O Warrants for Issues, E404/75/2
562. P. W. Hammond, *The Battles of Barnet and Tewkesbury* (Gloucester: Alan Sutton, 1990) p. 38

563. Calendar of Patent Rolls, Edward IV, Henry VI. AD 1467-1477 p. 261
564. Their lifestyle was extremely similar
565. *A Descriptive Catalogue of Ancient Deeds: Volume 5*, ed. H C Maxwell Lyte (London, 1906), *British History Online* http://www.british-history.ac.uk/ancient-deeds/vol5 [accessed 14 June 2020].
566. James Gairdner, *The Paston Letters, AD 1422–1509. Volume V* pp. 111-113
567. Document from the National Archives, C1/66/341, Document from the National Archives, C1/48/436
568. For example, it is recorded in the Calendar of Patent Rolls, Edward IV, Henry VI. AD 1467-1477, that on 22 March 1472, he granted out parts of the Lovell wardship
569. Document from the National Archives, C1/66/341, Document from the National Archives, C1/48/436
570. George Frederick Beltz, *Memorials of the Order of the Garter, from its foundation to the present time. Including the history of the order; biographical notices of the knights in the reigns of Edward III. and Richard II., the chronological succession of the members* (London: W. Pickering, 1841)
571. See below
572. Michèle Schindler, L*ovell Our Dogge. The Life of Viscount Lovell, Closest Friend of Richard III and Failed Regicide* (Stroud: Amberley Publishing, 2019) p. 73
573. ibid
574. J. A. F. Thomson, 'John De La Pole, Duke of Suffolk', Speculum (1979)
575. For example: Desmond Seward, *The Last White Rose* (London: Constable, 2010) p. 135
576. Inquisitions Post Mortem on William Lovell, Lord Morley, National Archives, C140/47/64
577. ibid
578. ibid
579. Calendar of Patent Rolls, Edward IV, Henry VI. AD 1467-1477, p. 603
580. His age is found in: Inquisitions Post Mortem on William Lovell
581. W. C. Metcalf, *A Book of Knights* (London, 1885)
582. This date is given in the inscription on her tomb, though her Inquisition Post Mortem states she died on 9 June.
583. Ed. Charles Lethbridge Kingsford, *The Stonor letters and papers, 1290–1483 Vol.* I p. 154
584. *Calendar of Close Rolls, Edward IV: Volume 2, 1468-1476*, ed. W H B Bird and K H Ledward (London, 1953), *British History Online* http://www.british-history.ac.uk/cal-close-rolls/edw4/vol2 [accessed 15 June 2020].

585. John's letters from then onwards were almost always written from Suffolk.
586. Charles Ross, *Edward IV* (New Haven and London: Yale University Press, 1974) 'The Invasion of France, 1475'
587. 'Edward IV: October 1472', in *Parliament Rolls of Medieval England*, ed. Chris Given-Wilson, Paul Brand, Seymour Phillips, Mark Ormrod, Geoffrey Martin, Anne Curry and Rosemary Horrox (Woodbridge, 2005), *British History Online* http://www.british-history.ac.uk/no-series/parliament-rolls-medieval/october-1472 [accessed 15 June 2020].
588. Mary Clive, *This Son of York. A biography of Edward IV* (London: Macmillan London Ltd, 1973). p. 201
589. Matthew Lewis, *Richard III: Loyalty Binds Me* (Stroud: Amberley Publishing, 2018) p. 237
590. Ed. Andrew R. Scoble, Esq., *The Memoirs of Philippe de Commines, Lord of Argenton, containing the histories of Louis XI and Charles VIII Kings of France and of Charles the Bold, Duke of Burgundy. To which is added the scandalous chronicle, or secret history of Louis XI, by Jean de Troyes* (London: George Bell and Sons, 1877) pp. 253-261
591. ibid
592. ibid
593. ibid, 277
594. No mention is made by him in Ed. Andrew R. Scoble, Esq., *The Memoirs of Philippe de Commines, Lord of Argenton, containing the histories of Louis XI and Charles VIII Kings of France and of Charles the Bold, Duke of Burgundy. To which is added the scandalous chronicle, or secret history of Louis XI, by Jean de Troyes* (London: George Bell and Sons, 1877)
595. Matthew Lewis, *Richard III: Loyalty Binds Me* (Stroud: Amberley Publishing, 2018), p. 248
596. ibid, p. 285
597. ibid
598. See above, chapter 5
599. ibid
600. https://www.vaticannews.va/en/saints/02/06.html
601. Anne F Sutton, *The Reburial of Richard, Duke of York* (Richard III Society, 1996) pp. 21-30
602. ibid
603. ibid
604. ibid
605. ibid
606. ibid
607. Michèle Schindler, *Lovell Our Dogge* p. 83
608. Ed. Charles Lethbridge Kingsford, *The Stonor letters and papers, 1290–1483 Vol.* pp. 14/5

609. ibid
610. ibid
611. ibid
612. ibid
613. ibid
614. Calendar of Patent Rolls, Edward IV, Henry VI. AD 1467-1477, quoted in:
615. *Calendar of Close Rolls, Edward IV: Volume 2, 1468-1476*, ed. W H B Bird and K H Ledward (London, 1953), *British History Online* http://www.british-history.ac.uk/cal-close-rolls/edw4/vol2 [accessed 15 June 2020].
616. ibid
617. ibid
618. ibid
619. John Ashdown-Hill, *The Third Plantagenet* (Stroud: The History Press, 2014) pp. 132/3
620. ibid, pp. 132–146
621. Luc Hommel: *Marguerite D'York ou La Duchesse Junon* (Paris: Librairie Hachette, 1959) pp. 92/3
622. H. T. Riley, *Ingulph's Chronicle of the Abbey of Croyland* (London: George Bell and Sons, 1908)pp. 143-145
623. See: Luc Hommel: *Marguerite D'York ou La Duchesse Junon* (Paris: Librairie Hachette, 1959)
624. ibid, pp. 92/3
625. Mary Clive, *This Son of York. A biography of Edward IV* (London: Macmillan London Ltd, 1973) p. 214
626. H. T. Riley, *Ingulph's Chronicle of the Abbey of Croyland* (London: George Bell and Sons, 1908)pp. 143-145
627. John Ashdown-Hill, *The Third Plantagenet* (Stroud: The History Press, 2014) p. 149
628. ibid, 132–146
629. ibid, p. 132
630. ibid
631. ibid, pp. 132/3
632. ibid, p. 149
633. ibid, pp. 143/4
634. See, for example: Paul Murray Kendall, *Richard the Third* (London: George Allan & Unwin, 1955–1956)
635. H. T. Riley, *Ingulph's Chronicle* pp. 145
636. John Ashdown-Hill, *The Third Plantagenet* (Stroud: The History Press, 2014) pp. 150
637. ibid
638. ibid
639. ibid. pp. 160-164
640. 'Edward IV: January 1478', in *Parliament Rolls of Medieval England*, ed. Chris Given-Wilson, Paul Brand, Seymour Phillips,

Mark Ormrod, Geoffrey Martin, Anne Curry and Rosemary Horrox (Woodbridge, 2005), *British History Online* http://www.british-history.ac.uk/no-series/parliament-rolls-medieval/january-1478 [accessed 16 June 2020].

641. J. Ashdown-Hill & A. Carson, 'The Execution of the Earl of Desmond', *Ricardian* 15 (2005) pp. 70–93
642. See: John Ashdown-Hill, *The Dublin King* (Stroud: The History Press, 2015)
643. ibid
644. See below, chapter 14
645. John Ashdown-Hill, *The Third Plantagenet* (Stroud: The History Press, 2014) pp. 149/150
646. James Gairdner, *The Paston Letters, AD 1422–1509. Volume V* pp. 300-303
647. Ed. W. H. Black, *Illustrations of Ancient State & Chivalry from the manuscripts preserved in the Ashmolean Museum* (London: Roxburghe Club, 1840) pp. 28-31
648. ibid
649. ibid
650. James Gairdner, *The Paston Letters, AD 1422–1509. Volume V* pp. 309/10
651. ibid
652. P.R.O Warrants for Issues, E404/76/4, no.26, 132
653. ibid
654. Edward IV: January 1478', in *Parliament Rolls of Medieval England*, ed. Chris Given-Wilson, Paul Brand, Seymour Phillips, Mark Ormrod, Geoffrey Martin, Anne Curry and Rosemary Horrox (Woodbridge, 2005), *British History Online* http://www.british-history.ac.uk/no-series/parliament-rolls-medieval/january-1478 [accessed 16 June 2020].
655. For example: Mary Clive, *This Son of York. A biography of Edward IV* (London: Macmillan London Ltd, 1973). pp. 218/9
656. Edward IV: January 1478', in *Parliament Rolls of Medieval England*, ed. Chris Given-Wilson, Paul Brand, Seymour Phillips, Mark Ormrod, Geoffrey Martin, Anne Curry and Rosemary Horrox (Woodbridge, 2005), *British History Online* http://www.british-history.ac.uk/no-series/parliament-rolls-medieval/january-1478 [accessed 16 June 2020].
657. John Ashdown-Hill, *The Third Plantagenet* (Stroud: The History Press, 2014) pp. 162
658. ibid, pp. 149-160
659. ibid, p. 162
660. Harleian Manuscripts 433 Vol. 3, p. 108
661. Ed. Andrew R. Scoble, Esq., *The Memoirs of Philippe de Commines, Lord of Argenton, containing the histories of Louis XI and Charles*

VIII Kings of France and of Charles the Bold, Duke of Burgundy. To which is added the scandalous chronicle, or secret history of Louis XI, by Jean de Troyes (London: George Bell and Sons, 1877) pp. 62/3

662. ibid
663. John Ashdown-Hill, *The Third Plantagenet* (Stroud: The History Press, 2014) pp. 167-174
664. James Gairdner, *The Paston Letters, AD 1422–1509. Volume V* pp. 126-131
665. ibid, pp. 318/9
666. ibid, 220-223
667. See below, chapter 10
668. See above, chapter 5
669. See, for instance The Ewelme Inventory p. 156
670. ibid
671. James Gairdner, *The Paston Letters, AD 1422–1509. Volume VI* pp. 1-3
672. *Calendar of Close Rolls, Edward IV, Edward V, Richard III. AD 1476-1485.* p. 90
673. George Frederick Beltz, *Memorials of the Order of the Garter, from its foundation to the present time. Including the history of the order; biographical notices of the knights in the reigns of Edward III. and Richard II., the chronological succession of the members* (London: W. Pickering, 1841)
674. *Calendar of Patent Rolls, Edward IV, Edward V, Richard III. AD 1476-1485.* p. 153
675. Ed. Henry Anstey, *Epistolae academicae Oxon* (*Registrum F*)
676. James Gairdner, *The Paston Letters, AD 1422–1509. Volume VI* pp. 21/2
677. *Calendar of Patent Rolls, Edward IV, Edward V, Richard III. AD 1476-1485*, p. 172
678. Proof of their marriage found, among other places: Cyril Flower, M. C. B. Dawes and A. C. Wood, 'Inquisitions Post Mortem, Henry VII, Entries 501-550', in *Calendar of Inquisitions Post Mortem: Series 2, Volume 3, Henry VII* (London, 1955), pp. 297-326. *British History Online* http://www.british-history.ac.uk/inquis-post-mortem/series2-vol3/pp297-326 [accessed 16 June 2020].
679. ibid
680. Little Margaret's grandmother was a sister of Warwick 'the Kingmaker'.
681. Cyril Flower, M. C. B. Dawes and A. C. Wood, 'Inquisitions Post Mortem, Henry VII, Entries 501-550', in *Calendar of Inquisitions Post Mortem: Series 2, Volume 3, Henry VII* (London, 1955), pp. 297-326. *British History Online* http://www.british-history.ac.uk/inquis-post-mortem/series2-vol3/pp297-326 [accessed 16 June 2020].

682. ibid
683. Henry Murray Lane, *The Royal Daughters of England, and their representatives : together with genealogical tables of the Royal Family from the Conquest to the present time ; v. 2* (London, Constable & Co., 1911) p. 334
684. ibid
685. 'Vatican Regesta 677: 1476-1484', in *Calendar of Papal Registers Relating To Great Britain and Ireland: Volume 13, 1471-1484*, ed. J. A. Twemlow (London, 1955), pp. 274-277. *British History Online* http://www.british-history.ac.uk/cal-papal-registers/brit-ie/vol13/pp274-277 [accessed 14 June 2020].
686. Calendar of the Patent Rolls, Henry VII, 1485-1509
687. Desmond Seward: *The Last White Rose* (London: Constable, 2010), p. 137
688. See below, chapter 16
689. Ed. Henry Anstey, *Epistolae academicae Oxon (Registrum F)*
690. ibid, pp. 454-456
691. Ed. G. E. C. Cokayne, *The Complete Peerage* (London: Cokayne, 1932)
692. Barrie Williams, 'The Mystery of Richard de la Pole', *Ricardian* 88 (March 1985) pp. 18-25
693. J. L. Laynesmith, *Cecily, Duchess of York* (London, New York: Bloomsbury Academic, 2017) p. 148
694. ibid
695. ibid
696. ibid
697. ibid
698. ibid
699. ibid
700. *Calendar of Patent Rolls, Edward IV, Edward V, Richard III. AD 1476-1485*. pp. 219/20
701. J. L. Laynesmith, *Cecily, Duchess of York* (London, New York: Bloomsbury Academic, 2017) p. 148
702. Ed. Henry Anstey, *Epistolae academicae Oxon (Registrum F);*
703. ibid
704. ibid, p. 484
705. ibid
706. Harleian Manuscript, no 364
707. ibid
708. ibid
709. Wendy E. A. Moorhen, 'Such was his Renown in Warfare', *Ricardian Bulletin* (2004) http://www.richardiii.net/2_3_0_riii_leadership.php military
710. ibid
711. ibid

712. Ed. Charles Lethbridge Kingsford, *The Stonor letters and papers, 1290–1483 Vol. II* p. 150
713. J. L. Laynesmith, *Cecily, Duchess of York* (London, New York: Bloomsbury Academic, 2017) p. 148
714. Henry Alfred Napier: *Historical Notices of the Parishes of Swyncombe and Ewelme in the County of Oxfordshire* (Oxford: James Wright, Printer to the University, 1863) p. 138
715. ibid
716. ibid
717. Charles Ross, *Edward IV* (New Haven and London: Yale University Press, 1974) p. 291
718. ibid, pp. 288-292
719. ibid
720. ibid
721. ibid
722. ibid, p. 291
723. Ed. G. E. C. Cokayne, *The Complete Peerage* (London: Cokayne, 1932)
724. This is detailed in: Barrie Williams, 'The Mystery of Richard de la Pole', *Ricardian* 88 (March 1985), pp. 18-25
725. ibid
726. ibid
727. Wendy E. A. Moorhen, 'Such was his Renown in Warfare', *Ricardian Bulletin* (2004) http://www.richardiii.net/2_3_0_riii_leadership.php military
728. Ed. Henry Anstey, *Epistolae academicae Oxon (Registrum F);*
729. ibid, pp. 463/4
730. https://www.british-history.ac.uk/cal-papal-registers/brit-ie/vol13/pp274-277?fbclid=IwAR0pD17V0BTCtnH5jbR2DQag4gekiVMc-hOjjxiKnIPa_WTFLMIVeceKSzw
731. XXXX.
732. Cyril Flower, M. C. B. Dawes and A. C. Wood, 'Inquisitions Post Mortem, Henry VII, Entries 501-550', in *Calendar of Inquisitions Post Mortem: Series 2, Volume 3, Henry VII* (London, 1955), pp. 297-326. *British History Online* http://www.british-history.ac.uk/inquis-post-mortem/series2-vol3/pp297-326 [accessed 16 June 2020].
733. ibid
734. The letter is quoted in: Henry Alfred Napier: *Historical Notices of the Parishes of Swyncombe and Ewelme in the County of Oxfordshire* (Oxford: James Wright, Printer to the University, 1863.) p. 139
735. Ed. J. Payne Collier, Esq, F.S.A, *Household books of John Duke of Norfolk and Thomas Earl of Surrey. Temp. 1481-1490. From the Original Manuscripts in the Library of the Society of Antiquaries,*

London (London: William Nicol, Shakespeare Press, 1841) p. 412

736. Wendy E. A. Moorhen, 'Such was his Renown in Warfare', *Ricardian Bulletin* (2004) http://www.richardiii.net/2_3_0_riii_leadership.php military
737. ibid
738. Joanna M. Williams, 'The Political Career of Francis, Viscount Lovell 1456–1487(?)',
739. ibid
740. Charles Ross, Edward IV (New Haven and London: Yale University Press, 1974) p. 402
741. ibid
742. ibid
743. ibid
744. ibid
745. Annette Carson, *Richard III, The Maligned King* (Stroud: The History Press, 2008) p. 16
746. ibid, p. 18
747. ibid, p. 17
748. H. T. Riley, *Ingulph's Chronicle of the Abbey of Croyland* (London: George Bell and Sons, 1908)
749. Annette Carson, *Richard III, The Maligned King* (Stroud: The History Press, 2008), p. 18
750. H. T. Riley, *Ingulph's Chronicle of the Abbey of Croyland* (London: George Bell and Sons, 1908)
751. Mary Clive, *This Son of York. A biography of Edward IV* (London: Macmillan London Ltd, 1973). pp. 253
752. Matthew Lewis, *Richard III: Loyalty Binds Me* (Stroud: Amberley Publishing, 2018) p. 237
753. ibid
754. ibid
755. Ed. C. A. J. Armstrong, The Usurpation of Richard III by Dominic Mancini
756. ibid
757. Wendy E. A. Moorhen, 'The Career of John de la Pole, Earl of Lincoln', *Ricardian* 13, pp. 347/8
758. ibid
759. ibid
760. ibid
761. ibid
762. Ed. C. A. J. Armstrong, The Usurpation of Richard III by Dominic Mancini
763. ibid
764. ibid
765. ibid

766. See, for example: Charles Ross, *Richard III* (York: Eyre Methuen Ltd, 1981)
767. See, for example: Annette Carson, *Richard III, The Maligned King* (Stroud: The History Press, 2008)
768. H. T. Riley, *Ingulph's Chronicle of the Abbey of Croyland* (London: George Bell and Sons, 1908)
769. Ed. C. A. J. Armstrong, *The Usurpation of Richard III by Dominic Mancini*
770. Annette Carson, *Richard III, The Maligned King* (Stroud: The History Press, 2008) pp. 46-50
771. ibid
772. Ed. C. A. J. Armstrong, *The Usurpation of Richard III by Dominic Mancini*
773. ibid
774. Matthew Lewis, *Richard III: Loyalty Binds Me* (Stroud: Amberley Publishing, 2018) p. 329
775. Ed. C. A. J. Armstrong, *The Usurpation of Richard III by Dominic Mancini*
776. ibid
777. ibid
778. See above, chapter 10
779. See: Ed. C. A. J. Armstrong, The Usurpation of Richard III by Dominic Mancini
780. See: *Calendar of Patent Rolls, Edward IV, Edward V, Richard III. AD 1476-1485*. pp. 219/20
781. H. T. Riley, *Ingulph's Chronicle* p. 487
782. Matthew Lewis, *Richard III: Loyalty Binds Me* (Stroud: Amberley Publishing, 2018) pp. 348/9
783. Ed. Charles Lethbridge Kingsford, *The Stonor letters and papers, 1290–1483*, p. 400
784. See, for example: H. A. Kelly, 'The Case against Edward IV's Marriage and Offspring: Secrecy; Witchcraft; Secrecy; Precontract', *Ricardian* 11 (September 1998) pp. 326-335
785. ibid
786. For example: Charles Ross, *Richard III* (York: Eyre Methuen Ltd, 1981)
787. For example: Annette Carson, *Richard III, The Maligned King* (Stroud: The History Press, 2008)
788. H. A. Kelly, 'The Case against Edward IV's Marriage and Offspring: Secrecy; Witchcraft; Secrecy; Precontract', *Ricardian*, 11 (September 1998), pp. 326-335
789. This is postulated, for example, in: Peter A Hancock, *Richard III and the Murder in the Tower* (Stroud: The History Press, 2009)
790. The Spanish ambassador Eustace Chapuys knew of it even 50 years later

791. Ed. Charles Lethbridge Kingsford, *The Stonor letters and papers, 1290–1483* p. 400
792. ibid
793. Ed. C. A. J. Armstrong, *The Usurpation of Richard III by Dominic Mancini*
794. An example being: Thomas More, The History of King Richard the Third, http://www.thomasmorestudies. org/docs/Richard.pdf
795. R. Davies, *Extracts from the Municipal Records of the City of York*
796. ibid
797. ibid
798. Ed. C. A. J. Armstrong, *The Usurpation of Richard III by Dominic Mancini*
799. Matthew Lewis, *Richard III: Loyalty Binds Me* (Stroud: Amberley Publishing, 2018) p. 351
800. ibid
801. Thomas More, *The History of King Richard the Third,* http://www. thomasmorestudies. org/docs/Richard.pdf
802. R. Davies, *Extracts from the Municipal Records of the City of York*
803. Matthew Lewis, *Richard III: Loyalty Binds Me* (Stroud: Amberley Publishing, 2018) p. 351
804. ibid
805. Ed. C. A. J. Armstrong, *The Usurpation of Richard III by Dominic Mancini*
806. ibid
807. ibid
808. Annette Carson, *Richard Duke of Gloucester as Lord Protector and High*
809. R. F. Green, *Historical Notes of a London Citizen, 1483-4,* (English Historical Review, Volume 96, 1981) p. 588
810. Thomas More, The History of King Richard the Third, http://www. thomasmorestudies. org/docs/Richard.pdf
811. Annette Carson, *Richard Duke of Gloucester as Lord Protector and High*
812. ibid
813. Ed. C. A. J. Armstrong, *The Usurpation of Richard III by Dominic Mancini*
814. ibid
815. ibid
816. Ed. J. Payne Collier, Esq, F.S.A, *Household books of John Duke of Norfolk and Thomas Earl of Surrey. Temp. 1481-1490* p. 407
817. R. F. Green, *Historical Notes of a London Citizen, 1483-4,* (English Historical Review, Volume 96, 1981) p. 588
818. ibid
819. ibid
820. See: Michèle Schindler, *Lovell Our Dogge* (Stroud: Amberley Publishing, 2019

821. L. G. Wickham Legg, *English Coronation Records* (Edinburgh: Archibald Constable
822. Peter W. Hammond, Anne F. Sutton, *The Coronation of Richard III: The*
823. ibid
824. ibid
825. ibid
826. ibid
827. ibid
828. ibid
829. ibid
830. ibid
831. L. G. Wickham Legg, *English Coronation Records* (Edinburgh: Archibald Constable
832. Peter W. Hammond, Anne F. Sutton, *The Coronation of Richard III: The*
833. Ed. J. Payne Collier, Esq, F.S.A, *Household books of John Duke of Norfolk and Thomas Earl of Surrey. Temp. 1481-1490* p. 407
834. See below, chapters 11
835. This letter is quoted in Charles Ross, *Richard III* (York: Eyre Methuen Ltd,
836. ibid
837. John Rous, *Joannis Rossi antiquarii Warwicensis Historia regum Angliae,*
838. ibid
839. Ed. William Dunn Macray, MA FSA, *A register of the members of St Mary*
840. ibid
841. John Ashdown-Hill, *Richard III's 'Beloved Cousyn'*, p. 133
842. For example: Stephen David, *Last Champion of York: Francis Lovell, Richard III's Truest Friend* (Marlborough: The Crowood Press, 2019)
843. The timeline of the princes' disappearance is given in Ed. C. A. J. Armstrong, *The Usurpation of Richard III by Dominic Mancini*
844. H. T. Riley, *Ingulph's Chronicle* p. 496
845. ibid
846. John Ashdown-Hill, *The Third Plantagenet* (Stroud: The History Press,
847. ibid
848. Calendar of Patent Rolls, Edward IV, Edward V, Richard III. AD 1476–1485, p. 365
849. John Rous, *Joannis Rossi antiquarii Warwicensis Historia regum Angliae,*
850. ibid
851. ibid
852. ibid

853. ibid
854. Peter W. Hammond, *The Children of Richard III* (Stroud: Fonthill Media, 2018) position 533
855. John Rous, *Joannis Rossi antiquarii Warwicensis Historia regum Angliae,*
856. H. T. Riley, *Ingulph's Chronicle of the Abbey of Croyland* (London: George Bell and Sons, 1908)
857. Annette Carson, *Richard III, The Maligned King* (Stroud: The History Press, 2008)
858. John Rous, *Joannis Rossi antiquarii Warwicensis Historia regum Angliae,*
859. L. C. Attreed, *The York House Books, Volume II* (Middlesbrough: A Sutton
860. Peter W. Hammond, *The Children of Richard III* (Stroud: Fonthill Media, 2018) position 371-384
861. Charles Ross, *Richard III* (York: Eyre Methuen Ltd, 1981), p. 101
862. ibid
863. Annette Carson, *Richard III, The Maligned King* (Stroud: The History Press, 2008) pp. 252-254
864. James Gairdner, *The Paston Letters, AD 1422–1509. Volume VI* p. 89/90 This letter is sometimes claimed to have been penned in 1485, in support for Henry VII, for example by James Gairdner himself. However, nothing in Henry's government indicates that the unrest had become so bad by October 1485 he needed such help.
865. Annette Carson, *Richard III, The Maligned King* (Stroud: The History Press, 2008) pp. 234-260
866. ibid
867. H. T. Riley, *Ingulph's Chronicle* p. 491
868. Calendar of Patent Rolls, Edward IV, Edward V, Richard III. AD 1476–1485
869. 'Richard III: January 1484', in *Parliament Rolls of Medieval England*, ed. Chris Given-Wilson, Paul Brand, Seymour Phillips, Mark Ormrod, Geoffrey Martin, Anne Curry and Rosemary Horrox (Woodbridge, 2005), *British History Online* http://www.british-history.ac.uk/no-series/parliament-rolls-medieval/january-1484 [accessed 19 June 2020].
870. ibid
871. Cyril Flower, M. C. B. Dawes and A. C. Wood, 'Inquisitions Post Mortem, Henry VII, Entries 501-550', in *Calendar of Inquisitions Post Mortem: Series 2, Volume 3, Henry VII* (London, 1955), pp. 297-326. *British History Online* http://www.british-history.ac.uk/inquis-post-mortem/series2-vol3/pp297-326 [accessed 16 June 2020].
872. 'Richard III: January 1484', in *Parliament Rolls of Medieval England.*

873. ibid
874. Paul Murray Kendall, *Richard the Third* (London: George Allan & Unwin, 1955–1956), p. 334
875. ibid
876. 'Richard III: January 1484', in *Parliament Rolls of Medieval England.*
877. Audrey Williamson, *The Mystery of the Princes* (Gloucester: Alan Sutton
878. Annette Carson, *Richard III, The Maligned King* (Stroud: The History Press, 2008) p. 271
879. 'Richard III: January 1484', in *Parliament Rolls of Medieval England*
880. ibid
881. Calendar of Patent Rolls, Edward IV, Edward V, Richard III.
882. For example, it is stated to have been so in Charles Ross, *Richard III* (York: Eyre Methuen Ltd, 1981) p. 101
883. ibid
884. Ed. C. A. J. Armstrong, *The Usurpation of Richard III by Dominic Mancini*
885. Annette Carson, *Richard III, The Maligned King* (Stroud: The History Press, 2008) p. 273
886. ibid
887. Charles Ross, *Richard III* (York: Eyre Methuen Ltd, 1981)p. 101
888. ibid
889. H. T. Riley, *Ingulph's Chronicle* pp. 496/7
890. Matthew Lewis, *Richard III: Loyalty Binds Me* (Stroud: Amberley Publishing, 2018) p. 473
891. H. T. Riley, *Ingulph's Chronicle* pp. 496/7
892. See: Paul Murray Kendall, *Richard the Third* (London: George Allan & Unwin, 1955–1956)
893. H. T. Riley, *Ingulph's Chronicle* pp. 496/7
894. ibid
895. Annette Carson, 'The Death of Edward of Middleham, Prince of Wales',
896. Matthew Lewis, *Richard III: Loyalty Binds Me* (Stroud: Amberley Publishing, 2018) pp. 473/4
897. 'Richard III: January 1484', in *Parliament Rolls of Medieval England*
898. For his birthdate, see: John Ashdown-Hill, *The Third Plantagenet* (Stroud: The History Press, 2014) p. 130
899. See below, footnote 918
900. For example: Edward Hall, *The Union Of The Two Noble And Illustre Famelies Lancastre & Yorke Beeyng Long In Continual Discension For The Croune Of This Noble Realme With All The Actes Done In Bothe The Tymes Of The Princes, Bothe Of The*

One Linage And Of The Other, Beginnyng At The Tyme Of Kyng Henry The Fowerth, The First Aucthor Of This Deuision, And So Successiuely Proceadyng To The Reigne Of The High And Prudent Prince Kyng Henry The Eight, the Undubitate Flower And Very Heire Of Both The Sayd Linages (1548)

901. Thomas Penn, *Winter King: Henry VII and the Dawn of Tudor England* (London: Penguin Books Ltd, 2011) p. 23
902. See below, chapter 13
903. See: Desmond Seward: *The Last White Rose* (London: Constable, 2010)
904. Ed. Piotr Radzikowsk, *Reisebeschreibung Niclas von Popplau, Ritters,*
905. ibid
906. *Paston Letters, AD 1422–1509. Volume II. New Complete Library Edition* (London: Chatto & Windus, Exeter: James G. Commin, 1904) p. 317
907. Peter W. Hammond, *The Children of Richard III* (Stroud: Fonthill Media, 2018) positions 878-890
908. ibid
909. Harleian Manuscripts 433 Vol. 3 p. 114
910. ibid
911. ibid
912. Peter W. Hammond, *The Children of Richard III* (Stroud: Fonthill Media, 2018) position 38
913. ibid
914. ibid, position 373
915. Harleian Manuscripts 433 Vol.3 pp. 107/8
916. Wendy E. A. Moorhen, 'The Career of John de la Pole, Earl of Lincoln', *Ricardian*, 13 (2003), pp. 341-358
917. Harleian Manuscripts 433 Vol.3 p. 14
918. H. T. Riley, *Ingulph's Chronicle*, pp. 497–8
919. Paul Murray Kendall, *Richard the Third*, pp. 349–350
920. ibid, pp. 360/1
921. ibid
922. ibid
923. Harleian Manuscripts 433 Vol 2, p. 168
924. Harleian Manuscripts 433 Vol 3, p. 114
925. ibid
926. ibid
927. L. C. Attreed, *The York House Books, Volume II* (Middlesbrough: A Sutton
928. ibid
929. Paul Murray Kendall, *Richard the Third*, pp. 362-3
930. Matthew Lewis, *Richard III*, Position 7137
931. Charles Ross, *Richard III*, p. xlvii
932. Matthew Lewis, *Richard III*, Position 7137

933. Paul Murray Kendall, *Richard the Third*, pp. 150–161
934. ibid
935. H. T. Riley, *Ingulph's Chronicle* p. 498
936. Ed. Jean Alexandre C. Bouchon, Chroniques de Jean Molinet, vol 3
937. H. T. Riley, *Ingulph's Chronicle* pp. 498/9
938. ibid
939. Wendy E. A. Moorhen, 'The Career of John de la Pole'
940. ibid
941. Calendar of Patent Rolls, Edward IV, Edward V, Richard III. AD 1476–1485. pp. 492, 567/8, 580
942. ibid
943. L. C. Attreed, *The York House Books, Volume II* (Middlesbrough: A Sutton
944. H. T. Riley, *Ingulph's Chronicle* p. 500
945. ibid
946. ibid
947. L. C. Attreed, *The York House Books, Volume II* (Middlesbrough: A Sutton
948. Calendar of Patent Rolls, Edward IV, Edward V, Richard III. AD 1476–1485, pp. 432/3
949. ibid
950. See below, chapter 14.
951. Wendy E. A. Moorhen, 'The Career of John de la Pole'
952. See above, chapter 6
953. H. T. Riley, *Ingulph's Chronicle* pp. 500/1
954. Marilyn Kilroy, *Edward and Humphrey de la Pole: Two Convenient Deaths* (Richard III Society, 2015)
955. For example: Matthew Lewis, *Richard III: Loyalty Binds Me* (Stroud: Amberley Publishing, 2018) p. 156
956. For example: Terry Breverton, *Henry VII, The Maligned Tudor King* (Stroud: Amberley Publishing, 2016)
957. Matthew Lewis, *The Survival of the Princes in the Tower: Murder, Mystery and Myth* (Stroud: The History Press, 2017) pp. 74-76
958. See below, chapter 14
959. Harleian Manuscripts 433 Vol 3, p. 114
960. See below, chapter 14
961. This theory is discussed in Wendy E. A. Moorhen, 'The Career of John de la Pole'
962. Barrie Williams, 'The Mystery of Richard de la Pole', *Ricardian* 88 (March 1985) pp. 18-25
963. Matthew Lewis, *Richard III: Loyalty Binds Me* (Stroud: Amberley Publishing, 2018) position 8156–8169
964. ibid
965. Matthew Lewis, *The Survival of the Princes in the Tower: Murder, Mystery and Myth* (Stroud: The History Press, 2017) pp. 75/6

966. Thomas Penn, *Winter King: Henry VII and the Dawn of Tudor England*
967. ibid
968. See below, chapter 13
969. It was given to Richard FitzHugh, Baron FitzHugh
970. 'Henry VII: November 1485, Part 1', in *Parliament Rolls of Medieval England*, ed. Chris Given-Wilson, Paul Brand, Seymour Phillips, Mark Ormrod, Geoffrey Martin, Anne Curry and Rosemary Horrox (Woodbridge, 2005), *British History Online* http://www.british-history.ac.uk/no-series/parliament-rolls-medieval/november-1485-pt-1 [accessed 20 June 2020].
971. Wendy E. A. Moorhen, 'The Career of John de la Pole'
972. ibid
973. ibid
974. L. G. Wickham Legg, *English Coronation Records* (Edinburgh: Archibald Constable
975. ibid
976. J. A. F. Thomson, 'John De La Pole, Duke of Suffolk', Speculum (1979)
977. L. C. Attreed, *The York House Books, Volume I* (Middlesbrough: A Sutton
978. ibid
979. J. A. F. Thomson, 'John De La Pole, Duke of Suffolk', Speculum (1979)
980. ibid
981. 'Henry VII: November 1485, Part 1', in *Parliament Rolls of Medieval England*
982. ibid
983. ibid
984. For example: Wendy E. A. Moorhen, 'The Career of John de la Pole'
985. Audrey Williamson, *The Mystery of the Princes* (Gloucester: Alan Sutton
986. Wendy E. A. Moorhen, 'The Career of John de la Pole'
987. E.g. Annette Carson, *Richard III: The Maligned King* (Stroud: The History
988. John Ashdown-Hill, *The Dublin King* (Stroud: The History Press, 2015), position 2340
989. ibid
990. ibid, positions 1803–2005
991. C. H. Williams, 'The Rebellion of Humphrey Stafford 1486', *The English*
992. Calendar of Patent Rolls, Henry VII, Vol I AD 1485–1494, p. 119
993. For example: Henry Alfred Napier: *Historical Notices of the Parishes of Swyncombe and Ewelme in the County of Oxfordshire* (Oxford: James Wright, Printer to the University, 1863)
994. See above, chapter 6

995. 'Henry VII: November 1485, Part 1', in *Parliament Rolls of Medieval England.*
996. Ed. Thomas Stapleton, Esq., FSA *Plumpton Correspondence. A Series of*
997. Ed. James Gairdner, *Letters and Papers Illustrative of the Reigns of*
998. L. C. Attreed, *The York House Books*, Volume I, p. 552
999. Calendar of Patent Rolls, Henry VII, Vol I AD 1485–1494 p. 106
1000. Polydore Vergil, Anglica Historica (1534), http://www.philological.bham.ac.uk/polverg/26eng.html
1001. Calendar of Patent Rolls, Henry VII, Vol I AD 1485–1494 pp. 106/7
1002. Polydore Vergil, Anglica Historica (1534)
1003. John Ashdown-Hill, *Richard III's 'Beloved Cousyn*, p. 149
1004. H. T. Riley, *Ingulph's Chronicle* p. 513
1005. C. H. Williams, 'The Rebellion of Humphrey Stafford 1486'
1006. ibid
1007. ibid
1008. ibid
1009. Polydore Vergil, Anglica Historica (1534)
1010. Calendar of Patent Rolls, Henry VII, Vol I AD 1485–1494, p. 119
1011. See above, chapter 5
1012. L. C. Attreed, *The York House Books*, Volume I, p. 552
1013. ibid
1014. See below, chapter 14
1015. Joanna M. Williams, 'The Political Career of Francis, Viscount Lovell
1016. H. T. Riley, *Ingulph's Chronicle* pp. 513/4
1017. Polydore Vergil, Anglica Historica (1534)
1018. ibid
1019. H. T. Riley, *Ingulph's Chronicle* pp. 513/4
1020. ibid
1021. ibid
1022. C. H. Williams, 'The Rebellion of Humphrey Stafford 1486', The English
1023. H. T. Riley, *Ingulph's Chronicle* pp. 513/4
1024. ibid
1025. See, for example: Desmond Seward: *The Last White Rose* (London: Constable, 2010)
1026. Calendar of Patent Rolls, Henry VII, Vol I AD 1485–1494, pp. 106/7
1027. ibid
1028. ibid
1029. ibid, p. 119
1030. C. H. Williams, 'The Rebellion of Humphrey Stafford 1486', The English
1031. ibid
1032. Wendy E. A. Moorhen, 'The Career of John de la Pole'

1033. ibid
1034. John Goodall: *God's House at Ewelme: Life, Devotion and Architecture in a Fifteenth-Century Almshouse* (London: Taylor & Francis, 2017) p. 128
1035. ibid
1036. ibid
1037. See above, chapter 12
1038. James Gairdner, *The Paston Letters, AD 1422–1509*. Vol VI, p. 95
1039. Polydore Vergil, Anglica Historica (1534)
1040. See Trans. and intro. Daniel Hobbins, *The life of Henry VII/ Bernard*
1041. Polydore Vergil, Anglica Historica (1534)
1042. ibid
1043. See Trans. and intro. Daniel Hobbins, *The life of Henry VII/ Bernard*
1044. 'Henry VII: November 1487', in *Parliament Rolls of Medieval England*, ed. Chris Given-Wilson, Paul Brand, Seymour Phillips, Mark Ormrod, Geoffrey Martin, Anne Curry and Rosemary Horrox (Woodbridge, 2005), *British History Online* http://www.british-history.ac.uk/no-series/parliament-rolls-medieval/november-1487 [accessed 20 June 2020].
1045. ibid
1046. David Baldwin, *Elizabeth Woodville: Mother of the Princes in the Tower*
1047. ibid
1048. ibid
1049. Terry Breverton, *Henry VII: The Maligned Tudor King* (Stroud: Amberley
1050. Polydore Vergil, Anglica Historica (1534)
1051. Matthew Lewis, *The Survival of the Princes in the Tower: Murder, Mystery and Myth* (Stroud: The History Press, 2017) p. 77
1052. Anne Crawford, The Yorkists: The History of a Dynasty (London: Continuum Books, 2007) p. 159
1053. John Ashdown-Hill, *The Dublin King*, Positions 2284
1054. See, for example: John Ashdown-Hill, *The Dublin King* (Stroud: The History Press, 2015)
1055. ibid
1056. See, for example: Matthew Lewis, *The Survival of the Princes in the Tower: Murder, Mystery and Myth* (Stroud: The History Press, 2017)
1057. Harleian Manuscripts 433 Vol.3, p. 114
1058. Matthew Lewis, *The Survival of the Princes in the Tower: Murder, Mystery and Myth* (Stroud: The History Press, 2017)
1059. Gordon Smith, 'Lambert Simnel and the King from Dublin', *Ricardian* (1996)
1060. Polydore Vergil, *Anglica Historica* (1534)
1061. ibid

1062. He was born on 2 November 1470
1063. See: Matthew Lewis, *The Survival of the Princes in the Tower: Murder, Mystery and Myth* (Stroud: The History Press, 2017)
1064. ibid, pp. 236/7
1065. ibid
1066. Calendar of Patent Rolls, Henry VII, Vol I AD 1485–1494, p. 179
1067. See: Polydore Vergil, Anglica Historica (1534)
1068. Jean Alexandre C. Bouchon, *Chroniques de Jean Molinet, vol 3*,
1069. ibid
1070. For a discussion on this, see: Matthew Lewis, *The Survival of the Princes in the Tower: Murder, Mystery and Myth* (Stroud: The History Press, 2017)
1071. Jean Alexandre C. Bouchon, *Chroniques de Jean Molinet, vol 3*,
1072. ibid
1073. John Ashdown-Hill, *The Dublin King* (Stroud: The History Press, 2015), positions 2759-2771
1074. ibid, position 2762
1075. Desmond Seward: *The Last White Rose* (London: Constable, 2010), p. 33
1076. ibid
1077. ibid. Actually, this all seems based on a letter by the archbishop of Armagh, in which he claimed Lincoln threatened him with unspecified legal actions if he did not participate, but Kendal stopped him from doing so
1078. David Baldwin, *Stoke Field: The Last Battle of the Wars of the Roses*
1079. ibid
1080. Jean Alexandre C. Bouchon, *Chroniques de Jean Molinet, vol 3*,
1081. She was certainly suspected of being involved, as can be seen in James Gairdner, *The Paston Letters, AD 1422–1509. Volume VI.*
1082. Ed. Angelo Raine, *York Civic Records* (York: Wakefield Society, 1939),
1083. Polydore Vergil, Anglica Historica (1534)
1084. Thomas Penn, *Winter King: Henry VII and the Dawn of Tudor England*
1085. Such as Ed. Rev. J. Rawson Lumby, D. D., *Bacon's History of the Reign of Henry VII* (Cambridge: Cambridge University Press, 1885), Polydore Vergil, Anglica Historica (1534)
1086. See Trans. and intro. Daniel Hobbins, *The life of Henry VII/ Bernard*
1087. Such as Polydore Vergil, Anglica Historica (1534)
1088. ibid
1089. ibid
1090. This is suggested, for example, in: Thomas Penn, *Winter King: Henry VII and the Dawn of Tudor England* (London: Penguin Books Ltd, 2011), p. 23

1091. 'Henry VII: November 1487', in *Parliament Rolls of Medieval England*, ed. Chris Given-Wilson, Paul Brand, Seymour Phillips, Mark Ormrod, Geoffrey Martin, Anne Curry and Rosemary Horrox (Woodbridge, 2005), *British History Online* http://www.british-history.ac.uk/no-series/parliament-rolls-medieval/november-1487 [accessed 21 June 2020].
1092. Cyril Flower, M. C. B. Dawes and A. C. Wood, 'Inquisitions Post Mortem, Henry VII, Entries 501-550', in *Calendar of Inquisitions Post Mortem: Series 2, Volume 3, Henry VII* (London, 1955), pp. 297-326. *British History Online* http://www.british-history.ac.uk/inquis-post-mortem/series2-vol3/pp297-326 [accessed 16 June 2020].
1093. Henry Alfred Napier: *Historical Notices of the Parishes of Swyncombe and Ewelme in the County of Oxfordshire* (Oxford: James Wright, Printer to the University, 1863) p. 152
1094. ibid
1095. ibid, p. 153
1096. ibid, p. 152
1097. ibid. p. 153
1098. ibid, pp. 152/3
1099. This is quoted in Henry Alfred Napier: *Historical Notices of the Parishes of Swyncombe and Ewelme in the County of Oxfordshire* (Oxford: James Wright, Printer to the University, 1863) p. 153
1100. Matthew Lewis, *Richard III: Loyalty Binds Me* (Stroud: Amberley Publishing, 2018) p. 227
1101. She is mentioned as 'prioress at Sion' in her grandmother Cecily's will, written in 1495: www.nationalarchives.gov.uk/pathways/citizenship/citizen_subject/transcripts/will_neville.htm
1102. For example: Terry Breverton, *Henry VII, The Maligned Tudor King* (Stroud: Amberley Publishing, 2016), chapter 6
1103. J. A. F. Thomson, 'John De La Pole, Duke of Suffolk', Speculum (1979)
1104. His writ of diem Clausit Extremum was issued on 24 July 1492. ibid.
1105. Handbook for Essex, Suffolk, Norfolk (London: John Murray, Ap. 178
1106. J. A. F. Thomson, 'John De La Pole, Duke of Suffolk', Speculum (1979)
1107. Anne Wroe, Perkin. *A Story of Deception* (London: Random House, 2003)
1108. Henry Alfred Napier: *Historical Notices of the Parishes of Swyncombe and Ewelme in the County of Oxfordshire* (Oxford: James Wright, Printer to the University, 1863) p. 172
1109. ibid
1110. ibid, p. 156
1111. ibid

Bibliography

Primary Sources

A Descriptive Catalogue of Ancient Deeds: Volume 5, ed. H C Maxwell Lyte (London, 1906), British History Online http://www.british-history.ac.uk/ancient-deeds/vol5 [accessed 14 June 2020].

Ed. Henry Anstey, *Epistolae academicae Oxon (Registrum F); a collection of letters and other miscellaneous documents illustrative of academical life and studies at Oxford in the fifteenth century. Volume II* (Oxford: Oxford Historical Society, 1898)

Ed. C. A. J. Armstrong, *The Usurpation of Richard III by Dominic Mancini* (Middlesbrough: A. Sutton Publishing, 1984)

L. C. Attreed, T*he York House Books, Volume I* (Middlesbrough: A Sutton Publishing, 1991)

Ed. Thomas Basin and Charles Samaran, *Histoire de Charles VII: Tome Premier, 1407–1444* (Paris: Les Classiques de l'Histoire de France Au Moyen Age. Volume 15, 1933)

S. Bentley, *Excerpta Historica or Illustrations of English history* (London, 1831)

Ed. W. H. Black, *Illustrations of Ancient State & Chivalry from the manuscripts preserved in the Ashmolean Museum* (London: Roxburghe Club, 1840)

Ed. Jean Alexandre C. Bouchon, *Chroniques de Jean Molinet, vol 3* (Paris: Verdière, 1828)

Ed. Edward A Bond, *Thomas de Burton, Chronica Monasterii de Melsa, a Fundatione Usque ad Annum 1396, Auctore Thoma de Burton, Abbate. Accedit Continuatio ad Annum 1406* (London: Longmans, Green, Reader and Dyer, 1868.)

Ed. Paul Brand, Anne Curry, Chris Given-Wilson, Rosemary Horrox, Geoffrey Martin, Mark Ormrod, Henry VI: November 1459, in Parliament Rolls of Medieval England (Woodbridge, Boydell, 2005)

'Brief notes of occurrences under Henry VI and Edward IV', in Three Fifteenth-Century Chronicles with Historical Memoranda by John

Stowe, ed. James Gairdner (London, 1880), pp. 148-163. British History Online http://www.british-history.ac.uk/camden-record-soc/vol28/pp148-163 [accessed 11 June 2020].

Ed. John Bruce, *Historie of the Arrivall of Edward IV in England and the Finall Recouerye of his Kingdomes from Henry VI AD M.CCCC. LXXI* (London: John Bower Nichols and Son, 1838)

Calendar of Close Rolls, Edward IV: Volume 1, 1461-1468, ed. W H B Bird and K H Ledward (London, 1949), British History Online http://www.british-history.ac.uk/cal-close-rolls/edw4/vol1 [accessed 13 June 2020].

Calendar of Close Rolls, Edward IV: Volume 2, 1468-1476, ed. W H B Bird and K H Ledward (London, 1953), British History Online http://www.british-history.ac.uk/cal-close-rolls/edw4/vol2 [accessed 14 June 2020].

Calendar of Fine Rolls, Henry VI, AD 1452–1461

Calendar of Papal Registers, X

Calendar of Patent Rolls, Richard II, Volume VI, AD 1396–1399

Calendar of Patent Rolls, Henry IV, Volume II, AD 1401–1405

Calendar of Patent Rolls, Henry VI, Volume III, AD 1436–1441

Calendar of Patent Rolls, Henry VI, Volume V, AD 1441–1446

Calendar of Patent Rolls, Henry VI, Volume V, AD 1446–1452

Calendar of Patent Rolls, Henry VI, Volume VI, AD 1452–1461

Calendar of Patent Rolls, Edward IV, AD 1461–1467

Calendar of Patent Rolls, Edward IV, Henry VI. AD 1467–1477

Calendar of Patent Rolls, Edward IV, Edward V, Richard III. AD 1476–1485

Calendar of Patent Rolls, Edward IV, Henry VI, Richard III, Volume I, AD 1461-1485

Calendar of Patent Rolls, Henry VII, Vol I. AD 1485–1494

Chancery Inquisitions Post Mortem, Henry VI, File 70, No.35

Ed. G. E. C. Cokayne, *The Complete Peerage* (London, Cokayne, 1932)

Ed. J. Payne Collier, Esq, F.S.A, *Household books of John Duke of Norfolk and Thomas Earl of Surrey. Temp. 1481-1490. From the Original Manuscripts in the Library of the Society of Antiquaries, London* (London: William Nicol, Shakespeare Press, 1841)

Ed. John Silvester Davies, *An English chronicle of the reigns of Richard II, Henry IV, Henry V, and Henry VI written before the year 1471; with an appendix, containing the 18th and 19th years of Richard II and the Parliament at Bury St. Edmund's, 25th Henry VI and supplementary additions from the Cotton. ms. chronicle called Eulogium* (London: Camden Society, 1856)

'Deeds: A.6301–A.6400', in A Descriptive Catalogue of Ancient Deeds: Volume 4, ed. H C Maxwell Lyte (London, 1902), pp. 22-34. British

History Online http://www.british-history.ac.uk/ancient-deeds/vol4/pp22-34 [accessed 10 June 2020].

R. Davies, *Extracts from the Municipal Records of the City of York* (London, 1843)

F. Devon, Issues of the Exchequer (London: John Murray, 1837)

Document from the National Archives, C1/48/436

Document from the National Archives, C1/66/341

'Edward IV: November 1461', in Parliament Rolls of Medieval England, ed. Chris Given-Wilson, Paul Brand, Seymour Phillips, Mark Ormrod, Geoffrey Martin, Anne Curry and Rosemary Horrox (Woodbridge, 2005), British History Online http://www.british-history.ac.uk/no-series/parliament-rolls-medieval/november-1461 [accessed 11 June 2020].

'Edward IV: October 1472', in Parliament Rolls of Medieval England, ed. Chris Given-Wilson, Paul Brand, Seymour Phillips, Mark Ormrod, Geoffrey Martin, Anne Curry and Rosemary Horrox (Woodbridge, 2005), British History Online http://www.british-history.ac.uk/no-series/parliament-rolls-medieval/october-1472 [accessed 15 June 2020].

'Edward IV: January 1478', in Parliament Rolls of Medieval England, ed. Chris Given-Wilson, Paul Brand, Seymour Phillips, Mark Ormrod, Geoffrey Martin, Anne Curry and Rosemary Horrox (Woodbridge, 2005), British History Online http://www.british-history.ac.uk/no-series/parliament-rolls-medieval/january-1478 [accessed 16 June 2020].

Piers de Fenin, *Mémoires de Pierre de Fenin comprenant le récit des événements: qui se sont passés en France et en Bourgogne sous les règnes de Charles VI et Charles VII, 1407-1427* (Histoire)

John Fisher, *Mornyng Rememberance*

Cyril Flower, M. C. B. Dawes and A. C. Wood,'Inquisitions Post Mortem, Henry VII, Entries 501-550', in Calendar of Inquisitions Post Mortem: Series 2, Volume 3, Henry VII (London, 1955), pp. 297-326. British History Online http://www.british-history.ac.uk/inquis-post-mortem/series2-vol3/pp297-326 [accessed 16 June 2020].

Ed. James Gairdner, *Memorials of King Henry VII* (London: Camden Society, 1858)

Ed. James Gairdner, *Letters and Papers Illustrative of the Reigns of Richard III and Henry VII Volume I* (London: Longman, Green, Longman, Roberts, and Green, 1863)

James Gairdner, *The Paston Letters, AD 1422–1509. Volume I. New Complete Library Edition* (London: Chatto & Windus, Exeter: James G. Commin, 1904)

James Gairdner, *The Paston Letters, AD 1422–1509. Volume II. New Complete Library Edition* (London: Chatto & Windus, Exeter: James G. Commin, 1904)

James Gairdner, *The Paston Letters, AD 1422–1509. Volume III. New CompleteLibrary Edition* (London: Chatto & Windus, Exeter: James G. Commin, 1904)

James Gairdner, *The Paston Letters, AD 1422–1509. Volume IV. New Complete Library Edition* (London: Chatto & Windus, Exeter: James G. Commin, 1904)

James Gairdner, *The Paston Letters, AD 1422–1509. Volume V. New Complete Library Edition* (London: Chatto & Windus, Exeter: James G. Commin, 1904)

James Gairdner, *The Paston Letters, AD 1422–1509. Volume VI. New Complete Library Edition* (London: Chatto & Windus, Exeter: James G. Commin, 1904)

R. F. Green, *Historical Notes of a London Citizen, 1483-4,* (English Historical Review, Volume 96, 1981)

Edward Hall, *The Union Of The Two Noble And Illustre Famelies Lancastre & Yorke Beeyng Long In Continual Discension For The Croune Of This Noble Realme With All The Actes Done In Bothe The Tymes Of The Princes, Bothe Of The One Linage And Of The Other, Beginnyng At The Tyme Of Kyng Henry The Fowerth, The First Aucthor Of This Deuision, And So Successiuely Proceadyng To The Reigne Of The High And Prudent Prince Kyng Henry The Eight, the Undubitate Flower And Very Heire Of Both The Sayd Linages* (1548)

Ed Alison Hanham, *John Benet's Chronicle, 1399-1462 An English Translation with New Introduction* (New York: Palgrave Macmillian, 2018)

Harleian Manuscript, no 364

Harleian Manuscripts 433 Vol. 2

Harleian Manuscripts 433 Vol. 3

'Henry V: November 1414', in Parliament Rolls of Medieval England, ed. Chris Given-Wilson, Paul Brand, Seymour Phillips, Mark Ormrod, Geoffrey Martin, Anne Curry and Rosemary Horrox (Woodbridge, 2005), British History Online http://www.british-history.ac.uk/no-series/parliament-rolls-medieval/november-1414 [accessed 7 June 2020].

'Henry V: November 1415', in Parliament Rolls of Medieval England, ed. Chris Given-Wilson, Paul Brand, Seymour Phillips, Mark Ormrod, Geoffrey Martin, Anne Curry and Rosemary Horrox (Woodbridge, 2005), British History Online http://www.british-history.ac.uk/no-series/parliament-rolls-medieval/november-1415 [accessed 7 June 2020].

'Henry VI: November 1449', in Parliament Rolls of Medieval England, ed. Chris Given-Wilson, Paul Brand, Seymour Phillips, Mark Ormrod, Geoffrey Martin, Anne Curry and Rosemary Horrox (Woodbridge, 2005), British History Online http://www.british-history.ac.uk/no-series/parliament-rolls-medieval/november-1449 [accessed 7 June 2020].

'Henry VII: November 1485, Part 1', in Parliament Rolls of Medieval England, ed. Chris Given-Wilson, Paul Brand, Seymour Phillips, Mark Ormrod, Geoffrey Martin, Anne Curry and Rosemary Horrox (Woodbridge, 2005), British History Online http://www.british-history.ac.uk/no-series/parliament-rolls-medieval/november-1485-pt-1 [accessed 20 June 2020].

'Henry VII: November 1487', in Parliament Rolls of Medieval England, ed. Chris Given-Wilson, Paul Brand, Seymour Phillips, Mark Ormrod, Geoffrey Martin, Anne Curry and Rosemary Horrox (Woodbridge, 2005), British History Online http://www.british-history.ac.uk/no-series/parliament-rolls-medieval/november-1487 [accessed 20 June 2020].

Trans. and intro. Daniel Hobbins, *The life of Henry VII/Bernard Andrés* (New York: Italica Press, 2011)

Raphael Holinshed, *Chronicles of England, Scotland and Ireland* (1577)

Leland's Collectana, Volume VI (London: 1770)

Inquisitions Post Mortem on William Lovell, Lord Morley, National Archives, C140/47/64

Ed. Charles Lethbridge Kingsford, *The Stonor letters and papers, 1290–1483 Vol. I* (London: Offices of the Society, 1919)

Ed. Charles Lethbridge Kingsford, *The Stonor letters and papers, 1290–1483 Vol. III* (London: Offices of the Society, 1919)

Ed. J. L. Kirby, Janet Stevenson, *Calendar of Inquisitions Post-Mortem and other Analogous Documents preserved in the Public Record Office XXI:6–10 Henry V* (1418–1422) (Woodbridge: Boydell Press, 2002)

J. L. Kirby, 'Inquisitions Post Mortem, Henry V, Entries 800-851', in Calendar of Inquisitions Post Mortem: Volume 20, Henry V (London, 1995), pp. 248-272. British History Online http://www.british-history.ac.uk/inquis-post-mortem/vol20/pp248-272 [accessed 7 June 2020]

L. G. Wickham Legg, English Coronation Records (Edinburgh: Archibald Constable & Co., 1901)

Ed. Malcolm Letts, *The Travels of Leo of Rozmital through Germany, Flanders, England, France, Spain, Portugal and Italy 1465-1467* (London: Hakluyt Society, 2017)

Ed. Rev. J. Rawson Lumby, D. D., *Bacon's History of the Reign of Henry VII* (Cambridge: Cambridge University Press, 1885)

Thomas More, *The History of King Richard the Third*, http://www.thomasmorestudies.org/docs/Richard.pdf

www.nationalarchives.gov.uk/pathways/citizenship/citizen_subject/transcripts/will_neville.htm

A. P. R. Obermann, H. Schoorl, *Koning Edward IV van Engeland op Texel*, Holland, Volume 13 (1981)

Christine de Pizan, *Das Buch von der Stadt der Frauen* (München: Deutscher Taschenbuch Verlag, 1995)

P.R.O Warrants for Issues, E404/75/2

P.R.O Warrants for Issues, E404/76/4

Ed. Piotr Radzikowsk, *Reisebeschreibung Niclas von Popplau, Ritters, bürtig von Breslau* (Kraków, 1998)

Ed. Angelo Raine, *York Civic Records* (York: Wakefield Society, 1939)

'Richard III: January 1484', in *Parliament Rolls of Medieval England*, ed. Chris Given-Wilson, Paul Brand, Seymour Phillips, Mark Ormrod, Geoffrey Martin, Anne Curry and Rosemary Horrox (Woodbridge, 2005), British History Online http://www.british-history.ac.uk/no-series/parliament-rolls-medieval/january-1484 [accessed 19 June 2020].

H. T. Riley, *Ingulph's Chronicle of the Abbey of Croyland* (London: George Bell and Sons, 1908)

Rotuli Parliamentorum, ut et petitiones, et placita in Parliamento, Ab Anno Duodecimo R. Edwardi IV. ad Finem eiusdem Regni Volume VI (London, 1777)

John Rous, Joannis Rossi antiquarii Warwicensis Historia regum Angliae

Rowland's Historical and Genealogical Account of the noble family of Neville

Ed. Andrew R. Scoble, Esq., *The Memoirs of Philippe de Commines, Lord of Argenton, containing the histories of Louis XI and Charles VIII Kings of France and of Charles the Bold, Duke of Burgundy. To which is added the scandalous chronicle, or secret history of Louis XI, by Jean de Troyes* (London: George Bell and Sons, 1877)

Sequitur generacio illustrissimi principis Ricardi, Ducis Eboraci & c ex serenissima principissa, uxore sua, Caecilia. T. Hearne, Liber Niger Scaccarii nec non Wilhelmi Worcestrii Annales Rerum Angelicarum, Volume 2 (London: 1774)

Reginald R. Sharpe, London and the kingdom: a history derived mainly from the archives at Guildhall in the custody of the corporation of the city of London, vol. III (London: Longmans, Green & Co., 1895)

Ed. Thomas Stapleton, Esq., FSA, Plumpton Correspondence: A Series of Letters, Chiefly Domestick, written in the reigns of Edward IV, Richard III, Henry VII and Henry VIII (London: John Bowyer and Son, 1839)

https://www.vaticannews.va/en/saints/02/06.html

'Vatican Regesta 677: 1476-1484', in Calendar of Papal Registers Relating To Great Britain and Ireland: Volume 13, 1471-1484, ed. J A Twemlow (London, 1955), pp. 274-277. British History Online http://www.british-history.ac.uk/cal-papal-registers/brit-ie/vol13/pp274-277 [accessed 14 June 2020].

Polydore Vergil, Anglica Historica (1534) http://www.philological.bham.ac.uk/polverg/26eng.html

Secondary Sources

Marjorie Anderson, *Alice Chaucer and Her Husbands*, PMLA Vol. 60, No. 1 (Mar., 1945), pp. 24-47

J. Ashdown-Hill & A. Carson, 'The Execution of the Earl of Desmond', *Ricardian* 15 (2005), pp. 70–93

John Ashdown-Hill, *Richard III's 'Beloved Cousyn': John Howard and the House of York* (Stroud: The History Press, 2009)

John Ashdown-Hill, *The Third Plantagenet* (Stroud: The History Press, 2014)

John Ashdown-Hill, *The Dublin King* (Stroud: The History Press, 2015)

John Ashdown-Hill, *The Mythology of Richard III* (Stroud: Amberley Publishing, 2015)

John Ashdown-Hill, *Cecily Neville, Mother of Richard III* (Yorkshire-Philadelphia: Pen & Sword, 2018)

John Ashdown Hill, *Elizabeth Widville, Lady Grey: Edward IV's Chief Mistress and the 'Pink Queen'* (Barnsley: Pen&Sword, 2019)

David Baldwin, *Elizabeth Woodville: Mother of the Princes in the Tower* (Stroud: Sutton Publishing Limited, 2002)

David Baldwin, *Stoke Field: The Last Battle of the Wars of the Roses* (Barnsley, Pen & Sword Military, 2006)

David Baldwin, *Richard III* (Stroud: Amberley Publishing, 2013)

George Frederick Beltz, *Memorials of the Order of the Garter, from its foundation to the present time. Including the history of the order; biographical notices of the knights in the reigns of Edward III. and Richard II., the chronological succession of the members* (London: W. Pickering, 1841)

Alex Brayson, *Deficit Finance During the Early Majority of Henry VI of England, 1436–1444. The 'Crisis' of the Medieval English 'Tax State'* (2019)

Terry Breverton, *Henry VII, The Maligned Tudor King* (Stroud: Amberley Publishing, 2016)

Annette Carson, *Richard III, The Maligned King* (Stroud: The History Press, 2008)

Annette Carson, *Richard Duke of Gloucester as Lord Protector and High Constable* (Horstead: Imprimis Imprimatur, 2015)

Annette Carson, 'Remembering Edward of Middleham', http://www.annettecarson.co.uk/357052365/4685305/posting/remembering-edward-of-middleham

Annette Carson, 'The Death of Edward of Middleham, Prince of Wales', http://www.annettecarson.co.uk/357052362

Helen Castor, *Joan of Arc. A history* (London: Faber and Faber Ltd, 2014)

K. L. Clark, *The Nevills of Middleham: England's Most Powerful Family in the Wars of the Roses* (Stroud: The History Press, 2016)

Mary Clive, *This Son of York. A biography of Edward IV* (London: Macmillan London Ltd, 1973).

Dr Anthony Corbet, *Edward IV, England's Forgotten Warrior King. His Life, His People and His Legacy* (Bloomington: iUniverse, 2015)

Susan Curran, *The English Friend* (Norwich: Lasse Press, 2011.)

Anne Curry, *Guide to the Hundred Years' War* (New York: Palgrave Macmillan, 2003.)

Anne Crawford, *The Yorkists: The History of a Dynasty* (London: Continuum Books, 2007)

Stephen David, *Last Champion of York: Francis Lovell, Richard III's Truest Friend* (Marlborough: The Crowood Press, 2019)

Rachel M. Delman, *Gendered viewing, childbirth and female authority in the residence of Alice Chaucer, duchess of Suffolk, at Ewelme, Oxfordshire* (2019) https://www.tandfonline.com/doi/full/10.1080/03044181.2019.1593619

Ed. Gwilym Dodd, Douglas Biggs, *Henry IV, The Establishment of the Regime, 1399-1406* (York: York Medieval Press, 2003)

Ed. Gwilym Dodd, Douglas Biggs, *The Reign of Henry IV: Rebellion and Survival, 1403-1413* (York: York Medieval Press, 2008)

James Gairdner, *History of the Life and Reign of Richard the Third, to which is added the story of Perkin Warbeck: from original documents* (Cambridge: Cambridge University Press, 1898)

Ute Gerhard, *Geschlechterstreit und Aufklärung. In: dies (Hrsg.): Frauenbewegung und Feminismus. Eine Geschichte seit 1789*. 2. Auflage (München: C. H. Beck, 2012)

Chris Given-Wilson, *Henry IV* (New Haven and London: Yale University Press, 2016)

John Goodall, *God's House at Ewelme: Life, Devotion and Architecture in a Fifteenth-Century Almshouse* (London: Taylor & Francis, 2017)

Peter W. Hammond, Anne F. Sutton, *The Coronation of Richard III: The Extant Documents* (Middlesbrough: A Sutton Publishing, 1984)

P. W. Hammond, *The Battles of Barnet and Tewkesbury* (Gloucester: Alan Sutton, 1990)

Peter W. Hammond, *The Children of Richard III* (Stroud: Fonthill Media, 2018)

Peter A Hancock, *Richard III and the Murder in the Tower* (Stroud: The History Press, 2009)

Michael Hicks, 'Pole, John de la, second duke of Suffolk', *Oxford Dictionary of National Biography* (Oxford University Press, 2004)

Luc Hommel, *Marguerite D'York ou La Duchesse Junon* (Paris: Librairie Hachette, 1959)

Rosemary Horrox, *Richard III: A Study of Service* (Cambridge: Cambridge University Press, 1989)

Lauren Johnson, *Shadow King. The Life and Death of Henry VI* (London: Head of Zeus Ltd, 2019)

Michael K. Jones, Malcolm G. Underwood, *The King's Mother. Lady Margaret Beaufort, Countess of Richmond and Derby* (New York: Cambridge University Press, 1992.)

H. A. Kelly, 'The Case against Edward IV's Marriage and Offspring: Secrecy; Witchcraft; Secrecy; Precontract', *Ricardian* 11 (September 1998), pp. 326-335

Paul Murray Kendall, *Richard the Third* (London: George Allan & Unwin, 1955–1956)

Marilyn Kilroy, *Edward and Humphrey de la Pole: Two Convenient Deaths* (Richard III Society, 2015)

Henry Murray Lane, *The Royal Daughters of England, and their representatives : together with genealogical tables of the Royal Family from the Conquest to the present time ; v. 2* (London, Constable & Co., 1911)

J. L. Laynesmith, *Cecily, Duchess of York* (London, New York: Bloomsbury Academic, 2017)

Matthew Lewis, *Richard, Duke of York: King by Right* (Stroud: Amberley Publishing, 2016)

Matthew Lewis, *The Survival of the Princes in the Tower: Murder, Mystery and Myth* (Stroud: The History Press, 2017)

Matthew Lewis, *Richard III: Loyalty Binds Me* (Stroud: Amberley Publishing, 2018)

W. C. Metcalf, *A Book of Knights* (London, 1885)

Wendy E. A. Moorhen, 'The Career of John de la Pole, Earl of Lincoln', *Ricardian*, 13 (2003), pp. 341-358

Wendy E. A. Moorhen, 'Such was his Renown in Warfare', *Ricardian Bulletin* (2004) http://www.richardiii.net/2_3_0_riii_leadership.php military

Ian Mortimer, *1415: Henry V's Year of Glory* (London: Random House, 2009)

Ian Mortimer, *Henry V, The Warrior King of 1415* (New York City: RosettaBooks, 2009, 2013)

Henry Alfred Napier, *Historical Notices of the Parishes of Swyncombe and Ewelme in the County of Oxfordshire* (Oxford: James Wright, Printer to the University, 1863)

Nicholas Orme, *Medieval Children* (New Haven and London: Yale University Press, 2001)

Thomas Penn, *Winter King: Henry VII and the Dawn of Tudor England* (London: Penguin Books Ltd, 2011)

Anthony J. Pollard, *Lord FitzHugh's Rising in 1470* (Bulletin of the Institute of Historical Research, 1979)

J. S. Roskell, '*Thomas Chaucer of Ewelme*', in Parl. and Pol. in Late Med. Eng. iii. 151-91

Charles Ross, *Edward IV* (New Haven and London: Yale University Press, 1974)

Charles Ross, *Richard III* (York: Eyre Methuen Ltd, 1981)

Michèle Schindler, *Lovell Our Dogge. The Life of Viscount Lovell, Closest Friend of Richard III and Failed Regicide* (Stroud: Amberley Publishing, 2019)

Desmond Seward, *The Last White Rose* (London: Constable, 2010)
Ed G. Smith, *The Coronation of Elizabeth Wydeville* (London, 1935)
Gordon Smith, 'Lambert Simnel and the King from Dublin', *Ricardian* (1996)
Peter Spring, *Sir John Tiptoft: 'Butcher of England': Earl of Worcester, Edward IV's Enforcer and Humanist Scholar* (Barnsley: Pen & Sword Military, 2018)
Ed. Thomas Stapleton, *De Antiquis Legibus Liber. Cronica Maiorum et Vicecomitum Londoniarum et quedam, que contigebant temporibis illis ab anno MCLXXVIII; cum appendice* (London: Camden Society, 1846)
Anne F Sutton, *The Reburial of Richard, Duke of York* (Richard III Society, 1996)
Nicola Tallis, *Uncrowned Queen: The Fateful Life of Margaret Beaufort, Tudor Matriarch* (London: Michael O'Mara Books Limited, 2019)
J. A. F. Thomson, 'John De La Pole, Duke of Suffolk', *Speculum* (1979)
Marion Turner, *Chaucer: A European Life* (Woodstock: Princeton University Press, 2019)
Christine Weightman, *Margaret of York: Diabolical Duchess* (Stroud: Amberley Publishing, 2012, first published 1989)
Barrie Williams, 'The Mystery of Richard de la Pole', *Ricardian* 88 (March 1985), pp. 18-25
C. H. Williams, 'The Rebellion of Humphrey Stafford 1486', *The English Historical Review* (1928)
Audrey Williamson, *The Mystery of the Princes* (Gloucester: Alan Sutton Publishing Limited, 1978)
Josephine Wilkinson, *The Princes in the Tower* (Stroud: Amberley Publishing, 2013)
Josephine Wilkinson, *Richard the Young King to Be* (Stroud: Amberley Publishing,2014)
Joanna M. Williams, 'The Political Career of Francis, Viscount Lovell 1456–1487(?)', *Ricardian* (1990)
Bertram Wolffe, *Henry VI* (New Haven and London: Yale University Press, 1981)
Anne Wroe, *Perkin. A Story of Deception* (London: Random House, 2003)

Index